The Longman handbook of modern British history 1714–1980

Also by Chris Cook and John Stevenson
The Slump: Society and Politics during the Depression
The Longman Atlas of Modern British History 1700–1970
British Historical Facts: 1760–1830

Other books by Chris Cook
Post-war Britain: a Political History (with Alan Sked)
The Age of Alignment: Electoral Politics in Britain 1922–1929
A Short History of the Liberal Party 1900–1976
By-elections in British Politics (*ed. with John Ramsden*)
The Politics of Reappraisal 1918–1939 (*ed. with Gillian Peele*)
The Decade of Disillusion (*ed. with David McKie*)
Crisis and Controversy: Essays in Honour of A. J. P. Taylor (*ed. with Alan Sked*)
Sources in British Political History 1900–1951 (*with Philip Jones et al.*)
The Labour Party (*ed. with Ian Taylor*)
Trade Unions in British Politics (*ed. with Ben Pimlott*)

Other books by John Stevenson
Popular Protest and Public Order (*with R. E. Quinault*)
Social Conditions in Britain Between the Wars
Popular Disturbances in England, 1700–1870

The Longman handbook of modern British history 1714 – 1980

Chris Cook and John Stevenson

Longman

London and New York

Longman Group Limited
Longman House, Burnt Mill, Harlow
Essex CM20 2JE, England
Associated companies throughout the world

*Published in the United States of America
by Longman Inc., New York*

First published 1983

British Library Cataloguing in Publication Data

Cook, Chris
The Longman handbook of modern British history 1714–1980.
1. Great Britain – History – 18th century
2. Great Britain – History – 19th century
3. Great Britain – History – 20th century
I. Title   II. Stevenson, John
941.07   DA470

ISBN 0-582-48581-9
ISBN 0-582-48582-7 Pbk

Library of Congress Cataloging in Publication Data

Cook, Chris, 1945–
The Longman handbook of modern British history,
1714–1980.

Bibliography: p. 299
1. Great Britain – History – 1714–1837.
2. Great Britain – History – Victoria, 1837–1901.
3. Great Britain – History – 20th century.
I. Stevenson, John, 1946–   . II. Title.
III. Title: Handbook of modern British history,
1714–1980.
DA470. C65   941.07   81–23621

ISBN 0-582-48581-9   AACR2
ISBN 0-582-48582-7 Pbk

Set in 9/10 pt Linotron 202 Univers Medium
Printed in Singapore by
Kyodo Shing Loong Printing Industries Pte Ltd.

Contents

95   Section II: Social and religious history

Preface and acknowledgements

This handbook has attempted to provide a convenient and highly usable companion for both teachers and students of British history from 1714 to the present day. It is a much condensed work, bringing together a wealth of chronological, statistical and tabular information which is not to be found elsewhere within the confines of a single volume. The book covers not only political and diplomatic events but also the broader fields of social and economic history. It has been designed as a handbook for use by teachers as well as by sixth formers, polytechnic and university students. No book of this type can be entirely comprehensive. Rather, we have included those facts, figures and statistics that we believe are most needed for courses in later modern British history.

Both authors would like to acknowledge the help and advice in the preparation of this book of Stephen Brooks, Richard Clayton, Peter Morgan, Louise Spitz and Judith Woods.

Chris Cook, Polytechnic of North London

John Stevenson, University of Sheffield

October 1982

Section I
Political history

Political chronology

Note: (i) In order to reflect the more personal character of politics and the less organised nature of parties in the eighteenth and the first half of the nineteenth centuries, governments up to 1868 are given the name of their principal minister or ministers. After 1868 governments are designated by their party label. (ii) In the eighteenth century leaders of administrations usually held the post of first lord of the Treasury or one of the secretaryships of state, no formal office of Prime Minister existing. From the early nineteenth century this term came into more common usage and has been adopted from the 1820s for the description of leaders of administrations.

1714 May   Schism Act passed. No person allowed to keep a school unless a member of the Anglican Church.

July   Harley St John (Bolingbroke) secures dismissal of the Earl of Oxford and begins attempt to pack administration with Jacobite sympathisers. Severe illness of Queen Anne forces calling of Privy Council. Pro-Hanoverian Duke of Shrewsbury appointed lord treasurer in place of Oxford (30th).

Aug.   Death of Queen Anne (1st); George I proclaimed King in London and leading cities. Bolingbroke dismissed from office.

Sept.   George I arrives in England (18th). *Whig administration* formed under Lord Stanhope. Principal figures: Lord Stanhope (secretary of state); Lord Halifax (first lord of the Treasury); Lord Townshend (secretary of state); Earl of Nottingham (lord president of the council); Lord Sunderland (lord lieutenant of Ireland).

1715 Mar.   Meeting of first parliament of George I with large Whig majority.

June   Bolingbroke, Ormonde and Oxford impeached. Flight of Bolingbroke and Ormonde; Oxford committed to the Tower. Widespread rioting followed by Riot Act strengthening power of magistrates by making many riots a capital offence.

Sept.   Jacobite rising in Scotland under the Earl of Mar.

Dec.   Pretender (James III) arrives in Scotland.

1716 Feb.   Pretender flees Scotland after failure of England to rise in support. Impeachment of Jacobite leaders; execution of Derwentwater and Kenmure.

May   Septennial Act extends maximum duration of parliaments to seven years.

1717 Jan.   Triple Alliance formed between England, France and Holland to uphold the treaty of Utrecht.

	Feb.	Convocation of the Church of England ceased to meet regularly.
	Apr.	Walpole and Townshend resign from administration.
1718	Aug.	Quadruple Alliance formed between England, France, the Emperor and Holland.
	Dec.	War between England and Spain. Repeal of the Occasional Conformity Act and the Schism Act.
1719	Dec.	Defeat of administration's Peerage Bill in House of Commons.
1720	Jan.	Spain joined Quadruple Alliance, ending hostilities with England.
	Feb.	South Sea Company's scheme for taking over part of the National Debt in return for exclusive trade in the South Seas accepted by the House of Commons.
	June	South Sea stock reaches record level.
	Aug.	South Sea stock falls rapidly in value.
	Dec.	Walpole begins restoration of public credit. Secret Committee appointed to investigate affairs of South Sea Company. Directors of company expelled from the House of Commons; chancellor of the exchequer (Aislabie) sent to the Tower.
1721	Feb.	Lord Townshend becomes secretary of state in place of Stanhope.
	Apr.	*Walpole administration* formed. Principal figures: Robert Walpole (first lord of the treasury); Lord Townshend (secretary of state); Carteret (secretary of state).
1722	Apr.	Death of Sunderland, Walpole's chief rival.
	May	Atterbury Plot by Jacobites discovered. Leading Jacobite sympathisers arrested. and non-jurors. Francis Atterbury (Bishop of Rochester) banished.
1724	Apr.	Carteret becomes lord lieutenant of Ireland, Duke of Newcastle becomes secretary of state and Henry Pelham secretary at war.
1725	Apr.	City Elections Act, regulating conduct of elections in London and increasing power of Court of Aldermen, passed by Walpole in spite of strong protests in the capital.
	Sept.	Treaty of Hanover between England, France and Prussia. Bolingbroke pardoned and returns to England where he helps to lead opposition to Walpole.
1727	June	Death of George I (11th); accession of George II.
1729	Nov.	Treaty of Seville with Spain; confirmation of *asiento* treaty allowing limited trade with Spanish colonies, Gibraltar ceded to England.

1730 May   Lord Harrington replaces Townshend as secretary of state.

1731 Mar.   Treaty of Vienna; Austrian Emperor agrees to disband Ostend East India Company.

1733 Mar.   Widespread opposition to Walpole's Excise Bill.
     Apr.   Walpole's majority in House of Commons reduced to 16 on Excise proposals; Walpole offers resignation to the King. Though remaining in office, Walpole postpones discussion of the Bill until June, effectively dropping the scheme.
     May   Walpole narrowly staves off defeat in the House of Lords over handling of South Sea Company affairs.

1734 Mar.   Motion to repeal Septennial Act defeated. Bolingbroke gives up active opposition to Walpole and retires to France.

1735 Jan.   Second parliament of George II's reign meets after general election of 1734, Walpole having lost 16 seats but still commanding a substantial majority.

1736 Sept. Porteous riots in Edinburgh.

1737   Frederick, Prince of Wales, quarrels with his father and sides openly with the opposition to Walpole.

1738 Mar.   Spanish ill-treatment of British sailors taken up by the opposition to Walpole in the Commons and City of London.

1739 Jan.   Convention of Pardo to settle differences with Spain submitted to parliament and approved by only 28 votes.
     Oct.   Walpole forced to accede to demand for war with Spain. War of Jenkins' Ear.
     Nov.   Capture of Porto Bello by Admiral Vernon.

1741 Feb.   Motion for Walpole's dismissal defeated by 184 votes.
     Apr.   Parliament dissolved. In subsequent general election Walpole's majority reduced to under 20 seats by defeats in Cornwall and Scotland.
     Dec.   Parliament reassembles and Walpole defeated in seven divisions.

1742 Feb.   Walpole decides to resign after defeat over Chippenham election petition. *Carteret administration* formed. Principal figures: John Carteret (secretary of state); Earl of Wilmington (first lord of the Treasury).

1743 Aug.   Henry Pelham becomes first lord of the Treasury in place of the Earl of Wilmington.

1744 Mar.   France declares war on Britain.
     Nov.   Carteret resigns after increasing disagreement in the cabinet and parliament about his foreign policy. *Pelham administration* formed. Principal figures: Henry Pelham (first

lord of the Treasury); Earl of Harrington (secretary of state); Duke of Bedford (first lord of the Admiralty).

1745 May   Battle of Fontenoy. Marshal Saxe defeats Duke of Cumberland.
     July   Second Jacobite rebellion. The Young Pretender, Charles Edward Stuart, lands in Scotland (25th) and proclaims his father as James VIII of Scotland and James III of England. Highland clans rise in support.
     Sept.   The Pretender enters Edinburgh with 2,000 men (11th); Jacobite victory at Prestonpans (21st).
     Dec.   Pretender reaches Derby, but decides to retreat to Scotland because of lack of support in England (4th).

1746 Feb.   Pelham, Newcastle, Hardwicke and Harrington resign after disagreements with the King over foreign policy. Bath and Granville attempt to form an administration. *Pelham administration* re-formed. Principal figures: H. Pelham (first lord of the Treasury); Earl of Harrington (secretary of state); Duke of Newcastle (secretary of state); William Pitt the Elder (vice-treasurer of Ireland).
     Apr.   Defeat of Young Pretender and Jacobite forces at battle of Culloden (16th).
     May   Pitt becomes paymaster-general of the Forces.
     Sept.   Flight of the Young Pretender to France.

1748 Oct.   Treaty of Aix-la-Chapelle ends War of Austrian Succession.

1751 May   Act passed for adoption of the reformed (Gregorian) calendar in England and the colonies. Year to begin from 1 January instead of 25 March; 11 days to be omitted from the calendar between 3 and 14 September 1752.

1753 June   Jewish Naturalisation Act passed, but repealed the following year because of popular opposition.

1754 Mar.   Death of Pelham. *Newcastle administration* formed. Principal figures: Duke of Newcastle (first lord of the Treasury); Earl of Holderness (secretary of state); Henry Fox (secretary at war); William Pitt (paymaster).

1755 May   Admiral Boscawen fails to prevent French reinforcements reaching North America. Subsidy treaties agreed with Hesse-Cassel and Russia to provide troops in the event of war.

1756 May   War declared against France. Seven Years War begins.
     June   Loss of Minorca after failure of Admiral Byng to defeat French invasion fleet.
     Oct.   Henry Fox announces intention to resign after severe criticism of the conduct of the war in the House of Commons. Newcastle resigns; the King asks Fox to form an administration, but he refuses. Devonshire agrees to form an administration with Pitt (29th).

	Nov.	*Pitt–Devonshire administration* formed. Principal figures: Duke of Devonshire (first lord of the Treasury); William Pitt (secretary of state).
1757	Apr.	The King demands Pitt's resignation after failures to achieve success in the war. George Grenville (treasurer of the navy) and Legge (chancellor of the exchequer) resign with Pitt. Widespread popular support shown for Pitt.
	July	After considerable negotiations *Pitt–Newcastle administration* formed. Principal figures: William Pitt (secretary of state); Duke of Newcastle (first lord of the Treasury); Henry Fox (paymaster of the Forces).
	Oct.	Failure of Rochefort expedition; news of defeats in India and Canada leads to criticism of the conduct of the war in Europe.
	Nov.	Victory for Britain's ally, Frederick the Great, at Rossbach.
	Dec.	Victory of Frederick at Leuthen.
1758	Apr.	At second treaty of Westminster, Prussia and Britain pledged themselves not to make a separate peace. Frederick granted an annual subsidy.
	July	Capture of Louisburg in North America (26th).
	Nov.	Occupation of Fort Duquesne by Colonel Forbes.
1759	May	Capture of Guadeloupe
	June	Capture of Fort Niagara in North America.
	July	Bombardment of Le Havre thwarts French plans for invasion of Britain.
	Aug.	Boscawen's defeat of French fleet at Lagos.
	Sept.	Wolfe's victory at battle of the Plains of Abraham (13th) and capture of Quebec (18th).
	Nov.	Defeat of French fleet by Admiral Hawke.
1760	Sept.	Surrender of Montreal to the British; virtual loss of Canada by the French.
	Oct.	Death of George II (25th); accession of George III.
1761	Oct.	Resignation of Pitt the Elder because of disagreements with colleagues about his war policy. *Bute–Newcastle administration* formed. Principal figures: Duke of Newcastle (first lord of the Treasury); Earl of Bute (secretary of state).
1762	May	Duke of Newcastle resigns from government because of quarrel with Bute over foreign policy. *Bute administration* formed. Principal figures: Earl of Bute (first lord of the Treasury); George Grenville (secretary of state).
	June	John Wilkes starts *The North Briton* to attack the Bute administration.
1763	Feb.	First treaty of Paris signed, ending Seven Years War (for provisions, see p. 223).
	Mar.	Introduction of cider tax increases Bute's unpopularity.
	Apr.	Bute resigns in the face of increasing attacks in the press

and parliament. *Grenville administration* formed. Principal figures: George Grenville (first lord of the Treasury and chancellor of the exchequer); Earl of Egremont (secretary of state, later first lord of the Admiralty). Earl of Halifax (secretary of state).   Wilkes arrested on a general warrant for an attack on the King in issue No. 45 of *The North Briton*.

Dec.   Wilkes' arrest declared illegal by Chief Justice Pratt. Wilkes forced into exile after publication of *An Essay on Woman*.

1765 Mar.   American Stamp Act passed to raise money for the defence of the American colonies by placing a charge on legal transactions. Six of the thirteen colonies petitioned against the Act. (For American affairs, see also pp. 205–6.)

July   Grenville administration dismissed by the King. *First Rockingham administration* formed. Principal figures: Marquess of Rockingham (first lord of the Treasury); Henry Seymour Conway (secretary of state).

1766 Jan.   Widespread petitioning movement against Stamp Act by English merchants.

Mar.   Repeal of the Stamp Act with strong support of Pitt (now Earl of Chatham).

July   *Chatham administration* formed. Principal figures: Earl of Chatham (lord privy seal); Duke of Grafton (first lord of the Treasury); Charles Townshend (chancellor of the exchequer).

1767 June   Townshend's Revenue Act passed, imposing duties on tea and other articles imported into America to pay for defence and administration of the colonies.

1768 Mar.   Wilkes elected MP for Middlesex.

May   Industrial and pro-Wilkes riots in London; 11 people killed by soldiers at the 'massacre' of St George's Fields.

Oct.   Resignation of Earl of Chatham. *Grafton administration* formed. Principal figures: Duke of Grafton (first lord of the Treasury); Lord North (chancellor of the exchequer).

1769 Feb.   House of Commons votes that Wilkes was guilty of a seditious libel for letter criticising the government for the 'massacre' of St George's Fields; Wilkes expelled from the Commons; formation of the 'Supporters of the Bill of Rights' to support Wilkes and the cause of parliamentary reform.

May   Cabinet decides to retain duties on tea in spite of strong opposition from the American colonists.

June–July   Petitioning movement for reform of parliament and reinstatement of Wilkes.

1770 Jan.   Grafton resigns after securing a majority of 44 in the House of Commons after a motion on the administration's handling of the Middlesex election issue. *North administration* formed. Principal figure: Lord North (first lord of the Treasury and chancellor of the exchequer).

Mar. Act repealing duties on paper, glass and paint, but retaining those on tea.
Apr. Edmund Burke publishes *Thoughts on the Causes of the Present Discontents*, accusing the King of dominating parliament through 'influence' and calling for a revival of 'party'.

1771 Mar. Printers' Case. London printers reprimanded for publishing parliamentary debates and Lord Mayor and two aldermen of London imprisoned for a breach of the privileges of the House of Commons. But no serious attempts made to interfere with parliamentary reporting thereafter.

1773 Oct. Tea Act passed to aid finances of the East India Company by allowing direct export of tea to North America. American colonists resist imports and payment of duty.
Dec. Boston Tea Party. Protestors dump 340 chests of East India Company tea in Boston harbour.

1774 Apr. Motion in the House of Commons to repeal tea duty and pacify the colonists. Quebec Act passed granting toleration to Roman Catholics in Canada. Continental Congress meets at Philadelphia and agrees to defy coercive measures. Quebec Act passed for government of Canada.

1775 Jan. Chatham's motion proposing conciliation with the American colonies defeated.
Mar. Burke's conciliation proposals defeated.
Apr. British and American forces skirmish at Lexington (18 April).
May Second Continental Congress meets at Philadelphia (10 May).
June Battle of Bunker's Hill, Boston.
Aug. King's proclamation of rebellion in American colonies.

1776 July American Declaration of Independence.
1777 Oct. Surrender of British forces at Saratoga.

1778 Feb. Treaty of Amity and Commerce signed between France and the American colonists. Charles James Fox's motion for virtual abandonment of the war against America defeated in the Commons.
Mar.–Apr. Motions criticising conduct of the war and urging reform of parliament by reduction of Crown influence only narrowly defeated in Commons.

1779 June Spain declares war on Britain. Siege of Gibraltar begins.
Dec. First meeting of Yorkshire reformers under Christopher Wyvill to concert plans for reform of parliament. Widespread agitation in Ireland for removal of trade and constitutional restrictions.

1780 Feb. Yorkshire petition for parliamentary reform presented. Beginning of widespread petitioning movement for 'economical reform'. Burke presents proposals for reform.

Mar. Convention of reformers in London.

Apr. Dunning's resolution 'that the influence of the Crown has increased, is increasing, and ought to be diminished' carried by 233 votes to 215. Further attempts to attack the Crown's influence defeated by the administration and its supporters.

June Protestant Association led by Lord George Gordon petitions parliament for repeal of the Catholic Relief Act of 1778; followed by widespread rioting in London – the 'Gordon riots'.

1781 Nov. News of Cornwallis' surrender at Yorktown reaches England.

1782 Feb. Motion asserting the impracticability of the continued war with America passed in the House of Commons.

Mar. North only narrowly escapes defeat on two motions of no confidence. The King accepts North's resignation. *Second Rockingham administration* formed. Principal figures: Marquess of Rockingham (first lord of the Treasury); Charles James Fox (foreign secretary).

May Clerke's Act passed disqualifying government contractors from sitting in the Commons.

June Crewe's Act passed disfranchising revenue officers of the Crown.

July Burke's Civil Establishment Act passed controlling royal expenditure, pensions and offices. Paymaster's Office regulated. Death of Rockingham (1st) leads to formation of *Shelburne administration.* Principal figures: Earl of Shelburne (first lord of the Treasury); William Pitt the Younger (chancellor of the exchequer); Thomas Townshend (home secretary).

Nov. Preliminaries of peace agreed with the American colonies.

1783 Jan. Preliminaries of peace signed with France and Spain.

Feb. Alliance of Fox and North and their supporters successfully challenges peace terms in the Commons; resignation of Shelburne.

Apr. *Fox–North administration* formed. Principal figures: Duke of Portland (first lord of the Treasury); Lord North (home secretary); Charles James Fox (foreign secretary).

Apr. Pitt's proposals for parliamentary reform defeated in the Commons.

Sept. Treaty of Versailles signed between England, France and Spain (for details, see p. 223).

Dec. Fox's India Bill. Designed by Burke to transfer the authority of the East India Company to commissioners nominated by parliament. Passes Commons but defeated in the Lords after pressure from the King. Ministers dismissed and *Pitt administration* formed. Principal figures: William Pitt (first lord of the Treasury and chancellor of the exchequer); Lord Sydney (home secretary); H. Dundas (treasurer of the navy, 1783–91, home secretary, 1791–4, war and colonies, 1794–1801).

1784 Mar.   Parliament dissolved for general election. Pitt and his
            supporters gain a majority of over 100.
     June   Pitt introduces first budget. Begins to reorganise
            government debts and finances. Duties reduced to deter
            smuggling, and window tax introduced. New loans raised
            and a large number of indirect taxes levied. 'Board for
            Taxes' set up to administer collection.
     July   Pitt's India Bill introduced, establishing a 'Board of Control'
            to administer the East India Company.

1785 Apr.   Pitt's proposals for limited parliamentary reform defeated by
            248 votes to 174. Pitt announces plans for a 'Sinking Fund'
            to liquidate the national debt. Sets up five commissioners to
            investigate waste in government departments.

1786 May   Pitt's 'Sinking Fund' established.
     Sept. Commercial treaty signed between Britain and France.
            Duties lowered on trade in manufactured goods and wine
            between the two countries.

1788 Nov.   King's illness starts 'Regency Crisis'. Fox and the Whigs
            demand unfettered powers for the Prince of Wales.

1789 Feb.   Recovery of the King ends crisis.
     July   Storming of the Bastille in Paris (14th).
     Nov.   Meeting of the Revolution Society in London to celebrate
            the 'Glorious Revolution' of 1688–9; sermon preached by Dr
            Price welcoming the French Revolution.

1790 Nov.   Burke publishes *Reflections on the Revolution in France*,
            bitterly attacking the revolution and its supporters.

1791 Mar.   Publication of Thomas Paine's *Rights of Man*, Pt I (Pt II
            published in February 1792).
     May   Burke and Fox quarrel publicly over the French Revolution.
     July   'Church and King' riots in Birmingham against dissenters.

1792 Jan.   Formation of London Corresponding Society, first
            artisan-based political society.
     May   Proclamation against seditious publications.
     Nov.   Formation of loyalist associations against 'Republicans and
            Levellers' begins.
     Dec.   Pitt fortifies the Tower, calls out the militia and begins
            preparations for war. Further proclamation against seditious
            writings and trial of Paine (in his absence) for seditious libel.

1793 Jan.   Execution of Louis XVI of France.
     Feb.   France declares war on Britain and Holland
     May   Grey's motion for reform defeated by 282 votes to 41 in the
            Commons.
     Oct.   British Convention meets at Edinburgh.
     Nov.–Dec.   British Convention reassembles; dispersed by
            authorities and leaders tried and harshly sentenced
            (January–September 1794).

1794 May   Arrest of leaders of English reform societies on charge of
            high treason. Secret committees appointed to investigate
            radical societies. Habeas Corpus suspended.
     July   Moderate Whigs under Portland join in the Pitt
            administration; Fox and his followers left in virtual isolation.
     Oct.–Nov.   Thomas Hardy and other radical leaders acquitted of
            high treason.

1795 July   Widespread food rioting in England; demonstrations against
            the war in London.
     Oct.   Mass meeting organised by London Corresponding Society
            in London. Attack on the king's coach by anti-war protestors
            at opening of parliament.
     Nov.–Dec.   Government introduces 'Two Acts'; extending the law
            of treason and prohibiting mass meetings unless approved
            by the magistracy.

1796 May   Failure of attempts to make peace with France.
     Dec.   Failure of French attempt to land at Bantry Bay, Ireland.
            Breakdown of further peace overtures to France.

1797 Feb.   Bank crisis in Britain; temporary suspension of cash
            payments by the Bank of England.   Defeat of Spanish
            fleet at Cape St Vincent. Failure of small French landing in
            Pembrokeshire.
     Apr.   Outbreak of naval mutiny at Spithead.
     May   Mutiny at Spithead settled; outbreak of mutiny at the Nore.
     June   Mutiny at the Nore suppressed and ringleaders hanged.
     Sept. Negotiations for peace with France broken off.
     Oct.   Duncan defeats Dutch fleet at Camperdown.
     Nov.   Pitt's Finance Bill proposes new indirect taxes as well as an
            income tax.

1798 Jan.   Pitt's Finance Bill approved by parliament.
     Apr.   Remaining leaders of London Corresponding Society
            arrested.
     May   Outbreak of rebellion in Ireland.
     June   Defeat of Irish rebels at Vinegar Hill and suppression of
            rising in Ulster.
     Aug.   Landing of General Humbert and French troops in
            Ireland.   Nelson defeats French fleet at the battle of the
            Nile.
     Sept. Humbert's troops surrender.
     Oct.   Failure of French expedition to Lough Swilly and capture of
            Wolfe Tone.

1799 Apr.   Pitt introduces income tax of 10 per cent.
     July   Combination Act passed, prohibiting combinations of
            workmen to raise wages. Act passed prohibiting certain
            named political societies, including the London
            Corresponding Society and the United Irishmen.

1800 Jan.   Peace overtures from Napoleon rejected by Pitt.
     July   Second Combination Act passed, partly relaxing provisions

of Act of 1799.

Aug.   Act of Union. Ireland merged with Great Britain and Irish parliament abolished.

1801 Feb.   Resignation of Pitt because of the King's refusal to permit the introduction of Catholic Emancipation. *Addington administration* formed. Principal figures: Henry Addington (first lord of the Treasury and chancellor of the exchequer); Duke of Portland (home secretary).

Apr.   Danish fleet destroyed at Copenhagen.

Oct.   Preliminary terms of peace agreed with France.

1802 Mar.   Peace of Amiens signed with France (for details, see p. 224).

1803 May   War resumed with France.

1804 May   Resignation of Addington. *Second Pitt administration* formed. Principal figures: William Pitt (first lord of the Treasury and chancellor of the exchequer); Lord Hawkesbury (home secretary).

July   Napoleon's invasion army of 100,000 men and 2,000 transports assembled at Boulogne. Extensive anti-invasion preparations in England.

1805 Aug.   Third Coalition formed with Britain, Austria and Russia. Napoleon begins movement of army of Boulogne to Central Europe.

Oct.   Nelson defeats Franco-Spanish fleet at Trafalgar.

1806 Jan.   Death of Pitt.

Feb.   *Grenville administration* formed, ('All the Talents'). Principal figures: Lord Grenville (first lord of the Treasury); Charles James Fox (foreign secretary).

Sept.   Death of Charles James Fox.

Nov.   Napoleon's Berlin decrees close all European ports to British shipping.

Jan.–Nov.   Orders in Council issued by Britain, in retaliation for Berlin decrees, ordering all neutral ships trading with Europe to proceed via Britain and pay duties.

1807 Mar.   Resignation of 'All the Talents' ministry. *Portland administration* formed. Principal figures: Duke of Portland (first lord of the Treasury); Spencer Perceval (chancellor of the exchequer).

May   Act abolishing the slave trade.

Sept.   Bombardment of Copenhagen.

Nov.   Napoleon issues Milan decrees for confiscation of all neutral shipping calling at British ports.

1808 Aug.   Convention of Cintra signed in Lisbon, allowing French to evacuate Portugal on easy terms. Widespread protests in England.

1809 Jan.   Committee appointed to investigate the Duke of York's
              involvement in the sale of army commissions.
      June   Motion for parliamentary reform defeated in the Commons.
      Sept. – Oct.   Failure of Walcheren expedition.   Resignation of
              Duke of Portland. *Perceval administration* formed. Principal
              figures: Spencer Perceval (first lord of the Treasury and
              chancellor of the exchequer); Earl of Liverpool (secretary
              for war and the colonies).

1810 Feb.   Government forced to appoint enquiry on the Walcheren
              expedition by vote in the House of Commons.
      Mar.   Government narrowly escapes defeat on motions of censure
              over Walcheren expedition.
      Apr.   Riots in London in support of radical MP Sir Francis Burdett.
      Oct.   George III suffers renewed bout of illness.

1811 Feb.   Prince of Wales given virtually full powers as Prince Regent
              (confirmed 1812).
      Mar.   Beginning of Luddite disturbances in Midlands.

1812 Jan.   Luddite disturbances spread to Yorkshire and Lancashire.
              Frame-breaking made capital offence.
      Mar.   Widespread petitions against Orders in Council.
      Apr.   Height of Luddite disturbances; attack on Rawfolds Mill;
              assassination of William Horsfall by Luddite sympathisers.
      May   Assassination of Spencer Perceval.
      June   *Liverpool administration* formed. Principal figures: Earl of
              Liverpool (first lord of the Treasury); Viscount Sidmouth
              (home secretary); Viscount Castlereagh (foreign secretary);
              Sir Robert Peel (home secretary). Orders in Council revoked.
      July   Wellington defeats French at Salamanca.

1813 June   Wellington's victory at Vittoria.
      Oct.   Defeat of Napoleon at battle of Leipzig.

1814 Apr.   Abdication of Napoleon.

1815 Mar.   Napoleon returns from Elba, beginning of the 'Hundred
              Days'.   Widespread petitioning movement and riots in
              London against passing of the Corn Laws, imposing a high
              protective tariff against imports of grain.
      June   Defeat of Napoleon at Waterloo. Peace of Vienna signed (see
              p. 224).

1816 Apr.   Income tax abolished after government defeat in the House
              of Commons.   Beginning of widespread riots against
              distress in East Anglia and manufacturing districts.
      Oct.   First cheap edition of Cobbett's *Political Register* issued, the
              'twopenny trash'.

1817 Jan.   Attack on Prince Regent's coach leads to introduction of
              'Gag Acts'; Habeas Corpus suspended, and restrictions
              placed on meetings.

| | Mar. | March of the 'blankcteers' broken up by troops. |
| | June | Pentrich 'rising' in Derbyshire led by Jeremiah Brandreth. |

1819 Aug.   Reform meeting at St Peter's Fields, Manchester, broken up by troops, 'Peterloo'; followed by 'Six Acts' restricting meetings and the press, and allowing magistrates to seize arms and prevent drilling.

1820 Jan.   Death of George III; accession of George IV.
     Feb.   Cato Street conspiracy uncovered.
     June   George IV's estranged wife Caroline returns to claim her rights as Queen.
     Nov.   Government forced to abandon its attempt to deprive Queen Caroline of her title and dissolve her marriage to the King after widespread popular opposition.

1821 Aug.   Riots in London at Queen Caroline's funeral.

1822 Jan.   Peel becomes home secretary in place of Lord Sidmouth.
     Aug.   Castlereagh commits suicide; George Canning becomes foreign secretary.

1823 Jan.   William Huskisson becomes president of the Board of Trade; Reciprocity of Duties Act passed (see p. 172).

1824 Feb.   Act to repeal the laws relative to combinations (see p. 142).

1825 Nov.–Dec.   Financial crisis in England, widespread bankruptcies and commercial failures.
     Dec.   Second Act relating to combinations of workmen, amending Act of 1824 (see p. 142).

1827 Feb.   Lord Liverpool paralysed by a stroke (17th).
     Apr.   *Canning administration* formed. Principal figures: Canning (first lord of the Treasury and chancellor the exchequer); Huskisson (president of the Board of Trade); Viscount Palmerston (secretary at war).
     July   Treaty with France and Russia for pacification of Greece.
     Aug.   Death of Canning. *Goderich administration* formed. Principal figures: Viscount Goderich (first lord of the Treasury); Huskisson (secretary of state for war and the colonies).

1828 Jan.   Resignation of Goderich after internal cabinet disputes with his colleagues. *Wellington administration* formed. Principal figures: Duke of Wellington (prime minister); Robert Peel (home secretary); Huskisson (secretary of state for war and the colonies).
     Feb.   Bill to repeal Test and Corporation Acts introduced by Lord John Russell and passed with minor amendments (May).
     May   Resignation of Huskisson and Canningites over failure of parliament to approve the transfer of the franchises of Penryn and East Retford to Manchester and Birmingham.

Catholic Emancipation Bill passes Commons but defeated in Lords.

1829 Feb. Wellington and Peel declare themselves in favour of Catholic Emancipation after election of Daniel O'Connell for County Clare. Widespread protests from 'Ultra' Tories.
Apr. Catholic Emancipation passed. Catholics admitted to parliament and to almost all public offices. Irish freehold qualification raised from 40s. to £10.
Sept. Metropolitan Police Act comes into operation. London given force of 3,314 professional police.

1830 June Death of George IV; accession of William IV.
July Dissolution of parliament for fresh elections.
Sept. Huskisson killed at inauguration of Liverpool and Manchester Railway.
Nov. Wellington declares against parliamentary reform (2nd); government defeated on a vote on the Civil List Accounts (15th); Wellington resigns (16th). *Grey administration* formed. Principal figures: Earl Grey (prime minister); Lord John Russell (paymaster-general); Viscount Melbourne (home secretary); Viscount Palmerston (foreign secretary); H. Brougham (lord chancellor).

1831 Mar. First Reform Bill introduced into House of Commons by Lord John Russell. Passes second reading. (For fuller details of the reform movement see pp. 57–9.)
Apr. Government defeated on Gascoyne's amendment objecting to the reduction in numbers of MPs for England and Wales. Parliament dissolved.
June Whigs returned after general election and second Reform Bill introduced into Parliament.
July Reform Bill receives second reading.
Sept. Reform Bill receives third reading.
Oct. Reform Bill rejected by House of Lords (8th). Riots in Nottingham and Derby (8–10th); riots in Bristol (29th–31st).
Dec. New Reform Bill introduced into Commons; passes second reading (18th).

1832 Jan. William IV agrees to creation of peers in order to obtain passage of reform.
Mar. Reform Bill passes third reading by 355 votes to 239 (22nd).
Apr. Reform Bill passes second reading in Lords.
May Government defeated on Lyndhurst's motion; resignation of ministers. 'May days' (9th–15th); Wellington asked to form an administration but unable to do so; the King forced to recall Grey and confirm assurances that peers will be created as necessary to ensure passage of Reform Bill.
June Reform Bill receives third reading in Lords and royal assent (4th and 7th). (For provisions of Reform Act, see pp. 59–60).
July Scottish Reform Act passed.
Aug. Irish Reform Act passed.

1833 Apr.   Irish Coercion Act passed.
     Aug.   Slavery abolished throughout British Empire; £20 million
            allocated as compensation to slave-owners.

1834 July   Resignation of Earl Grey over question of extending Irish
            Coercion Act. Lord Melbourne becomes prime minister with
            leading ministers retaining places.
     Aug.   Poor Law Amendment Act passed, the 'New Poor Law'.
            Central board of commissioners appointed to administer
            system (for further details, see p. 110).
     Nov.   Ministry dismissed by the King and caretaker administration
            formed under Duke of Wellington. Principal figures: Duke of
            Wellington (prime minister and secretary of state); Lord
            Lyndhurst (lord chancellor).
     Dec.   *Peel administration* formed. Principal figures: Sir Robert
            Peel (prime minister and chancellor of the exchequer); Lord
            Lyndhurst (lord chancellor); Duke of Wellington (foreign
            secretary). Parliament dissolved because majority in the
            Commons against the ministry. Peel issues 'Tamworth
            Manifesto' in an attempt to broaden base of support.

1835 Feb.   New parliament meets.
     Apr.   Sir Robert Peel resigns after Whigs and Irish members
            combine in the 'Lichfield House Compact' to defeat Peel on
            the use of surplus revenues from the Irish Church. *Second
            Melbourne administration* formed. Principal figures: Lord
            Melbourne (prime minister); Viscount Palmerston (foreign
            secretary); Lord John Russell (home secretary).
     Sept. Municipal Corporations Act. Members of town councils to be
            elected by ratepayers; town councils to publish accounts
            and budgets.

1836 Aug.   Commutation of Tithes Act. Tithes to be paid in money and
            calculated on basis of average price of corn in previous
            seven years.

1837 June   Death of William IV; accession of Queen Victoria.
     Nov.   First parliament of Queen Victoria's reign meets; Lord
            Melbourne continues as prime minister.

1838 Aug.   National Charter drawn up (for fuller details of the
            development of Chartism, see pp. 151–2).
     Sept. Anti-Corn Law League set up at Manchester under the
            leadership of John Bright and Richard Cobden.

1840 Jan.   Penny postage introduced.
     Feb.   Marriage of Victoria and Prince Albert of
            Saxe-Coburg-Gotha.

1841 Aug.   Following defeat of the government, *second Peel
            administration* formed. Principal figures: Sir Robert Peel
            (prime minister); Duke of Wellington (minister without
            portfolio); Sir James Graham (home secretary); William

Ewart Gladstone (president of the Board of Trade, from 1843).

1842 June   New sliding scale of duties introduced to regulate the corn trade; duties on over 700 articles removed or reduced; income tax reimposed.

1844 May   Bank Charter Act. Note-issuing and credit functions of Bank of England separated. Note circulation limited.

1845 Oct.   First effects of Irish potato blight felt. Beginning of the Irish famine.

Dec.   Peel resigns over desire to repeal Corn Laws (6th); resumes office (20th).

1846 Jan.   Peel declares for a total repeal of the Corn Laws.

June   Royal assent given to repeal of the Corn Laws; sliding scale abolished; duty retained until 1849; only a nominal duty of 1s. retained thereafter.   Resignation of Peel after defeat of government on Irish Coercion Bill. *Russell administration* formed. Principal figures: Lord John Russell (prime minister); Lord Palmerston (foreign secretary); Thomas B. Macaulay (paymaster-general).

1848 Apr.   Chartist demonstration at Kennington Common in support of third petition.

1849 June   Repeal of the Navigation Laws.

1850 Sept.   Re-establishment of Roman Catholic hierarchy in England.

1851 Feb.   Russell announces intention of government to resign after defeat over Bill to reduce the county franchise to £10 (24th).

Mar.   Russell announces that ministers to resume office after failure of attempts to form a new ministry.

May   Opening of Great Exhibition in Hyde Park.

Dec.   Dismissal of Palmerston for interference with internal affairs of France.

1852 Feb.   *Earl of Derby's administration* formed. Principal figures: Earl of Derby (prime minister); Benjamin Disraeli (chancellor of the exchequer).

Sept.   Death of Duke of Wellington.

1853 Dec.   *Aberdeen administration* formed. Principal figures: Earl of Aberdeen (prime minister); Lord John Russell (foreign secretary); W. E. Gladstone (chancellor of the exchequer); Viscount Palmerston (home secretary).

1854 Mar.   Alliance of Britain and France with Turkey. Declaration of war by England and France on Russia (28th), beginning of Crimean War (for details, see p. 212).

1855 Jan. Resignation of Lord Aberdeen after criticism of the conduct of the Crimean War.
     Feb. *Palmerston administration* formed. Principal figures: Lord Palmerston (prime minister); W. E. Gladstone (chancellor of the exchequer).

1856 Mar. Treaty of Paris concludes Crimean War (for details, see p. 225).

1857 Nov. Commercial crisis in England. Bank Charter Act of 1844 suspended.

1858 Feb. Rejection of Palmerston's Conspiracy to Murder Bill leads to his resignation. *Second Derby administration* formed. Principal figures: Earl of Derby (prime minister); Disraeli (chancellor of the exchequer).
     June Property qualification for members of parliament abolished.
     July Jews admitted to parliament. Act for the better government of India.

1859 Mar. Defeat of government on Reform Bill introduced by Disraeli.
     Apr. Parliament dissolved.
     May   Government resigns after finding itself in a minority in new parliament.
     June *Second Palmerston administration* formed. Principal figures: Lord Palmerston (prime minister); W. E. Gladstone (chancellor of the exchequer); Earl Russell (foreign secretary).

1860 Jan. Commercial treaty between Great Britain and France.

1861 Nov. 'Trent incident'. Two Confederate commissioners, Mason and Slidell, taken from the British steamer *Trent* by Federal (USA) warship.
     Dec. Death of Prince Albert.

1865 Oct. Death of Lord Palmerston; Earl Russell assumes premiership.

1866 Feb. Gladstone introduces a Reform Bill.
     Mar. The 'Cave of Adullam' formed (see Adullamites, p. 284).
     May   Financial crisis in England; widespread bank failures.
     June Gladstone introduces Reform Bill to lower franchise qualifications in the boroughs and the counties. Defeat of the Bill by the revolt of the Adullamites led to the resignation of the ministry. *Third Derby administration* formed. Principal figures: Earl of Derby (prime minister); Disraeli (chancellor of the exchequer).
     July Demonstrations by Reform League in London; Hyde Park railings broken down by crowds (23rd).

1867 Feb. Disraeli introduces reform proposals.   Fenians attempt to seize arsenal at Chester Castle and release prisoners at

Clerkenwell prison. Rising in Ireland suppressed.

May   Reform demonstration held in Hyde Park in defiance of
       government ban; resignation of home secretary, Spencer
       Walpole.
Aug.   Second Reform Act passed (for details, see pp. 60–1).

1868 Feb.   Resignation of Lord Derby; Disraeli becomes prime minister.
     Dec.   Resignation of Disraeli and Conservatives following the
             general election. *Liberal government* formed. Principal
             figures: W.E. Gladstone (prime minister and chancellor of the
             exchequer); J. Bright (Board of Trade); E. Cardwell (War
             Office).

1869 July   Disestablishment and disendowment of the Irish Church.
     Oct.   Opening of Suez Canal.

1870 Jan.   Bankruptcy Act comes into force; imprisonment for debt
             ended.
     Aug.   Irish Land Act passed, providing for compensation for
             outgoing tenants, loans to be spent on improvements,
             restraint on evictions and establishment of courts of
             arbitration.   Forster's Elementary Education Act.
             Establishment of School Boards made compulsory where
             educational provision deemed inadequate (for further
             details, see p. 103).

1871 June   Abolition of religious tests at Oxford and
             Cambridge.   Trade Union Act gives legal recognition to
             trade unions and protection of funds, though unions to
             remain liable to prosecution under provisions of 1825 Act.
     Aug.   Purchase of commissions in the army abolished.

1872 July   Ballot Act passed.
     Aug.   Licensing Act restricting sale of intoxicating liquors.

1873 Mar.   Gladstone defeated on Irish University Bill and resigned, but
             resumed office in the same month.
     June   Beginning of Ashanti War.

1874 Feb.   Gladstone resigned following losses in general election.
             Conservative government formed. Principal figures: B.
             Disraeli (prime minister); Sir Stafford Northcote (chancellor
             of the exchequer); Earl of Derby (foreign secretary).
     July   New Licensing Act passed.

1875 June   Artisans Dwellings Act.
     Aug.   Conspiracy and Protection to Property Act ends use of law of
             conspiracy in trade disputes and legalises peaceful
             picketing.   Employers and Workmen Act limits penalties
             for breach of contract.
     Dec.   British government purchases shares in the Suez Canal
             Company owned by the Khedive of Egypt for £4,000,000.

1877 Jan.   Proclamation of Queen Victoria as Empress of India.

1878 July   Treaty of Berlin (for details, see p. 225).

1879 Jan.   Beginning of Zulu War in South Africa.

1880 Feb.   Dissolution of parliament for general election.
     Apr.   Resignation of ministers, following general election. *Liberal
             government* formed. Principal figures: W. E. Gladstone
             (prime minister and chancellor of the exchequer); Sir William
             Harcourt (home secretary); Earl Granville (foreign secretary).

1881 Mar.   Irish Coercion Act.
     Aug.   Irish Land Act (for details see p. 234).

1882 May   Murder of Lord Frederick Cavendish in Phoenix Park, Dublin
             (see p. 234).
     July   Bombardment of Alexandria.   Resignation of John Bright
             as Chancellor of the Duchy of Lancaster.   New Irish
             Coercion Act.

1883 Aug.   Corrupt and Illegal Practices Act.

1884 Mar.   Franchise Bill introduced.
     July   Franchise Bill blocked in the House of Lords.
     Nov.   Agreement reached between government and opposition on
             redistribution of seats.   Third Reform Act passed (see p. 61).

1885 Mar.   Redistribution Act passed (see p. 61).
     June   Resignation of Gladstone administration. *Conservative
             government* formed. Principal figures: Marquess of
             Salisbury (prime minister and foreign secretary); Lord
             Randolph Churchill (secretary for India); J. Chamberlain
             (president of local government board).
     Nov.   General election.
     Dec.   Results of general election leave Liberals as largest single
             party. 'Hawarden Kite'; Gladstone's support for Home Rule
             for Ireland widely reported.

1886 Feb.   *Liberal government* formed. Principal figures: W. E.
             Gladstone (prime minister); Earl of Rosebery (foreign
             secretary); H. Campbell-Bannerman (secretary for war).
             Gladstone announces intention to examine 'going nearer to
             the source and seat of the mischief' in Ireland. Lord
             Randolph Churchill in Belfast urges loyalists to resist
             attempts at repeal of the Union. Unemployed riots in
             London.
     Mar.   Resignation of Joseph Chamberlain and George Trevelyan
             from government.
     Apr.   Gladstone introduces Irish Home Rule Bill.
     June   Defeat of Home Rule Bill on second reading in Commons.
             Dissolution of parliament and general election called.
     July   As a result of general election Gladstone resigned.

Conservative government formed. Principal figures:
Marquess of Salisbury (prime minister and foreign
secretary); Lord Randolph Churchill (chancellor of the
exchequer).

Sept. Parnell's Tenant Relief Bill defeated.

Dec. Resignation of Lord Randolph Churchill after disagreements
over his budget proposals. G. J. Goschen becomes
chancellor of exchequer.

1887 June Celebration of Queen Victoria's Jubilee (21st).

Aug. Irish Tenants' Act and new Coercion Act passed.

Nov. 'Bloody Sunday'; meeting of Social Democratic Federation
in Trafalgar Square broken up by police and troops.

1888 Aug. County Councils Act.

Sept. Commission formed to investigate complicity of Parnell and
his colleagues in outrages in Ireland.

1889 Aug. Beginning of London dock strike led by Ben Tillett, Tom
Mann and John Burns.

Sept. Dock companies concede 'docker's tanner', ending strike.

1890 Feb. Parnell cleared of involvement in Irish outrages.

Nov. Parnell cited as co-respondent in O'Shea divorce. Calls for
Parnell to resign as leader of Irish Party.

Dec. Irish Nationalist Party split, majority seceding from Parnell's
leadership.

1891 Aug. Abolition of fees for elementary education.

Oct. Gladstone outlines 'Newcastle Programme'. Death of
Parnell.

Nov. Chamberlain renounces hope of Liberal Unionists rejoining
Liberal Party.

1892 July General election returns small Liberal majority over
Conservatives, but in a minority against all other parties.

Aug. Conservative administration defeated on vote of confidence.
Liberal government formed. Principal figures: W. E.
Gladstone (prime minister); H. H. Asquith (home secretary);
Earl of Rosebery (foreign secretary); H.
Campbell-Bannerman (secretary for war).

1893 Jan. Bradford Conference leads to formation of Independent
Labour Party.

Feb. Gladstone introduces Second Irish Home Rule Bill.

Sept. Home Rule Bill passes third reading in the Commons by 34
votes (1st); defeated in the House of Lords by 419 votes to
41 (8th).

1894 Feb. Employers' Liability Act defeated in the House of Lords.

Mar. Local Government Act passed, creating elected parish
councils, urban district and rural district
councils.   Resignation of Gladstone. Queen summons

Earl of Rosebery to take premiership.   Death duties introduced in Harcourt's budget.

1895 June   Resignation of Liberal government after defeat on 'cordite' vote.

July   General election returns Conservatives as largest single party. *Conservative government* formed. Principal figures: Marquess of Salisbury (prime minister and foreign secretary); A. J. Balfour (first lord of the Treasury); Marquess of Lansdowne (secretary for war); Joseph Chamberlain (colonial secretary).

Dec.   Boundary dispute between British Guiana and Venezuela leads to crisis in relations between Britain and the United States (settled by Treaty of Washington, 1897).   Jameson raid launched in South Africa.

1896 Jan.   Chamberlain repudiates Jameson raid; 'Kruger telegram' of support from German Emperor to President Kruger on defeat of Jameson raid (3rd).

Oct.   Lord Rosebery resigns Liberal leadership; Sir William Harcourt becomes effective party leader.

1897 July   Committee of House of Commons reports on Jameson raid, censuring Rhodes but acquitting Chamberlain and the Colonial Office.

Aug.   Workmen's Compensation Act passed; accidents at work to be paid for by employers.

1898 June   Anglo-French Convention settles colonial boundaries in West Africa.

Sept.   Defeat of dervishes at Omdurman and capture of Khartoum.   Confrontation of French and British forces at Fashoda – the 'Fashoda Crisis'.

Nov.   Marchand marches French forces away from Fashoda.

Dec.   Campbell-Bannerman becomes leader of the Liberal Party, following departure of Harcourt and Morley from the leading circles of the party.

1899 Mar.   Anglo-French Convention resolves spheres of influence dispute concerning Congo and Nile basins.

Mar.–Apr.   Inconclusive talks with Germany about possibility of an alliance.

May   Hague Conference to discuss disarmament and peace, leading to revision of laws of war and setting up of Court of Arbitration.

May–June   Conference between Milner and Kruger to resolve differences between Boers and Uitlanders breaks down (31 May–5 June).

Oct.   Outbreak of Boer War.

Nov.   British overtures for an alliance with Germany rejected.

Dec.   'Black Week' (10th–15th); British defeats at Stormberg (10th), Magersfontein (11th) and Colenso (15th). Buller superseded by Lord Roberts with Lord Kitchener as chief of staff.

1900 Feb.   Relief of Ladysmith (28th).
    Feb.   Labour Representation Committee (LRC) formed after a meeting at Memorial Hall in London, with aim of electing members of parliament 'sympathetic with the needs and demands of the Labour movement'; political levy from unions agreed.   Irish nationalists recombine under the leadership of John Redmond.
    May   Relief of Mafeking; widespread rejoicing in England (17th).
    Oct.   General election, known as the 'Khaki' election. Conservatives returned with reduced majority.
    Nov.   Salisbury gives up Foreign Office and replaced by Lansdowne.

1901 Jan.   Death of Queen Victoria; accession of Edward VII (22nd).
    Feb.   Breakdown of peace negotiations between Kitchener and Botha at Middelburg.

1902 Jan.   Alliance signed between Britain and Japan.
    Mar.   Boers sue for peace. Education Bill introduced.
    May   Peace with Boers signed at Vereeniging.
    July   Salisbury succeeded as premier by A. J. Balfour.
    Dec.   Education Act passed (see p. 103).

1903 Mar.   Irish Land Purchase Act passed, sponsored by George Wyndham, secretary for Ireland.
    May   Chamberlain announces his support for imperial preference at speech in Birmingham.   Edward VII's visit to Paris opens way to more cordial relations with France.
    Sept.   Chamberlain and leading tariff reformers resign from cabinet to prosecute their campaign in the country at large. Cabinet reconstruction. Austen Chamberlain becomes chancellor of the exchequer; Alfred Lyttelton becomes colonial secretary.

1904 Apr.   *Entente Cordiale* between Britain and France. Agreement over Morocco, followed by agreement over Siam, Egypt and Newfoundland.
    Oct.   Sir John ('Jacky') Fisher appointed first sea lord.   Dogger Bank incident involving Russian fleet and British fishing vessels.

1905 Apr.   Anglo-French military convention.
    Aug.   Anglo-Japanese Alliance.   Unemployed Workmen Act passed. Unemployed registers formed under auspices of local government boards. Expenses to be defrayed by voluntary contribution.
    Nov.   Sinn Fein Party founded in Dublin.
    Dec.   Resignation of Balfour. *Liberal government* formed. Principal figures: Campbell-Bannerman (prime minister), Asquith (chancellor of the exchequer), Sir E. Grey (foreign secretary), Lord Haldane (secretary for war), Lloyd George (president of Board of Trade).

1906 Jan. General election; Liberals returned with an overall majority of 84. Twenty-nine Labour MPs elected.
     Feb. Parliament met.
     Apr. Education Bill introduced.
     July Joseph Chamberlain paralysed by a stroke; effective end of his political career.
     Dec. Trades Disputes Act passed, reversing Taff Vale decision.   Government drop Education Bill after it has been mutilated by amendments in Lords.

1907 Mar. Third Imperial (Colonial) Conference in London.
     May Introduction of the Territorial and Reserve Forces Bill to establish the Territorial Army.
     June House of Commons approves Campbell-Bannerman's resolutions that if a Bill passed all its stages in the Commons three times it should become law, notwithstanding opposition by the Lords.
     Aug. Anglo-Russian Agreement on Asia. Russia joins the *Entente*.

1908 Apr. Campbell-Bannerman resigns and Asquith becomes prime minister. Lloyd George becomes chancellor of the exchequer.
     July Old Age Pensions Bill passed by Parliament.
     Oct. Suffragette disturbances in Trafalgar Square.
     Nov. Lords reject the Licensing Bill.

1909 Mar. Introduction of Navy Bill, a result of alarm at German shipbuilding. Four keels to be laid at once and four more if needed.
     Apr. Lloyd George introduces his 'People's Budget'.
     July Laying of the other four Dreadnought keels (provided for by Navy Act) is sanctioned by the government.
     Nov. Lords reject the Budget.   House of Lords upholds Osborne Judgment.
     Dec. Parliament dissolved.

1910 Jan. General election. *Minority Liberal government* formed, dependent upon the support of the Irish Nationalist and Labour Parties.
     Apr. Lloyd George Budget passed. Parliament Bill introduced with aim of reforming the House of Lords.
     May Death of Edward VII. George V ascends the throne.
     June Constitutional Conference between the leaders of the Liberal and Unionist Parties. A 'party truce' called while Conference tries to reach a compromise on the question of reform of the House of Lords.
     Oct. Unionists reject Lloyd George's suggestion of a coalition.
     Nov. Conference dissolves, having failed to reach agreement. Asquith secures the King's pledge to create enough peers to pass the Parliament Bill if the Liberals win the election.
     Dec. Liberals returned to power with very little change in the relative strengths of the parties.

1911 May   National Insurance Bill introduced by Lloyd George.
     Aug. Parliament Act passes House of Lords. The Lords lose their
           power of veto.   House of Commons resolves to pay MPs
           £400 p.a.
     Aug. Dock strike.   Two-day railway strike.
     Oct. Churchill becomes first lord of the admiralty.
     Nov. Balfour resigns leadership of the Unionist Party and is
           succeeded by Andrew Bonar Law.   Suffragette riots,
           entailing extensive damage to property in London's West
           End.
     Dec. National Insurance Bill receives royal assent.

1912 Feb. Miners' strike begins with the aim of securing a national
           minimum wage for miners.
     Mar. A Bill to establish minimum district wages for miners is
           rushed through parliament.
     Apr. End of miners' strike.   Introduction of third Irish Home
           Rule Bill.
     May   Strike of London dockers.
     Aug. End of dockers' strike.
     Sept. Two hundred thousand Ulstermen sign a 'Solemn Covenant'
           to oppose Home Rule.   Anglo-French naval convention.

1913 Jan. Home Rule Bill rejected by House of Lords.
     July Home Rule Bill again rejected by Lords.
     Oct. Lloyd George begins his 'Land Campaign' for reform of rural
           social conditions.

1914 Mar. Suffragette riots in London.   Curragh officers resign their
           commissions rather than act against Ulster resistance to
           Home Rule.
     May   Third reading of Home Rule Bill and Welsh Church
           (Disestablishment) Bill in Commons.
     June Third reading of Plural Voting Bill.   Assassination of Franz
           Ferdinand, Crown Prince of Austria, at Sarajevo.
     July Buckingham Palace Conference attempts and fails to reach
           compromise on the exclusion of Ulster from the Home Rule
           Bill.
     Aug. Britain declares war on Germany and Austria.
     Nov. First battle of Ypres. Britain declares war on Turkey.

1915 Apr. Anglo-French landings at Gallipoli.
     May   Formation of *Coalition government*, which Conservatives
           join, under Asquith. Bonar Law becomes colonial secretary,
           Balfour replaces Churchill at the Admiralty, Curzon becomes
           lord privy seal.   Second battle of Ypres.
     Dec. Robertson appointed chief of imperial general staff. Haig
           succeeds French as British C. in C. on the Western Front.

1916 Jan. Allies evacuate Gallipoli peninsula. Introduction of
           conscription.
     Apr. Easter Rising in Dublin suppressed.

June   Naval battle at Jutland establishes British naval superiority.
July–Nov.   Battle of the Somme.
July   Lloyd George made secretary for war.
Dec.   Asquith resigns; Lloyd George forms new *Coalition government*. War cabinet established with five members: Lloyd George (prime minister), Bonar Law (chancellor of the exchequer and leader of the House), and Milner, Curzon and Arthur Henderson (Labour), who had no departmental responsibilities.

1917 Feb.   Revolution in Russia led by Kerensky.
Apr.   Battle of Vimy Ridge.
June   Allenby takes command in Palestine.
July   Hundred-day battle of Flanders begins.
Oct.   Bolshevik Revolution in Russia.
Nov.   British take Gaza.   British take Passchendaele.   Balfour Declaration that Britain favoured the establishment of a 'national home' for the Jewish people in Palestine.
Dec.   Allenby enters Jerusalem.

1918 Feb.   Representation of the People Act creates universal male and limited female suffrage.
July   Second battle of the Marne.
Sept.   General allied offensive in West.
Oct.   Turkey surrenders.
Nov.   Allies grant armistice to Austria and then to Germany.
Dec.   General election returns Lloyd George to power as head of a *Coalition government*, with 478 'Coalition' MPs returned, the vast majority being Conservatives. Lloyd George (prime minister), Bonar Law (leader of the house), Austen Chamberlain (chancellor of the exchequer), Balfour (foreign secretary), Birkenhead (lord chancellor).   Seventy Sinn Fein MPs refuse to take their seats.

1919 Jan.   Paris Peace Conference begins.   First Dáil Eireann elected. Irish Free State proclaimed.
Jan.–Feb.   Engineers strike at Clyde and Belfast.
Feb.   National Industrial Conference established.   Sankey Commission appointed into mining industry in order to avoid miners' strike.
Apr.   De Valera elected President of Sinn Fein Executive.
Aug.   Sinn Fein declared an illegal organisation.
Sept.   Railway strike.   Dáil Eireann proscribed; increase in acts of violence by Irish Republican Army.
Oct.   End of railway strike.   End of war cabinet. Curzon replaces Balfour as foreign secretary.
Dec.   Viscountess Astor becomes first woman MP to take her seat in parliament.

1920 Jan.   Versailles treaty comes into force (for details, see p. 227).
Apr.   Conscription abolished.
June   Government begins recruiting 'Black and Tans', volunteers to suppress IRA.

Oct.   Miners' strike.
Nov.   Miners' strike ends.
Dec.   Black and Tåns set fire to the city of Cork. Government of Ireland Act passed, partitioning Ireland into six counties of Ulster, and the South. Each has a separate parliament.

1921 Mar.   Anglo-Russian trade agreement signed.   Coal Mines (Decontrol) Act returns mines to their owners after wartime government control.
Apr.   Miners' strike. State of Emergency declared.
May   Elections to Irish parliaments. Sinn Fein win overwhelming majority of seats in southern parliament, but do not recognise it.
June   Miners' strike ends.
Oct.   Conference to negotiate an Irish treaty in London.
Dec.   'Articles of Agreement for a Treaty' signed, When ratified Southern Ireland will be the 'Irish Free State' with Dominion status within the Empire.

1922 Sept.   'Chanak crisis' caused by Turko-Greek war.
Oct.   Carlton Club meeting of Conservative Party decides not to continue their coalition with Lloyd George. Lloyd George resigns. Formation of *Conservative government* under Bonar Law.
Nov.   General election. Conservatives gain a comfortable majority (73 seats). Principal figures: Bonar Law (prime minister), Stanley Baldwin (chancellor of the exchequer), Curzon (foreign secretary).
Dec.   Irish Free State comes into formal existence.

1923 May   Bonar Law resigns because of ill-health and Baldwin becomes prime minister.
Dec.   General election. No party is returned with an overall majority. Conservatives the largest party with 258 seats. Baldwin resumes office.

1924 Jan.   Conservative government defeated on an amendment to the Address. Baldwin resigns. *First Labour government* takes office, dependent upon Liberal support in parliament. Principal figures: James Ramsay MacDonald (prime minister and foreign secretary), Philip Snowden (chancellor of the exchequer), John Wheatley (minister of health).
Feb.   Britain recognises Soviet Russia.
July   Beginning of London Conference on Reparations.
Aug.   Conference accepts Dawes plan.
Sept.   Hastings, the attorney-general, withdraws a prosecution against J. R. Campbell for incitement to mutiny.
Oct.   Labour government defeated on vote of censure over Campbell case. MacDonald resigns office. In general election. Conservatives win a large majority of seats.
Nov.   Formation of *Conservative government*. Principal figures: Baldwin (prime minister), Churchill (chancellor of the exchequer), Austen Chamberlain (foreign secretary),

Neville Chamberlain (minister of health), Birkenhead
(secretary for India).

1925 Apr.   Britain returns to Gold Standard.
    July   'Red Friday'; Triple Alliance of miners, railway, and transport
            unions threatens an embargo on transport of coal if miners'
            wages cut. Government averts strike by nine-month subsidy
            and setting up a Royal Commission into mining industry
            under Herbert Samuel.
    Dec.   Widows, Orphans and Old Age Pensions Act introduces
            contributory pensions; pensions to be given at 65 instead of
            70.   Treaty of Locarno signed in London.   Irish
            Boundary Agreement.

1926 Mar.   Samuel Commission reports: finds the government subsidy
            unsound, which signifies wage cuts.
    May   Miners refuse wage cuts and are 'locked out'. Nine-day
            General Strike.
    Oct. – Nov.   Imperial Conference in London. Britain and her
            Dominions are to be regarded as autonomous units of equal
            status.
    Nov.   Miners return to work.

1927 May   Passage of Trade Disputes and Trade Unions Act: General
            Strikes made illegal and 'contracting-in' instituted as basis of
            trade union political levy to Labour Party.
    Aug   Failure of conference on naval disarmament between
            Britain, USA and Japan.
            Unemployed Insurance Act reduces benefits.

1928 Apr.   Voting age of women lowered from 30 to 21.
    May   Parliament rejects Revised Prayer Book.

1929 Mar.   Passing of Local Government Act abolishes the guardians of
            the poor and transfers their responsibilities to county councils.
    May   General election. No party secures an overall majority.
            Labour has most seats (289).
    June   Formation of Labour government. Principal figures:
            MacDonald (prime minister), Arthur Henderson (foreign
            secretary), Snowden (chancellor of exchequer), J. H.
            Thomas (lord privy seal), Margaret Bondfield (minister of
            labour).
    Oct.   'Crash' of New York Stock Exchange.   Anglo-Russian
            relations resumed.   Irwin, viceroy of India, makes a public
            promise of Dominion status for India.

1930 Apr.   Naval Disarmament Conference in London. Naval treaty
            between Britain, France, Italy, Japan and USA.
    May   Sir Oswald Mosley resigns from government when cabinet
            rejects his unemployment policy.
    Nov.   Round Table Conference on India in London.
    Dec.   Two and a half million unemployed.

1931 Feb.   Mosley founds the 'New Party'.   May Committee on
             economy established by government.
     July   Financial crisis in Europe. The May Committee recommends
             economies, including reduction of unemployment benefits.
     Aug.   Labour government breaks up on question of reducing
             unemployment benefits.   Formation of *National
             Government* by MacDonald with four Labour, four
             Conservative and two Liberal cabinet ministers. Principal
             figures: MacDonald (prime minister), Snowden (chancellor
             of the exchequer), Thomas, Sankey, Baldwin, Neville
             Chamberlain, Hoare, Cunliffe-Lister, Samuel (home
             secretary) and Reading (foreign secretary).
     Sept.   Britain goes off the Gold Standard.   Second India
             Conference begins in London. Economy measures
             introduced.
     Oct.   General election. National Government win an
             overwhelming majority of seats (largely a Conservative
             majority). Labour badly beaten.
     Nov.   MacDonald forms second 'National' cabinet. Principal
             figures: MacDonald (prime minister), Baldwin (lord
             president), Neville Chamberlain (chancellor of the
             exchequer), Snowden (lord privy seal), Sir John Simon
             (foreign secretary).

1932 Feb.   Beginning of two-year Disarmament Conference at Geneva.
     Mar.   Import Duties Act imposes 10 per cent general duty on
             imports.
     Apr.   Exchange Equalisation Fund established to smooth
             variations in exchange rates. Import duty on manufactured
             goods raised to between 20 and 33⅓ per cent.
     July   Anglo-French Pact of friendship signed at Lausanne.
     July–Aug.   Ottawa Imperial Economic Conference.
     Sept.   Snowden, Samuel and Sinclair resign from government in
             protest at its protectionist policies
     Oct.   Mosley launches British Union of Fascists.
     Nov.–Dec.   Third India Conference in London.

1933 Jan.   Unemployment reaches almost 3 million.   Hitler becomes
             Chancellor of Germany.
     Apr.   Anglo-German Trade Pact.
     Apr.–July   Embargo on Russian exports.
     June–July   World Monetary and Economic Conference in London.

1934 Feb.   Anglo-Russian Trade Agreement.
     Oct.   Failure of Naval Disarmament Conference in London.

1935 Apr.   Stresa Conference of Britain, France and Italy.
     June   MacDonald resigns. Baldwin becomes prime minister.
             Reconstruction of National Government: Simon (home
             secretary), Hoare (foreign secretary), Neville Chamberlain
             (chancellor of the exchequer), Cunliffe-Lister (secretary for
             air).

	Aug.	Government of India Bill passed.
	Nov.	General election returns National Government with a large majority, largely made up of Conservatives.
	Dec.	Hoare–Laval Pact between Britain and France over Abyssinia. Hoare resigns; Anthony Eden the new foreign secretary. Clement Attlee elected leader of the Labour Party.

1936	Jan.	Death of George V. Edward VIII succeeds to the throne.
	Mar.	London Naval Convention signed by Britain, USA and France.
	July	Beginning of Spanish Civil War.
	Aug.	Anglo-Egyptian treaty terminates British military occupation.
	Sept.	'Non-Intervention (in Spain) Committee' of all European powers meets in London.
	Oct.	Russia accedes to London Naval Convention.
	Dec.	Edward VIII abdicates. Accession of George VI. Irish Constitution (Amendment) and Executive Authority Acts abolish chief functions of governor-general and retains King for external relations only.

1937	Jan.	Anglo-Italian Agreement signed.
	Apr.	Indian Constitution comes into force.
	May	Baldwin resigns. Neville Chamberlain becomes prime minister, with Simon (chancellor of exchequer), Eden (foreign secretary), Hoare (home secretary).
	June	Imperial Conference in London.
	July	Anglo-Russian and Anglo-German Naval Agreements signed.

1938	Feb.	Eden resigns and is succeeded by Lord Halifax.
	Apr.	Agreement signed between Britain and Eire. Anglo-Italian Agreement on East Mediterranean and Red Sea.
	Sept.	Chamberlain meets Hitler at Berchtesgarden. British fleet mobilised. Munich Conference on Czechoslovakia, attended by Chamberlain, Daladier, Hitler and Mussolini.
	Oct.	Duff Cooper resigns as first lord of the Admiralty.
	Nov.	Anglo-Italian Pact comes into force.

1939	Mar.	British guarantee to Poland.
	Apr.	Russia proposes alliance with Britain and France against German aggression. Compulsory military service announced (operative from June).
	July	Ministry of Supply set up.
	Aug.	Emergency Powers Act.
	Sept.	Anglo-Polish Pact of mutual assistance. German–Soviet Non-aggression Pact. War declared on Germany (3rd).

1940	Apr.	Germans invade Denmark and Norway.
	May	Invasion of France. Chamberlain resigns. Formation of *Coalition government* under Churchill. War cabinet formed with Churchill as P.M. and minister of defence, Chamberlain (lord president), Attlee (lord privy seal),

Halifax (foreign secretary), Arthur Greenwood (minister without portfolio). British troops evacuate Norway.

June British troops evacuate France at Dunkirk. Italy declares war on Britain.

July Germans occupy Channel Islands.

July–Sept. Battle of Britain.

Sept.–Oct. London 'Blitz'.

Oct. British troops land in Greece.

Nov. German air raids on Coventry.

1941 Mar. Roosevelt signs Lend-Lease Bill.

May Raid on London damages House of Commons. HMS *Hood* sunk. *Bismarck* sunk.

June Germans invade Russia.

July Anglo-Russian Alliance.

Aug. Roosevelt and Churchill issue Atlantic Charter.

Dec. Japanese attack US fleet at Pearl Harbor without warning.   Germany and Italy declare war on USA.

1942 Feb. Fall of Singapore to Japanese.

May Anglo-Soviet treaty for 20 years. First 1,000-bomber raid on Cologne.

Aug. Raid on Dieppe.   Alexander takes command of Middle East Army.   Montgomery in command of 8th Army.

Oct.–Nov. Battle of El Alamein.

Dec. Publication of Beveridge report on *Social Insurance and Allied Services*.

1943 Jan. Casablanca Conference: Allies demand unconditional surrender of Germany, Italy and Japan.

Feb. Ministry of Town and Country Planning set up.

Sept. Allies invade Italy.

Oct. Foreign secretaries of Britain, USA and USSR agree to found United Nations on the basis of their wartime alliance.

Nov.–Dec. Churchill, Roosevelt and Stalin meet at Tehran Conference.

1944 June Allies enter Rome.   'D-Day': Allied landing in Normandy.

Aug. Passage of Butler Education Act.

Sept. Battle of Arnhem.

Oct. Moscow Conference of Churchill and Stalin.

Nov. Address from the throne refers to a comprehensive health service and a uniform system of national insurance.

1945 Feb. Yalta Conference of Churchill, Stalin and Roosevelt.

May Germany surrenders.   Labour Party leaves coalition and Churchill forms 'caretaker' government.

July General election gives Labour a huge majority. Formation of *first majority Labour government*. Principal figures: Attlee (prime minister), Herbert Morrison (leader of the House), Aneurin Bevan (minister of health), Ernest Bevin (foreign secretary), Hugh Dalton (chancellor of the exchequer), Stafford Cripps (president of the Board of Trade).

July–Aug.   Potsdam Conference.
Aug.   British troops liberate Burma.   Atom bombs dropped on
       Hiroshima and Nagasaki.
Sept.   Japan surrenders.
Dec.   Britain, USA and USSR agree in Moscow to provisional
       democratic government in Korea. Anglo-American Financial
       Agreement.

1946 Mar.   Bank of England nationalised. Churchill's 'Iron Curtain'
            speech at Fulton, Missouri, USA.
     July   Coal Industry Nationalisation Act passed.   Irgun terrorists
            blow up British military HQ in King David Hotel, Jerusalem.
     Nov.   National Health Service Act passed (to take effect from July
            1948).
     Dec.   Britain and USA arrange economic merger of their zones in
            Germany

1947 Jan.   Coal Industry Nationalisation Act comes into effect.
     Feb.   Government announces that India will become independent
            by June 1948.
     Mar.   Anglo-French treaty of alliance.
     Apr.   School-leaving age raised to 15.
     June   US secretary of state Marshall suggests US aid for Europe.
     Aug.   Act nationalising electricity is passed.   Inland Transport
            Act passes.   India becomes independent.
     Nov.   Budget leak. Dalton resigns; Cripps becomes chancellor of
            the exchequer.

1948 Jan.   Inland Transport Act becomes effective; railways are
            nationalised.   Burma becomes independent.
     Apr.   US Economic Cooperation Act becomes effective, with $980
            million of 'Marshall Aid' to be at Britain's disposal.   Act
            nationalising electricity becomes effective.
     May   Jews proclaim new state of Israel.
     July   1947 Town and Country Planning Act becomes
            effective.   Representation of the People Act
            passed.   Berlin airlift by Britain and USA.   End of
            bread rationing.

1949 Mar.   End of clothes rationing.
     Apr.   North Atlantic Treaty Organisation (NATO) established.
            Conference of Commonwealth P.M.s redefines
            'Commonwealth'. Independent republics who accept the
            Crown as a 'symbol of the free association of its
            independent member states' are to remain in
            Commonwealth. Ireland becomes a republic.
     May   Gas industry nationalised.
     Sept.   Sterling devalued from $4.03 to $2.80.
     Nov.   Royal assent given to Iron and Steel Nationalisation Bill, but
            it is not to be effective until January 1951.

1950 Jan.   Britain recognises Communist government of China.
     Feb.   General election: Labour returned to office with a greatly
            reduced majority.

May	Petrol rationing ends.
June	North Korean troops enter South Korea. UN Security Council authorises military aid to South Korea.
Sept.	British troops in action in Korea.
Oct.	Chinese troops enter Korean War. Cripps retires. Hugh Gaitskell becomes chancellor of the exchequer.

1951	Jan.	New rearmament programme of £4,700 million announced.
	Feb.	Nationalisation of iron and steel takes effect. Bevin resigns from Foreign Office and is replaced by Herbert Morrison.
	April	Bevan resigns in protest at cabinet decision to impose prescription charges (along with Harold Wilson and John Freeman).
	Oct.	General election. Establishment of *Conservative government* with majority of 16 seats. Principal figures: Churchill (prime minister), Eden (foreign secretary), R. A. Butler (chancellor of the exchequer), Maxwell Fyfe (home secretary).
	Dec.	London Foreign Exchange Market reopens after 12 years.

1952	Jan.	Commonwealth Finance Ministers Conference in London to coordinate policy of the sterling area. Restrictions imposed on imports and hire-purchase.
	Feb.	Death of George VI. Queen Elizabeth II ascends throne.
	Mar.	Fifty-seven Labour M.P.s dissent from 'Party line' and vote against government defence motion.
	Oct.	Britain's first atom bomb exploded off Monte Bello Islands, Western Australia.

1953	Feb.	Amnesty for wartime deserters declared.
	Mar.	Steel denationalised.
	Apr.	Road transport denationalised.
	June	Coronation of Elizabeth II. Britain gives *de facto* recognition to the Republic of Egypt.
	July	Korean armistice signed at Panmunjon.
	Sept.	End of sugar rationing after 14 years.

1954	Mar.	London Gold Market reopened after 15 years.
	Apr.	Geneva Conference on Indo-China opens. Bevan resigns from Labour Party shadow cabinet over the party's Far Eastern policy.
	July	All food rationing ends. Anglo-Egyptian Agreement in Cairo to withdraw British troops from Suez Canal zone.

1954	Aug.	End of hire-purchase controls.
	Oct.	Anglo-Egyptian Suez Canal Agreement reached.

1955	Feb.	Decision to proceed with manufacture of hydrogen bombs announced. Hire-purchase restrictions reintroduced.
	Apr.	Paris Agreement ratified: West Germany to join NATO and Britain to maintain four divisions and tactical air force on the Continent. USSR denounces 1942 treaty with Britain and France. Churchill resigns: Eden becomes prime minister,

	Harold Macmillan, foreign secretary, Selwyn Lloyd, minister of defence.
May	General election gives Conservatives a majority of nearly 60.
July	Summit Conference of Britain, France, USA and USSR at Geneva. Further hire-purchase restrictions.
Dec.	Attlee retires. Gaitskell elected leader of the Labour Party. Cabinet reshuffle. Macmillan becomes chancellor of the exchequer, Selwyn Lloyd, foreign secretary, Butler lord privy seal and leader of the House.

1956 Feb.	House of Commons rejects motion to abolish the death penalty.
June	British troops leave Suez.
July	Nasser nationalises Suez Canal.
Aug.	Britain rejects request for independence by Central African Federation. Tripartite Declaration by Britain, France and USA against nationalisation of Suez Canal.
Oct.	Anglo-French invasion of Suez. British outline plan of a European Free Trade Area announced.
Nov.	Ceasefire in Suez.
Dec.	Anglo-French troops evacuate Suez. Britain draws £201 million from International Monetary Fund (IMF).

1957 Jan.	Eden retires. Macmillan becomes prime minister and Peter Thorneycroft becomes chancellor of the exchequer.
Mar.	Gold Coast given independence as Ghana.
Apr.	Decision to discontinue 'call up' for national service after 1960. Labour Party calls for an end to planned British hydrogen bomb tests.
May	First British hydrogen bomb explosion in the Central Pacific.
July	Electricity Bill enacted: Central Electricity Generating Board and Electricity Council replace Central Electricity Authority. Federation of Malaya Independence Act is given royal assent.
Aug.	Council on Prices, Productivity and Incomes established.
Sept.	Disarmament discussions in London end without agreement. Publication of Wolfenden report on prostitution.

1958 Jan.	Treaties establishing European Economic Community (EEC) and Euratom come into force. Thorneycroft resigns in protest at failure of cabinet to cut government expenditure. Heathcoat Amory becomes chancellor of the exchequer. Russia proposes 19-nation summit negotiations.
Feb.	Britain and USA agree on the establishment of American missile bases in Britain. Campaign for Nuclear Disarmament (CND) set up with Earl (Bertrand) Russell as president.
Apr.	First Aldermaston march organised by CND.
June	British plan for Cyprus rejected by Greek government.
July	Government decides to resume British nuclear tests. First life peers created.

Oct.	Hire-purchase restrictions removed.
Nov.	France formally rejects British proposal for a European Free Trade Area.
Dec.	Partial convertibility between sterling and the American dollar announced.

1959 Jan. Britain recognises Castro regime in Cuba.
Feb. London Agreement between Britain, Greece and Turkey on independence for Cyprus.   Macmillan visits Moscow.
Mar. Air services agreement between Britain and USSR.
Oct. General election returns Conservatives with a majority of 100.
Nov. European Free Trade Association (EFTA) convention agreed.
Dec. Anglo-Russian Cultural Agreement reached.

1960 Feb. Macmillan addresses South African parliament on African nationalism– 'wind of change' speech.   Britain agrees to the establishment of a US ballistic missile early warning system in Britain.
Apr. Blue Streak rocket abandoned as a military weapon.   Hire-purchase restrictions reintroduced and credit squeeze begins.   Togoland becomes independent.
May Opening and breakdown of Paris Summit Conference.   EFTA treaty comes into effect.
June Somaliland given independence.   Commons rejects Wolfenden Commission's recommendations on homosexuality.
July Selwyn Lloyd replaces Amory as chancellor of the exchequer.
Aug. Cyprus becomes independent.
Oct. Federation of Nigeria becomes independent.   Labour Party Conference votes against existing party defence policy.   Royal Navy's first nuclear submarine *Dreadnought* launched.
Nov. Gaitskell re-elected leader of the Labour Party.   Britain announces that she will provide facilities for US Polaris submarines at Holy Loch.

1961 Jan. Hire-purchase controls relaxed.
Feb. Government announce an increase in National Health Service prescription charges.
Mar. First US nuclear submarine arrives at Holy Loch Conference on discontinuance of nuclear weapons tests between Britain, USA and USSR begins at Geneva.
July British troops land in Kuwait following an appeal from Kuwaiti government.   Macmillan announces government decision to apply for EEC membership.   Anglo-American agreement to establish US Missile Defence Alarm Station in Britain.   'Pay pause' announced by Selwyn Lloyd; National Economic Development Council (NEDC) established.
Aug. IMF places £714 million at Britain's disposal.   Failure of Geneva Conference. USSR to resume nuclear weapons tests.

	Oct.	Labour Party Conference votes against Polaris bases and German troops being stationed in Britain.
	Nov.	Official opening of negotiations for British entry into EEC at Brussels.
	Dec.	Tanganyika receives independence. Macmillan meets President Kennedy in Bermuda.
1962	Mar.	Liberal wins Orpington by-election.
	Apr.	End of government's 'Pay pause'.
	July	Macmillan asks seven senior ministers for their resignations. Cabinet reconstructed. Butler (deputy prime minister and first secretary of state), Henry Brooke (home secretary), Reginald Maudling (chancellor of the exchequer). Government announces setting up of the National Incomes Commission.
	Aug.	Jamaica, Trinidad and Tobago become independent.
	Dec.	British troops quell uprising in Brunei. Macmillan meets Kennedy at Nassau. USA offers Polaris missiles for use on British submarines as part of a multilateral NATO force. British Railways Board replaces British Transport Commission under terms of the 1976 Transport Act. Beeching made chairman.
1963	Jan.	Britain refused entry to the EEC. Death of Gaitskell.
	Feb.	Harold Wilson elected leader of the Labour Party.
	Mar.	Publication of Beeching Report on British Railways.
	Apr.	Polaris missile agreement signed by Britain and USA.
	June	House of Commons censure John Profumo, ex-minister for war, for lying to House.
	July	Peerage Bill receives royal assent. Peers can now renounce titles.
	Aug.	Partial nuclear test ban treaty signed by Britain, USA and USSR
	Oct.	Macmillan retires. Sir Alec Douglas-Home becomes prime minister. Iain Macleod and Enoch Powell refuse to serve under Home. Butler becomes foreign secretary, Lloyd, leader of the House, Anthony Barber, minister of health, Edward Heath, secretary of state for industry.
	Dec.	Zanzibar and Kenya become independent. Federation of Rhodesia and Nyasaland is dissolved.
1964	Apr.	First GLC election won by Labour – majority of 27. Retail Price Maintenance abolished.
	Sept.	Malta gains independence. Northern Rhodesia becomes independent as Zambia.
	Oct.	General election. Formation of *Labour government*, with an overall majority of five. Principal figures: Harold Wilson (prime minister), James Callaghan (chancellor of the exchequer), George Brown (deputy P.M. and minister for economic affairs – a new department), Patrick Gordon Walker (foreign secretary). Fifteen per cent import surcharge announced.
	Nov.	Ban on sale of arms to South Africa.

Dec. IMF lends Britain $1,000 million. Statement of Intent on Productivity, Prices and Incomes signed by TUC and employers' organisations.

1965 Jan. National Health prescription charges abolished.   Defeat of Patrick Gordon Walker in Leyton by-election. Succeeded as foreign secretary by Michael Stewart.
Feb. Establishment of National Board for Prices and Incomes.   Gambia becomes independent.
Apr. Import surcharge cut to 10 per cent.   TSR-2 fighter plane development cancelled.
May Britain draws $1,400 million from the IMF.
June Hire-purchase terms stiffened.
July Tightening of Exchange Controls.   Home resigns leadership of Conservative Party. Edward Heath elected to replace him.
Sept. Five-Year National Plan aiming at a 25 per cent increase in GNP by 1970 announced.
Oct. Parliament passes Bill abolishing death penalty.
Nov. Rhodesia makes a Unilateral Declaration of Independence (UDI). Economic sanctions announced.

1966 Jan. White Paper announces proposed Industrial Reorganisation Corporation.   British government bans all trade with Rhodesia.
Feb. Hire-purchase terms stiffened.
Mar. General election. Labour win overall majority of 97.
May Official seamen's strike.
July End of seamen's strike.   Minister of technology, Frank Cousins, resigns in protest against government incomes policy.   Prices and Incomes Bill introduced providing for an 'early warning' system on prices and incomes. Six-month wage freeze and stiff deflationary measures announced.   George Brown resigns, but is persuaded to remain in office.
Aug. George Brown exchanges office with foreign secretary Michael Stewart. Sir Edward Compton named Britain's first parliamentary commissioner (Ombudsman).
Nov. End of import surcharge.
Dec. Wilson and Rhodesian leader Ian Smith hold negotiations on Rhodesia on board HMS *Tiger*. United Nations Security Council approves British resolution for mandatory sanctions against Rhodesia.

1967 Jan. Prime minister and foreign secretary in Rome for EEC negotiations.   Jeremy Thorpe elected leader of the Liberal Party following Jo Grimond's resignation.
Feb. Russian prime minister Kosygin in London; meets Queen at Buckingham Palace. Downing Street–Kremlin 'hot line' agreed upon.
May Wilson announces Britain's formal application to join the EEC.
June Arab–Israeli War. Arab oil embargo on Britain.   Relaxation of hire-purchase restrictions.

July	Defence cuts announced: withdrawal from East of Suez by mid-1970. Vesting date of British Steel Corporation.
Aug.	Douglas Jay sacked in cabinet reshuffle. Wilson takes over Department of Economic Affairs. Further relaxation of hire-purchase controls.
Sept.	Arabs lift oil embargo. Dock strike begins in London and Liverpool.
Oct.	Liverpool dockers return to work. HMS *Resolution*, Britain's first Polaris submarine, is commissioned.
Nov.	Sterling devalued to $2.40 to the £. Aden becomes independent. Chancellor of the exchequer, James Callaghan, exchanges offices with Roy Jenkins (home secretary).
Dec.	France vetoes British application to join EEC.

1968 Jan.	Public expenditure cuts announced.
Mar.	Rush for gold in leading financial centres. Stock Exchange and banks closed in Britain. Resignation of foreign secretary George Brown. Summit meeting of Western Central Bankers agrees two-tier system for price of gold.
Apr.	Cabinet reshuffle. Barbara Castle becomes minister for employment and productivity. Birmingham immigration speech by Enoch Powell. Heath sacks him from shadow cabinet.
June	National Health Service prescription charges re-introduced.
Sept.	Basle arrangement for sterling area agreed. Swaziland becomes independent.
Oct.	Failure of HMS *Fearless* talks on Rhodesia. Massive demonstration in London against the US involvement in Vietnam War.
Nov.	Hire-purchase restrictions tightened. Credit squeeze imposed.

1969 May	Voting age reduced to 18.
June	Government drops its plans for legal restraints on unofficial strikes in return for a TUC pledge to deal with such disputes.
Aug.	Three-day street battle in Londonderry following Apprentice Boys march. Army takes over security and police functions in Northern Ireland.
Oct.	Department of Economic Affairs abolished.
Dec.	EEC summit meeting at The Hague agrees to negotiations for British entry by June 1970. Parliament votes for permanent abolition of death penalty.

1970 Jan.	Age of majority reduced to 18.
June	General election. Formation of Conservative government with a majority of 30. Principal figures; Heath (prime minister), Macleod (chancellor of the exchequer), Home (foreign secretary), Maudling (home secretary).
July	Death of Macleod. Barber becomes chancellor of the exchequer.
Oct.	Government establishes new conglomerate ministries: Department of Trade and Industry; Department of the Environment.

Dec. Industrial Relations Bill introduced (became law in 1971).

1971 Jan. 'Angry Brigade' bomb attack on home of Robert Carr, secretary for employment.

Feb. Financial collapse of Rolls-Royce Limited. Aero-engine interests nationalised.   First British soldier killed in Belfast.

Mar. One-day strike by 1.5 million engineers against Industrial Relations Bill.   Chichester-Clark resigns Northern Ireland premiership and is succeeded by Brian Faulkner.

June EEC negotiations completed. Parliament endorses British entry.

Aug. Internment without trial introduced in Ulster.

Sept. TUC votes against registration under Industrial Relations Act.

Oct. Labour Party Conference overwhelmingly carries anti-EEC resolution.

Nov. Draft agreement signed between Britain and Rhodesia: Rhodesia to be independent if majority of population agree to negotiated terms.

1972 Jan. Miners' strike begins.   Britain signs EEC treaty.   'Bloody Sunday' – 13 civilians killed by paratroopers in Londonderry.

Feb. State of Emergency declared in power crisis: large-scale power cuts begin, with 1.5 million workers laid off at the height of the crisis. Wilberforce enquiry's terms for settling miners dispute published. Miners vote to return to work.

Mar. National Industrial Relations Court (NIRC) fines TGWU for contempt.   'Direct Rule' established for Northern Ireland: William Whitelaw, secretary of state.

Apr. 'Work-to-rule' on British Rail. NIRC orders 'cooling-off' period.   NIRC imposes further fine for contempt on TGWU.   Roy Jenkins, George Thompson and Harold Lever resign from Labour shadow cabinet over EEC.

May Pearce Commission concludes that the Rhodesian people are not generally in favour of the settlement plan: sanctions continue.

June Government decision to 'float' the pound.

July Robert Carr replaces Maudling as home secretary, when Maudling resigns due to 'Poulson' corruption examination.   Start of national dock strike following rejection of Jones–Aldington proposals for modernisation of the docks.

Aug. President Amin orders expulsion of 40,000 British Asians from Uganda.   Intervention of official solicitor to release dockers imprisoned under Industrial Relations Act.

Sept. Thirty-two unions suspended by TUC for registering under Industrial Relations Act.

Nov. Government imposes immediate 90-day freeze on prices, pay, rent and dividend increases.   Government defeat on new immigration rules.

1973 Jan. Britain becomes a member of EEC.

Feb.   Start of foreign exchange crisis. Dollar devalued by 10 per cent.

Mar.   Ulster referendum: overwhelming majority in favour of retaining links with Britain. White Paper proposes a Northern Ireland Assembly, elected by proportional representation.

Apr.   Phase Two of counter-inflation policy comes into operation: £1 plus 4 per cent and a price code supervised by new Price Commission.

June   New Northern Ireland Assembly elected.

July   Assembly's first sitting ends in chaos.

Oct.   Arab-Israeli War. Arabs cut oil supplies to West.   Firemen begin series of unofficial strikes.   Phase Three of counter-inflation policy launched: 7 per cent or £2.25 a week with threshold safeguards.

Nov.   Electrical Power Engineers Association ban out-of-hours work.   Miners ban overtime.   Major rise in oil prices by the Organisation of Petroleum Exporting Countries (OPEC).   Eleven-man power-sharing executive proposed for Northern Ireland.

Dec.   Rail drivers' union, the Amalgamated Society of Locomotive Engineers and Firemen (ASLEF), bans overtime. Emergency measures taken to conserve fuel: 50 mph speed limit, temperature control in offices, three-day working week announced from 31 December.   Power engineers call off ban on out-of-hours working.   Tripartite Conference (UK government, Northern Ireland executive-designate and Irish government) agree to establish a Council of Ireland – the Sunningdale Agreement.

1974 Jan.   End of Direct Rule in Northern Ireland. New executive takes office.   Lord Carrington made secretary of new Energy Department.   Parliament recalled for two-day debate on energy crisis.   Loyalists expelled from Northern Ireland Assembly after angry scenes.

Feb.   Eighty-one per cent majority favour strike action in ballot of miners.   Heath calls general election and miners' strike begins. No party wins a clear majority in election and Heath enters abortive coalition negotiations with Liberals.

Mar.   Wilson forms a minority Labour government. Principal figures: Callaghan (foreign secretary), Denis Healey (chancellor of the exchequer), Michael Foot (secretary for employment).   End of three-day week and miners' strike.   Food subsidies begin.

Apr.   Britain demands renegotiation of EEC terms of entry.

May   State of Emergency in Northern Ireland due to Protestant General Strike in protest at Sunningdale agreement. Plan to establish a Council of Ireland postponed. General Strike called off. Northern Ireland Assembly suspended and Direct Rule from Westminster resumed.

July   Industrial Relations Act 1971 repealed. Pay Board and statutory incomes policy abolished. NIRC abolished.

Oct.   Guildford pub bombings by Provisional IRA; 5 killed and 70 injured.   General election gives Labour an overall majority of three.

Nov.   Birmingham pub bombings by Provisionals: 21 killed and 120 injured.   Prevention of Terrorism Act passed, proscribing the IRA and giving police wider powers.

Dec.   Government announce aid to British Leyland.

1975 Jan.   Industry Bill introduced proposing National Enterprise Board and planning agreements.   Referendum on EEC membership announced.

Feb.   Heath withdraws as Conservative leader after defeat by Mrs Margaret Thatcher in first ballot of leadership election. Thatcher elected leader.   Wilson – Brezhnev summit meeting in Moscow.

Mar.   Meriden motor cycle co-operative set up.   EEC summit meeting agreement on British renegotiation terms. British cabinet accepts the terms.

Apr.   Government accepts Ryder plan to invest £1,400 million in British Leyland over eight years.

May   *Scottish Daily News* published by workers' cooperative. Elections for Northern Ireland Convention.

June   Referendum gives two-to-one majority for remaining in EEC. In cabinet reshuffle, Benn demoted from Employment to Energy.

July   Government announce anti-inflation policy: £6 a week limit on pay increases until August 1976. TUC supports policy.

Nov.   Chequers meeting of government, TUC, CBI and NEDC on strategy to regenerate British industry.   Britain applies to IMF for £975 million loan.

Dec.   End of internment without trial in Northern Ireland.   Sex Discrimination and Equal Pay Acts come into force.

1976 Mar.   Northern Ireland Convention dissolved: Direct Rule from Westminster continued.   Wilson resigns as prime minister.

Apr.   Callaghan defeats Foot in Parliamentary Labour Party ballot for leadership and becomes prime minister. Foot becomes lord president of the council, Crosland becomes foreign secretary.

May   TUC endorses Stage 2 of government incomes policy (minimum £2.50, maximum £4 per week increases).   Jeremy Thorpe resigns Liberal leadership; Grimond resumes leadership on a caretaker basis.

June   Britain secures £3 billion standby credit from European and American Central Banks.

July   David Steel elected Liberal leader.

Sept.   Roy Jenkins resigns as home secretary to become president of the European Commission (succeeded by Merlyn Rees).   Government seeks £2,300 million loan from IMF.   Ian Smith accepts Anglo-American proposals for majority rule in Rhodesia in two years.

Dec.   British Letter of Intent to IMF. Public spending cuts of £2,500 million, increased indirect taxation and BP share sale.

1977 Jan.   Ian Smith rejects British proposals for transition to majority
             rule.   Bullock Report on industrial democracy published:
             recommends worker-directors.
     Feb.   Death of Crosland; David Owen made foreign secretary
             British Leyland toolroom workers strike.   Government
             defeated on guillotine motion on Devolution Bills for
             Scotland and Wales.
     Mar.   Lib–Lab Pact arranged, enabling government to defeat
             Conservative no-confidence motion.
     May   Eleven-day Loyalist general strike in Ulster called by United
             Ulster Action Council. Collapses through lack of support.
     July   Trade union demonstrations at Grunwick factory in support
             of claims for union recognition.   Stage 3 of incomes
             policy announced: 10 per cent limit on earnings increases.
     Aug.   Violent clashes at National Front march, Lewisham, London.
     Sept.   Owen presents Ian Smith with Anglo-American proposals
             for Rhodesian settlement.   National Front march in
             Manchester banned.
     Nov.   Firemen's strike for a 30 per cent pay increase.

1978 Jan.   End of firemen's strike.   Special Liberal Party Assembly
             votes to continue Lib–Lab pact until July.   Government
             suffers serious defeats in Commons on Scottish Devolution
             Bill. Amendments carried requiring minimum 'Yes' vote of
             40 per cent of the whole electorate.
     Mar.   'Internal settlement' agreed in Rhodesia between Ian Smith
             and three black nationalist leaders.   Stricter controls on
             immigration proposed by House of Commons Select
             Committee.
     May   Ban on Zimbabwe African National Union (ZANU) and
             Zimbabwe African People's Union (ZAPU) lifted in
             Rhodesia.   Labour government suffers several defeats on
             Budget – thresholds for higher tax rates raised to
             £8,000.   Steel announces that Lib–Lab Pact will end in
             August.
     July   Government proposes 5 per cent pay guideline for 12
             months beginning 1 August.   Devolution Bills for
             Scotland and Wales receive royal assent.
     Oct.   Labour Party Conference at Blackpool rejects government's
             5 per cent pay guidelines.
     Nov.   TUC General Council refuses to endorse government's 5 per
             cent pay limit.
     Dec.   Government wins vote of confidence following previous
             day's defeat on imposition of sanctions against private
             companies giving wage increases above 5 per cent.

1979 Jan.   Secondary picketing in road haulage strike creates growing
             difficulties. About 150,000 laid off due to strike.   White
             Rhodesians vote for limited form of majority rule.   Labour
             government survives Commons vote on its handling of
             industrial relations.
     Feb.   Government–TUC 'concordat' with agreement on 5 per cent
             inflation within three years.

Mar.   Devolution Referendums. Wales votes 'no'
        overwhelmingly. Scotland has insufficient 'yes' vote (i.e. not
        40 per cent of total electorate).   Government is defeated
        in no-confidence vote, for first time since 1924. General
        election called.
May   General election: formation of *Conservative government* with
        majority of 41. Principal figures: Thatcher (prime minister),
        Carrington (foreign secretary), Whitelaw (home secretary),
        Geoffrey Howe (chancellor of the exchequer).
June   First direct elections to European Parliament. Conservatives
        win 60 of the 78 British seats.
Aug.   Commonwealth Conference in Lusaka clears the ground for
        Lancaster House conference on Rhodesian settlement,
        which agrees to free elections.
Dec.   Government introduces Employment Bill on picketing,
        secret ballot and closed shop.   End of UDI in Rhodesia,
        Lord Soames arrives as governor to supervise elections.

British monarchs, 1702–1980

	Accession	Coronation
House of Stuart		
Anne (1665–1714)	8 Mar. 1702	23 Apr. 1702
House of Hanover		
George I (1660–1727)	1 Aug. 1714	20 Oct. 1714
George II (1683–1760)	14 June 1727	11 Oct. 1727
George III (1738–1820)	25 Oct. 1760	22 Sept. 1761
George IV (1762–1830)	29 Jan. 1820 (Prince Regent since 5 Feb. 1811)	19 July 1821
William IV (1765–1837)	26 June 1830	8 Sept. 1831
Victoria (1819–1901)	20 June 1837	28 June 1838
House of Saxe-Coburg-Gotha (after 1917 House of Windsor)		
Edward VII (1841–1910)	22 Jan. 1901	9 Aug. 1902
George V (1865–1936)	6 May 1910	22 June 1914
Edward VIII (1894–1972)	20 Jan. 1936	– (Abdicated, 11 Dec. 1936)
George VI (1895–1952)	11 Dec. 1936	12 May 1937
Elizabeth II (1926–)	6 Feb. 1952	2 June 1953

Genealogical charts

The Stuart and Hanoverian lines

Unless otherwise stated, the dates are those of accession.

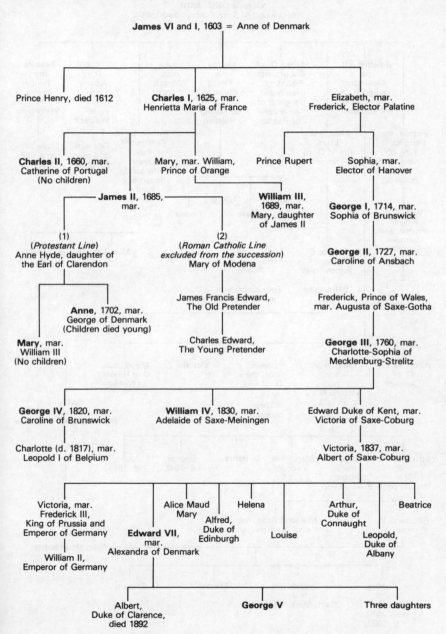

The family of Queen Victoria

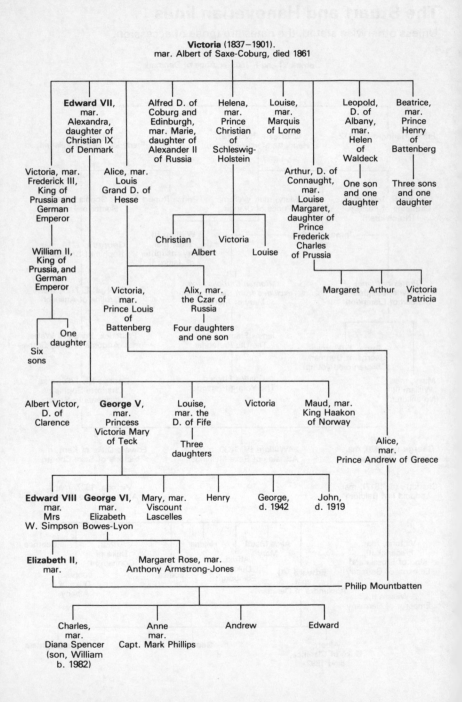

Victoria (1837–1901).
mar. Albert of Saxe-Coburg, died 1861

Edward VII, mar. Alexandra, daughter of Christian IX of Denmark

Alfred D. of Coburg and Edinburgh, mar. Marie, daughter of Alexander II of Russia

Helena, mar. Prince Christian of Schleswig-Holstein

Louise, mar. Marquis of Lorne

Leopold, D. of Albany, mar. Helen of Waldeck

Beatrice, mar. Prince Henry of Battenberg

Victoria, mar. Frederick III, King of Prussia and German Emperor

Alice, mar. Louis Grand D. of Hesse

Arthur, D. of Connaught, mar. Louise Margaret, daughter of Prince Frederick Charles of Prussia

One son and one daughter

Three sons and one daughter

William II, King of Prussia, and German Emperor

Christian   Victoria
Albert   Louise

Victoria, mar. Prince Louis of Battenberg

Alix, mar. the Czar of Russia

Four daughters and one son

Margaret   Arthur   Victoria
Patricia

Six sons

One daughter

Albert Victor, D. of Clarence

George V, mar. Princess Victoria Mary of Teck

Louise, mar. the D. of Fife

Victoria

Maud, mar. King Haakon of Norway

Three daughters

Alice, mar. Prince Andrew of Greece

Edward VIII mar. Mrs W. Simpson

George VI, mar. Elizabeth Bowes-Lyon

Mary, mar. Viscount Lascelles

Henry

George, d. 1942

John, d. 1919

Elizabeth II, mar.

Margaret Rose, mar. Anthony Armstrong-Jones

Philip Mountbatten

Charles, mar. Diana Spencer (son, William b. 1982)

Anne mar. Capt. Mark Phillips

Andrew

Edward

Lists of principal ministers

Prime Ministers

1721	4 Apr.	Sir Robert Walpole (Earl of Orford)
1741	16 Feb.	Earl of Wilmington
1743	27 Aug.	Henry Pelham
1754	16 Mar.	Duke of Newcastle
1756	16 Nov.	Duke of Devonshire
1757	2 July	Duke of Newcastle
1760	25 Oct.	Duke of Newcastle (on the death of George II Newcastle resumed office the same day as first lord of the Treasury under George III)
1762	26 May	Earl of Bute
1763	16 Apr.	George Grenville
1765	13 July	Marquess of Rockingham
1766	30 July	Earl of Chatham
1768	14 Oct.	Duke of Grafton
1770	28 Jan.	Lord North (Earl of Guildford)
1782	27 Mar.	Marquess of Rockingham
1782	4 July	Earl of Shelburne
1783	2 Apr.	Duke of Portland
1783	19 Dec.	William Pitt (the Younger)
1801	17 Mar.	Henry Addington (1st Viscount Sidmouth)
1804	10 May	William Pitt
1806	11 Feb.	Lord William Wyndham Grenville
1807	31 Mar.	Duke of Portland
1809	4 Oct.	Spencer Perceval
1812	8 June	Earl of Liverpool
1820	29 Jan.	Earl of Liverpool (resumed office on accession of George IV)
1827	10 Apr.	George Canning
1827	31 Aug.	Viscount Goderich

1828	22 Jan.	Duke of Wellington
1830	22 Nov.	Earl Grey
1834	16 July	Viscount Melbourne
1834	17 Nov.	Duke of Wellington
1834	10 Dec.	Sir Robert Peel
1835	18 Apr.	Viscount Melbourne
1837	20 June	Viscount Melbourne (resumed office on accession of Queen Victoria)
1841	30 Aug.	Sir Robert Peel
1846	30 June	Lord John Russell (Earl Russell)
1852	23 Feb.	Earl of Derby
1852	19 Dec.	Earl of Aberdeen
1855	6 Feb.	Viscount Palmerston
1858	20 Feb.	Earl of Derby
1859	12 June	Viscount Palmerston
1865	29 Oct.	Earl Russell
1866	28 June	Earl of Derby
1868	27 Feb.	Benjamin Disraeli (Earl of Beaconsfield)
1868	3 Dec.	William Ewart Gladstone
1874	20 Feb.	Benjamin Disraeli (Earl of Beaconsfield)
1880	23 Apr.	William Ewart Gladstone
1885	23 June	Marquess of Salisbury
1886	1 Feb.	William Ewart Gladstone
1886	25 July	Marquess of Salisbury
1892	15 Aug.	William Ewart Gladstone
1894	5 Mar.	Earl of Rosebery (Earl of Midlothian)
1895	25 June	Marquess of Salisbury
1901	23 Jan.	Marquess of Salisbury (resumed office on the accession of Edward VII)
1902	12 July	Arthur James Balfour (Earl of Balfour)
1905	5 Dec.	Sir Henry Campbell-Bannerman
1908	7 Apr.	Herbert Henry Asquith (Earl of Oxford and Asquith)
1910	8 May	Herbert Henry Asquith (Earl of Oxford and Asquith) (resumed office on accession of George V)
1916	7 Dec.	David Lloyd George (Earl Lloyd-George of Dwyfor and Viscount Gwynedd)
1922	23 Oct.	Andrew Bonar Law

1923	22 May	Stanley Baldwin (Earl Baldwin of Bewdley)
1924	22 Jan.	James Ramsay MacDonald
1924	4 Nov.	Stanley Baldwin (Earl Baldwin of Bewdley)
1929	5 June	James Ramsay MacDonald
1935	7 June	Stanley Baldwin (Earl Baldwin of Bewdley)
1936	21 Jan.	Stanley Baldwin (Earl Baldwin of Bewdley) (resumed office on accession of Edward VIII)
1936	12 Dec.	Stanley Baldwin (Earl Baldwin of Bewdley) (resumed office on accession of George VI)
1937	28 May	(Arthur) Neville Chamberlain
1940	10 May	Winston Leonard Spencer Churchill (Sir)
1945	26 July	Clement Richard Attlee (Earl Attlee)
1951	26 Oct.	Winston Leonard Spencer Churchill (Sir)
1952	7 Feb.	Winston Leonard Spencer Churchill (resumed office on accession of Elizabeth II)
1955	6 Apr.	Sir (Robert) Anthony Eden (Earl of Avon)
1957	10 Jan.	Harold Macmillan
1963	19 Oct.	Sir Alec (Alexander Frederick) Douglas-Home (Lord Home of the Hirsel)
1964	16 Oct.	(James) Harold Wilson (Sir)
1970	19 June	Edward Heath
1974	4 Mar.	(James) Harold Wilson (Sir)
1976	5 Apr.	(Leonard) James Callaghan
1979	4 May	Margaret Hilda Thatcher

Secretaries of state for the Northern Department

Prior to 1782 there were two secretaries of state; one for the Southern Department and one for the Northern Department, who shared domestic and foreign business. In 1782 the Southern Department became the Home Office and the Northern Department was converted into the Foreign Office.

1714	17 Sept.	Charles Townshend (Viscount Townshend)
1716	12 Dec.	James Stanhope (Earl Stanhope)
1717	15 Apr.	Earl of Sunderland
1718	18–21 Mar.	Lord Stanhope
1721	10 Feb.	Viscount Townshend

1723	29 May	Sir Robert Walpole (Earl of Orford)
1730	19 June	William Stanhope (Earl of Harrington)
1742	12 Feb.	Lord Carteret
1744	24 Nov.	Earl of Harrington
1746	10 Feb.	Earl Granville
1746	14 Feb.	Earl of Harrington
1746	29 Oct.	Earl of Chesterfield
1748	6–12 Feb.	Duke of Newcastle
1754	23 Mar.	Earl of Holderness
1761	25 Mar.	Earl of Bute
1762	27 May	George Grenville
1762	14 Oct.	Earl of Halifax
1763	9 Sept.	Earl of Sandwich
1765	10–12 July	Duke of Grafton
1766	23 May	Henry Seymour Conway
1768	20 Jan.	Viscount Weymouth (Marquess of Bath)
1768	21 Oct.	Earl of Rochford
1770	19 Dec.	Earl of Sandwich
1771	22 Jan.	Earl of Halifax
1771	12 June	Earl of Suffolk
1779	7 Mar.	Viscount Weymouth
1779	27 Oct.	Viscount Stormont (Earl of Mansfield)

Secretaries of state for Foreign Affairs

1782	27 Mar.	Charles James Fox
1782	17 July	Lord Grantham
1783	2 Apr.	Charles James Fox
1783	19 Dec.	Earl Temple (Marquess of Buckingham)
1783	23 Dec.	Marquess of Carmarthen (Duke of Leeds)
1791	8 June	Lord Grenville
1801	20 Feb.	Lord Hawkesbury (Earl of Liverpool)
1804	14 May	Lord Harrowby (Earl of Harrowby)
1805	11 Jan.	Lord Mulgrave (Earl of Mulgrave)
1806	7 Feb.	Charles James Fox

1806	24 Sept.	Viscount Howick (Earl Grey)
1807	25 Mar.	George Canning
1809	11 Oct.	Earl Bathurst
1809	6 Dec.	Marquess Wellesley
1812	4 Mar.	Viscount Castlereagh (Marquess of Londonderry)
1822	16 Sept.	George Canning
1827	30 April	Viscount Dudley and Ward (Earl of Dudley)
1828	2 June	Earl of Aberdeen
1830	22 Nov.	Viscount Palmerston
1834	15 Nov.	Duke of Wellington
1835	18 Apr.	Viscount Palmerston
1841	2 Sept.	Earl of Aberdeen
1846	6 July	Viscount Palmerston
1851	26 Dec.	Earl Granville
1852	27 Feb.	Earl of Malmesbury
1852	28 Dec.	Lord John Russell (Earl Russell)
1853	21 Feb.	Earl of Clarendon
1858	26 Feb.	Earl of Malmesbury
1859	18 June	Lord John Russell (Earl Russell)
1865	3 Nov.	Earl of Clarendon
1866	6 July	Lord Stanley (Earl of Derby)
1868	9 Dec.	Earl of Clarendon
1870	6 July	Earl Granville
1874	21 Feb.	Earl of Derby
1878	2 Apr.	Marquess of Salisbury
1880	28 Apr.	Earl Granville
1885	24 June	Marquess of Salisbury
1886	6 Feb.	Lord Rosebery (Earl of Midlothian)
1886	3 Aug.	Earl of Iddesleigh
1887	14 Jan.	Marquess of Salisbury
1892	18 Aug.	Lord Rosebery (Earl of Midlothian)
1894	11 Mar.	Earl of Kimberley
1895	29 June	Marquess of Salisbury
1900	12 Nov.	Marquess of Lansdowne
1905	11 Dec	Sir Edward Grey (Viscount Grey of Falloden)

1916 11 Dec.	Arthur James Balfour (Earl of Balfour)
1919 24 Oct.	Earl Curzon (Marquess Curzon)
1924 23 Jan.	James Ramsay MacDonald
1924 7 Nov.	(Sir) (Joseph) Austen Chamberlain
1929 8 June	Arthur Henderson
1931 26 Aug.	Marquess of Reading
1931 9 Nov.	Sir John Allesbrook Simon (Viscount Simon)
1935 7 June	Sir Samuel John Gurney Hoare (Viscount Templewood)
1935 22 Dec.	Sir (Robert) Anthony Eden (Earl of Avon)
1938 1 Mar.	Viscount Halifax
1940 22 Dec.	Sir (Robert) Anthony Eden (Earl of Avon)
1945 27 July	Ernest Bevin
1951 9 Mar.	Herbert Stanley Morrison (Baron Morrison of Lambeth)
1951 28 Oct.	Sir (Robert) Anthony Eden (Earl of Avon)
1955 20 Dec.	(John) Selwyn Brooke Lloyd (Baron Selwyn-Lloyd)
1960 27 July	Earl of Home (Lord Home of the Hirsel)
1963 20 Oct.	Richard Austen Butler (Baron Butler of Saffron Walden)
1964 16 Oct.	Patrick Chrestien Gordon Walker (Baron Gordon-Walker)
1965 22 Jan.	(Robert) Michael Maitland Stewart (Baron Stewart of Fulham)
1966 11 Aug.	George Alfred Brown (Baron George-Brown)

Secretaries of state for Foreign and Commonwealth Affairs

1968 16 Mar.	(Robert) Michael Maitland Stewart (Baron Stewart of Fulham)
1970 19 June	Sir Alec (Alexander Frederick) Douglas-Home (Lord Home of the Hirsel)
1974 4 Mar.	(Leonard) James Callaghan
1976 5 Apr.	(Charles) Anthony Raven Crosland
1977 21 Feb.	David Anthony Llewellyn Owen
1979 5 May	Lord Carrington

Secretaries of state for the Southern Department

1714	27 Sept.	James Stanhope (Earl Stanhope)
1716	22 June	Paul Methuen
1717	16 April	Joseph Addison
1718	16 Mar.	James Craggs
1721	4 Mar.	Lord Carteret (Earl Granville)
1724	6 Apr.	Duke of Newcastle upon Tyne
1748	6–12 Feb.	Duke of Bedford
1751	18 June	Earl of Holderness
1754	23 Mar.	Sir Thomas Robinson (Lord Grantham)
1755	14 Nov.	Henry Fox (Lord Holland)
1756	4 Dec.	William Pitt (Earl of Chatham)
1761	9 Oct.	Earl of Egremont
1763	9 Sept.	Earl of Halifax
1765	10 July	Henry Seymour Conway
1766	23 May	Duke of Richmond
1766	30 July	Lord Wycombe (Marquess of Lansdowne)
1768	21 Oct.	Viscount Weymouth
1770	19 Dec.	Earl of Rochford
1775	9 Nov.	Viscount Weymouth
1779	24 Nov.	Earl of Hillsborough (Marquess of Downshire)

Secretaries of state for Home Affairs

1782	27 Mar.	Earl of Shelburne
1782	10 July	Thomas Townshend (Viscount Sydney of St Leonards)
1783	2 Apr.	Lord North (Earl of Guildford)
1783	19 Dec.	Earl Temple (Marquess of Buckingham)
1783	23 Dec.	Lord Sydney (Viscount Sydney of St Leonards)
1789	5 June	Lord William Wyndham Grenville
1791	8 June	Henry Dundas (Viscount Melville)
1794	11 July	Duke of Portland
1801	30 July	Thomas Pelham (Earl of Chichester)

1803	17 Aug.	Charles Philip Yorke
1804	12 May	Lord Hawkesbury (Earl of Liverpool)
1806	5 Feb.	Earl Spencer
1807	25 Mar.	Lord Hawkesbury (Earl of Liverpool)
1809	1 Nov.	Richard Ryder
1812	11 June	Viscount Sidmouth
1822	17 Jan.	Sir Robert Peel
1827	30 Apr.	William Sturges-Bourne
1827	16 July	Marquess of Lansdowne
1828	26 Jan.	Sir Robert Peel
1830	22 Nov.	Viscount Melbourne
1834	19 July	Lord Duncannon (Earl of Bessborough)
1834	15 Dec.	Henry Goulburn
1835	18 Apr.	Lord John Russell (Earl Russell)
1839	30 Aug.	Marquess of Normanby
1841	6 Sept.	Sir James Robert George Graham
1846	6 July	Sir George Grey
1852	27 Feb.	Spencer Horatio Walpole
1852	28 Dec.	Viscount Palmerston
1855	8 Feb.	Sir George Grey
1858	26 Feb.	Spencer Horatio Walpole
1859	3 Mar.	Thomas Henry Sutton Sotherton Estcourt
1859	18 June	Sir George Cornewall Lewis
1861	25 July	Sir George Grey
1866	6 July	Spencer Horatio Walpole
1867	17 May	Gathorne Hardy (Earl of Cranbrook)
1868	9 Dec.	Lord Aberdare
1873	9 Aug.	Robert Lowe (Viscount Sherbrooke)
1874	21 Feb.	Richard Assheton Cross (Viscount Cross)
1880	28 Apr.	Sir William George Granville Venables Vernon Harcourt
1885	24 June	Sir Richard Assheton Cross (Viscount Cross)
1886	6 Feb.	Hugh Culling Eardley Childers
1886	3 Aug.	Henry Matthews (Viscount Llandaff)
1892	18 Aug.	Herbert Henry Asquith (Earl of Oxford and Asquith)
1895	29 June	Sir Matthew White Ridley (Viscount Ridley)

1900	12 Nov.	Charles Thompson Ritchie (Lord Ritchie)
1902	12 July	Aretas Akers-Douglas (Viscount Chilston)
1905	11 Dec.	Herbert John Gladstone (Viscount Gladstone)
1910	19 Feb.	Winston Leonard Spencer Churchill (Sir)
1911	24 Oct.	Reginald McKenna
1915	27 May	Sir John Allesbrook Simon (Viscount Simon)
1916	12 Jan.	Herbert Louis Samuel (Viscount Samuel)
1916	11 Dec.	Sir George Cave (Viscount Cave)
1919	14 Jan.	Edward Shortt
1922	25 Oct.	William Clive Bridgeman (Viscount Bridgeman)
1924	23 Jan.	Arthur Henderson
1924	7 Nov.	Sir William Joynson-Hicks (Viscount Brentford)
1929	8 June	John Robert Clynes
1931	26 Aug.	Sir Herbert Louis Samuel (Viscount Samuel)
1932	1 Oct.	Sir John Gilmour
1935	7 June	Sir John Allesbrook Simon (Viscount Simon)
1937	28 May	Sir Samuel John Gurney Hoare (Viscount Templewood)
1939	3 Sept.	Sir John Anderson (Viscount Waverley)
1940	3 Oct.	Herbert Stanley Morrison (Baron Morrison of Lambeth)
1945	25 May	Sir Donald Bradley Somervell (Baron Somervell of Harrow)
1945	3 Aug.	James Chuter Ede (Baron Chuter-Ede)
1951	28 Oct.	Sir David Maxwell Fyfe (Earl of Kilmuir)
1954	18 Oct.	Gwilym Lloyd-George (Viscount Tenby)
1957	13 Jan.	Richard Austen Butler (Baron Butler of Saffron Walden)
1962	13 July	Henry Brooke (Baron Brooke of Cumnor)
1964	18 Oct.	Sir Frank Soskice (Baron Stow Hill)
1965	23 Dec.	Roy Harris Jenkins
1967	30 Nov.	(Leonard) James Callaghan
1970	20 June	Reginald Maudling
1972	19 July	(Leonard) Robert Carr (Baron Carr of Hadley)
1974	5 Mar.	Roy Harris Jenkins
1976	10 Sept.	Merlyn Rees
1979	5 May	William Stephen Ian Whitelaw

Parliamentary reform

The unreformed House of Commons

The franchise (prior to 1832)

England and Wales: in the counties the voting qualification was the possession of freehold property valued for the land tax at 40 shillings per annum – the 40*s*. freeholder. In the boroughs various qualifications applied. The main types were:

(i) Scot and lot: right of voting vested in inhabitant householders paying poor rate.

(ii) Householder or 'potwalloper': right of voting vested in all inhabitant householders not receiving alms or poor relief.

(iii) Burgage: voting rights attached to property in the borough.

(iv) Corporation: right of voting confined to the corporation.

(v) Freeman: right of voting rested in the freemen of the borough.

(vi) Freeholder: right of voting lay with the freeholders.

Scotland: In the Scottish counties the franchise belonged to freeholders possessing land valued at 40*s*. 'of old extent' or to owners of land rated at £400 Scots (*c*. £35 sterling). In Sutherland the vote also extended to tenants of the Earl of Sutherland. The Scottish boroughs, or burghs, were combined in groups for the purpose of electing MPs by a process of indirect election. Voting was vested in the small burgh councils.

The composition of the House of Commons in 1790

Constituencies	MPs
English boroughs	
196 boroughs each returning 2 members	392
5 boroughs each returning 1 member	5
2 boroughs (City of London and Weymouth) each returning 4 members	8
English counties	
40 counties each returning 2 members	80

Constituencies	MPs
English universities	
2 universities each returning 2 members	4
Welsh boroughs	
5 boroughs each returning 1 member	5
7 groups of boroughs each returning 1 member	7
Welsh counties	
12 counties each returning 1 member	12
Scottish burghs	
15 burghs each returning 1 member	15
Scottish counties	
27 counties each returning 1 member	27
6 counties, grouped in pairs, 1 of each pair alternately returning 1 member	3
Total constituencies 314	**Total MPs 558**

As a result of the Act of Union in 1800, 100 extra members representing Ireland were added to the existing members of the House of Commons.

Size of electorates in English boroughs *c.* 1790

Electors	Number of boroughs
Under 500	149
500–1,000	32
Over 1,000	22

The Reform Movement, 1714–1830

1716 Septennial Act extends duration of parliaments to 7 years.

1729 Last Determinations Act fixes representation in disputed constituencies in perpetuity at the size 'last determined'.

1739 'Patriot' opposition begins to articulate programme for shorter parliaments and a reduction of patronage.

1768   Wilkes' expulsion from the House of Commons after election for Middlesex focuses attention on the subject of parliamentary reform.

1776   Major Cartwright's *Take Your Choice* outlines radical reform programme including universal suffrage and annual parliaments. Wilkes seeks leave to bring in a Bill for 'a just and equal Representation of the People of England in Parliament'.

1779   Yorkshire Association formed led by Christopher Wyvill to campaign for parliamentary reform.

1780   Convention of reformers in London, and petitions for reform sent in by several counties and towns. Dunning's motion passed condemning the increased power of the Crown over parliament.   Society for Constitutional Information founded.

1782   Economical reform' measures passed, limiting the number of government placeholders in the House of Commons.

1783   Pitt's proposals for a limited reform of parliament defeated in the House of Commons by 293 votes to 149.

1785   Pitt's proposals to redistribute 72 seats from 'decayed boroughs' to the counties and to slightly increase the electorate defeated in the House of Commons by 248 votes to 174.

1789   Meeting of London Revolution Society to celebrate the 'Glorious Revolution' of 1688 addressed by Dr Price welcoming the French Revolution for its stimulus to parliamentary reform and religious toleration.

1791   Publication of Thomas Paine's *Rights of Man* (Part I; Part II, 1792). Formation of reform societies in Sheffield and Manchester.

1792   London Corresponding Society founded by London artisans led by Thomas Hardy and demands annual elections and 'an equal Representation of the Whole Body of the People'.   Whig Society of the Friends of the People established.

1793   Charles Grey's motion for parliamentary reform defeated in the House of Commons by 282 votes to 41. British Convention of Reformers meets in Edinburgh.

1794   Leading reformers put on trial for high treason after plans for a new convention alarm government. Habeas Corpus suspended. Reformers acquitted.

1795   Mass meetings for reform in London and Sheffield.   'Two Acts' passed extending the law of treason to cover spoken words and banning most mass meetings.

1797   Last mass meeting of London Corresponding Society dispersed by police and troops.   Rejection of Charles Grey's motion for parliamentary reform in the House of Commons by 256 votes to 91.

1798   Remaining leaders of London Corresponding Society arrested and imprisoned.

1799   London Corresponding Society and United Societies banned.

1800   Act of Union adds 100 extra members for Ireland to the House of Commons.

1806   William Cobbett lends support to cause of parliamentary reform.

1807   Sir Francis Burdett and Lord Cochrane elected as radical MPs for
        Westminster.

1809   Anti-bribery Act of J. C. Curwen passed. Burdett's motion for
        limiting duration of parliaments and extending franchise defeated.

1810   Thomas Brand's motion for limited parliamentary reform defeated.

1812   London Hampden Club founded to promote cause of
        parliamentary reform.

1816   Cobbett produces first cheap edition of the *Political Register*,
        disseminating reform ideas among the poorer classes.   Spa
        Fields meetings in London addressed by Henry Hunt; petition for
        reform.

1817   Convention of reformers in London. Burdett's motion for reform
        defeated in the House of Commons.

1818   Sir Robert Heron's motion for triennial parliaments defeated in the
        House of Commons. Burdett's motions for annual parliaments,
        manhood suffrage, secret ballot and equal electoral districts
        defeated by 106 votes to nil.

1819   Reform meetings at Birmingham, Stockport and Manchester.
        Meeting at St Peter's Fields (Peterloo) broken up by magistrates
        and troops. Henry Hunt arrested. Widespread protests.

1821   Seats of Grampound transferred to Yorkshire. Lord Durham's Bill
        advocating triennial parliaments, equal electoral districts and
        ratepayer franchise defeated.

1822   Lord John Russell's motion to redistribute 100 members from the
        smallest boroughs defeated. County meetings organised by
        leading Whigs to promote cause of reform.

1826   Further reform proposals by Russell defeated in the House of
        Commons.

1827   Bill to redistribute seats of Penryn to Manchester and Birmingham
        defeated by the House of Lords.

1829   Formation of Birmingham Political Union.

1830   Wellington declares against need for parliamentary reform.
        Wellington's resignation leads to Grey and the Whigs taking office
        on a pledge to reform parliament.

(*Note: for events leading up to the first Reform Act see Political
chronology, pp. 14–15.*)

The Reform Act of 1832

1. Disfranchisement clauses
(a) Fifty-six nomination or rotten boroughs returning 111 members of
    parliament lost representation.

(b) Thirty boroughs with less than 4,000 inhabitants lost 1 member of parliament each.

(c) Weymouth and Melcombe Regis gave up 2 of their 4 members.
   One hundred and forty-three seats made available for redistribution.

2. Enfranchisement
(a) Sixty-five seats awarded to the counties.
(b) Forty-four seats distributed to 22 large towns, including Birmingham, Manchester, Leeds, Sheffield and the new London metropolitan districts.
(c) Twenty-one smaller towns given 1 member each.
(d) Scotland awarded 8 extra seats.
(e) Ireland given 5 extra seats.

3. Franchise qualifications:
(a) Borough franchise regularised, right of voting vested in all householders paying a yearly rental of £10 and, subject to 1 year residence qualification, £10 lodgers (if sharing a house and the landlord not in occupation).
(b) In the counties, franchise granted to 40s. freeholders; £10 copyholders; £50 tenants, £10 long leaseholders; £50 medium leaseholders. Borough freeholders could vote in counties if their freehold was between 40s. and £10, or if it was over £10 and occupied by a tenant.

The Reform Act of 1867 (and Scotland, 1868)

1. Disfranchisement clauses:
(a) Six boroughs returning 2 members and 5 boroughs returning 1 member totally disfranchised.
(b) Thirty-five boroughs returning 2 members deprived of 1 member.
(c) Peeblesshire and Selkirkshire to return 1 member conjointly instead of 1 each.
   Fifty-three seats made available for redistribution.

2. Enfranchisement clauses:
(a) Nine new boroughs and London University to return 1 member each.
(b) Five seats awarded to increase representation of Leeds, Liverpool, Birmingham, Manchester (from 2 seats to 3) and Salford (from 1 seat to 2).
(c) Chelsea and Hackney each created 2-member seats.
(d) Twenty-five seats awarded to the English counties.
(e) One extra seat awarded to Wales (Merthyr Tydfil became 2-member seat).
(f) Five additional seats awarded to Scottish burghs.
(g) Three extra seats awarded to Scottish counties.

3. Franchise qualifications:
(a) Borough franchise extended to all householders paying rates and to lodgers paying a rental of £10, subject to a one-year residence qualification.
(b) County franchise extended to occupiers of property rated at £12 a year (£14 in Scotland) and to those with lands worth £5 a year.

The Reform and Redistribution Acts of 1884–1885

1. Disfranchisement clauses:
(a) Thirteen boroughs returning 2 members and 66 boroughs returning 1 member in England and Wales merged in the counties.
(b) Thirty-six boroughs returning 2 members in England and Wales deprived of 1 member.
(c) Two 2-member boroughs, Macclesfield and Sandwich, disfranchised.
(d) Two boroughs returning 1 member each in Scotland merged in the counties.
(e) Twenty-two boroughs returning 1 member each in Ireland merged in the counties.
(f) Three boroughs returning 2 members each in Ireland deprived of 1 member.
    One hundred and thirty-eight seats made available for redistribution.

2. Enfranchisement clauses:
(a) London (including Croydon) to return 62 members instead of 22.
(b) Twenty-six seats added to provincial English boroughs.
(c) Six new provincial boroughs created in England and Wales returning 1 member each.
(d) Sixty-six additional members allocated to English and Welsh counties.
(e) Seven seats added to Scottish counties.
(f) Seven seats added to Aberdeen, Edinburgh and Glasgow.
(g) Twenty-one extra seats allocated to Irish counties.
(h) Four seats allocated to Belfast and Dublin.

3. Franchise qualifications
The Representation of the People Act 1884 created a uniform franchise in both boroughs and counties of the United Kingdom on the basis of the 1867 borough franchise, to include:
(a) householders, subject to a one-year residential qualification and payment of rates;
(b) lodgers who occupied lodgings worth £10 a year, subject to a one-year residential qualification;
(c) an occupation franchise for those with lands or tenements worth £10 a year.

The Electorate

	Electorate (000s)		Population (000s)	
	England and Wales	UK	England and Wales	UK
1831	435	516	14,000	24,000
1833	700	813	14,000	24,000
1866	1,000	1,310	22,000	31,000
1868	2,000	2,500	22,000	31,000
1883	2,600	3,100	26,000	35,000
1885	4,400	5,600	27,000	36,000

Percentage of all adults (male and female) entitled to vote (approx.)

	(%)
1831	5
1833	7
1867	16
1884	28½
1918	74
1928	97*

* This figure is less than 100 per cent due to a six-month residence qualification before voters went onto the register.

Adult males able to vote

	England and Wales	Scotland	Ireland
1833	1 in 5	1 in 8	1 in 20
1869	1 in 3	1 in 3	1 in 6
1885	2 in 3	3 in 5	1 in 2

Legislation governing parliamentary representation and the conduct of elections, 1828–1980

1828   Polling limited in boroughs to eight days and providing for several polling places where necessary.

1832   First Reform Act (for detailed franchise and redistribution provisions, see pp. 59–60) Time allowed for polling in each constituency reduced to two days (after 1853 reduced to one day in the boroughs); general elections still to take place over the course of a fortnight. Electoral register introduced.

1854   Corrupt Practices Prevention Act. Sponsored by Lord John Russell, the Act levied small fines for bribery, cheating and the use of undue influence and intimidation. Itemised accounts to be produced by candidates of their expenditure for examination by an election auditor.

1863   Office of election auditor replaced by that of returning officer.

1867   Representation of the People Act (for detailed franchise and redistribution provisions, see pp. 60–61).

1868   Parliamentary Elections Act transferred jurisdiction over disputed elections from selected committees of the House of Commons to the judges in the high court. Penalties for bribery strengthened.

1872   Ballot Act, introduced voting by secret ballot and increased the number of polling places.

1878   Registration system in English boroughs overhauled, regularising electoral rolls.

1883   Corrupt and Illegal Practices Act. Maximum election expenses laid down for parliamentary elections. Severe penalties (including imprisonment) introduced for anyone found guilty of corrupt practices.

1884   Representation of the People Act (for detailed provisions, see p. 61).

1885   Redistribution of Seats Act (for detailed provisions, see p. 61).

1918   Representation of the People Act. Vote given to all men over 21 and to women over 30 if they were ratepayers or wives of ratepayers.

1928   Representation of the People (Equal Franchise) Act. Vote given to all women over 21.

1948   Representation of the People Act abolished plural voting – the practice of having one vote in the constituency in place of residence, *and* in the place of business or university where educated.

1969   Representation of the People Act, reduced the minimum age of voting from 21 to 18 years.

Elections and party politics

Elections 1832–1979

Prior to 1832, the computation of election results is complicated by the vagueness of party lines, the number of uncontested elections and the presence of 'independent' candidates. All of these factors continued to operate to a greater or lesser degree after 1832, but the Reform Act of 1832 has generally been taken as the point from which an overall assessment of election results can be made in two-party terms. It should be noted, however, that the terms 'Conservative' (Tory) and 'Liberal' (Whig) represented for much of the nineteenth century only imprecise descriptions of political allegiance and cannot be regarded in the same way as the more definitive party labels of the twentieth century. For the complexity of political and party allegiance in the aftermath of the 1832 Reform Act, see N. Gash, *Reaction and Reconstruction in English Politics, 1832–52*, Oxford, Clarendon Press, 1965. The fullest reference source for election results in this period is F. W. S. Craig, *British Parliamentary Election Results, Volume 1: 1832–1885*, London, Macmillan, 1977.

1832   The election followed the extension of the franchise by the 1832 Reform Act.

	Seats
Conservatives (*Tories*)	175
Liberals (*Whigs*)	483
Total	658

1835   Melbourne refused to serve as prime minister without Lord Althorp (who in November 1834 was elevated to the House of Lords as 3rd Earl Spencer) to lead in the Commons. His only alternative suggestion to Althorp was Lord John Russell, whom the King would not accept. Consequently, Melbourne offered his resignation and William IV accepted it. Peel took office with a minority government. Eager to consolidate his party support and to show Conservative acceptance of the 1832 Reform Act, he decided to go to the country after three defeats in the House on the Irish Tithe Bill.

Conservatives	273
Liberals	385
Total	658

1837   By law parliament had to dissolve within six months of the death of the monarch, in this case William IV.

Conservatives   313
Liberals   345

            Total   658

1841   The Whig government, aware it was losing the confidence of the
       country, decided to go to the polls on what it hoped was a popular
       platform: vote by ballot and repeal of the Corn Laws.

Conservatives   367
Liberals   291

            Total   658

1847   Peel resigned office following the defeat of an Irish 'coercion' Bill,
       though a more significant factor in his departure was the
       opposition of the Tory protectionists to his repeal of the Corn
       Laws in 1846.

Conservatives   324
(*Peelites and Protectionists*)
Liberals   332

            Total   656

1852   Derby's insistence that the Conservative Party adhere to
       Protection weakened the position of the government. Following a
       powerful attack by Gladstone on Disraeli's budget the government
       was defeated and resigned. Dissolution followed.

Conservatives (*including*   330
Peelites)
Liberals   324

            Total   654

1857   Dissolution following the defeat of Palmerston's government on a
       motion of censure of its Chinese policy.

Conservatives   264
Liberals (*including*   390
Peelites)

            Total   654

1859   Palmerston's government, weakened by the appointment of the
       disreputable Lord Clanricarde to the cabinet in 1857, was defeated
       on the Conspiracy to Murder Bill, introduced in consequence of
       the Orsini bomb attempt on the life of Napoleon III.

Conservatives   297
Liberals   357

            Total   654

1865   Parliament was reaching the end of its seven-year life and many
       Liberals were anxious for an opportunity to state to the country
       their opinion on the question of franchise reform. In view of the
       unlikelihood of Palmerston, an opponent of reform, living the

length of another parliament, yet sensing that Palmerston's personality might still prove an electoral asset, it was decided to dissolve.

Conservatives	288
Liberals	370
Total	658

1868 Parliament dissolved following the considerable extension of the franchise by the 1867 Reform Act.

Conservatives	271
Liberals	387
Total	658

1874 After six years of office Gladstone sensed the growing unpopularity of the government in the country, and its increasing weakness in parliament. This, coupled with internal party difficulties which eventually prompted him secretly to resign the leadership, led him to dissolve on the question of finance, hoping to save the government's position by the popularity of a budget surplus.

Conservatives	342
Liberals	251
Irish Nationalists	59
Total	652

1880 The cabinet faced the difficulty of carrying a highly unpopular Water Bill, or dropping it with loss of face. Suddenly by-election results appeared to indicate a movement of public opinion in the Conservatives' favour and Disraeli dissolved parliament.

Conservatives	238
Liberals	353
Irish Nationalists	61
Total	652

1885 Despite the passage of the 1884 Reform Bill, the failures of the Liberal government at home and abroad, coupled with internal party divisions between Whigs, Moderates and Radicals, had weakened the Administration. The Irish Nationalist MPs, annoyed at the attitude of the government towards Irish Home Rule, and tempted by the prospect of a Conservative government proving more sympathetic on the question, allied with the Conservatives to defeat the government on an increase in the beer and spirit duties. Gladstone resigned and the minority Conservative government which replaced him, as 'caretaker' government, soon called the dissolution.

Conservatives	249
Liberals	335
Irish Nationalists	86
Total	670

1886   The Liberal Party split on the question of Home Rule. Gladstone's
        Home Rule Bill was defeated by a combination of Conservatives
        and Liberal Unionists and a dissolution followed.

Conservatives	317
Liberal Unionists	77
Liberals	191
Irish Nationalists	85
Total	670

1892   Having fulfilled almost all his legislative commitments during a
        six-year parliament, Salisbury advised the Queen to dissolve
        Parliament. He probably hoped that the timing of the election
        would marginally favour the Unionist forces, and would return a
        Liberal government with only a small majority and a weak
        parliamentary position.

Conservatives	268
Liberal Unionists	46
Liberals	272
Irish Nationalists	80
Others	4
Total	670

1895   A weak Liberal government, which had failed to carry many of its
        major legislative proposals was defeated, probably willingly, on
        the Army Estimates and resigned. Lord Salisbury became P.M.
        and dissolved in order to gain the parliamentary strength the new
        cabinet required.

Conservatives	340
Liberal Unionists	71
Liberals	177
Irish Nationalists	82
Total	670

1900   Knowing the Liberal Party to be divided on the question of the
        South African War, Salisbury dissolved when the war turned in
        Britain's favour, thus taking advantage of the extreme patriotism it
        had engendered.

	Seats	Total votes	% share of total vote
Conservatives	334]	1,797,444	51.1
Liberal Unionists	68]		
Liberals	184	1,568,141	44.6
Irish Nationalists	82	90,076	2.5
Labour	2	63,304	1.8
Others	0	544	0.0
Total	670	3,519,509	100.0

1906   In 1905, with his party hopelessly divided on the tariff question,
        Balfour decided to resign. He hoped that the Liberals might split
        on the questions of Home Rule and the composition of a Liberal

cabinet, but Campbell-Bannerman succeeding in holding the party leadership and keeping his party together, and lost no time in going to the country to exploit the unpopularity and divisions of the Conservatives.

	Seats	Total votes	% share of total vote
Conservatives (*Free Trade and Tariff Reform*)	133 ⎤		
	⎬	2,451,454	43.6
Liberal Unionists (*Free Trade and Tariff Reform*)	24 ⎦		
Liberals	400	2,757,883	49.0
Irish Nationalists	83	35,031	0.6
Labour	30	329,748	5.9
Others	0	52,387	0.9
Total	670	5,626,503	100.0

1910 January. The House of Lords having rejected Lloyd George's 1909 'People's Budget', the government turned to the electorate for a mandate to force the Budget through the Lords.

	Seats	Total votes	% share of total vote
Conservatives	241 ⎤		
	⎬	3,127,887	46.9
Liberal Unionists	32 ⎦		
Liberals	275	2,880,581	43.2
Irish Nationalists	82	124,586	1.9
Labour	40	505,657	7.6
Others	0	28,693	0.4
Total	670	6,667,404	100.0

1910 December. Having failed to reach a compromise with the Unionists on the question of reform of the House of Lords, and under pressure from his Irish Nationalist and Labour allies to carry out its reform, Asquith sought a clear mandate from the electorate for reform. Given such a mandate, he had the King's assurance that enough new peers would be created to pass a Reform Bill.

	Seats	Total votes	% share of total vote
Conservatives	237 ⎤		
	⎬	2,420,566	46.3
Liberal Unionists	35 ⎦		
Liberals	272	2,295,888	43.9
Irish Nationalists	84	131,375	2.5
Labour	42	371,772	7.1
Others	0	8,768	0.2
Total	670	5,228,369	100.0

1918 Parliament had sat beyond its legal term due to the First World War. Lloyd George had made an electoral pact with the Conservative Party, and both wings of the wartime coalition government were eager to exploit the popularity victory gave them.

	Seats	Total vote	% share of total vote
Coalition Unionist	335	3,504,198	32.6
Coalition Liberal	133	1,455,640	13.5
Coalition Labour	10	161,521	1.5
(Coalition)	(478)	(5,121,359)	(47.6)
Conservative	23	370,375	3.4
Irish Unionist	25	292,722	2.7
Liberal	28	1,298,808	12.1
Labour	63	2,385,472	22.2
Irish Nationalist	7	238,477	2.2
Sinn Fein	73	486,867	4.5
Independent and others	10	572,503	5.3
Total	707	10,766,583	100.0

1922   The growing unpopularity of coalition with Lloyd George among the Conservative MPs and rank and file led to a split in the party, the majority of Conservatives refusing to continue the coalition for another election. Lloyd George therefore resigned office, and Bonar Law, the new P.M. and leader of the anti-coalition Conservatives, dissolved parliament to consolidate a parliamentary base for his government.

Conservative	345	5,500,382	38.2
National Liberal	62	1,673,240	11.6
Liberal	54	2,516,287	17.5
Labour	142	4,241,383	29.5
Others	12	462,340	3.2
Total	615	14,393,632	100.0

1923   Bonar Law had pledged that his government would not raise the issue of Tariff Reform during the life of the 1922 parliament. Possibly because he thought Lloyd George was about to take up a protectionist policy, Law's successor Baldwin spoke in favour of Tariff Reform in October. This indicated that an election was likely, but the reasons for calling it so quickly (December) are not clear. Possibly it was to forestall a prolonged campaign by the opposition in favour of Free Trade.

Conservative	258	5,538,824	38.1
Liberal	159	4,311,147	29.6
Labour	191	4,438,508	30.5
Others	7	260,042	1.8
Total	615	14,548,521	100.0

1924   The Liberals refused to support the minority Labour government over the Campbell case – an allegation that for political reasons a prosecution for incitement to mutiny had been withdrawn. After defeat in the House of Commons, MacDonald sought a dissolution.

	Seats	Total vote	% share of total vote
Conservative	419	8,039,598	48.3
Liberal	40	2,928,747	17.6
Labour	151	5,489,077	33.0
Others	5	181,857	1.1
Total	615	16,639,279	100.0

1929 Parliament was nearing the end of its (five-year) legal term. With by-elections going against the government Baldwin dissolved, seeking to save the position (before it deteriorated further) by fighting on the government's record and its 'safety first' approach.

Conservative	260	8,656,473	38.2
Liberal	59	5,308,510	23.4
Labour	288	8,389,512	37.1
Others	8	293,880	1.3
Total	615	22,648,375	100.0

1931 The Labour cabinet split on the question of reduction of unemployment benefits. Ramsay MacDonald formed a coalition or National Government of Conservatives, Liberals and those Labour ministers who would serve. The new government dissolved quickly, partly to gain a mandate to administer the country, partly to exploit the difficulties of the weakened Labour opposition.

Conservative	473	11,978,745	55.2
National Labour	13	341,370	1.6
Liberal National	35	809,302	3.7
Liberal	33	1,403,102	6.5
(National Government)	(554)	(14,532,519)	(67.0)
Independent Liberal	4	106,106	0.5
Labour	52	6,649,630	30.6
Others	5	656,373	1.7
Total	615	21,656,373	100.0

1935 Following the resignation of MacDonald and the reorganisation of the National Government in June, an election was predictable. Parliament was already four years old. The international tension between Italy and Abyssinia persuaded Baldwin that the time was opportune for dissolution and a campaign on the need for rearmament and collective security, thus 'stealing the clothes' of the Liberal and Labour parties.

Conservative (including National Labour and Liberal Nationals)	432	11,810,158	53.7
Liberal	21	1,422,116	6.4
Labour	154	8,325,491	37.9
Others	9	439,289	2.0
Total	615	21,997,054	100.0

1945   Parliament having been extended because of the war, Churchill
wished to continue the coalition until the defeat of Japan. But with
the defeat of Germany the Labour Party wished to dissolve the
coalition and hold an election in the autumn. Churchill decided
that the government could not function efficiently with the
prospect of an election hanging over it. He ended the coalition
and formed a 'caretaker' government which supervised the
election.

	Seats	Total vote	% share of total vote
Conservative	213	9,988,306	39.8
Liberal	12	2,248,226	9.0
Labour	393	11,995,152	47.8
Others	22	854,294	2.8
Total	640	25,085,978	100.0

1950   Their term of office coming to an end, and having carried much
important legislation, Labour decided to go to the country.

	Seats	Total vote	% share
Conservative	298	12,502,567	43.5
Liberal	9	2,621,548	9.1
Labour	315	13,266,592	46.1
Others	3	381,964	1.3
Total	625	28,772,671	100.0

1951   With a narrow Commons majority constantly harassed by the
opposition, and the government's impetus spent, Attlee decided
that to postpone an election would only lead to further
deterioration in the government's position.

	Seats	Total vote	% share
Conservative	321	13,717,538	48.0
Liberal	6	730,556	2.5
Labour	295	13,948,605	48.8
Others	3	198,969	0.7
Total	625	28,595,668	100.0

1955   Churchill's retirement from the premiership obviously meant a
change of party leadership. Eden, the new P.M., with the
advantage of a rising standard of living and splits in the Labour
Party, decided to dissolve after Butler's Budget had reduced
income tax by 6d. in the pound.

	Seats	Total vote	% share
Conservative	344	13,286,569	49.7
Liberal	6	722,405	2.7
Labour	277	12,404,970	46.4
Others	3	346,554	1.2
Total	630	26,760,498	100.0

1959   Improvement in opinion polls and the economy, plus an easing of
foreign problems and a recovery of party morale, persuaded
Macmillan to take the opportunity to dissolve.

	Seats	Total vote	% share of total vote
Conservative	365	13,749,830	49.4
Liberal	6	1,638,571	5.9
Labour	258	12,215,538	43.8
Others	1	255,302	0.9
Total	630	27,589,241	100.0

1964   With parliament nearing the end of its statutory life, Sir Alec Douglas-Home delayed dissolution for as long as possible in the hope of economic improvement and to let the party recover from the divisions resulting from a change of leadership.

Conservative	304	12,001,396	43.4
Liberal	9	3,092,878	11.2
Labour	317	12,205,814	44.1
Others	0	348,914	1.3
Total	630	27,655,374	100.0

1966   Having only a precarious parliamentary majority, Wilson and his party decided to take the opportunity of an upswing in popularity, reflected in the Hull North by-election, to dissolve and improve their position.

Conservatives	253	11,418,433	41.9
Liberal	12	2,327,533	8.5
Labour	363	13,064,951	47.9
Others	2	452,689	1.7
Total	630	27,263,606	100.0

1970   From opinion polls and by-election trends Wilson believed he detected a ground swell of support for Labour and dissolved.

Conservatives	330	13,145,123	46.4
Labour	287	12,179,341	43.0
Liberal	6	2,117,035	7.5
Others	7	903,299	3.1
Total	630	28,347,798	100.0

1974   February. The confrontation between the miners and the Heath government, combined with the three-day week led Heath to dissolve in order to seek a fresh mandate for his policy.

Conservatives	297	11,868,906	37.9
Labour	301	11,639,243	37.1
Liberal	14	6,063,470	19.3
Others (Northern Ireland)	12	717,986	2.3
Scottish National Party	7	632,032	2.0
Plaid Cymru	2	171,364	0.6
Others	2	260,665	0.8
Total	635	31,333,226	100.0

1974   October. Having made numerous policy statements during the summer, the Labour government decided that the opinion polls signified a Labour victory and dissolved the shortest parliament of the century. This, it was hoped, would gain a new mandate for the numerically weak government.

	Seats	Total vote	% share of total vote
Conservatives	277	10,464,817	35.8
Labour	319	11,457,079	39.2
Liberal	13	5,346,754	18.3
Others (Northern Ireland)	12	702,094	2.4
Scottish Nationalists	11	839,617	2.9
Plaid Cymru	3	166,321	0.6
Others		212,496	0.8
Total	635	29,189,178	100.0

1979   A minority Labour government towards the end of its term of office, was defeated on a vote of confidence.

Conservatives	339	13,697,690	43.9
Labour	269	11,532,148	36.9
Liberal	11	4,313,811	13.8
Others (Northern Ireland)	12	695,889	2.2
Scottish Nationalists	2	504,259	1.6
Plaid Cymru	2	132,544	0.4
Others	0	343,674	1.2
Total	635	31,222,279	100.0

Conservative Party

The origins of the Conservative Party have been variously traced to the seventeenth century, the era of party strife under Queen Anne, and the administration of Pitt the Younger. Other historians have preferred to date the decisive emergence of the Conservative Party from the resignation of Peel in 1846 or even from the Second Reform Act of 1867. Certainly the evolution of the Conservative Party represented no sharp break either in ideas or institutions with the older Tory Party. According to one authority the term 'Conservative Party' was first used in its modern political sense in an article in the *Quarterly Review* in January 1830 (R. Blake, *The Conservative Party from Peel to Churchill*, Eyre and Spottiswoode, London, 1970, pp. 6–7) and the use of the term 'Conservative' by individuals has been recorded earlier. By 1832 the phrase 'Conservative Party' was in common use by politicians and journalists to describe the personalities, ideas and institutions previously referred to as Tory, though the latter remained in use.

1832   One hundred and seventy-five Conservative MPs returned at general election; Carlton Club founded.

1834   Peel forms cabinet and is thus recognised as party leader. Publication of Peel's 'Tamworth Manifesto' identifying the Conservative Party as a party of moderate reform and attempting to extend the social composition of support for the party to the middle classes.

1834–5   Appearance of Conservative and Constitutional Associations.

1835   Peel's government leaves office after defeats on Irish Tithes Bill. Conservatives win 273 seats in general election.

1837   Conservatives win 313 seats and lose general election.

1839   Stanley and his Whig followers join Peel.

1841   Conservatives win general election with a majority of 78 (367 seats). Peel forms his second cabinet.

1846   Party splits on Peel's repeal of the Corn Laws. Peel retains most of the cabinet, the chief whip Sir J. Young and Bonham the party's election manager. The 'Protectionists' are led by Lord George Bentinck, supported by Stanley and Disraeli.

1847   A divided Conservative Party wins 324 seats to the Liberals' 332. The party fund is used to support 'Peelite' candidates of whom 89 are elected. Stanley now leads the Protectionist Conservatives in the Lords. Bentinck leads in the Commons.

1848   Death of Bentinck. Leadership of party in the Commons put into commission under a committee of Granby, J. C. Herries and Disraeli, but Disraeli is the effective leader.

1850   Death of Peel.

1852   In February Lord Derby (Stanley) forms a cabinet. It falls on Disraeli's budget. In the general election 330 Conservatives are returned, but in December the Peelites join a coalition government with the Liberals under Aberdeen. Sir William Jolliffe made chief whip and Philip Rose, Disraeli's solicitor, made principal agent.

1855   Derby refuses to form a government when Aberdeen's ministry falls.

1857   Conservatives win 264 seats in general election.

1858   In February Derby forms the 'Who? Who?' ministry.

1859   Derby resigns office and Palmerston forms a Whig government. M. Spofforth succeeds Rose as principal agent.

1865   Conservatives lose general election (288 seats).

1866   Liberal government defeated on Reform Bill by an alliance of Whigs and Conservatives. Derby forms a government in June.

1867   Disraeli introduces a Reform Bill which considerably extends the franchise. It is passed.   April: Conference of Conservative Working Men's Associations in London. November: Inaugural meeting of the National Union of Conservative and Constitutional Associations.

1868   Derby retires and is succeeded by Disraeli who forms a government in February. M. Spofforth forms a Central Board to organise for the election. Conservatives lose the November election (276 seats).

1870   J. E. Gorst succeeds Spofforth as principal agent and sets up a
        Central Conservative Office.

1871   Gorst and Keith-Falconer become honorary secretaries of the
        National Union.

1872   Disraeli's Crystal Palace speech at London conference of the
        National Union links Conservative Party with the Empire and
        claims the working class should support both.

1874   Conservatives win 350 seats and Disraeli forms a cabinet. Gorst's
        engagement as party agent ends.

1877   W. B. Skene becomes principal Conservative agent. Gorst ceases
        to be secretary of National Union.

1880   Conservatives lose general election, winning only 236 seats.
        Skene resigns. Central Committee set up under chairmanship of
        W. H. Smith to enquire into state of party organisation. July:
        Gorst resumes position as principal agent. Rowland Winn
        becomes chief whip. Fourth Party ginger group of Lord Randolph
        Churchill, J. E. Gorst, A. J. Balfour and H. Drummond-Wolff
        emerges.

1881   Lord Beaconsfield (Disraeli) dies. Party is now led by Lord
        Salisbury in the Lords and Sir H. Stafford-Northcote in the
        Commons – a dual leadership.

1882   E. Stanhope becomes chairman of the Central Committee – Gorst
        resigns as principal agent.

1883   G. C. T. Bartley becomes principal agent.

1883   Lord Randolph Churchill attacks party leaders at a National Union
        Conference. Primrose League founded by Churchill and
        Drummond-Wolff.

1884   Split in party organisation. National Union threatened with
        eviction from Conservative Central Office premises. July quarrel
        between Churchill and leaders resolved. Hicks-Beach elected
        chairman of National Union Council. Central Committee
        abolished. Primrose League officially recognised.

1885   Lord Salisbury invited to form a cabinet. Is thus recognised as
        party leader. Conservatives win 249 seats in general election (a
        defeat). Captain R. W. E. Middleton becomes principal agent (the
        first time the title is officially used) and Akers-Douglas becomes
        chief whip.

1886   Salisbury's minority government falls on Jesse Colling's 'three
        acres and a cow' amendment to the Address. Liberal Party splits
        on Home Rule. Conservatives and Liberal Unionists ally to defeat
        Home Rule Bill. Conservatives win election (317 seats). Salisbury
        P.M., Churchill leader in Commons. In December Churchill resigns
        and a Liberal Unionist, Goschen joins cabinet as chancellor of the
        exchequer. W. H. Smith becomes leader of the House.

1891   Smith dies, and A. J. Balfour becomes leader of the House.

1892   Conservatives lose general election (268 seats).

1895   Conservatives win election (341 seats). Salisbury forms a
       government composed of Conservatives and Liberal Unionists.

1900   Conservatives win 'Khaki' election (334 seats). Salisbury forms
       another joint Conservative–Liberal Unionist government. Sir
       W. H. Walrond becomes chief whip.

1902   Salisbury retires and Balfour becomes P.M. Liberal Unionist Duke
       of Devonshire leads in the Lords. A. Acland Hood is chief whip.

1903   Party splits on 'Tariff Reform' into Balfourites, Chamberlainites
       and Free Traders. Major cabinet reconstruction. Lord Lansdowne
       (a Liberal Unionist) leads the 'Unionists' in the Lords. Middleton
       retires as principal agent and is succeeded by L. Wells.

1905   Balfour resigns as prime minister.

1906   Conservatives defeated in general election, Unionist forces
       winning only 157 seats. Reorganisation of party to give more
       strength to the regions is started. Percival Hughes succeeds A.
       Haig (appointed 1905) as principal agent.

1910   Party loses two general elections. Wins 273 seats in January, 272
       in December.

1911   Party again reorganised. Acland-Hood resigns as chief whip and is
       replaced by Balcarres, and new office of chairman of the Party
       Organisation is given to A. Steel-Maitland. Balfour resigns. Austen
       Chamberlain (a Liberal Unionist) and Walter Long enter leadership
       election, but withdraw in favour of Bonar Law. Lansdowne still
       leads in the Lords.

1912   Formal amalgamation of Conservative and Liberal Unionist
       parties. J. Boraston becomes principal agent.

1915   Conservatives enter wartime coalition cabinet. Eight
       Conservatives given posts, and Bonar Law becomes colonial
       secretary.

1916   Conservatives withdraw support for Asquith and Lloyd George
       succeeds him as P.M. Bonar Law becomes chancellor of the
       exchequer.

1918   'Coupon election' in which Conservatives have an electoral pact
       with Lloyd George Liberals. Three hundred and thirty-five
       'Coalition Unionists', and 23 other Conservatives are returned to
       support Lloyd George government.

1921   Law retires due to ill health. Austen Chamberlain elected leader at
       the Carlton Club.

1922   Party meeting at the Carlton declares against fighting another
       election alongside Lloyd George. Bonar Law returns and is given
       the title, 'Leader of the Conservative and Unionist Party', the first
       time the Commons leader is officially recognised as leader of the
       whole party while in opposition. Party splits, Chamberlain, F. E.
       Smith and others adhering to Lloyd George. Conservatives win
       election (345 seats).

1923   Law retires and dies. Contest for premiership between Baldwin and Curzon. King appoints Baldwin. Baldwin calls an election on the tariff issue; Conservatives lose (258 seats).

1924   Conservatives win general election (419 seats). Party reunited and W. Churchill finally leaves Liberals to become chancellor of the exchequer.

1929   J. C. C. Davidson founds Research Department. Party loses general election (260 seats)

1931   Conservatives join the National Government. Four Conservative ministers serve in MacDonald's cabinet, with Baldwin as the lord president of the council. Conservatives win 473 seats in general election and dominate the National Government. R. Topping becomes first general director.

1935   Baldwin becomes prime minister when MacDonald resigns. Tacit electoral agreement with Simonite National Liberals. At general election 432 Conservatives are returned.

1937   Baldwin retires and the King invites Neville Chamberlain to form a government.

1938   Eden, the foreign secretary, resigns in protest against the government's policy of appeasement.

1940   Neville Chamberlain resigns as prime minister due to dissatisfaction of Conservative backbenchers with his handling of the war, and Labour's refusal to serve under him in a coalition (May). Halifax renounces his claim to leadership and allows Churchill to become P.M. of coalition government; party leader from October 1940.

1945   Victory in Europe leads to break-up of the coalition and a general election. Conservatives lose (213 seats). R. A. Butler becomes chairman of the Research Department. Formation of the Conservative Political Centre. Assheton, chairman of Party Organisation, organises Parliamentary Secretariat.

1946   Woolton becomes chairman of Party Organisation.

1947   Woolton–Teviot agreement provides for union of Conservative and Liberal National parties at the constituency level, and the adoption of candidates who might be recommended by either headquarters.

1948   Maxwell Fyfe Committee Report is adopted by annual conference. Its proposals are aimed at democratising the process of selection of candidates and securing more efficient party funding.

1950   Conservatives lose general election, but reduce Labour's majority (298 seats)

1951   Conservatives win general election (321 seats)

1955   Churchill retires as P.M. Eden succeeds him. Conservatives win general election (344 seats).

1956   Suez crisis.

1957   Eden retires due to ill health. The Queen, following advice from senior conservatives, chooses Harold Macmillan rather than R. A. Butler as his successor.

1958   Peter Thorneycroft resigns as chancellor of the exchequer and Enoch Powell as financial secretary to the treasury: a 'little local difficulty'.

1959   Conservatives win general election (365 seats)

1963   Macmillan retires due to ill health. Sir Alec Douglas-Home emerges as leader, despite the challenge of R. A. Butler, Q. Hogg and R. Maudling. Macleod and Powell refuse to serve in government.

1964   Conservatives lose general election (304 seats).

1965   Under some pressure from the party, Home resigns. Edward Heath becomes the party's first elected leader, defeating Maudling and Powell in the ballot. *Putting Britain Right Ahead* is published and is basis of the Conservative election manifesto.

1966   Conservatives lose general election (257 seats).

1967   Conservatives win GLC elections.

1968   Powell raises the immigration issue in 'rivers of blood' speech and Heath dismisses him from the shadow cabinet.

1969   GLC Young Conservatives publish *Set the Party Free*, urging greater party democracy.

1970   Selsdon Park meeting of shadow cabinet. Manifesto published: *A Better Tomorrow*. Conservatives win general election (330 seats). Heath becomes P.M.

1974   Three-day week. Conservatives win 296 seats in February general election and Wilson forms government. Conservatives lose October election (277 seats). Lord Home's Rules Committee rejects National Union Executive recommendation for an electoral college of area chairmen to select leader.

1975   Heath under pressure from the party stands for re-election. In ballot for party leadership Margaret Thatcher defeats Heath in first round, and H. Fraser, W. Whitelaw, J. Prior, G. Howe and J. Peyton in second.

1979   Conservatives win general election (339 seats). M. Thatcher becomes first woman prime minister.

Liberal Party

As with the term 'Conservative', 'Liberal' only emerged gradually in the nineteenth century to describe one of the major groupings in British politics. The parliamentary Liberal Party was only formed in the late 1850s through a fusion of Whigs, 'Peelites' and radicals, but the term was used earlier to describe the opponents of the Conservatives. Historians have used both the terms 'Liberal' and 'Whig' for the period 1832–67.

Thereafter 'Whig' is normally applied to the landed, upper-class element in the Liberal Party.

1832   Liberals win 483 seats. Grey becomes P.M.

1834   Grey resigns when Althorp, leader in the Commons, refuses to support the Irish Coercion Bill. Melbourne becomes P.M., but resigns when Althorp is elevated to House of Lords.

1835   Liberals win 385 seats and Melbourne forms second cabinet.

1836   Reform Club founded.

1837   Liberals win general election (345 seats).

1839   Melbourne resigns. Bedchamber crisis and Melbourne returns.

1841   Liberals lose general election (291 seats). Liberal government defeated in Commons and resigns.

1846   Conservative ministry breaks up. Lord John Russell forms a Liberal cabinet.

1847   Liberals win general election (332 seats). Lord John Russell P.M.

1852   General election. Liberals win 324 seats. Whigs will no longer endure Russell's leadership and join a coalition with the Peelites under Aberdeen.

1855   Aberdeen government falls over conduct of Crimean War. Palmerston becomes P.M. when Russell fails to form a government.

1857   Liberals (including Peelites) win 390 seats. Palmerston defeated in a motion of censure on his Chinese policy.

1859   Palmerston's government defeated on Conspiracy to Murder Bill. Palmerston wins general election (357 seats). Willis' Rooms meeting where Whigs, Radicals and Peelites agree to serve under Palmerston.

1860   Liberal Registration Association founded.

1865   Liberals win general election (370 seats). Palmerston dies. Russell becomes P.M.

1868   Liberals win general election (387 seats). Gladstone becomes P.M.

1874   Liberals lose election (251 seats). Gladstone resigns leadership. Liberal Registration Association recognised and becomes known as Liberal Central Association.

1875   Meeting of Liberal MP's elects Hartington leader in the Commons.

1877   Foundation of the National Liberal Federation; first president is Joseph Chamberlain.

1880   Liberals win general election (353 seats). Hartington refuses premiership and advises the Queen to make Gladstone P.M., which she does.

1885   Government defeated on spirit duties and Gladstone resigns office. Liberals win general election (335 seats).

1886   Party splits on Home Rule Bill. Liberal Unionists led by
        Chamberlain and Hartington help Conservatives defeat the Bill. In
        general election Gladstonian Liberals badly beaten (191 seats). F.
        Schnadhorst becomes party agent (until 1892).

1887   National Liberal Club opened. Liberal Publication Department
        founded.

1891   'Newcastle Programme' adopted by conference, advocating
        extensive social reforms.

1892   Liberals win general election by a narrow majority (272 seats).

1894   Gladstone retires. Rosebery becomes P.M. Harcourt leads the
        party in the Commons.

1895   Liberals lose the general election (177 seats). Rosebery privately
        refuses to work with Harcourt, and is titular leader only. Harcourt
        leads the party in the Commons, Kimberley in the Lords.

1896   Rosebery formally resigns leadership.

1898   Harcourt resigns leadership of Liberal MPs.

1899   Campbell-Bannerman elected leader of Liberals in the Commons.
        Herbert Gladstone becomes chief whip. Party divided on question
        of South African War.

1900   Three-way split in party on motion of censure on Joseph
        Chamberlain, colonial secretary. Liberals lose general election
        (184 seats). Liberal Imperialists found Liberal Imperialist Council
        under chairmanship of Sir Edward Grey.

1902   Foundation of Liberal League by the Liberal Imperialists, with
        Rosebery as president, Asquith, Fowler and Grey vice-presidents.

1903   Confidential electoral pact made with Labour Representation
        Committee, allowing a number of Labour candidates to stand
        unopposed by Liberals.

1905   Campbell-Bannerman becomes P.M. Leading Liberal Imperialists
        join government.

1906   Liberals win general election (400 seats).

1908   Death of Campbell-Bannerman. Asquith becomes P.M.

1909   Lloyd George's Budget rejected by Lords.

1910   January: Liberals win 275 seats in general election and Asquith
        forms minority government. December: they win 271 seats and
        Asquith is again P.M.

1914   Outbreak of war. Morley, Burns and C. P. Trevelyan resign from
        the government as Liberal pacifists.

1915   Coalition with Conservatives with Asquith remaining P.M.

1916   Conservatives withdraw support from Asquith. He resigns and
        Lloyd George becomes P.M. Party in parliament therefore split,
        with two sets of whips – Lloyd George's government whips and
        Asquith's official Liberal whips.

1918   Lloyd George and the Coalition Liberals fight the general election
        in alliance with the Conservatives – the 'Coupon election'. One
        hundred and thirty-eight Coalition Liberals returned, 27
        Asquithian Liberals. Asquith himself defeated, Lloyd George again
        P.M.

1919   With Asquith out of parliament, Maclean is elected sessional
        chairman of the parliamentary party. Thorne and Hogge
        appointed joint whips. Asquithian Liberals refuse the Lloyd
        George whip.

1920   Asquith wins Paisley by-election. Lloyd George floats the idea of
        Conservative–Liberal fusion. Liberal backbenchers oppose the
        idea. Coalition Liberals begin to form their own organisation of
        constituency 'area advisory committees'.

1922   Carlton Club revolt of Conservative backbenchers against the
        coalition. Lloyd George resigns. Sixty-two Coalition Liberals and
        54 Liberals returned in general election.

1923   Thorne resigns and Asquith makes V. Phillipps chief whip. Party
        agrees to reunion when Baldwin calls a general election on the
        question of 'Protection'. Joint manifesto by Asquith and Lloyd
        George and merger of organisations, but Lloyd George maintains
        his own headquarters and political fund. Liberals win 159 seats.

1924   Liberals help defeat Labour government over Campbell case.
        Forty Liberal MPs returned in general election.

1925   Asquith elevated to Lords as Lord Oxford and Asquith. Lloyd
        George elected chairman of the parliamentary party. Collins made
        chief whip. Seven MPs who voted against Lloyd George as
        chairman form the Radical Group, chaired by Runciman.
        Launching of the 'Liberal Million Fund'. Green Book, *The Land and
        the Nation* published by the Liberal Land Committee. Lloyd
        George founds 'Land and Nation League'.

1926   Liberal Land Conference. Lloyd George and Asquith split over
        General Strike. Asquith resigns party leadership, succeeded by
        Lloyd George.

1927   Asquithians in Party Organisation replaced by Lloyd George
        supporters. Hutchinson made chief whip. Asquithians form the
        Liberal Council. Samuel made chairman of the Organisation
        Committee.

1928   Liberal Yellow Book, *Britain's Industrial Future* published, the
        basis of *We Can Conquer Unemployment*, the Liberal election
        manifesto.

1929   Fifty-nine Liberals returned in general election. Liberals split on
        Labour government's Coal Bill.

1930   Hutchinson resigns demanding an anti-government policy.
        Sinclair made chief whip.

1931   Simon, Hutchinson and Brown resign Liberal whip in protest
        against the party's attitude to the Labour Budget. Formation of
        National Government. Several Liberals, led by Samuel accept

office in the coalition, and 21 MPs led by Simon establish a body to support the National Government. In general election, 35 Liberal National group (Simonites), 33 Liberals led by Samuel and 4 Independent Liberals (Lloyd Georgites) returned. Samuel and Simon, plus several of their followers, accept office in the National Government.

1933   Samuelites leave government in protest against its protectionist policies. Simonites remain.

1935   General election: 17 Samuelites and 4 Lloyd George Independents returned. Sinclair elected chairman of the parliamentary party.

1936   Foundation of Liberal Party Organisation, incorporates all Liberal bodies except the Liberal Central Association. The National Liberal Federation is wound up.

1939   Liberals refuse to join a coalition under Chamberlain when Sinclair is not offered a post in the war cabinet.

1940   Liberals join Churchill coalition, Sinclair becoming secretary for air.

1945   Liberals win 12 seats in general election. Sinclair loses seat and Clement Davies elected chairman of parliamentary party.

1946   Liberal Council wound up.

1947   Woolton–Teviot agreement for formal union of Conservatives and Liberal Nationals.

1950   Nine Liberal MPs returned in general election. Out of 475 Liberal candidates, 319 lose their deposits.

1951   Six Liberals returned at general election. Churchill offers Clement Davies the Ministry of Education. He declines the offer.

1952   H. F. P. Harris appointed to a new post of general director of the party.

1956   Davies resigns leadership. Jo Grimond elected chairman of the Liberal MPs.

1958   Mark Bonham-Carter wins Torrington by-election, first Liberal by-election victory since 1929.

1959   Liberals win six seats at general election.

1962   Eric Lubbock wins Orpington by-election.

1964   Liberals win nine seats in general election.

1965   David Steel wins Roxburgh, Selkirk and Peebles by-election.

1966   Liberals win 12 seats in general election.

1967   Grimond resigns. Jeremy Thorpe elected chairman of Liberal MPs.

1969   W. Lawler wins Birmingham Ladywood by-election for Liberals from Labour.

1970   Liberals win six seats in general election.

1972–3   Dramatic series of by-election victories in Rochdale, Sutton, Ely, Ripon and Berwick.

1974   February: Liberals win 14 seats in general election. Heath approaches Thorpe with offer of a coalition, but talks fail when Heath refuses to promise electoral reform.   October: Liberals win 13 seats in general election.

1976   Thorpe resigns after party pressure due to his involvement with Norman Scott. An 'interregnum' leadership by Grimond until David Steel elected leader of the party.

1977   Liberals enter Lib–Lab Pact to sustain minority Callaghan government.

1978   End of Lib–Lab Pact.

1979   Liberals win by-election victory in Liverpool Edge Hill, and win 11 seats in general election.

1981   Liberals enter alliance with Social Democratic Party to fight next general election and agree to ally with each other in by-elections.

1982   Victory of Roy Jenkins (SDP/Alliance) at Glasgow Hillhead.

Labour Party

1900   Labour Representation Committee (LRC) formed (27 February). J. R. MacDonald secretary. Two MPs returned in 1900 election.

1902   Taff Vale decision undermines legal position of the trade unions.

1903   Electoral pact between MacDonald and Herbert Gladstone, the Liberal whip.

1906   Twenty-nine LRC MPs returned in general election. On their arrival in parliament they assume the title 'Labour Party'. K. Hardie becomes chairman.

1910   Two general elections: 40 Labour MPs returned in the January election, 42 in December.

1914   MacDonald resigns because the party will not oppose the War Estimates and Arthur Henderson becomes chairman of the parliamentary party

1917   W. Adamson becomes chairman of the parliamentary party.

1918   Promulgation of new Labour Party Constitution prepared by Henderson and Sidney Webb. It allows individual membership of the party and formally commits it to a socialist programme. Sixty-three Labour MPs returned in general election. *Labour and the New Social Order* published and adopted by conference – it forms basis of policy for next 30 years.

1921   J. Clynes becomes chairman of the parliamentary party.

1922   MacDonald becomes chairman of parliamentary party. In the general election 142 Labour MPs are returned.

1923   General election returns 191 Labour MPs.

1924   January: MacDonald forms a minority Labour government. In October it is defeated over the Campbell case, and the 'Red' or 'Zinoviev' Letter' election follows, with 151 Labour MPs returned.

1926   May: General Strike.

1927   Electoral agreement with Co-operative Party.

1929   Labour wins 288 seats in the general election and forms a second minority government.

1931   Cabinet splits on question of reduction of unemployment benefits. MacDonald forms a National Government. Henderson becomes leader of the party. General election follows in which MacDonald and Snowden attack Labour Party. Labour win only 52 seats.

1932   George Lansbury elected party leader. Labour Party Conference disaffiliates ILP.

1934   Publication of *For Socialism and Peace*.

1935   Labour win 154 seats in the general election. Clement Attlee elected leader by parliamentary party.

1937   Local constituency parties given more power by a change in party constitution.

1940   Labour leaders refuse to serve under Chamberlain, but enter Churchill's coalition government and accept wartime electoral truce.

1942   Publication of policy statement *The Old World and the New Society* which advocates retention of controls, planned production and public ownership.

1945   Labour withdraw from coalition which leads to a dissolution of parliament. A massive Labour victory (393 seats) allows Attlee to form the first majority Labour government. It begins a programme of nationalisation and social reform, and establishes the National Health Service.

1950   Labour win election by a narrow majority. Total of Labour seats is 315.

1951   Resignations of Bevan, Wilson and Freeman from the government in protest at the imposition of prescription charges. General election sees Labour defeated with 295 seats, though they gain highest total vote.

1955   Division in party when Bevanites oppose manufacture and use of the hydrogen bomb. General election defeat for Labour, who win 277 seats. Attlee retires and Hugh Gaitskell elected leader.

1956   Publication of *The Future of Socialism* by Anthony Crosland.

1959   Labour defeated in general election, followed by Gaitskell's attempts to revise clause IV of the party constitution.

1960   Death of Bevan. Leadership defeated over unilateral nuclear disarmament. Gaitskell makes 'fight and fight again' speech.

1961   *Signposts for the Sixties* adopted by annual conference. It plans for economic growth under Labour, upon which the social services and standard of living will depend. Unilateralists are defeated.

1963   Death of Hugh Gaitskell. Wilson defeats George Brown and James Callaghan in ballot to become leader.

1964   Labour win election with 317 seats; Wilson forms government with only a precarious majority.

1966   Wilson dissolves parliament and Labour return to power with 363 seats.

1969   Struggle with the trade unions over the proposals for reform of trade union law embodied in *In Place of Strife*. Cabinet forced to drop its proposals.

1970   Labour defeated in general election, winning 287 seats.

1972   Formation of a TUC–Labour Party Liaison Committee.

1974   March: Wilson forms minority government with 301 seats after a stalemate election. Enters a 'social contract' with the trade unions as an alternative to a statutory incomes policy. In October Labour win a second close election, taking 319 seats.

1975   Labour ministers campaign for and against EEC in referendum campaign.

1976   Wilson resigns. Callaghan elected leader.

1977   In March the Labour government face almost certain defeat in a 'no confidence' vote. Callaghan and the Liberal leader, Steel, conclude the 'Lib-Lab' Pact which secures the government's position.

1978   End of Lib-Lab Pact.

1979   Government defeated. Labour lose general election (268 seats).

1980   Michael Foot takes over from James Callaghan as leader of the Labour Party.

Other parties

British Union of Fascists
(*See entry for New Party*)

Common Wealth

The party was founded by Sir Richard Acland (Liberal MP for Barnstaple) in 1942. During the prevailing electoral truce (due to the war and the coalition government) its aim was to contest by-elections against 'reactionary' candidates, and it was not opposed by Labour or 'progressive' candidates. But in 1943 membership of the Common Wealth was proscribed by the Labour Party. Although it won three by-elections (Eddisbury 1943, Skipton 1944 and Chelmsford 1945) only 1 of the 23 candidates it ran in the 1945 general election was sucessful. This victory was at Chelmsford, where no Labour candidate ran, and the Common Wealth victor, E. Millington, subsequently joined the Labour Party. So too did Acland when the election results became known. Common Wealth contested no more elections, but survived for a time as an organisation.

Communist Party of Great Britain

The Communist Party (CP) was founded at a Unity Convention held in London in July–August 1920. Most of the delegates at the conference were representatives of the British Socialist Party which had previously agreed to merge into the new party. Attempts in the early years to affiliate to the Labour Party were rebuffed. J. T. W. Newbold became the first Communist MP (for Motherwell) in 1922. In 1924 S. Saklatvala was elected for Battersea North (he had won the seat for Labour in 1923, even though he was CP member). That same year the Labour Party declared that Communists could not become individual members of the Labour Party, and turned down Communist requests for affiliation in 1935, 1943 and 1946. Willie Gallagher was elected Communist MP for West Fife in 1935 and again in 1945, when he was joined by P. Piratin (Stepney, Mile End). Since the 1945 general election the CP have failed to return an MP, and there has been a steady decline in the total votes cast for it. In the October 1974 general election all 29 Communist candidates lost their deposits. This may well explain the reappraisal of the party's position in 1977–8. The party was rent by internal division over the revision of its programme, *The British Road to Socialism*, and proposals to adopt a strategy based on building a 'Broad Democratic Alliance', laying emphasis on parliamentary methods and 'Euro-Communist' in tone. In the 1979 general election the party's candidates polled a total of 16,858 votes.

Independent Labour Party

During the 1880s the idea of an independent party of labour proved slow to gain acceptance. Yet in 1892 J. K. Hardie, one of its main advocates, and three other candidates, were returned as independent labour members at the general election. These successes were followed by the foundation of a national organisation, the Independent Labour Party (ILP), at Bradford in 1893.

In the 1895 election the ILP fielded 28 candidates but did not elect a single MP. Hardie lost his West Ham seat. In 1900 the ILP was one of the founding bodies of the Labour Representation Committee. Although affiliated to the Labour Party the ILP held its own conferences, sponsored its own candidates and maintained its own policies, even after the 1918 revision of the Labour Party Constitution. Throughout the 1920s differences with the Labour Party grew and the 37 ILP members among the 288 Labour MPs elected in 1929 were strong critics of MacDonald's government. Indeed the 1930 ILP Conference decided to vote against the policy of the Labour government where it contradicted the ILP line. In 1932 the Labour Party Conference disaffiliated the ILP. Accordingly, all 17 ILP candidates stood against Labour candidates in the 1935 election, and 4 were returned for various Glasgow divisions. In 1945 the ILP ran five candidates and three were successful, but after the death of the party's leader, James Maxton, in 1946, the ILP MPs joined the Labour Party.

In the 1950 and 1951 elections the ILP ran three candidates, in the 1955 and 1959 elections, two. All lost their deposits, a tale repeated in the cases of the three ILP candidates who stood at by-elections in the 1960s.

There were no ILP candidates at the 1964 and 1966 general elections, and in the 1970 general election, the one ILP candidate (Graham, Halifax) also lost his deposit.

There were no ILP candidates in the 1974 and 1979 elections.

Irish Nationalist Party

The Home Rule League was founded in Dublin in November 1873, with the object of winning self-government for Ireland. In the 1874 general election 59 Home Rulers were returned for Irish constituencies, with all but 2 of these victories outside Ulster. The Home Rule MPs constituted themselves an independent and separate party at Westminster, with their own executive council, whips and secretaries. Their leader was Isaac Butt, but more active than he were C. S. Parnell and J. G. Biggar, who in 1875 devised the policy of parliamentary obstruction.

On Butt's death in 1879, W.Shaw was elected chairman. In the 1880 general election 61 Home Rulers were elected, and Parnell defeated Shaw in the election for chairman. The followers of Shaw refused to serve under Parnell, but did not form a separate party, and Parnell's party remained the one effective Home Rule organisation in the House.

In 1885 the Parnellites won 86 seats (including 1 in England). This allowed Parnell to hold the balance between Conservatives and Liberals and helped persuade Gladstone to introduce his Home Rule Bill in 1886. In 1886 the Home Rulers won 85 seats but the party split in 1890 over Parnell's divorce case. Forty-five Nationalists demanded he resign his leadership, 26 continued to support him. He died in 1891, but the party remained divided, returning 9 Parnellites and 71 anti-Parnellites in the 1892 election. John Redmond led the Parnellites following Parnell's death, J. McCarthy the anti-Parnellites. In 1895 12 Parnellites and 70 anti-Parnellites were returned. Only in 1900 did the Nationalists reunite under Redmond's leadership. Eight-two Nationalists were returned in 1900, 83 in 1906. In 1910 they found themselves again holding the balance between Liberals and Conservatives, having over 80 seats, and pressed Asquith to remove the House of Lords veto, thus opening the way for a Home Rule Bill to pass. But the First World War prevented implementation of the Act, and divisions over the war and the 1916 Easter Rebellion broke the hold of the party on the Irish electorate.

In 1918 only 7 of its 58 candidates were elected, compared to Sinn Fein's 73, although T. P. O'Connor (the solitary Irish Nationalist MP for an English seat) was returned unopposed for Liverpool Scotland division until his death in 1929.

Liberal National Party (National Liberal Party after 1948)

The Liberal National Group was formed in 1931 by 23 Liberal MPs who split from the official party to join the ranks of the National Government. In the 1931 general election they were opposed by Liberals, but not by Conservatives. They won 35 of the 41 seats they contested. In 1932 the 'Samuelite' Liberals left the National Government in protest at its protectionist policies, but the other Liberal Nationals, the 'Simonites' remained. In 1935, 33 of the 44 Liberal National candidates were returned. Between joining the National Government in 1931 and 1945 the Liberal Nationals were only opposed twice by Liberals (Denbigh 1935 and St Ives 1937). They were not opposed by a Conservative until 1946 (Scottish Universities). In 1940 E. Brown succeeded Sir J. Simon as Leader. In the 1945 election Brown was defeated, and only 13 of the Liberal Nationals' 51 candidates were returned. The Woolton–Teviot agreement of May 1947 urged the constituency parties of the Conservatives and Liberal Nationals to combine, and in 1948 the party adopted the name National Liberal Party. In the 1966 parliament only two MPs styled themselves Conservative and National Liberals, though two other members of the group were elected as Conservatives by Joint Associations. These four relinquished the room assigned to them in the

House in 1966 and the group became fully integrated into the
Conservative Party.

Liberal Unionist Party

The Liberal Unionist Party was formed by those Liberals who left the
party in opposition to Gladstone's 1886 Home Rule Bill. Ninety-three
Liberals voted against the Bill, 46 of them radical Unionists who followed
Joseph Chamberlain, the rest Whig and moderate Liberal Unionists who
followed the Marquess of Hartington. Both groups set up organisations
to fight the 1886 election: Hartington founded the Liberal Unionist
Association, Chamberlain the National Radical Union. An electoral
agreement with the Conservatives secured the return of 77 Liberal
Unionists, mainly Hartingtonians. In 1889 Chamberlain restyled his
organisation the National Liberal Union and the two groups virtually
amalgamated. In 1891 Hartington was elevated to the Lords as the Duke
of Devonshire, and Chamberlain was elected leader of the Liberal
Unionists in the Commons. In 1895 the Liberal Unionists took office in
the Conservative government and the two parties became virtually fused.
Separate organisations and funds were maintained until the two parties
merged in 1912, but the merger was really a recognition of a *fait
accompli.*

National Front

The National Front (NF) was formed in early 1967 following the merger of
the League of Empire Loyalists, the British National Party and members
of the Racial Preservation Society. Shortly afterwards the Greater Britain
Movement merged with the Front. The Party's aims include an end to all
coloured immigration, repatriation of immigrants living in Britain,
withdrawal from the Common Market, support for Ulster Unionists and
stronger penalties for criminals.

   In the 1970 municipal elections the NF won 10 per cent of the poll in
some places, but in the General Election all 10 NF candidates lost their
deposits, despite an average NF vote of 3.6 per cent of the poll. That year
Chesterton resigned from the NF after another internal struggle. O'Brien
became chairman of the National Directorate. In 1972 John Tyndall
replaced O'Brien. The NF polled 10,000 votes in the Leicester local
elections of 1973, and won an average 6.8 per cent of the poll in the GLC
elections. At the West Bromwich by-election Martin Webster obtained 10
per cent of the votes cast, but at Hove the NF candidate won only 3 per
cent of the votes.

   The Front ran 36 candidates in the 1974 GLC elections and 54 in the
February general election. All 54 lost their deposits, but won an average
of 3.3 per cent of the votes. At the Newham by-election the Front
candidate beat the Conservative candidate into third place, though losing
the election. Ninety candidates were run in October of that year, all

losing their deposits. In the same year Kingsley Read replaced John Tyndall.

In 1975 membership of the NF began to fall. Read, again voted head of the Directorate, expelled Tyndall who was reinstated by court action. A split occurred, with Read and others leaving to form the National Party.

At the 1979 general election, the Front ran 303 candidates. They polled 190,747 votes and shortly afterwards further internal rifts occurred.

New Party
(*British Union of Fascists after 1932*)

Sir Oswald Mosley resigned from the Labour government in May 1930 when the cabinet rejected his 'Memorandum' on unemployment. In October 1930 a resolution at the Labour Party Conference, calling upon the NEC to consider the Memorandum, was narrowly defeated. In December the main points of the Memorandum were published as the *Mosley Manifesto*. Seventeen Labour MPs signed the *Manifesto*, six of whom (Sir Oswald Mosley, Lady Cynthia Mosley, J. Strachey, O. Baldwin, W. J. Brown and R. Forgan) left the party to form the New Party in February 1931. Baldwin and Brown resigned from the New Party almost immediately and Strachey left four months later. But a Conservative MP (Allen) and a Liberal (Dudgeon) joined the party. In the 1931 general election the New Party's 24 candidates were all defeated and only Mosley saved his deposit.

In 1932, after Mosley's visit to Italy, the New Party changed its name to the British Union of Fascists (BUF), adopting uniforms and mass rallies on the model of continental fascist parties. The BUF urged a radical economic programme to solve the problem of unemployment and envisaged itself taking power in the event of a breakdown of conventional politics. By 1934 the BUF had obtained as many as 40,000 members and the backing of influential people, including Lord Rothermere, the proprietor of the *Daily Mail*. The violence of Mosley's supporters towards their opponents at the Olympia Meeting of June 1934, however, alienated public opinion, and improving economic circumstances limited the movement's appeal. The BUF did not contest the 1935 election and advised its members not to vote. In 1936 it changed its name to the British Union of Fascists and National Socialists (BUFNS) and adopted a distinctly anti-Semitic tone. A series of provocative marches through Jewish districts in London led to clashes between the police and anti-fascist demonstrators, notably at Cable Street in October 1936, leading to the Public Order Act which banned the wearing of uniforms and provided for the prohibition of marches. The BUFNS gained some support in the London County Council elections of 1937 in the East End of London, but failed to secure any seats. In May 1940 Mosley and other leading members were detained under the Emergency Powers Defence Regulations and in July the British Union was banned. In 1948 Mosley re-entered active politics by forming the Union Movement which adopted a neo-fascist stance and called for a ban on immigration.

Peelites

In 1846 112 Tories voted with Peel for repeal of the Corn Laws, but 242 voted with Bentinck for Protection. Many of those who went into the lobby with Peel did so not out of love of Free Trade, but because of their personal loyalty to Peel and the desire to maintain him as prime minister. Among the followers of Peel were all but three of the cabinet ministers, the chief whip, Sir J. Young, and Bonham, the party's election manager. Peel thus had the support of the most important elements in the Conservative Party. Accordingly, the party fund was used to finance Peelite candidates in the 1847 general election, and 89 of them were returned.

The Peelites constituted not only the intellectual leadership, the administratively able and the middle class of the Tory party, but also formed a body of centre opinion which overlapped with moderate Liberalism, yet Peel failed to organise his followers in parliament, up to his death in 1850. But in December 1852 they were able to join the coalition formed by the Peelite P.M. Aberdeen on favourable terms, being given half the cabinet offices.

Plaid Cymru (Welsh Nationalist Party)

The party was founded in 1925 by John Saunders Lewis with the aim of obtaining independence for Wales. Since then it has run candidates at every general election and numerous by-elections, but without success until its president, Gwynfor Evans, won the 1966 Camarthen by-election. In 1970 the Plaid ran 36 candidates and polled 175,000 votes, although none were elected. The party tended to attract a new influx of working-class support from South Wales to supplement the 'hard core' membership of the Welsh-speaking rural North Wales region. It also broadened its appeal by pursuing economic regeneration for the Welsh economy, encouragement for Welsh cultural activities, as well as full self-government for Wales. The adverse publicity attracted by the activities of the 'Free Wales Army' may have injured the party's prospects for a time, but in the February 1974 election it won two seats (Caernarvon and Merioneth) and in October 1974 Gwynfor Evans added a third, by again winning at Carmarthen. The lack of support for devolution in the Welsh referendum in early 1979 was taken as marking some decline in enthusiasm for Welsh nationalism. In the 1979 general election the party fielded 36 candidates, polling 132,000 votes and retaining two seats, with Evans again losing Carmarthen.

Scottish Crofters' Party

This party represented the protest of Highland smallholders against the Liberal Party's neglect of their grievances. The 1884 Reform Act opened

the way for them to channel their protest into electoral activity of an
effective nature. In the Highlands they possessed their own organisation,
and fought the 1885 election in alliance with the Highland Land League.
Six candidates stood (three closely associated with the League) and five
were returned, for Caithness-shire, Ross-shire, Argyllshire, Wick Burghs
and Inverness Burghs. In 1886 victories followed at North-west
Lanarkshire and Sutherlandshire. At the 1892 general election the
Crofter's candidates threw in their lot with Gladstone, and stood as
Gladstonian Liberals.

Scottish National Party

The Scottish National Party (SNP) was formed in 1934 as a merger of two
earlier groups: the National Party of Scotland founded in 1928 and the
Scottish Party in 1930. From 1929 onwards the National Party contested
elections, but it was not until 1945 that the SNP won its first seat. R. D.
McIntyre won the Motherwell by-election, but was defeated at the
general election three months later. In 1964 the party contested 15 seats,
and in 1966 23 seats, but with no success. Then in 1967 Mrs W. Ewing
won the Hamilton by-election. This encouraged the SNP to field 65
candidates in the 1970 general election, but of these only 1, Stewart in
the Western Isles, was elected, and 43 lost their deposits. It appeared that
the SNP was again in decline, yet in 1973 Mrs Mcdonald won the
Glasgow, Govan, by-election. In 1974 the party won 7 seats in the
February general election and in October won 11 seats. Poor
performances in the Hamilton by-election and the 1978 local elections
signified a wane in Scottish nationalism. In 1979 the country voted only
narrowly for devolution, thus relinquishing the possibility of devolution
under the terms of the Act. In the 1979 general election the SNP won only
two seats.

Sinn Fein

Gaelic for 'Ourselves alone'. Irish nationalist party founded in 1902 by
Arthur Griffiths (1872–1922) and formed into the Sinn Fein League in
1907–8 when it absorbed other nationalist groups. The group rose to
prominence in the 1913–14 Home Rule crisis when many Sinn Feiners
joined the Irish Volunteers and many Dublin workers joined the
organisation. Sinn Fein members were involved in the Easter Rising in
1916 and one of the battalion commanders, Eamon de Valera
(1882–1979), took over as leader in October 1917. It successfully
contested by-elections in 1917 and in 1918 won 73 out of 105 Irish seats,
but its members refused to take their seats at Westminster, setting up an
Irish parliament in Dublin. Banned by the British, Sinn Fein provided the
main political organisation in the campaign against British forces from
1919 to 1921. In 1922 it split over the treaty with Britain setting up the
Irish Free State, De Valera leading the breakaway group who refused to

accept the exclusion of Ulster. After the civil war between 'Free-Staters' and 'Republicans' in 1922–3, Sinn Fein continued to contest elections, but its elected representatives refused to take their seats in the Dail and take an oath of allegiance to the Crown. In 1926 De Valera formed a new party, Fianna Fail, abandoning the fundamentalist Sinn Feiners to a minority role, as a consequence of which they failed to return any seats in the general election of September 1927. Sinn Fein continued in existence as the 'political wing' of the Irish Republican Army, winning four seats in the 1957 general election and operating as a fund-raising and propaganda body into the 1970s.

Social Democratic Party (SDP)

The SDP originated on 25 January 1981 as the Council for Social Democracy, an organisation led by four disillusioned Labour politicians (Shirley Williams, David Owen, William Rodgers and Roy Jenkins). The broad aims of the new party were set out in the Limehouse Declaration, followed on 26 March 1981 by the setting up of the Social Democratic Party as a separate political party. Although its aims are to be decided by reference to its members, its leading members have expressed support for electoral reform through proportional representation, continued membership of the EEC, multilateral disarmament and a reflationary economic strategy with an incomes policy and inflation tax. In September 1981 the party joined an alliance with the Liberal Party to fight the next general election and to reach mutual agreement on the fighting of by-elections and local government elections. Party membership in October 1981 stood at 66,000. The first SDP candidate, Shirley Williams, was elected at the Crosby by-election in November 1981. Roy Jenkins won Glasgow Hillhead in 1982 and was subsequently elected leader of the party.

Union Movement
(*See entry for New Party.*)

Welsh Nationalist Party
(*See entry for Plaid Cymru.*)

Section II
Social and religious history

Population

The population of England and Wales, 1695–1791

	Population (m.)		Rate of growth (% per annum)
1695	5.2	1695–1701	1.2
1701	5.8	1701–11	0.3
1711	6.0	1711–21	0.1
1721	6.0	1721–31	0.1
1731	6.1	1731–41	0.2
1741	6.2	1741–51	0.4
1751	6.5	1751–61	0.4
1761	6.7	1761–71	0.6
1771	7.2	1771–81	0.5
1781	7.5	1781–91	1.0
1791	8.3	1791–1801	1.1

(*Source*: N. Tranter, *Population since the Industrial Revolution: the case of England and Wales*, London, Croom Helm, 1973, p. 41. Census returns are only available from 1801; these figures are estimates based on data contained in the Parish Register Abstracts for baptisms, burials and marriages.)

Population, 1801–1977

	Population (m.)			Rate of growth
	England and Wales	Scotland	Ireland	England and Wales annual av. % increase
1801	8.9	1.6	5.2	1.1
1811	10.2	1.8	6.0	1.43
1821	12.0	2.1	6.8	1.81
1831	13.9	2.4	7.8	1.58

1841	15.9	2.6	8.2	1.43
1851	17.9	2.9	6.5	1.27
1861	20.1	3.1	5.8	1.19
1871	22.7	3.4	5.4	1.32
1881	26.0	3.7	5.2	1.44
1891	29.0	4.0	4.7	1.17
1901	32.5	4.5	4.5	1.22
1911	36.1	4.8	4.4	1.09
1921	37.9	4.9	4.3 (1926)	0.49
1931	40.0	4.8	4.3 (1936)	0.55
1951	43.8	5.1	4.3	0.48
1961	46.1	5.2	4.3	0.52
1971	48.7	5.2	4.5	0.26
1977	49.1	5.2	n.a.	0.01

Note: figures for 1801 to 1971 based upon decennial census returns, with the exception of Irish figures based on census returns in 1926 and 1936, and figures for 1977 which are mid-year estimates. Figures for Ireland after 1911 represent the combined population totals for Northern Ireland and the Republic of Ireland.

(Source: B. R. Mitchell and P. Deane, Abstract of British Historical Statistics, Cambridge University Press, 1962, pp. 6–7; Britain 1979, London, HMSO, 1979, p. 7.)

Comparative population growth

(annual average percentage increases)

	1700–50	1750–1800	1800–50	1850–1910	1910–40
England and Wales	0.2	0.7	1.8	1.6	0.5
Scotland	0.6	0.5	1.6	0.9	0.4
Ireland	0.6	1.1	0.6	0.6	0.1
France	0.1	0.6	0.7	0.2	0.1
Holland	0.7	0.8	0.8	1.5	1.7
Belgium	0.8	0.7	0.9	1.2	0.4
Norway	0.4	1.0	1.3	1.0	0.8

(Source: N. Tranter, Population since the Industrial Revolution: the case of England and Wales, London, Croom Helm, 1973, p. 43.)

Birth-rates and death-rates in England and Wales, 1841–1978

	Births per 000 population	Deaths per 000 population
1841–5	35.2	21.4
1846–50	34.8	23.3
1851–5	35.5	22.7
1856–60	35.5	21.8
1861–5	35.8	22.6
1866–70	35.7	22.4
1871–5	35.7	22.0
1876–80	35.4	20.8
1881–5	33.5	19.4
1886–90	31.4	18.9
1891–5	30.5	18.7
1895–1900	29.3	17.7
1901–5	28.2	16.1
1906–10	26.3	14.7
1911–15	23.6	14.3
1916–20	20.1	14.4
1921–5	19.9	12.1
1926–30	16.7	12.1
1931–5	15.0	12.0
1936–40	14.7	12.2
1941–5	15.9	12.8
1946–50	18.0	11.8
1951–5	15.3	11.7
1956–60	16.4	11.6
1961–5	18.1	11.8
1966–70	16.9	11.7
1970–5	13.4	11.7
1976–8	12.1	11.7

(*Source*: B. R. Mitchell and P. Deane, *Abstract of British Historical Statistics*, Cambridge University Press, 1962, pp. 8–10, 29–30, 34–5, 36–7; B. R. Mitchell and H. G. Jones, *Second Abstract of British Historical Statistics*, Cambridge University Press, 1971, pp. 21–2.)

Birth-rates and death-rates in Scotland and Ireland, 1855–1969

	Scotland		Ireland	
	Births per 000 population	Deaths per 000 population	Births per 000 population	Deaths per 000 population
1855–9	33.8	20.4	—	—
1860–4	35.1	22.2	—	—
1865–9	35.1	21.8	26.4	17.0
1870–4	34.9	22.5	27.5	18.0
1875–9	35.1	21.2	25.8	18.9
1880–4	33.5	19.8	24.1	18.6
1885–9	31.9	18.7	23.1	18.1
1890–4	30.6	19.1	22.8	18.4
1895–9	30.1	18.1	23.4	17.9
1900–4	29.4	17.5	23.0	18.1
1905–9	28.1	16.3	23.4	17.2
1910–14	25.9	15.3	23.0	16.7
1915–19	21.7	15.6	20.5	17.2
1920–4	24.3	14.0	20.9	14.5
1925–9	20.3	13.7	21.4	15.1
1930–4	18.6	13.2	20.2	14.1
1935–9	17.7	13.2	19.8	14.3
1940–4	17.8	14.1	21.7	13.9
1945–9	19.6	12.8	21.9	12.0
1950–4	17.9	12.2	20.7	11.4
1955–9	18.9	12.1	21.4	10.9
1960–4	19.8	12.1	22.9	10.8
1965–9	18.4	12.1	22.3	10.6

* Figures before 1925 refer to the whole of Ireland, after 1925 to Northern Ireland only.

(*Source*: B. R. Mitchell, *European Historical Statistics, 1750–1970*, London, Macmillan, 1975, pp. 110, 113, 117, 120, 122, 124.)

Selected urban populations, 1801–1977

	(000s) 1801	1851	1901	1951	1977
Greater London*	1,117	2,685	6,586	8,348	6,970
Birmingham	71	233	522	1,113	1,050
Glasgow	77	357	762	1,090	832
Leeds	53	172	429	505	735
Sheffield	46	135	381	513	547
Liverpool	82	376	685	789	536
Manchester	75	303	645	703	491
Bradford	13	104	280	292	462
Edinburgh	83	202	394	467	463
Bristol	61	137	339	443	409
Belfast	(1821) 37	103	349	444	357
Coventry	16	36	70	258	340
Cardiff	2	18	164	244	278

* Up to 1951 'Greater London' was defined as the Metropolitan Police District, an area reaching up to 15 miles from the centre of London. In 1951 it was redefined to refer to a slightly lesser area, but which still stretched beyond the boundaries of the London County Council to include built-up areas which formed part of the London conurbation. The 1977 figures relate to the most recent definition of 'Greater London' which is the area administered by the Greater London Council as established by the London Government Act of 1963.

(*Source*: B. R. Mitchell and P. Deane, *Abstract of British Historical Statistics*, Cambridge University Press, 1962, pp. 24–7; *Britain 1979*, London, HMSO, 1979, p. 11.)

Migration to and from the United Kingdom, 1820–1976

	External movement (000s)	Internal movement (000s)
1820–9	216	—
1830–9	668	—
1840–9	1,495	—

	External movement (000s)	Internal movement (000s)
1850–9	2,440	—
1860–9	1,841	300
1870–9	2,149	744
1880–9	3,570	1,089
1890–9	2,680	1,567
1900–9	4,404	2,287
1910–19	3,526	2,224
1920–9	3,960	2,492
1930–9	2,273	2,361
1940–9	590	240
1950–9	1,327	676
1960–9	1,916	1,243
1970–6	2,079	1,440

Note: Figures up to 1919 refer to all movements of citizen passengers to and from UK ports, including Ireland; figures from 1919 to 1963 are for UK and Commonwealth citizens migrating for permanent residence; figures from 1964 refer to all migration of UK and Commonwealth citizens, other than to and from Ireland.

(Source: B. R. Mitchell and P. Deane, Abstract of British Historical Statistics, Cambridge University Press, 1962, pp. 47–9; B. R. Mitchell, European Historical Statistics, 1750–1970, London, Macmillan, 1975, pp. 142, 146; D. Butler and A. Sloman, British Political Facts, 1900–1979, London, Macmillan, 1980, p. 298.)

Education

Education legislation and principal events

1780 Robert Raikes opened three Sunday schools in Gloucestershire and begins spread of the Sunday School Movement to other parts of the country.

1796 William Pitt as prime minister proposed extending the system of industrial schools for pauper children to all children working in industry, but the proposals are not implemented.

1798 Joseph Lancaster opened a school for 1,000 pupils in Borough Road, London, using the monitorial system in which the older children taught the younger.

1801 Royal Lancastrian Society founded and opens a number of voluntary schools using the monitorial system.

1811 The National Society for the Education of the Poor in accordance with the Principles of the Established Church is founded as an Anglican organisation to rival the Nonconformist-based Royal Lancastrian Society. It also used the monitorial system, but only children who were regular churchgoers could attend National Schools.

1814 British and Foreign School Society formed out of the Royal Lancastrian Society. No religious barriers were imposed and with the National Society it provided the basis on which the state system was to develop.

1828 The Revd Thomas Arnold becomes headmaster of Rugby and begins the process of reform in the public schools by introducing the prefect system, the ideal of Christian duty and a more rigorous intellectual atmosphere. This influence spread to other schools through Vaughan at Harrow, Pears at Repton and Thring at Uppingham. Many public schools were founded from the 1830s on the new principles providing education for the sons and daughters of the new middle classes.

1833 The Factory Act provided for the education of children working in textile factories. The first government grant, of £20,000, was made to education, shared between the British and Foreign Schools and the National Societies. A Committee of the Privy Council on Education set up in England and Wales, with the lord president as head.

1839 The grant to the two educational societies was increased to £30,000 and government inspectors were appointed to supervise schools receiving the grant. Thereafter the subsidy was regularly increased.

1840   The Grammar School Act gave the Court of Chancery the power to alter the original statutes of the schools, thereby adapting them to meet new needs.

1844   Lord Shaftesbury organises 'Ragged Schools' for free education of the poorest children.

1858   The Newcastle Commission was appointed to survey the state of elementary education. One result of its recommendations was the establishment of the system of 'payment by results' in which the size of the government grant was dictated by the numbers of children in regular attendance and the number passing an annual examination in the three 'Rs' conducted by the school inspector.

1868   Public Schools Act. The Act regulated the administration of public schools and provided for the adaptation of their original charters to meet new circumstances.

1870   Education Act (Forster's). The first major Education Act. The existing 20,000 voluntary schools were given slightly increased grants. Where school places were insufficient, new school boards could be set up, or where the ratepayers demanded it, school boards could be rate-aided with powers to build schools and compel attendance. Board schools could provide religious instruction so long as it was not 'distinctive of any particular denomination'. School fees of a few pence each week were charged, but poorer parents could be excused payment. As a result of the Act voluntary schools and the new board schools constituted a dual system, each school's management committee dealing directly with Whitehall. Voluntary schools received no more rate aid and no more building grants.

1876   Education Act (Sandon's). The Act created school attendance committees for districts where there were no school boards and could compel attendance.

1880   Education Act. This made it compulsory for children to go to school between the age of 5 and 10, when they could be exempted to work part-time in factories, if they had reached a certain educational standard.

1889   Education Act. County councils were empowered to levy a 1d. rate for technical education. The Board of Education was set up.

1891   Assisted Education Act. This made available a capitation grant of 10s. to all schools, enabling them to cease charging fees.

1891–5   From 1890 the system of payment by results was gradually dismantled and replaced by a system of block grants.

1893   Education (Blind and Deaf Children) Act. Made possible the establishment of special schools for the blind and deaf.

1902   Education Act (Balfour's). School boards were abolished and replaced by new local education authorities which were given the power to provide secondary education. In many cases new secondary schools were built and grants given to grammar schools.

1903   The Association to Promote the Higher Education of Working Men (from 1905 the Workers' Educational Association) founded by Albert Mansbridge. First branch opened in Reading in 1904.

1907   All secondary schools receiving grants from local education authorities to reserve 25 to 40 per cent of free places for children from elementary schools.

1918   Education Act (Fisher's), introduced by H. A. L. Fisher, president of the Board of Education. The Act raised the school-leaving age to 14 and abolished the remaining fees for elementary education in some schools. Provisions for the compulsory part-time education for children from 14 to 18 were not implemented because of government economies.

1926   Hadow Report published, recommending the division of schools into primary and secondary tiers, with transfer between tiers at the age of 11. The old 'elementary' schools would now become primary schools and different types of secondary education were envisaged with the school-leaving age raised to 15. The report was not implemented immediately because of government economies.

1936   Education Act. The Act raised the school-leaving age to 15, but was not enforced until 1944.

1944   Education Act (Butler's), introduced by R. A. Butler, minister of education. The Act raised the school-leaving age to 15 and provided free secondary education for all children, divided into three types – grammar schools, technical schools and secondary modern schools, selection for which was to be by an '11-plus' examination. Primary education was reorganised into infant and junior schools. Free school milk, subsidised meals and free medical and dental inspections to be provided in schools. Provisions were made for raising the school-leaving age to 16 (not implemented until 1973).

1951   General Certificate of Education (GCE) replaces School Certificate as principal examination leading to university entrance.

1959   McMeeking Committee reports in favour of improved technical training, including more apprenticeships and greater facilities for day-release schemes.

1960   Robbins Committee on higher education set up.

1963   Crowther Report recommends raising the school-leaving age to 16 and the provision of part-time education after 16.   Conservative administration under Sir Alec Douglas-Home accepts the recommendation of the Robbins Committee for a doubling of university places over the next 10 years to 218,000, with an expansion in other areas of higher education to provide another 172,000 places. Colleges of technology to be developed as technological universities and postgraduate business schools to be established.   Newsom Committee on secondary education recommends raising of school-leaving age and an alternative examination to GCE Ordinary Level.

1964 Labour Party elected to power with pledge to reorganise secondary education along comprehensive lines.

1965 Certificate of Secondary Education (CSE) introduced.

1969 Open University established, offering part-time degree studies to students of all ages via correspondence and broadcasting.

1973 School-leaving age raised to 16, having first been announced in 1964.

1976 Education Act requires local education authorities to submit proposals for comprehensive reorganisation and limits the scope for taking up places in independent and direct-grant schools.

1980 Education Act by Conservative government strengthens position of parents on school governing bodies; relaxes obligations to provide milk and meals; and sets up scheme to finance able pupils to attend independent schools.

Expenditure on education in UK 1840–1978

	(£ m.)		(£ m.)
1840	0.17	1930	50.1
1850	0.37	1940	65.0
1860	1.27	1950	272.0
1870	1.62	1955	410.6
1880	4.0	1960	917.3
1890	5.8	1965	1,114.9
1900	12.2	1970	2,592.0
1910	17.9	1975	5,348.3
1920	43.2	1978	8,658.1

(*Sources*: B. R. Mitchell and P. Deane, *Abstract of British Historical Statistics*, Cambridge University Press, 1962, pp. 396–9; A. H. Halsey (ed.), *Trends in British Society since 1900*, London, Macmillan, 1972, p. 168.)

Percentage of children in different age groups attending schools in England and Wales, 1901–1968

	2–4 years	5–11 years	12–14 years	15–18 years
1901	2.8	89.3	41.5	0.3
1911	–	–	57.5	1.5
1921	–	–	65.8	3.2

	2–4 years	5–11 years	12–14 years	15–18 years
1931	8.8	91.7	73.0	6.0
1938	10.0	92.4	74.5	6.6

	2–4 years	5–10 years	11–14 years	15–18 years
1951	7.7	97.2	93.1	12.5
1961	10.8	99.9	99.1	19.6
1968	10.7	99.3	100.0	30.0

	2–4 years	5–14 years	15–18 years
1977	24.3	96.1	34.9

(*Source*: A. H. Halsey (ed.), *Trends in British Society since 1900*, London, Macmillan, 1972, p. 163; *Annual Abstract of Statistics*, HMSO, 1978.)

Social reform

Factory and industrial legislation

1802 Health and Morals of Apprentices Act. The Act prohibited
workhouse children apprenticed to textile factories from working
more than 11 hours a day. They were also to have better
accommodation and be provided with elementary education. The
Overseer of the Poor and the local magistrates were to supervise
the Act, but it failed to provide an efficient and independent
inspectorate.

1819 Factory Act. Children under 9 years prohibited from working in
cotton mills; those over 9 restricted to a 12-hour day.

1831 Truck Act. The Act prohibited payment in goods and tokens. All
workers other than domestic servants to be paid entirely in
coin.   Factory Act. No young people under 18 to work more
than 12 hours a day.

1833 Factory Act ((also known as Althorp's Act). The Act applied only to
textile factories and limited the hours of work for children and
youths. Children aged from 9 to 12 to work a maximum of 9 hours
a day and no more than 48 hours a week. Youths from 13 to 18 to
work a maximum of 12 hours a day and no more than 69 hours a
week. The employment of children under 9 was prohibited, except
in silk factories, and night work by workers under 18 was banned,
except in lace factories. Children from 9 to 11 (later raised to 13)
were to have 2 hours' compulsory education every day. The first
four factory inspectors were appointed.

1842 Mines Act. This followed on a Royal Commission into mining
conditions. The Act prohibited women and girls and boys under 10
years of age from being employed underground. Inspectors of
mines were appointed.

1842 Factory Act. The Act applied to textile factories and laid down that
women and youths and young girls between 13 and 18 were not
to work more than 12 hours a day. Hours of work for children
under 13 were reduced from 9 to 6½ hours a day with 3 hours'
education. The age at which children could start work was
lowered from 9 to 8.

1847 Factory Act. The Act restricted working hours for women and
young persons in textile factories to 10 a day.

1850 Factory Act. The Act specified the hours within which women and
young persons could work. They were allowed to work only
between 6 a.m. and 6 p.m. with an hour's break for meals. They

were not allowed to work after 2 p.m. on Saturdays. Although the Act effectively extended the permitted hours of work to 10½ per day, it was intended to imply limitations for men's hours by restricting the availability of assistance from women and young persons. This intention was circumvented by using child labour to do shift work alongside male workers.

1853   Factory Act. Intended to prevent the use of child labour for shift work, the Act laid down that children were to be employed only from 6 a.m. to 6 p.m. with 1½ hours for meals.

1864   Factory Acts (Extension) Act. Special regulations for health and safety were made for six 'dangerous' industries including match-making, cartridge-making and pottery. Existing Factory Acts were made to apply to these industries, extending their provisions for the first time beyond textile mills and mines.

1867   Factory Acts (Extension) Act. The Act extended all existing Factory Acts to places employing more than 50 people.

1874   Factory Act. The Act raised the minimum working age to 9. Women and young people were to work no more than 10 hours a day in the textile industry. Children up to 14 only to work for half a day.

1878   Factory and Workshops Act. Regulations made governing conditions in workshops.

1891   Factory and Workshops (Consolidation) Act. Safety and sanitary regulations extended. Minimum working age in factories raised to 11.

1901   Factory and Workshops Act. Minimum working age raised to 12.

1901   Trade Boards Act. Boards were set up to fix minimum wages in a number of sweated industries, such as tailoring, paper box-making, chain and lace-making.

1918   Trade Boards Act. Trade boards extended to all low-paid trades and industries.

1937   Factory Act. Young persons under 16 not to work more than 44 hours in a week; those between 16 and 18, and women, no more than 48 hours a week. New regulations introduced governing lighting, ventilation and cleaning.

1946   National Insurance (Industrial Injuries) Act. In return for contributions collected under the National Insurance Act, benefits payable for injuries sustained at work or industrial diseases.

1961   Factories Act. Consolidated safety regulations in industrial premises, including all factories, warehouses, shipyards, docks and construction sites.

1963   Offices, Shops and Railway Premises Act. Consolidated safety regulations for commercial premises, including prevention of accidents and conditions of employment.

1965   Redundancy Payments Act. Provided graduated redundancy payments according to length of service of workers concerned.   Nuclear Installations Act. Regulations governing the granting of licences and safety in nuclear installations.

1974   Health and Safety at Work Act. Reorganised system under which safety and health at work was safeguarded and extended it to cover all those at work.

1975   Petroleum and Submarine Pipelines Act. Provided for the health and safety of all persons working in the offshore oil and gas industry.

Poor relief, health and social welfare

At the beginning of the eighteenth century the administration of poor relief was based upon the Poor Laws of 1597–8 and of 1601. By the former a poor rate was raised from the members of the parish for the support of the poor. Relief was given 'indoors', in the workhouse, and 'outdoors' to people in their own homes. The Act of 1597–8 empowered the overseers to erect a poorhouse out of the poor rates. Parish overseers were to provide work for paupers and were given the power to apprentice pauper children. Under the Act of 1601, the churchwardens of each parish and other substantial property owners were appointed overseers of the poor. Paupers were to be maintained out of poor rates with provisions for them to be set to work. Vagrants could be committed to Houses of Correction. By the 1662 Act of Settlement a stranger could be removed from the parish if he had no prospect of work within 40 days. Itinerant workmen had to carry a certificate from their own parish stating that they would be taken back. Settlement would otherwise be granted after 40 days' residence.

1691   Register of parishioners in receipt of poor relief to be kept.

1697   Settlement Act. Non-parishioners allowed into a parish if in possession of a Settlement Certificate from their own parish. Paupers and their families to carry a 'P' on their clothing to distinguish them.

1722   Knatchbull's Act. Parishes encouraged to build workhouses and permitted to contract out the care of paupers. 'Unions' could be formed between parishes too small to support a workhouse on their own. Illegitimate children were not to receive a Settlement Certificate and vagrant children could be apprenticed without their parents' consent.

1733   Bastardy Act. Obliged women with illegitimate children to name the father.

1782   Gilbert's Act. Parishes permitted to combine for more effective administration; able-bodied and infirm paupers to be separated and only the latter sent to the workhouse; work to be provided for able-bodied poor and wages supplemented from the poor rates if necessary. Orphan children to be boarded out and children under 7 not to be separated from parents. Requirement to wear pauper's badge no longer necessary for paupers of good character. 'Guardians' to be appointed to administer relief.

1795   Speenhamland system. Resolution of the Berkshire magistrates at meeting at Speenhamland near Newbury in May 1795 to supplement wages from poor rates on a sliding scale dictated by the price of bread. Elements of the 'system' had been adopted informally as a result of Gilbert's Act, and the practice now became widespread in the agricultural counties of southern England. The system was later widely criticised because it encouraged farmers to pay low wages and demoralised the rural labourer.

1819   Poor Relief Act (also known as Sturges Bourne Act). This enabled parishes to appoint a representative Poor Law Committee with voting powers determined by their contribution to the poor rates. The Act was an attempt to ensure that substantial property owners had an influential say in the conduct of poor relief.

1834   Poor Law Amendment Act. The Act followed from the *Report of the Royal Commission on the Poor Laws, 1834* which expressed widespread dissatisfaction with the administration, effects and growing cost of poor relief. The Act attempted to abolish 'outdoor' relief for the able-bodied; relief was only to be granted to those who entered the workhouse after passing the 'workhouse test'. The workhouse regime was to be made as spartan as possible to discourage all but the truly needy from applying for relief. Parishes were to be united into Unions and Union workhouses substituted for parish workhouses, to be run by elected Boards of Guardians. The Act also established three central Poor Law Commissioners to supervise the implementation of the Act.

1836   Registration of births, marriages and deaths made compulsory.

1842   *Enquiry into the Sanitary Conditions of the Labouring Population of Great Britain*, written by Edwin Chadwick, secretary to the Poor Law Commissioners, revealed the totally inadequate drainage, sewerage and sanitation in the industrial areas.

1844   Poor Law Amendment Act. Owners and ratepayers were allowed votes for the election of guardians on a level with their assessment for poor rate. The Act also empowered mothers of illegitimate children to apply to the justices in petty sessions for a maintenance order against the father.

1845   Lunacy Act. Board of Commissioners set up to inspect asylums and other places where mentally ill were kept.

1847   Poor Law Commission abolished following the abuses revealed in the Andover Workhouse, replaced by a Poor Law Board responsible to a minister.

1848   Public Health Act allowed local boards of health to be set up and appoint medical officers of health.

1871   Local Government Board set up to supervise poor law and public health.

1872   Public Health Act. Appointment of medical officers of health made
        compulsory and sanitary authorities set up.

1875   Public Health Act. Local sanitary authorities given power to
        enforce sanitary regulations including drainage, sanitation and
        water supplies.

1906   Local authorities allowed to provide school meals.

1907   School medical examinations made compulsory and school
        medical services established.

1909   Old Age Pensions Act came into force, giving 5s. per week
        pension to people over 70 years old with incomes less than £31
        10s. a year.   Labour Exchanges set up to register vacant jobs
        and provide contact between employers and those requiring work.

1911   National Insurance Act. The Act provided insurance against
        sickness and unemployment to be paid for by contributions from
        the state, the employer and the employee. It covered those
        between 16 and 70 years old, but was limited to industries where
        unemployment was recurrent. Maternity grants introduced.

1918   Ministry of Health established.

1919   Pensions raised to 10s. per week.

1925   Widows Pension Act provided contributory pensions for widows,
        orphans and the elderly.

1926   Pensions made contributory, and qualifying age became 65 for
        men and 60 for women.

1929   Local Government Act. Boards of Guardians abolished and their
        functions transferred to county councils and county boroughs.
        Public assistance committees and public health committees set up
        by county and county borough councils.

1930   Poor Law Act. The Poor Law was renamed Public Assistance.
        Only the aged and the infirm now to apply for the workhouse, and
        outdoor relief could be granted.   Mental Treatment Act made
        voluntary treatment possible for mental illness.

1931   Under the economy measures of the National Government a
        'Means Test' was introduced for unemployment benefit.

1934   Local authorities allowed to provide subsidised or free milk at
        schools. Unemployment Assistance Board set up to administer
        unemployment benefit.

1942   Publication of Beveridge Report advocating a system of national
        insurance, comprehensive welfare and the deliberate maintenance
        of a high level of employment.

1946   National Insurance Act established a comprehensive 'Welfare
        State' on the lines advocated by the Beveridge Report.
        Compulsory insurance provided for unemployment, sickness and
        maternity benefits, old age and widows' pensions, and funeral
        grants.   National Health Service Act provided a free medical
        service for everyone, including free hospital treatment, dental care

and opticians' services. The Act came into force in 1948. Doctors and dentists now worked within the National Health Service though they continued to be able to treat private patients as well.   Free milk for all schoolchildren introduced.

1948   National Assistance Act. The Act abolished all the Poor Law still in existence and provided cash payments for those in need and without any other source of income.

1961   Graduated pension scheme introduced in addition to flat-rate old age pension.

1966   System of earnings-related supplements for unemployment and sickness benefits introduced.

1967   Abortion Act provides for the legal termination of pregnancy if two registered doctors believe that continuation may injure the physical or mental health of the pregnant woman (or members of her family) or where there is substantial risk of mental or physical abnormalities.   Family Planning Act allows local health authorities to provide a family-planning service for all who seek it, either directly or through a voluntary body. Advice provided free with graduated charges for contraceptive devices according to the means of the patient.

1971   Abolition of free milk for schoolchildren. Introduction of Family Income Supplement to provide a cash benefit for poorer families with children.

1973   National Health Service Reorganisation Act creates Area Health Authorities to coordinate health services within the new local government boundaries set up in 1972.

1978   Health Services Act provides for the withdrawal of private medicine from National Health Service hospitals.

Housing

Housing developments

1840   Select Committee on the Health of Towns exposes slum conditions in many industrial towns.

1851   Labouring Classes Lodging Houses Act, permitted local authorities to appoint commissioners to erect or purchase lodging houses for the working classes. Little used.

1868   Artisans' and Labourers' Dwellings Act (also known as Torrens' Act) gave local authorities powers to compel owners to demolish or repair insanitary houses.

1875   Artisans and Labourers Dwellings Improvement Act gave local authorities powers of compulsory purchase of areas 'unfit for human habitation'.

1885   Royal Commission on the Housing of the Working Classes revealed the poor state of housing in London and other major cities. The Commission recommended the appointment of additional sanitary inspectors, the rating of derelict land and government loans to build working-class housing.

1890   Housing of the Working Classes Act granted local councils further powers to close insanitary houses and to build council houses using money from the local rates.

1903   Ebenezer Howard founded a company to develop the first 'garden city' at Letchworth in Hertfordshire.

1915   Rent Restrictions Act introduced rent controls as a wartime measure.

1919   Housing and Town Planning Act or 'Addison' Act (after Dr C. Addison, minister of health) gave open-ended subsidies to local authorities to cover the cost of municipal housing schemes. Local authorities with populations over 20,000 were obliged to survey the housing needs of their district and draw up plans for housing development. A second Act provided a subsidy of £260 for houses built for sale or rent by private builders. Over 200,000 houses built under the two Acts.

1920   Wartime rent controls continued and extended to higher-rated property.   Welwyn 'garden city' started.

1922   Fresh grants under the Addison scheme cease as a result of economy measures.

1923   Housing Act offered a subsidy of £6 annually for 20 years for houses built by local authorities or private builders to agreed specifications. Almost 500,000 houses built under its provisions before the subsidy was withdrawn in 1929, mainly by private builders for sale. Act regarded as a failure in terms of council-house building.

1924   Housing Act or 'Wheatley' Act (after C. I. Wheatley, minister of health) increased the state subsidy to £9 a year for 40 years on houses built for rent at controlled rents and made provision for the expansion of the building trades. Over 500,000 council houses built under the Act before it was suspended in 1932.

1930   Housing Act or 'Greenwood' Act (after A. Greenwood, minister of health) provided for slum clearance by the local authorities with graduated subsidies according to the number of families rehoused and the cost of clearance. Local authorities obliged to produce five-year plans for slum clearance. Its operation was interrupted by the financial crisis of 1931 and the economy drive of 1931–3.

1933   Housing Act drew up fresh plans for slum clearance with subsidies under the Greenwood Act, aiming to clear 266,000 slum dwellings, build 285,000 houses and rehouse 1¼ million people.

1935   Housing Act or 'Hilton Young' Act (after E. Hilton Young, minister of health) provided for an Overcrowding Survey and obliged local authorities to make plans to end overcrowding.

1938   Rent Act removed rent control from houses worth more than £20 (£135 in London), but retained it on those below.

1946   New Towns Act set up a number of development corporations entrusted with the building of new towns in various parts of the country.

1947   Town and Country Planning Act. County councils compelled to prepare plans for the development of their areas and given powers of compulsory purchase. Planning permission required for major alterations to buildings or changes in land use by owners.

1951   Conservative government pledges itself to building 300,000 houses per year. Housing subsidies for local authority housing raised from £22 to £35 per home. Local authorities empowered to license private contractors to build a greater number of council houses and encouragement given to private house-building.

1957   Rent Act of Conservative government abolished rent control on 810,000 houses and allowed rent increases for 4,300,000 houses still controlled.

1965   Rent Act of Labour government reintroduced rent control over the great majority of privately owned, unfurnished accommodation.

1972   Housing Finance Act forced local councils to charge 'fair rents' for subsidised council houses. Rent rebates and allowances to be given to those unable to afford the new rents.

1974   Housing Act increased aid to housing associations and introduced

Housing Action Areas. Rent Act introduced protection for tenants in furnished accommodation; extended rent tribunal powers and tenants' rights.

1975   Community Land Act introduced a plan to bring development land within public control. Repealed 1979.

1976   Agricultural Rent Act. 'Tied' cottages abolished in rural areas.

1980   Housing Act gives council tenants right to buy their houses.

Houses built in England and Wales, 1919–1978

	Local authority	Private	Total
1919–24	176,914	221,543	398,457
1925–9	326,353	673,344	999,697
1930–4	286,350	804,251	1,090,601
1935–9	346,840	1,269,912	1,616,752
1940–4	—	—	151,000
1945–9	432,098	126,317	588,415
1950–4	912,805	228,616	1,141,421
1955–9	688,585	623,024	1,311,609
1960–4	545,729	878,756	1,424,485
1965–9	761,224	994,361	1,755,585
1970–4	524,400	885,300	1,409,700
1975–8	465,100	621,200	1,086,300

(*Source*: A. H. Halsey (ed.), *Trends in British Society since 1900*, London, Macmillan, 1971, p. 311; *Annual Abstract of Statistics*, London, HMSO, 1969).

Types of housing tenure in England and Wales

	Owner-occupiers	Rented from local authority	Rented from private landlords	Others
1914	10.0	1.0	80.0	9.0
1939	31.0	14.0	46.0	9.0
1966	46.7	25.7	22.5	5.1

	Owner-occupiers	Rented from local authority	Rented from private landlords	Others
1970	50.0	30.0	15.0	5.0
1977	54.0	32.0	9.0	5.0

(*Source*: A. H. Halsey (ed.), *Trends in British Society since 1900*, London, Macmillan, 1971, p. 308; *Facts in Focus*, Harmondsworth, Penguin Books, 1972, p. 51.)

Slum clearance in England and Wales, 1930–1968

	Houses demolished or closed	Persons moved
1930	27,564	91,109
1934–9	245,272	1,001,417
1940–4	—	—
1945–9	29,350	98,950
1950–4	60,532	211,090
1955–9	213,402	682,228
1960–4	303,621	833,746
1965–8	270,186	722,905

(*Source*: A. H. Halsey (ed.), *Trends in British Society since 1900*, London, Macmillan, 1971, p. 312.)

Women

The status of women

1792 Mary Wollstonecraft's, *Vindication of the Rights of Women* presents the first, clear statement of the need for political and civil equality for women.

1839 Custody of Infants Act gave mothers of 'unblemished character' access to their children in the event of separation or divorce.

1848 Women admitted to London University.

1850 North London Collegiate Day School for girls established.

1854 Cheltenham Ladies' College founded.

1857 Matrimonial Causes Act set up divorce courts. Women obtained limited access to divorce, though, unlike for men, this could only be obtained on a specific cause other than adultery. Rights of access to children after divorce extended. Women given right to their property after a legal separation or a protection order given as a result of husband's desertion.

1867 John Stuart Mill publishes speech on *Admission of Women to Electoral Franchise*; followed by *The Subjection of Women* (1869).

1870 Married Women's Property Act allowed women to retain £200 of their own earnings.   Education Act provided elementary education for girls as well as boys.

1871 Newnham College, Cambridge, founded.

1872 London School of Medicine for Women opened. Hitchin College (later Girton College) moves to Cambridge.

1873 Custody of Infants Act extended access to children to all women in the event of separation or divorce.

1876 Medical schools opened to women.

1882 Married Women's Property Act allowed women to own and administer their property.

1884 Married Women's Property Act makes a woman no longer a 'chattel' but an independent and separate person.

1886 Guardianship of Infants Act. Women could be made sole guardian of children if husband died.

1894 Local Government Act. Women eligible to vote for parochial councils.

1897   Foundation of National Union of Women's Suffrage Societies, a federation of existing women's suffrage groups under the presidency of Mrs Millicent Fawcett.

1903   Women's Social and Political Union formed by Mrs Emmeline Pankhurst and her daughters Christabel and Sylvia to campaign more militantly for female suffrage ('suffragettes').

1907   Qualification of Women (County and Borough Councils) Act. Women allowed to become councillors.

1910   Violent campaign for women's suffrage including demonstrations, arson attacks and picture slashing. Government only prepared to consider women's suffrage as part of a wider extension of the franchise. 'Hunger strikes' mounted in prisons.

1913   Emily Davidson kills herself by throwing herself in front of the King's horse at the Derby. 'Cat and Mouse' Act passed to permit release and reimprisonment of suffragettes on hunger strike.

1918   Representation of the People Act gives the vote to women over 30. Rights to vote given in local elections on similar terms. Women entitled to become MPs.

1919   Sex Disqualification Removal Act opens all professions to women except the Church.   Lady Astor becomes first woman MP to take her seat.

1923   Women allowed to obtain divorce on grounds of adultery alone. Husband only allowed access to children if a desirable influence.

1925   Married Women's Property Act required husband and wife to be treated as separate individuals in any property transaction.

1928   Representation of the People Act. Women over 21 were given the vote in parliamentary and local elections.

1937   Divorce Act makes desertion and insanity grounds for divorce.

1967   Abortion Act provides for legal termination of pregnancy (see p. 112).   Family Planning Act allows local health authorities to provide a family planning service (see p. 112).

1969   Divorce Act liberalises divorce laws by granting divorce on any grounds showing an 'irretrievable breakdown' in a marriage.

1970   Equal Pay Act designed to prevent discrimination in pay between men and women doing equal work; to come into operation by December 1975.

1975   Sex Discrimination Act made discrimination between men and women unlawful in employment, education, training and the provision of housing, goods, facilities and services. Discriminatory advertisements made illegal. Sex discrimination defined as treating a person less favourably than another on the grounds of his or her sex. Equal Opportunities Commission set up to assist enforcement of Equal Pay and Sex Discrimination Acts.

Press and broadcasting

Major developments in the press

1702 First daily paper produced, the *Daily Courant*.

1712 Stamp Act introduced; newspapers subjected to tax and price increased.

1771 Printers' Case effectively frees the press to report parliamentary debates.

1785 *The Times* founded as the *Daily Universal Register*.

1797 Newspaper Act increases Stamp Duty on newspapers.

1814 Steam presses used to print *The Times*.

1821 *Manchester Guardian*, later *The Guardian*, founded.

1836 Reduction of Stamp Tax from 4*d.* to 1*d.*

1837 Invention of electric telegraph greatly facilitates collection of news.

1843 *News of the World* founded as Sunday newspaper.

1851 First news agency, Reuters, formed in London.

1855 Repeal of Stamp Duty on newspapers permits cheap press.

1870 Education Act provides basis of mass reading public.

1881 George Newnes produces *Tit-Bits* magazine for mass audience.

1896 *Daily Mail* founded by Alfred Harmsworth, later Lord Northcliffe (1865–1922); first mass circulation newspaper, priced at ½*d.*

1900 *Daily Express* started by Arthur Pearson (1866–1921).

1904 *Daily Mirror* refounded as ½*d.* illustrated newspaper, the first to make regular use of halftone photographs.

1908 Harmsworth acquires *The Times*.

1914 Press censorship introduced under Defence of the Realm Act of August 1914 and strengthened in subsequent amendments.

1922 Death of Lord Northcliffe. His newspaper empire passes to his brother, Lord Rothermere (1868–1940).

1926 *British Gazette* produced as official government organ during General Strike. TUC produced the *British Worker* as a response.

1932–3 Major circulation war between main newspapers. *Daily Herald* and *Daily Express* achieve circulations of over 2 million copies each per day.

1937   Total sale of all national dailies estimated at 10 million copies per day.

1939   Restrictions upon the press reintroduced during the Second World War under Defence Regulations.

1940   Newspapers limited in size, and circulations pegged at present rate due to shortage of newsprint. *Daily Worker* suppressed.

1949   First Royal Commission on the Press recommends setting up of Press Council to oversee all aspects of the press and handle complaints from the public.

1950   Total sale of all national daily newspapers reaches all-time peak of 17 million copies per day.

1953   Press Council set up according to recommendations of the Royal Commission of 1949.

1960   *News Chronicle* closed.

1962   Shawcross Commission on the Press reveals falling share of advertising revenue going to the press; expresses concern about growing concentration of the press; criticises the growth of newspaper involvement with television; and advised admission of lay members and an independent chairman to the Press Council.

1973   Following the Report of the Committee on Privacy, further lay members appointed to the Press Council.

1977   Report of McGregor Commission on the Press reveals fresh increase in newspaper advertising; continued concentration of ownership; growing economic difficulties due to increasing costs and overmanning, and greater division between 'quality' and 'popular' press.

1979   Total sales of all national daily newspapers estimated at 14 million copies per day and 19 million on Sundays.

Major developments in broadcasting

1901 First transatlantic radio message.

1922 Radio broadcasting begun by British Broadcasting Company.

1924 Baird transmits first successful television pictures.

1926 British Broadcasting Corporation (BBC) set up as a public corporation to take over radio broadcasting from the British Broadcasting Company.

1929 Experimental television broadcasts begun.

1936 First regular television broadcasts started from Alexandra Palace in North London.

1939 Television transmissions suspended for duration of the war.

1946 Television transmissions resumed.

1949 Report of the Broadcasting Committee rejected introduction of advertising and any breach in the BBC's monopoly.

1954 Television Act establishes commercial television under the overall control of the Independent Broadcasting Authority (IBA); programmes to be financed by advertising and transmitted by regionally based companies.

1955 First commercial television transmissions.

1962 Report of Pilkington Committee on Broadcasting criticises 'trivial' nature of many television programmes, especially on the commercial channels. Recommendation that greater powers be given to the IBA over its programme companies rejected by the government.

1964 Partly as a response to the Pilkington Report, only the BBC permitted to go ahead with a second channel, BBC-2, which began transmission in April.

1966 Colour television introduced.

1972 Sound Broadcasting Act ends BBC monopoly of radio by allowing setting up of commercial radio stations.

1973 First commercial radio stations begin broadcasting.

1978 Government publishes proposals on future of broadcasting following report of Annan Committee. A fourth television channel to be established in which priority to be given to the minority and educational interests not catered for on existing channels, including a Welsh language service for Wales, to be financed by advertising and government grants.

Crime and police

The development of the police

1792 Middlesex Justices Act provides for a force of professional magistrates and constables to operate in London.

1798 Thames Police Office set up to patrol the riverside districts of London.

1829 Metropolitan Police Act set up a paid, uniformed police force for the metropolitan area excluding the City of London, under the authority of two commissioners and the home secretary.

1833 Lighting and Watching Act permitted any town with over 5,000 population to appoint paid watchmen.

1835 Municipal Corporation Act required each of the 178 boroughs to appoint a watch committee and to set up a force of constables.

1839 County Police Act permitting justices to set up a paid county police force. In 1840 it was authorised to amalgamate borough and county forces where desired.

1856 County and Borough Police Act compelled all counties and boroughs to establish and maintain a police force. Three Inspectors of Constabulary appointed to assess their efficiency and report to parliament; forces certified as efficient to qualify for an exchequer grant towards the cost of the force. Boroughs of under 5,000 people, maintaining their own forces, not to be eligible for a grant.

1877 Municipal Corporations (New Charters) Act prohibited newly incorporated boroughs of under 20,000 population from setting up police forces.

1888 Local Government Act abolished police forces run by boroughs with less than 10,000 population. Control of the county police forces transferred to standing joint committees of county councillors and justices.

1919 Police Act, passed following strikes among metropolitan and provincial forces. It created the Police Federation and gave the home secretary powers to set nationwide pay and conditions of service.

1946 Police Act abolished and amalgamated 45 of the smaller non-county police forces.

1964 Police Act encouraged the setting up of joint crime and traffic squads. In 1966 amalgamation reduced the number of police forces in England and Wales from 117 to 49. Complaints against forces to be handled by an officer from an outside force.

1965 Metropolitan Police set up 'Special Patrol Group' (SPG) of 100 volunteers specially trained for riot control, gun use and intervention to support particular divisions at the command of Scotland Yard.

1969 Police National Computer Unit set up at Hendon to store information and provide direct links with the 800 police stations in England and Wales. Became operational in 1974.

1974 Diplomatic Protection Group of armed constables set up to provide protection for diplomatic premises in London.

1976 Police Act set up a Police Complaints Board to deal with complaints from the public against the police.

1977 Members of Scotland Yard Obscene Publications Squad jailed for corruption. Sir Robert Mark, Commissioner of Metropolitan Police, reveals that almost 400 officers had left or been required to leave the Metropolitan Police since 1972 following investigations of corruption.

Committals for indictable offences in England and Wales 1805–1856

	Total		Total		Total		Total
1805	4,605	1818	13,567	1831	19,647	1844	26,542
1806	4,346	1819	14,254	1832	20,829	1845	24,303
1807	4,446	1820	13,710	1833	20,072	1846	25,107
1808	4,735	1821	13,115	1834	20,168	1847	28,833
1809	5,330	1822	12,241	1835	20,731	1848	30,349
1810	5,146	1823	12,263	1836	20,984	1849	27,816
1811	5,337	1824	13,698	1837	23,612	1850	26,813
1812	6,576	1825	14,437	1838	23,094	1851	27,960
1813	7,164	1826	16,164	1839	24,443	1852	27,510
1814	6,390	1827	17,921	1840	27,187	1853	27,057
1815	7,818	1828	16,564	1841	27,760	1854	29,359
1816	9,091	1829	18,675	1842	31,309	1855	25,972
1817	13,932	1830	18,107	1843	29,591	1856	19,437

Note: The judicial statistics were altered and extended in 1857 to contain new categories of information.

(Source: British Parliamentary Papers, 1836–1857.)

Crimes known to the police, 1857–1978

	England and Wales	Scotland		England and Wales	Scotland
1857	91,671	—	1925	113,986	33.070
1865	92,522	—	1930	147,031	36,723
1870	90,532	118,105	1935	234,372	59,753
1875	82,316	123,169	1940	305,114	62,266
1880	98,440	122,656	1945	478,394	86,075
1885	86,905	114,865	1950	461,435	74,640
1890	81,773	136,505	1955	438,085	74,773
1895	81,323	134,357	1960	743,713	102,617
1900	77,934	33,492	1965	1,133,882	140,141
1905	94,654	39,804	1970	1,568,400	167,200
1910	103,132	38,376	1975	2,105,600	232,482
1915	77,972	33,915	1978	2,395,800	277,213
1920	100,827	39,444			

Note: Figures relate to indictable, generally more serious, offences, reported to or discovered by the police. Figures for Scotland up to 1895 also include minor, non-indictable, offences. The Theft Act, 1969, altered the categories of indictable offence, and the figures from 1970 are not strictly comparable to those before.

Numbers transported to Australia from Great Britain and Ireland (males and females), 1788–1853

	Total		Total		Total		Total
1788	759	1797	399	1806	519	1815	1,093
1789	—	1798	392	1807	313	1816	1,288
1790	1,246	1799	297	1808	299	1817	2,013
1791	2,035	1800	683	1809	340	1818	3,350
1792	780	1801	749	1810	521	1819	2,706
1793	322	1802	789	1811	479	1820	3,989
1794	84	1803	1,661	1812	526	1821	2,750
1795	—	1804	340	1813	602	1822	2,421
1796	370	1805	—	1814	1,262	1823	2,735

	Total		Total		Total		Total
1824	1,887	1832	4,522	1840	3,754	1847	1,705
1825	2,750	1833	6,871	1841	3,489	1848	1,634
1826	2,178	1834	4,675	1842	5,528	1849	3,416
1827	3,693	1835	6,077	1843	3,730	1850	3,204
1828	3,925	1836	6,028	1844	4,468	1851	2,111
1829	4,797	1837	4,933	1845	3,632	1852	2,578
1830	5,416	1838	5,178	1846	2,106	1853	1,569
1831	5,064	1839	3,711				

Note: Transportation became increasingly common in the late eighteenth century as a substitute for capital punishment, but was gradually replaced by long-term imprisonment in the United Kingdom after 1840. As a result the numbers of those transported gradually declined, falling to almost negligible proportions after 1853, until it was finally ended in 1867.

(*Source*: A. G. L. Shaw, *Convicts and the Colonies*, London, Faber, 1966, pp. 361–8.)

Criminal statistics: minor (non-indictable) offences, 1900–1970

	Adults proceeded against	Adults found guilty	Juveniles proceeded against	Juveniles found guilty
1900	672,989	557,489	—	—
1910	551,395	483,111	18,059	14,694
1920	427,556	374,565	16,953	14,956
1930	317,231	287,691	8,842	7,577
1938	236,752	216,759	16,873	15,310
1950	220,188	202,286	19,810	18,410
1960	247,133	232,992	28,025	26,337
1970	394,540	360,041	25,184	22,521

(*Source*: A. H. Halsey (ed.), *Trends in British Society since 1900*, London, Macmillan, 1971, pp. 527–8.)

Traffic offences, England and Wales, 1900–1970

	Numbers found guilty of traffic offences	Traffic offences as a percentage of all offences
1900	2,548	0.4
1910	55,633	9.1
1920	157,875	24.9
1930	267,616	42.8
1938	475,124	60.3
1950	357,832	52.6
1960	622,551	60.1
1970	991,200	59.2

(*Source: The Criminal Statistics for England and Wales*, 1900–70)

Prison population in England and Wales, 1880–1977 (daily average)

	(*000s*)		(*000s*)
1880	28.7	1940	9.3
1890	18.3	1950	20.0
1900	17.5	1960	27.1
1910	22.0	1970	39.0
1920	9.9	1977	41.6
1930	11.3		

(*Source: Annual Reports* of the Prison Commissioners and Prison Department of the Home Office.)

Major popular disturbances and demonstrations

1715   Attacks upon dissenting meeting houses and chapels in the North-West and the Midlands by pro-Tory/Jacobite demonstrators. Most serious disturbances at Manchester,

Birmingham and Oxford. Riot Act introduced to provide severer penalties against rioters.

1736   Porteus riots. Captain Porteus was the commander of a troop of soldiers in Edinburgh who opened fire on a crowd at the execution of a smuggler. Porteus was tried and condemned to death, but reprieved. A crowd attacked the prison he was held in and lynched Porteus (September). The magistrates were reprimanded and the city fined £12,000.   Attacks on Irish by English workmen in London.   Attacks on informers.

1739–40   Food riots in East Anglia and West Country.

1740   Destruction of Newcastle Guildhall by pitmen and others after a man killed during a food riot.

1756–7   Widespread food riots in the Midlands and Forest of Dean; 'Shudehill fight' at Manchester.

1757   Militia Act riots against being balloted for the militia, mainly in Lincolnshire and Yorkshire.

1763–5   Machine-breaking by Spitalfields weavers and demonstrations against imports of foreign textiles.

1766   Widespread food riots. Major areas of disturbances in the West Country, Thames Valley, Midlands and East Anglia.

1768   Demonstrations in support of John Wilkes in London. 'Massacre' of St George's Fields: some of Wilkes's supporters killed by soldiers when demonstrating outside the King's Bench Prison (May).

1772–3   Renewed wave of food riots, mainly in East Anglia, the West Country, the Midlands and on Tayside.

1780   Gordon riots in London. Lord George Gordon led the Protestant Association in a campaign to repeal the Catholic Relief Act of 1778. A mass lobby of parliament to present a petition on 2 June led to almost a week of rioting with attacks on the property of Catholics and prominent public buildings. Newgate prison burned and over 300 people killed or executed as a result of the riots.

1791   'Church and King' riots in Birmingham. House and property of Joseph Priestley and other dissenters destroyed by loyalists (July).

1794   'Crimp house' riots in London; attacks on recruiting houses for illegally obtaining recruits.

1795–6   Widespread food riots following poor harvests in 1794 and 1795.

1795   Attack on the King's coach at the opening of parliament during huge anti-war demonstrations (29 October).

1796   Riots against implementation of Supplementary Militia Act in Lincolnshire and Wales.

1797   Mutinies among fleets at Spithead and the Nore (May–June).

1800–1   Widespread food riots following harvest failures in 1799 and 1800.

1809   'Old Price' riots at Drury Lane theatre, London, against increased admission charges.

1810   Burdett riots. Demonstrations in London in support of radical MP Sir Francis Burdett.

1811–12   Luddite machine-breaking outbreaks (begin March 1811) in Midlands, Yorkshire, Lancashire and Cheshire. Renewed outbreaks occurred in 1814 and 1816.

1816   Widespread disturbances against high prices and unemployment on the conclusion of the Napoleonic Wars. Main centres in East Anglia and manufacturing districts. Spa Fields riot in London. Attack on gunshops and Tower of London by group of revolutionary followers of Thomas Spence.

1817   Attack on Prince Regent's coach at state opening of Parliament (January).   March of the 'blanketeers' from Manchester to present a petition for reform and against distress broken up by troops (March).   Failure of Pentrich 'rising' in Derbyshire led by Jeremiah Brandreth (June). Brandreth executed.

1819   Reform demonstration broken up at St Peter's Fields, Manchester. Eleven killed and nearly 200 wounded – the 'Peterloo Massacre'.

1820   Cato Street conspiracy to assassinate the cabinet discovered. Arthur Thistlewood and fellow conspirators executed (February).   'Battle of Bonnymuir' near Glasgow between weavers and troops.'

1821   Two killed during riots at funeral of Queen Caroline (August).

1826   Power-looms destroyed in Lancashire (April–May).

1830–3   'Captain Swing' disturbances among agricultural districts in southern England. Hundreds of demonstrations, riots, machine-breakings and arson attempts. Several hundred labourers transported. Reform disturbances in London (November 1830).

1831   Riots in Bristol, Nottingham and Derby following Lords' rejection of the Reform Bill.

1833   Clerkenwell riot; reform demonstration broken up by police.

1839   'Bull Ring' riots in Birmingham. Pro-Chartist demonstrations (July).   Newport 'rising' led by John Frost suppressed (November).

1840   Chartist 'rising' in Dewsbury and Sheffield.

1842   'Plug-plot' riots and Chartist General Strike in the North and Potteries (July–August).

1848   Chartist demonstration at Kennington Common (10 April).

1852   Stockport riots between Catholics and Protestants; two Catholic churches sacked.

1855 'Sunday Trading' riots in Hyde Park, London, against Act prohibiting trading on Sundays.

1862 'Garibaldi' riots in Hyde Park, London between Irish and Italians.

1866 Reform demonstration breaks down Hyde Park railings (July).   Sheffield 'outrages': attacks upon non-union labour by Sheffield cutlers (October).

1867 Reform League demonstration at Hyde Park in defiance of home secretary's ban (May).   Fenian rescue of prisoners in Manchester (September). Gunpowder attack by Fenians on Clerkenwell Prison (December).

1868 'Murphy' riots in Ashton and Stalybridge; attacks on Irish Catholics provoked by anti-Catholic lecturer, William Murphy.

1886 'Black Monday'; unemployed riots in West End of London, following meeting of Social Democratic Federation in Trafalgar Square (8 February).

1887 'Bloody Sunday'; meeting of Social Democratic Federation in Trafalgar Square broken up by police and troops (13 November).

1893 Two people killed during clashes between troops and strikers at Acton Hall Colliery, near Featherstone.

1909 Serious sectarian riots in Liverpool.

1910 Disturbances during Cambrian Combine strike at Tonypandy in South Wales. Troops called out to disperse demonstrators.

1911 Clashes between police and strikers in Liverpool on 'Bloody Sunday' (13 August) and two strikers shot by troops (15 August). Two men shot at Llanelli (17 August).

1919 Clashes between police and strikers during General Strike in Glasgow, known as 'Bloody Friday' (31 June). Troops called to patrol city.   Demobilisation disturbances in London and at Rhyl, North Wales (March).   Police strike in Liverpool followed by rioting in central districts (August).

1926 General Strike. Clashes between strikers and police in Glasgow, Hull, London and elsewhere. Four thousand strikers prosecuted for violence or incitement to violence; about 1,000 imprisoned.

1931 Widespread demonstrations against government economy measures. Clashes between National Unemployed Workers' Movement (NUWM) demonstrators and police in Bristol, Salford, Manchester, Dundee and other places (October–November).

1932 Clashes between unemployed demonstrators and police in Birkenhead and Liverpool (September).   NUWM 'hunger march' to London followed by clashes with police in Hyde Park and Central London (October–November). Serious riot in Dartmoor prison.

1934 'Hunger march' to London mounted by the NUWM followed by mass lobby of Parliament (February).   Olympia meeting of British Union of Fascists (BUF) (June).

1934–5   Demonstrations mounted against new Unemployment
Assistance Board regulations governing unemployment relief in
South Wales, Scotland and Yorkshire. Some disturbances in
South Wales (October–February).

1936   'Battle of Cable Street'; fighting between police and anti-fascist
demonstrators attempting to prevent BUF march through the
Jewish districts of East London (4 October).   'Jarrow March' of
unemployed to London (October). Further NUWM 'hunger march'
to London protesting against unemployment (November).

1937   Proposed march by BUF through East End prohibited under Public
Order Act. March through Bermondsey leads to 113 arrests and 28
injured (July).

1938–9   Demonstrations in London by NUWM as part of campaign for
'winter relief' for the unemployed.

1958   Race riots in London (Notting Hill) and the Midlands.

1961   'Sit-down' demonstrations in London organised by Campaign for
Nuclear Disarmament (CND).

1964–6   'Mods' versus 'Rockers' disturbances at seaside resorts, usually
at Bank Holiday weekends.

1967   'Sit-in' at London School of Economics begins wave of similar
demonstrations in several universities (March). Anti-Vietnam War
demonstration mounted by Vietnam Solidarity Campaign leads to
disturbances outside American Embassy in Grosvenor Square
(October).

1968   Anti-Vietnam demonstrations in London lead to clashes with
police in Grosvenor Square (March and October).

1973   Riot in Parkhurst prison.

1974   Red Lion Square clashes between National Front and opponents,
one man killed (June).

1976   Disturbances at West Indian carnival in London (September). Hull
prison riot; an estimated £1 million worth of damage
(August–September).

1977   Clashes between police and mass pickets at Grunwick strike
(July–September).

1979   Southall disturbances between police and anti-National Front
demonstrators; one man killed (April).

1980   Rioting in St Paul's area of Bristol by coloured youths (April).

1981   Rioting in Brixton (April), leads to setting up of Scarman Enquiry.
Serious riots in Toxteth, Liverpool and Moss Side, Manchester,
followed by 'copycat' rioting by youths in many other towns and
cities (July).

Local government

Local government and representation

1818 Vestries Act (also known as Sturges Bourne Act) established a system of voting according to land-ownership in electing parish officers.

1831 Vestries Act (also known as Hobhouse Act) provided for the election of members of parish vestries and a secret ballot if requested by five ratepayers. One-third of elected representatives to retire each year.

1835 Municipal Reform Act. All members of town councils to be elected by the ratepayers, and town councils to publish their accounts. Franchise in local elections extended to all males over 21 who had been owners or tenants of property for two and a half years and had paid rates. Towns with over 6,000 population were divided into wards for voting. Property qualifications introduced, restricting election of town councillors to property owners.

1855 Metropolis Management Act. The Act set up the Metropolitan Board of Works as the main authority for London.

1888 Local Government Act. Administration of counties, including levying of rates, maintenance of roads, bridges, lunatic asylums and poor relief transferred to county councils elected by ratepayers.

1889 Establishment of London County Council (LCC).

1894 Local Government Act created rural and urban district councils. All county and parliamentary electors given the vote in local elections. Civil functions of parish vestries were transferred to new parish councils and parish meetings.

1899 Local Government Act converted the London vestries into borough councils.

1918 Representation of the People Act established a common franchise for county councils, boroughs, parishes and urban and district councils. Men entitled to vote with six month occupancy of premises or land within the area. Women over 30 entitled to vote under the same provisions or if married to a man entitled to vote.

1928 Representation of the People Act allowed women over 21 to vote at local elections.

1929 Local Government Act gave county and county borough councils control over public assistance to the poor and sick.

1945   Representation of the People Act extended franchise in local government to all those registered for parliamentary elections.

1965   Two-tier system of local government established in London. Greater London Council (GLC) set up; responsible for general services and borough councils amalgamated to form larger units.

1972   Local Government reorganisation in England and Wales creates six metropolitan counties to run services in the major conurbations. Thirty-nine county councils with new boundaries established to run major services. A second tier of 375 district councils to provide local services and amenities. Abolition of 1,200 councils, including old county borough councils, but 7,000 smaller parish councils retained as a third tier of local government. Subsequent legislation introduced to reform local government along similar lines in Scotland.

Occupations and social structure

Gregory King's estimate of the population and wealth of England and Wales, calculated for 1696

Rank	Number of families	Persons	Yearly income per family (£)	Yearly expenditure per family (£)	Total income of groups (£)
Temporal lords	160	6,400	2,800	2,400	448,000
Spiritual lords	26	520	1,300	1,100	33,800
Baronets	800	12,800	880	816	70,400
Knights	600	7,800	650	498	39,000
Esquires	3,000	30,000	450	420	1,350,000
Gentlemen	12,000	96,000	280	268	3,360,000
Clergy, superior	2,000	12,000	60	54	120,000
Clergy, inferior	8,000	40,000	45	40	360,000
Persons in the law	10,000	70,000	140	119	1,400,000
Sciences and liberal arts	16,000	80,000	60	57.10s.	960,000
Persons in offices (higher)	5,000	40,000	240	216	1,200,000
Persons in offices (lower)	5,000	30,000	120	108	600,000
Naval officers	5,000	20,000	80	72	400,000
Military officers	4,000	16,000	60	56	240,000

Rank	Number of families	Persons	Yearly income per family (£)	Yearly expenditure per family (£)	Total income of groups (£)
Common soldiers	35,000	70,000	14	15	490,000
Freeholders (better sort)	40,000	280,000	84	77	3,360,000
Freeholders (lesser)	140,000	700,000	50	45.10s.	7,000,000
Farmers	150,000	750,000	44	42.15s.	6,600,000
Labouring people and servants	364,000	1,275,000	15	15.5s.	5,460,000
Cottagers and paupers	400,000	1,300,000	6.10s.	7.6.3d.	2,600,000
Artisans, handicrafts	60,000	240,000	40	38	2,400,000
Merchants by sea	2,000	16,000	400	320	800,000
Merchants by land	8,000	48,000	200	170	1,600,000
Shopkeepers, tradesmen	40,000	180,000	45	42.15s.	1,800,000
Common seamen	50,000	150,000	20	21.10s.	1,000,000
Vagrants		30,000	2	3	60,000

(*Source*: G. N. Clark, *The Wealth of England from 1496 to 1760*, Oxford, 1946, pp. 192–3.)

Patrick Colquhoun's estimate of the social structure of the United Kingdom, *c.* 1815 (000s)

	(*000s*)
Royalty and nobility	3
Baronets, knights and squires	50

	(000s)
Upper clergy, merchants and bankers	40
Upper civil servants and lawyers	40
Independent gentry	150
Upper doctors and other professionals	20
Army and navy officers	70
Lesser clergy	75
Upper freeholders	300
Shipowners, lesser merchants, shipbuilders, engineers and builders	200
Lesser professionals, civil servants and dissenting ministers	250
Innkeepers	375
Shopkeepers and hawkers	600
Master craftsmen and manufacturers	450
Lesser freeholders	900
Farmers	1,300
Teachers, actors, clerks and shopmen	320
Artisans and other skilled workers	4,500
Agricultural labourers, miners, road and canal workers and seamen	3,500
Personal and household servants	1,300
Soldiers and sailors	800
Paupers, vagrants, prisoners and lunatics	1,900

(*Source*: G. D. H. Cole and R. Postgate, *The Common People, 1746–1946*, London, Methuen, 6th edn, 1963, p. 71.)

Principal occupation groups in Britain in 1851 in order of size

	Male	*Female*
Total population	10,224,000	10,736,000
Population of 10 years old and upwards	7,616,000	8,155,000
Agriculture: farmer, grazier, labourer, servant	1,563,000	227,000
Domestic service (excluding farm service)	134,000	905,000

	Male	Female
Cotton worker, every kind, with printer, dyer	255,000	272,000
Building craftsman: carpenter, bricklayer, mason, plasterer, plumber, etc.	442,000	1,000
Labourer (unspecified)	367,000	9,000
Milliner, dressmaker, seamstress (seamster)	494	340,000
Wool-worker, every kind, with carpet-weaver	171,000	113,000
Shoemaker	243,000	31,000
Coal-miner	216,000	3,000
Tailor	135,000	18,000
Washerwoman		145,000
Seaman (merchant), pilot	144,000	
Silk worker	53,000	80,000
Blacksmith	112,000	592
Linen, flax-worker	47,000	56,000
Carter, carman, coachman, postboy, cabman, busman, etc.	83,000	1,000
Ironworker, founder, moulder (excluding iron-mining, nails, hardware, cutlery, files, tools, machines)	79,000	590
Railway driver, etc. porter, etc. labourer, platelayer	65,000	54
Hosiery worker	35,000	30,000
Lace worker	10,000	54,000
Machine, boiler-maker	63,000	647
Baker	56,000	7,000
Copper, tin, lead-miner	53,000	7,000
Charwoman		55,000
Commercial clerk	44,000	19
Fisherman	37,000	1,000
Miller	37,000	562
Earthenware worker	25,000	11,000
Sawyer	35,000	23
Shipwright, boat-builder, block- and mast-maker	32,000	28
Straw-plait worker	4,000	28,000

	Male	Female
Wheelwright	30,000	106
Glover	4,500	25,000
Nailer	19,000	10,000
Iron-miner	27,000	910
Tanner, currier, fellmonger	25,000	276
Printer	22,000	222

(*Source*: Compiled from figures collected in 1851 census, *Parliamentary Papers* (1691), LXXXVIII, 1852–3.)

Occupational groups in Britain, 1911–1961

	1911 Number (000s)	%	1931 Number (000s)	%	1961 Number (000s)	%
Employers and proprietors	1,232	6.7	1,407	6.7	1,139	4.7
White-collar workers	3,433	18.7	4,841	23.0	8,478	35.9
(a) Managers and administrators	631	3.4	770	3.7	1,268	5.4
(b) Higher professionals and technicians	184	1.0	240	1.1	718	3.0
(c) Lower professionals and technicians	560	3.1	728	3.5	1,418	6.0
(d) Foremen and inspectors	237	1.3	323	1.5	682	2.9
(e) Clerks	832	4.5	1,404	6.7	2,994	12.7
(f) Salesmen and shop assistants	989	5.4	1,376	6.5	1,398	5.9
Manual workers	13,685	74.6	14,776	70.3	14,022	59.3
(a) Skilled	5,608	30.5	5,618	26.7	5,981	25.3
(b) Semi-skilled	6,310	34.4	6,044	28.7	6,004	25.4
(c) Unskilled	1,767	9.6	3,114	14.8	2,037	8.6
Total occupied population	18,350	100.0	21,024	100.0	23,639	100.0

(*Source*: A. H. Halsey (ed.), *Trends in British Society since 1900*, London, Macmillan, 1972, p. 113.)

Employment in Britain, 1977

	Number (000s)	%
Agriculture, forestry and fishing	391	1.6
Mining and quarrying	349	1.4
Chemicals and allied industries	466	1.9
Metals, engineering and vehicles	3,795	15.5
Textiles	516	2.1
Clothing and footwear	390	1.6
Food, drink and tobacco	723	2.9
Other manufactures	1,453	5.9
Construction	1,265	5.2
Gas, electricity and water	350	1.4
Transport and communications	1,449	5.9
Distributive trades	2,734	11.1
Professional, financial, scientific and miscellaneous services	7,144	29.1
National and local government service	1,633	6.7
Employers and self-employed	1,886	7.7
Total in civil employment	24,547	100.0
Armed forces	327	—
Unemployed	1,450	—
Total working population	26,367	—

(*Source: Britain 1979: an official handbook*, London, HMSO, 1979, pp. 310–11.)

Labour

Chronology of trade union history

1717 Reports of widespread combination of wool-workers in Devon and Somerset.

1718 Royal Proclamation against 'lawless clubs and societies'.

1719 Weavers' riots in Norwich and Colchester over the use of foreign calico; attacks on people wearing calico in London and campaign for an Act prohibiting their use mounted by the Weavers' Company.   Keelmen's strike in the North-East.

1720 Weavers' riots in Tiverton over use of imported wool.   Renewed rioting in London over delay in passing a Calico Act.

1723–6 Widespread stoppage and disturbances in the West Country woollen industry during a wage dispute. Acts passed in 1726 and 1728 to regulate wages.

1738–40 Renewed strikes and disturbances in the West Country over wage rates.

1740 Colliers' disturbances in the North-East to obtain wage rises.

1744 Keelmen's strike in the North-East against overloading of keels and a 'Contract' agreed with masters regulating wages and conditions.

1750 Disturbances in the West Country over the use of imported Irish wool.   Strike of keelmen on the Tyne and Wear in defence of terms of 'Contract'. Strike broken by the use of troops.

1755 Act obtained by Gloucestershire weavers to regulate wages ignored by clothiers; widespread disorder suppressed by the use of troops.

1752 Strike of Norwich weavers to enforce regulation of the trade.

1758 London coal-heavers obtain an Act regulating the trade and placing them under the direction of the alderman for Billingsgate.

1762 Seamen's strike in Liverpool.

1765 Protracted colliers' strike in the North-East over the yearly 'bond'.   Campaign of Spitalfields' weavers against imports of French silks achieves prohibitory Act.

1767–8 Widespread industrial disputes among the London trades including silk-weavers, coal-heavers, seamen, hatters, tailors, watermen, sawyers and coopers.

1768   Seamen's and keelmen's strikes in the North-East.

1773   Spitalfields Act obtained to regulate wages of London silk-weavers.

1775   Liverpool sailors' strike.

1778–9   Framework knitters' campaign for Act regulating wages defeated in Parliament. Disturbances in Nottingham following rejection of Bill.   Machine-breaking in Lancashire directed at large spinning-jennies. Arkwright's factory at Birkacre, near Chorley, destroyed.

1792   Strikes of seamen along the East coast, of shipyard workers, Lancashire miners and several London trades.   Power loom factory of Messrs Grimshaw burnt down by Manchester weavers.

1793   Friendly Societies Act gives societies legal status and protection for their funds.

1797   Unlawful Oaths Act passed in wake of naval mutinies makes secret oath-taking illegal. Used subsequently to restrict trade union organisation.   Campaign of London watchmakers against taxes on their trade.

1799   Combination Act: passed as a result of petition of master millwrights of London for a Bill to outlaw combinations in the trade. Although combinations of workmen could already be prosecuted as conspiracies and for other offences in common law, the petition sought an Act similar to another 40 or so Acts passed during the eighteenth century to provide for summary prosecution (i.e. before a magistrate) of combinations in particular trades. On behalf of the government, Wilberforce suggested that the Act should apply to *all* combinations and this was supported by Pitt. The Act provided for summary prosecution before a single magistrate on the evidence of one or more witnesses. Workmen could be sentenced to three months in gaol or two months in a House of Correction with hard labour for: (a) combining to improve conditions or raise wages; (b) inducing others to leave work; (c) refusing to work with others; (d) attending meetings with the purpose of improving wages and conditions or persuading others to attend such a meeting or raise money for such a meeting; (e) contributing to the expenses of anyone tried under the Act; (f) holding money for a combination and refusing to answer questions about it.

1800   Objections to the 1799 Combination Act complained about the vagueness of its language; the use of summary jurisdiction; the possibility of employer-magistrates trying their own workmen; the compulsion to answer questions about money possibly held for a combination, thereby incriminating oneself or else face automatic sentence under the Act. Petitions for total repeal led by the Whig, Sheridan, were resisted by Pitt who claimed that provisions for summary prosecution of combinations were essential. The Combination Act of 1800, therefore, retained the principal features of the 1799 Act, but modified some of its features, notably: (a) two magistrates instead of one to try cases; (b) employer-magistrates prohibited from trying cases of men in their own trade; (c) an arbitration provision was introduced; (d) masters were prohibited from combining to reduce wages, increase hours or worsen conditions.

1801   Extensive strike of shipwrights in government dockyards led and organised by John Gast.

1802   Strike in civilian shipyards on Thames.   Petition of clothiers in the South-West against gig-mills, followed by strikes and machine-breaking in the South-West and Yorkshire.

1803   First annual suspension of statutes regulating woollen industry.   Strike of Tyne keelmen.

1805   Wool-workers petition for regulation of trade.

1807   Cotton weavers petition for minimum wage bill.

1808   Manchester cotton weavers' strike leads to widespread stoppage throughout the cotton district; 60,000 looms idle by June.

1809   Repeal of protective legislation in the woollen industry.   Further strike of the Tyne keelmen.

1810   London printers of *The Times* prosecuted for conspiracy.   Strike of Lancashire and Cheshire cotton spinners, organised by 'General Union of Spinners'. Strike collapsed after four months.

1811   Beginning of Luddite campaign in Nottinghamshire directed at hosiers who refused to raise wages and end abuses in the trade. Frame-breaking spreads through hosiery districts of Nottinghamshire, Derbyshire and northern Leicestershire.

1812   Rejection of framework-knitters Bill to regulate the trade leads to continued frame-breaking. Machine-breaking spreads to the Yorkshire croppers with attacks on mills around Huddersfield and Leeds and to Lancashire and Cheshire where attacks were made on power looms. Frame-breaking made a capital offence. In Scotland, cotton weavers mount a six-week strike covering the area from Aberdeen to Carlisle.   Luddite attacks in Yorkshire reach climax in April with unsuccessful attack on Rawfold's Mill of William Cartwright and in Lancashire with attacks on Westhoughton. Arrests of leaders and garrisoning of the North with over 10,000 troops gradually ends the main wave of machine-breaking.

1813   Clauses in Elizabethan Statute of Artificers empowering judges to fix wages repealed.

1814   Clauses in Elizabethan Statute of Artificers regulating apprenticeship abolished.   Francis Place begins collecting evidence for campaign against the Combination Laws.

1815   Seamen's strike in north-eastern ports. Compromise settlement reached with shipowners.

1816   Strikes against lay-offs and wage reductions in iron-working districts. Renewed machine-breaking in textile districts.

1817   March of the 'blanketeers' (distressed Lancashire weavers) from
       Manchester for relief and parliamentary reform broken up by
       troops.

1818   Weavers' and spinners' strikes in Lancashire and attempts to form
       a 'General Union of the Trades'. Metropolitan Trades Committee
       sets up early general union, the 'Philanthropic Hercules'.

1819   Keelmen's strike on Tyneside.

1820   Scottish weavers strike, and clashes with troops.

1821   Strikes and riots in Shropshire iron districts.

1824   Campaign for repeal of the Combination Laws managed by
       Francis Place and Joseph Hume, MP. In February 1824 Hume
       moved resolutions in the House of Commons for committee to
       consider the laws on the emigration of artisans, the exportation of
       machinery and combinations of workmen. As a result
       Combination Act of 1824 was passed, virtually repealing all the
       provisions of the 1800 Act. Combination to alter wages or
       conditions now legal and freed from prosecution for conspiracy or
       other offences existing prior to the Combination Laws. Violence or
       threats in trade disputes made punishable by two months' hard
       labour on summary conviction before two magistrates not
       engaged in, or related to persons engaged in, the trade.

1825   The 1824 Act led to a rapid increase in trade union activity with
       extensive strikes, including some violence. This resulted in a new
       Act, the Combination Act of 1825, repealing the 1824 Act. It
       exempted from prosecution combinations which met to bargain
       over wages and conditions, but did not explicitly confer a right to
       strike. Violence, intimidation, molestation and obstruction
       (including picketing) in furtherance of a dispute made offenders
       liable to three months' imprisonment. The effect was to impose a
       narrow definition of legal activity for trade unions, confining them
       to peaceful collective bargaining over wages and hours only.
       Combinations to negotiate outside these limits could be
       prosecuted as criminal conspiracy 'in restraint of trade'. Also,
       many of the methods which unions might employ were liable to
       prosecution and were still ill-defined in law.   *Trades
       Newspaper* founded by John Gast and others.

1829   General Union of Spinners formed by John Doherty in
       Manchester. Also launches Union of Trades.

1830   Union of Trades changes name to National Association for the
       Protection of Labour and forms branches in cotton districts,
       Midlands and Potteries.   Strike of Northumberland and
       Durham Colliers' Union under leadership of Thomas Hepburn.
       Strike broken by eviction of colliers from their houses.

1831   Collapse of spinners' union after strikes early in the year; Doherty
       founds *Voice of the People* journal.

1832   Industrial unrest in South Wales. Merthyr occupied by
       miners.   Exchange of goods made by cooperative production

facilitated by National Equitable Labour Exchange.   National Association for the Protection of Labour collapses.   Operative Builders' Union formed as federation of building unions; executive was Grand Committee, appointed by Grand Lodge of 'Builders' Parliament' which met twice a year. Involved in a series of strikes and lock-outs to change contract system of labour.   William Benbow's *Grand National Holiday and Congress of the Productive Classes* suggests idea of a General Strike.

1833   Widespread 'turn-outs' of workmen lead to moves for general unions. Owenite Grand National Moral Union of the Productive Classes formed in October at conference of delegates from Co-operative and Trade Societies 'to establish for the productive classes a complete dominion over the fruits of their own industry'. In November Robert Owen and John Fielden establish the Society for Promoting National Regeneration with the intention of securing an eight-hour day by means of a limited General Strike on 1 March 1834.

1834   On 13 February conference of trade union delegates in London decide to consolidate all trade unions in a single body with Central Committee and district lodges, The Grand National Consolidated Trades' Union (GNCTU) of Great Britain and Ireland. It had up to 16,000 fee-paying members, mainly in London and provincial skilled trades, but gained little support from several important groups, such as builders, potters, cotton spinners and Yorkshire cloth workers. Widespread strike movement by GNCTU defeated by lock-outs and internal divisions.   Owen became Grand Master of reconstituted union known as British and Foreign Consolidated Association of Industry, Humanity and Knowledge, but most unions had seceded from the body and it was virtually defunct by the end of 1834.   In March 1834 six labourers (the 'Tolpuddle Martyrs') convicted and sentenced to transportation for seven years for administering illegal oaths in connection with the Agricultural Labourer's Friendly Society at Tolpuddle, Dorset. Widespread protests all over the country, including a peaceful demonstration of 40,000–50,000 in London. The men were eventually pardoned and allowed to return to England.

1837   Leader of the Cotton Spinners' Association deported after he had been charged with conspiracy over the murder of a 'blackleg' in Glasgow.

1842   Strikes of coal-miners and other workers merge into General Strike for the Charter. Widespread stoppage of work enforced over much of northern England by drawing plugs from engine boilers, hence called the 'Plug-plot' riots.

1844   Miners' Association strike in the North-East and Yorkshire. Strike defeated after four months in a spate of mass evictions and use of strike-breakers.

1851   Amalgamated Society of Engineers founded, the beginning of 'New Model Unionism'. Initial membership 12,000; rising to 33,000 in 1868 and 71,000 in 1891.

1853   Amalgamated Association of Operative Cotton Spinners formed.

1854   Imported Irish labour used to defeat Preston cotton spinners' strike.

1855   Society benefit funds protected by Friendly Societies Act.

1858   Formation of National Miners' Association by Alexander MacDonald, and of Glasgow Trades Council. Nine-week strike in the Staffordshire collieries.

1859   Peaceful picketing allowed by Molestation of Workmen Act.   Building workers' strike in London and intimidation in the Manchester building trade.

1860   London Trades Council and Amalgamated Society of Carpenters and Joiners formed.   Coal Mines Regulation Act abolishes truck payment and regulates conditions of employment.

1864   First national conference of trade union delegates.

1865   Reform League formed to win enfranchisement for the working class.

1866   'Sheffield Outrages' (October); attacks on non-union cutlery workers by fellow workmen. As a result, Royal Commission on Trade Unions established.   Hornby v. Close case, decision against trade union trying to recoup funds from a defaulting local treasurer raises doubts over the degree of protection for funds given by Friendly Societies Act of 1855. Short-lived United Kingdom Alliance of Organised Trades formed.

1867   Master and Servant Act amended to limit prosecution of strikers for breach of contract, but unions remained dissatisfied because criminal action still possible for 'aggravated cases'. The 'Junta' – Applegarth, Allan, Coulson, Odger and Guile – mastermind trade union case for Royal Commission, with Frederic Harrison as their nominee. Report of Royal Commission recommended legalisation of trade unions.

1868   First Trades Union Congress (TUC) at Manchester; 34 delegates with no formal organisation.

1869   Second TUC at Birmingham; 40 delegates representing 250,000 members.

1871   Trade Union Act and Criminal Law Amendment Act; gave unions legal recognition and right to protect their funds, although picketing was made illegal in any form. The TUC established its Parliamentary Committee and the Amalgamated Society of Railway Servants was formed. 'Nine Hours' strike by engineers in the North-East secures shorter hours.

1872   National Agricultural Union formed by Joseph Arch. Soon had 10,000 members and a weekly journal, Labourers' Chronicle, which reached a circulation of 30,000.

1874   Trade unionists Alexander MacDonald and Thomas Burt elected as MPs for Stafford and Morpeth respectively.   Royal Commission on Labour laws set up.

1875   Conspiracy and Protection of Property Act, allowed peaceful picketing and eliminated conspiracy from trades disputes unless they were illegal.   Employers and Workmen Act limited penalty in breach of contract to civil damages.   Henry Broadhurst becomes secretary of the TUC.

1878   Nine-week strike of cotton weavers in Lancashire; disturbances at Preston and Blackburn.

1880   Employers' Liability Act.   Re-emergence of socialist influence in next few years.

1886   National Federation of Labour formed on Tyneside.

1887   Attack launched on Broadhurst at TUC, Keir Hardie accusing him of not properly serving the movement by collaborating with the employers.

1888   H. H. Champion's *Labour Elector* launched, advocating the establishment of an Independent Labour Party.   Strike of the women match-makers of Bryant & May in London.   The start of 'New Unionism'.

1889   In March, Will Thorn begins to organise gas workers, who successfully fought to reduce hours from 12 to 8 per day.   In August, the London dockers' strike saw the dockers winning 6d. per hour,, and was followed by the establishment of the Dock, Wharf, Riverside and General Labourers Union under Ben Tillett.   Miners Federation of Great Britain (MFGB) formed.

1890   Formation of Shipping Federation, the employers response to New Unionism.

1892   Keir Hardie carries motion for a labour representation fund at TUC, although little progress is made.

1893   Independent Labour Party set up and National Free Labour Association established.   Two people killed after clashes between strikers and soldiers at Ackton Hall Colliery, near Featherstone.

1894   Change in Standing Orders of TUC; representation now related to the number of members affiliated to TUC.

1896   *Lyons* v. *Wilkins* case; injunction against Amalgamated Trade Society of Fancy Leather Workers prevented them from picketing Lyons' premises.   Employers Federation of Engineering Associations formed.

1897–8   July 1897 to January 1898, national lock-out in engineering industry ends in success for employers.   Scottish TUC formed.

1898   Employers' Parliamentary Council formed to counter effects of TUC Parliamentary Committee.

1899   Formation of General Federation of Trade Unions to control a fund for mutual support in the event of strikes.

1900   Labour Representation Committee (LRC) formed, following Scottish Workers Parliamentary Election Committee.

1901   Taff Vale case. A strike against the Taff Vale Railway Co., sanctioned by the Amalgamated Society of Railway Servants (ASRS), was opposed legally by Ammon Beasley, the company manager, on the strength of the *Lyons* v. *Wilkins* case. The legal case continued after the strike had ended, with the Law Lords under Lord Halsbury granting the injunction against the ASRS to stop picketing, and making the funds of the union liable for damages amounting to £23,000.

1905   'Caxton Hall Concordat' – mutual support by LRC and Parliamentary Committee of TUC for members standing for parliamentary election.

1906   Twenty-six Labour MPs elected in January general election, following secret agreement between Ramsay MacDonald, secretary of the LRC and Herbert Gladstone, Liberal Whip, aimed at securing trade union and working-class representation. Parliamentary Labour Party formed. Trades Disputes Act freed trade unions from liability for damages by strike, reversing Taff Vale judgment.

1907   ASRS threaten national railway strike, but government intervention secured agreement.

1908   Strike of Amalgamated Engineers in North-East ends in defeat after seven months.

1909   Miners Federation formally affiliate to Labour Party.   Trade Boards set up by Winston Churchill to fix wages in industries liable to cheap labour.   Osborne judgment; judgment against ASRS prevented the trade unions from using their funds for political purposes.

1910   Ten months' strike by miners in South Wales, accompanied by rioting and the despatch of troops.   Tom Mann published *Industrial Syndicalist* and then joined with Tillett and Havelock Wilson to form the National Transport Workers' Federation.

1911   Strikes of dockers and seamen joined in August by railway unions, but settled after two days by Lloyd George's intervention. Two men killed by troops during clashes in Liverpool.

1912   February: miners' national strike for minimum wage, which continues until April. District minimum wages achieved.   May: London dock strike collapses after use of blackleg labour to break the strike.

1913   Trade Union Act: reversed the Osborne judgment, allowing the unions to use their funds for political purposes under certain circumstances.   Eight-month strike of Irish Transport Union.   National Union of Railwaymen formed by amalgamation of ASRS and other railway unions. ASLEF and Clerk's Union remain independent.

1914   Attempt to organise 'Triple Alliance' of miners, railwaymen and transport workers. Not able to organise properly before outbreak of First World War.   Strike truce declared shortly after outbreak of the war by TUC.

1915   Beginning of Clydeside movement against 'dilution' of skilled
       trades by unskilled labour.   'Treasury agreement' negotiated
       between government and trade unions, relaxing trade practices
       and accepting compulsory arbitration. Later passed into law as
       Munitions of War Act.   Arthur Henderson for Labour Party
       joined cabinet in May.   July: miners' strike in South Wales in
       defiance of Treasury agreement; further unrest on Clydeside.

1916   Clyde Workers' Committee formed, leaders arrested and journals
       suppressed.   December: Henderson enters War Cabinet, other
       Labour MPs join government.

1917   Continuing strikes and unrest in munitions and other factories
       over dilution, conscription of skilled workers and rising prices,
       many led by unofficial committees of shop stewards. Government
       Commission of Enquiry into Industrial Unrest appointed.   TUC
       decide to levy affiliate societies to increase efficiency of
       organisation.   Whitley Committee set up to report on 'Relations
       of Employers and Employees'. Recommends setting up of Whitley
       Councils, composed of employers and union leaders in each
       industry to discuss wages and conditions and more general
       problems. Not universally accepted, but Whitley Councils became
       established in sphere of government employment to bring sides
       together when in dispute.

1918   Widespread strikes against dilution and conscription, largest
       number of days lost for any year of the war.   Police strikes in
       London and Merseyside.

1919   Forty Hours' strike in Glasgow called on 27 January, organised by
       Scottish TUC and Clyde Workers' Committee. Clashes with police
       on Friday, 31 January ('Bloody Friday'), lead to arrest of strike
       leaders, calling in of troops and collapse of strike.   Industrial
       Courts Act set up permanent arbitration tribunal, known as the
       Industrial Court; could only advise.   Sankey Commission
       looked into wages and nationalisation in mining after threat of
       miners' strike; it accepted the principle of nationalisation, but this
       was repudiated by the government and
       mine-owners.   September: national railway strike in opposition
       to 'Geddes Axe'. Liverpool police strike leads to rioting. Police
       strikes in other cities fail; police forces purged of militants.

1920   Continuing widespread industrial unrest among miners and
       railwaymen, but most notably in transport, with the London dock
       strike. Performance before the Industrial Court earned Ernest
       Bevin the title of 'the dockers' KC'. 'Council of Action' formed to
       stop government interfering in Russian Revolution; loading of
       Jolly George with munitions blacked.

1921   March–April: attempted action by revived Triple Alliance, but
       J. H. Thomas of railwaymen calls on miners to negotiate. April 15:
       'Black Friday' when only the miners strike. TUC Coordinating
       Committee led by Gosling and Bevin of transport workers,
       recommend a General Council with larger and wider powers than
       Parliamentary Committee.

1921–4 Number of amalgamations: Amalgamated Engineering Union (AEU), Transport and General Workers Union (TGWU) and National Union of General and Municipal Workers established.

1925 Walter Citrine appointed TUC general secretary.

1925–6 Miners strike, leading to General Strike. In 1924 the mine-owners agreed to pay rises, but could not give them after the return to the Gold Standard and the fall of exports. Baldwin set up a Royal Commission under Herbert Samuel, but its report was unfavourable to the miners who, led by A. J. Cook, coined the slogan 'not a penny off the pay, not a second on the day'. A temporary government subsidy ran out in 1 May 1926, and all sides prepared for a lock-out. The TUC agreed to support the miners and when negotiations were broken off on 3 May because compositors stopped production of the *Daily Mail*, the General Strike began. The government, using the time gained by the Samuel Commission and the subsidy, was prepared, and troops, police and volunteers maintained essential services. Moderate union leaders became worried about the direction of the strike, and led by J. H. Thomas set up a Negotiating Committee to meet with Samuel and seek a solution. They accepted the cabinet offer, though many saw this as a surrender, and work was resumed on 12 May. The miners continued their strike for almost six months, but were eventually forced to accept wage cuts and longer hours.

1927 Trades Disputes and Trade Union Act amended 1913 Act and imposed 'contracting in' for political levy, stopping some money going to Labour Party, and outlawed general strikes and sympathetic strikes.

1928 Amalgamation of TGWU with Workers' Union, third largest of general unions.   The Mond–Turner talks initiated a new policy of union–business cooperation in industry. They went on through 1929 and were supported at the TUC despite left-wing protests.

1929 *Daily Herald* becomes official newspaper for trade union and Labour Party views.

1931 Fall of second Labour government; the General Council of the TUC refused to accept spending cuts and Ramsay MacDonald formed National Government. The TUC, led by Bevin, maintain support for Labour Party as independent body.

1931–2 Reconstruction of National Joint Council, which became National Council of Labour, formalising links between the TUC and the political side of the Labour movement. This gave the General Council more political influence.

1932 Cotton strike against wage cuts in textile industry.

1930–5 Economic depression reduces union membership. Miners badly hit, falling from 804,236 members in1929, to 588,321 in 1939; surpassed in 1935 as largest union by TGWU. Some unions grew, like the AEU, the Electrical Trades Union and the General and Municipal Workers.

1938   Government officially approach TUC on mobilisation for war effort.

1939–45   Wide legislation by government in industrial sphere. Bevin becomes minister of labour. Control of Employment Act gave government power to direct labour. Order 1305 legally restricted strikes and lock-outs and imposed compulsory arbitration.   The Bridlington Agreement, 1939, between TUC affiliated unions restricted 'poaching' members from each other. Increase in memberships of most unions during war years.

1944   National Union of Mineworkers formed to replace MFGB with more centralised organisation.

1946   Repeal of 1927 Trades Disputes and Trade Union Act.

1951   Order 1305 withdrawn after unsuccessful prosecution of dock strikers.

1956   Frank Cousins becomes General Secretary of TGWU.   *Bonsor* v. *Musicians' Union*; decided that a member was wrongfully expelled from trade union and was entitled to damages for breach of contract.

1958   National Arbitration Tribunal, remnant of Order 1305 and valued by unions, went out of existence.   London busmen's strike.

1956–62   Struggle in Electrical Trades Union over alleged malpractices of Communist leadership. Moderates led by Byrne, Cannon and Chapple defeat Communists, but only after litigation and expulsion of the union from the TUC and Labour Party.

1962   National Economic Development Council formed with TUC participation.

1964   Department of Economic Affairs set up under George Brown, Prices and Incomes Board under Aubrey Jones.   *Rookes* v. *Barnard* case, made threat to strike to injure a third party illegal, even if in furtherance of a trade dispute; *Stratford* v. *Lindley* case determined that strike action not in furtherance of a trade dispute was not protected by 1906 Act.

1965   Trades Disputes Act; reversed Rookes–Barnard judgment and gave trade unions further legal immunities.

1966   National seamen's strike defeated. Prices and Incomes Bill passed into law. Cousins resigns from Cabinet.

1968   May 15: one-day national stoppage by Amalgamated Union of Engineering and Foundry Workers against government's prices and incomes policy.   June: Report of Donovan Commission on Industrial Relations; led by Woodcock, Clegg and Kahn-Freund it argued against legal intervention and for improved voluntary agreements in industrial relations.

1969   Government White Paper *In Place of Strife* contemplates state intervention in industrial relations and legal sanctions against 'wildcat' strikes. Dropped after opposition from the TUC.

1970–1   Conservative government, committed to new legal framework for industrial relations, pass Industrial Relations Act in August 1971, which gives the government wide-ranging and unique powers, and sets up a National Industrial Relations Court and system of registration for unions. Schemes provoke massive TUC opposition and most unions refuse to register or cooperate with it in any way.

1972   January: miners' strike begins with widespread power cuts and industrial disruption.   February: State of Emergency declared as power crisis worsens and 1½ million workers laid off. Wilberforce Committee reports and grants many of miners' demands; strike called off.   March: *Heaton* v. *TGWU*: first test for the National Industrial Relations Court set up under the Industrial Relations Act. It decided against the union in a blacking dispute, fining them £5,000 and a further £50,000 for contempt, the TGWU refusing to acknowledge the Court. Further fine in April for contempt.   April: attempt by railway unions to start industrial action led to government initiating its 'cooling-off' period and compulsory ballot allowed under the Act. Ballot voted six to one in favour of action and not used by government again.   July: Union action over decasualisation of labour in docks led to the imprisonment of the 'Pentonville Five' when they ignored an order from the NIRC to stop blacking containers; led to national dock strike. *Goad* v. *AUEW*: James Goad excluded from union, and appealed to NIRC. Union refused to acknowledge the Court and were fined £5,000, with £50,000 for contempt. Highest number of days lost in strikes since 1926.

1974   January: miners' strike again, following 81 per cent poll in favour of strike. Heath defeated in February election called on the union issue. Labour government's Trade Union and Labour Relations Act, repealed most of the Industrial Relations Act, although the NIRC survived for a short while, sequestering £280,000 of the AEU's funds for non-payment of fines. Fines paid anonymously when AEU threatened a national stoppage. Court abolished in July. 'Social Contract' initiated between trade unions and government: attempt to achieve industrial peace by agreement and without legal intervention.

1975   July: TUC accept flat-rate pay increase norm.   November: Employment Protection Act gave statutory authority to the Advisory, Conciliation and Arbitration Service to arbitrate, if requested, in industrial disputes, and extended the rights of individual employees and trade unions.

1976   Stage Two 4½ per cent pay limit agreed with TUC.   Employment Protection Act comes into force.

1977   Stage Three sets earnings increase limit at 10 per cent.   Firemen's strike; servicemen called in to deal with fires.

1978   October: unions reject 5 per cent wage norm; beginning of widespread industrial action during winter months by lorry drivers, water workers, hospital and municipal workers, the so-called 'winter of discontent'.

1979   May: Conservative government wins general election pledged to
        reform various aspects of trade union law, including the 'closed
        shop', secondary picketing and use of secret ballot before strikes.

1980   January–March: first national steel strike since 1926. Parliament
        passes Employment Act to carry through its election pledges.

Chartism: table of events
Note: For definition of Chartism see Glossary (p. 285).

1832   Reform Act.

1834   March: Tolpuddle Martyrs sentenced.   July: New Poor Law.

1835   Municipal Reform Act (including provision for reform of borough
        police).

1836   April: Foundation of Association of Working Men to procure a
        Cheap and Honest Press.   May: Newspaper duty reduced to
        1*d*.   June: Foundation of London Working Men's Association
        (LWMA).

1837   January: Foundation of East London Democratic Association.
        May: Birmingham Political Union revived; committee of LWMA
        and radical MPs prepare the Charter.   November: *Northern
        Star* issued for first time (at 4½*d*.) at Leeds.

1838   May: People's Charter published, London. National Petition
        published, Birmingham.   June: Foundation of Great Northern
        Union, Leeds by Feargus O'Connor. Foundation of Northern
        Political Union, Newcastle.   December: The first arrest: Revd.
        J. R. Stephens for addressing open-air meeting in Hyde.

1839   February: General Convention of the Industrious Classes opens
        (4th) at British Hotel, Charing Cross.   March: Major-General Sir
        C. Napier takes command of Northern District (until September
        1841).   May: Convention moves to Birmingham; divisions
        appear between 'Physical' and 'Moral' Force Chartists. Several
        moderate delegates leave.

1839   June: Chartist petition with 1,280,000 signatures presented to
        parliament (14th); rejected (12 July) by 235 votes to 46.   July:
        Bull Ring riots, leading to the Birmingham, Bolton and
        Manchester Police Acts (repealed 1842).   September:
        Convention dissolved (after failure of Sacred Month.)
        November: Newport rising, to free Vincent. John Frost and other
        participants arrested, tried and transported.

1840   January: Abortive 'risings' in Dewsbury and Sheffield.   July:
        National Charter Association (NCA) founded (Manchester).
        Lovett released (imprisoned since July 1839).

1841   April: Foundation by Lovett of the National Association of the
        United Kingdom for Promoting the Political and Social
        Improvement of the People.   August: General election.
        O'Connor released (imprisoned since March 1840).

1842   April: First Complete Suffrage Union Conference at Birmingham.
April: NCA Convention (London) (12th).   May: Second National
Petition rejected by parliament.   August: Plug riots.   Trough
of trade cycle, meaning wage cuts and
unemployment.   December: Collapse of Second Complete
Suffrage Union Conference (Birmingham).

1843   September: Chartist Convention at Birmingham accepts Land
Plan.

1844   August: O'Connor–Cobden debate, Northampton.

1845   September: Agricultural Co-operative Society founded.
Foundation of the Society of Fraternal Democrats.

1846   June: Repeal of the Corn Laws.

1847   May: Ten Hours Act.   O'Connorville, first land settlement
opened.

1848   February: French Revolution.   Publication of *Communist
Manifesto.*   April: Chartist Convention, London. Kennington
Common meeting. O'Connor presents the National Petition (10th);
it is rejected.   May: National Assembly. Arrests of Chartist
leaders in North.   June: Clashes between police and Chartists
in East End of London.   August: Abortive risings at Ashton,
Dukinfield, Stalybridge and Oldham.

1849   December: Chartist Delegate Conference.

1850   January: Foundation of the National Reform League (Bronterre
O'Brien).   March: National Charter League (O'Connorite).
August: Chartist Land Company dissolved by Act of parliament.

1851   January: O'Connorite Convention (Manchester).   March:
London Conference adopts wide programme.

1852   January: Harney buys *Northern Star*, which becomes the *Star of
Freedom.*   Ernest Jones and Harney quarrel: O'Connor insane.

1854   March: Labour parliament, Manchester (Jones).

1858   February: Last Chartist Convention.

Trade union membership and trade disputes

Year	Total number of trade unions	Total number of union members	Total number of trade union members affiliated to TUC	Number of stoppages beginning in year	Aggregate duration in working days of stoppages in progress in year
1893	1,279	1,559,000	1,100,000	599	30,440,000
1894	1,314	1,530,000	1,000,000	903	9,510,000
1895	1,340	1,504,000	1,076,000	728	5,700,000

Year	Total number of trade unions	Total number of union members	Total number of trade union members affiliated to TUC	Number of stoppages beginning in year	Aggregate duration in working days of stoppages in progress in year
1896	1,358	1,608,000	1,093,191	906	3,560,000
1897	1,353	1,731,000	1,184,241	848	10,330,000
1898	1,326	1,752,000	1,200,000	695	15,260,000
1899	1,325	1,911,000	1,250,000	710	2,500,000
1900	1,323	2,022,000	1,200,000	633	3,090,000
1901	1,322	2,025,000	1,400,000	631	4,130,000
1902	1,297	2,013,000	1,500,000	432	3,440,000
1903	1,285	1,994,000	1,422,518	380	2,320,000
1904	1,256	1,967,000	1,541,000	346	1,460,000
1905	1,244	1,997,000	1,555,000	349	2,370,000
1906	1,282	2,210,000	1,700,000	479	3,020,000
1907	1,283	2,513,000	1,777,000	585	2,150,000
1908	1,268	2,485,000	1,705,000	389	10,790,000
1909	1,260	2,477,000	1,647,715	422	2,690,000
1910	1,269	2,565,000	1,662,133	521	9,870,000
1911	1,290	3,139,000	2,001,633	872	10,160,000
1912	1,252	3,416,000	2,232,446	834	40,890,000
1913	1,269	4,135,000	—	1,459	9,800,000
1914	1,260	4,145,000	2,682,357	972	9,880,000
1915	1,229	4,359,000	2,850,547	672	2,950,000
1916	1,225	4,644,000	3,082,352	532	2,450,000
1917	1,241	5,499,000	4,532,085	730	5,650,000
1918	1,264	6,533,000	5,283,676	1,165	5,880,000
1919	1,360	7,926,000	6,505,482	1,352	34,970,000
1920	1,384	8,348,000	6,417,910	1,607	26,570,000
1921	1,275	6,633,000	5,128,648	763	85,870,000
1922	1,232	5,625,000	4,369,268	576	19,850,000
1923	1,192	5,429,000	4,328,235	628	10,670,000
1924	1,194	5,544,000	4,350,982	710	8,420,000
1925	1,176	5,506,000	4,365,619	603	7,950,000
1926	1,164	5,219,000	4,163,994	323	162,233,000

Year	Total number of trade unions	Total number of union members	Total number of trade union members affiliated to TUC	Number of stoppages beginning in year	Aggregate duration in working days of stoppages in progress in year
1927	1,159	4,919,000	3,874,842	308	1,170,000
1928	1,142	4,806,000	3,673,144	302	1,390,000
1929	1,133	4,858,000	3,744,320	431	8,290,000
1930	1,121	4,842,000	3,719,401	422	4,400,000
1931	1,108	4,624,000	3,613,273	420	6,980,000
1932	1,081	4,444,000	3,367,911	389	6,490,000
1933	1,081	4,392,000	3,294,581	357	1,070,000
1934	1,063	4,590,000	3,388,810	471	960,000
1935	1,049	4,867,000	3,614,351	553	1,960,000
1936	1,036	5,295,000	4,008,647	818	1,830,000
1937	1,032	5,842,000	4,460,617	1,129	3,410,000
1938	1,024	6,053,000	4,669,186	875	1,330,000
1939	1,019	6,298,000	4,866,711	940	1,360,000
1940	1,004	6,613,000	5,079,094	922	940,000
1941	996	7,165,000	5,432,844	1,251	1,080,000
1942	991	7,867,000	6,024,411	1,303	1,527,000
1943	987	8,174,000	6,642,317	1,785	1,808,000
1944	963	8,087,000	6,575,654	2,194	3,714,000
1945	781	7,875,000	6,671,120	2,293	2,835,000
1946	757	8,803,000	7,540,397	2,205	2,158,000
1947	734	9,145,000	7,791,470	1,721	2,433,000
1948	735	9,319,000	7,937,091	1,759	1,944,000
1949	726	9,274,000	7,883,355	1,426	1,807,000
1950	732	9,289,000	7,827,945	1,339	1,389,000
1951	735	9,535,000	8,202,079	1,719	1,694,000
1952	719	9,583,000	8,088,450	1,714	1,792,000
1953	717	9,523,000	8,093,837	1,746	2,184,000
1954	703	9,556,000	8,106,958	1,989	2,457,000
1955	694	9,726,000	8,263,741	2,419	3,781,000
1956	674	9,762,000	8,304,709	2,648	2,083,000
1957	674	9,813,000	8,337,325	2,859	8,412,000

Year	Total number of trade unions	Total number of union members	Total number of trade union members affiliated to TUC	Number of stoppages beginning in year	Aggregate duration in working days of stoppages in progress in year
1958	665	9,626,000	8,176,252	2,629	3,462,000
1959	658	9,610,000	8,128,251	2,093	5,270,000
1960	654	9,821,000	8,299,393	2,849	3,024,000
1961	635	9,883,000	8,312,875	2,701	3,046,000
1962	626	10,014,000	8,313,000	2,449	5,795,000
1963	607	10,067,000	8,315,000	2,068	1,755,000
1964	598	10,218,000	8,326,000	2,524	2,277,000
1965	630	10,325,000	8,771,000	2,354	2,925,000
1966	622	10,259,000	8,868,000	1,937	2,398,000
1967	603	10,194,000	8,789,000	2,116	2,787,000
1968	584	10,200,000	8,726,000	2,378	4,690,000
1969	563	10,479,000	8,875,000	3,116	6,846,000
1970	540	11,187,000	9,402,000	3,906	10,980,000
1971	523	11,135,000	10,002,000	2,228	13,551,000
1972	502	11,359,000	9,895,000	2,497	23,909,000
1973	513	11,456,000	10,001,000	2,873	7,197,000
1974	498	11,764,000	10,002,000	2,922	14,750,000
1975	488	12,026,000	10,364,000	2,282	6,012,000
1976	462	12,386,000	11,036,000	2,016	3,284,000
1977	485	12,707,000	11,516,000	2,703	10,142,000
1978	485	—	—	2,349	9,306,000

(Source: H. Pelling, A History of British Trade Unionism, Harmondsworth, Penguin, 1963, pp. 261–3; G. S. Bain and R. Price, Profiles of Union Growth: A Comparative Statistical Portrait of Eight Countries, Oxford, Blackwell, 1980, pp. 37–8; Department of Employment Gazette, London, HMSO.)

Religion

Major events in British Church history, 1714–1980

1714   Bolingbroke passes Schism Act by which teachers were required to declare their conformity to the Established Church; aimed at restricting the dissenting academies.

1716   Dr Williams founds the Williams Library. Non-jurors negotiate for reunion with the Greek Church, but fail.

1717   Convocation prorogued by government after it censures Bishop Hoadly's *The Nature of the Kingdom, or Church of Christ* which declares against tests of orthodoxy and argues that sincerity is the only requirement of Christian profession. Convocation does not meet for business again until 1852.

1719   Repeal of Occasional Conformity and Schism Acts. Presbyterians meet at Salter's Hall to protest against the subscription to a belief in the Trinity by the clergy.

1721   Toleration Act passed by Irish parliament.

1722   Francis Atterbury, Bishop of Rochester, arrested and banished for corresponding with the Pretender.

1723   Penal levy of £100,000 placed on Catholics.

1727   Walpole introduces first annual Bill of Indemnity allowing Dissenters to escape penalties of the Test and Corporation Acts by taking the Sacrament after rather than before election to office. Independent, Baptist and Presbyterian congregations form General Body of Protestant Dissenting Ministers.

1728   Moravian mission established in England.

1729   John Wesley, Junior Fellow of Lincoln College, Oxford, and friends begin to meet at Oxford in a strict religious society, dubbed as 'Methodists'. Doddridge establishes a Presbyterian Academy at Market Harborough.

1730   Tindal's *Christianity as Old as the Creation* declares that Christ merely confirmed the law revealed by the light of nature.

1732   Organisation of Protestant dissenting deputies to act as pressure group for dissenters.

1736   Bishop Warburton's *Alliance of Church and State* argues for the Established Church and a Test Act.   Attempt to relieve Quakers from tithes fails.

1738   John Wesley returns from America, falls under the influence of Peter Böhler, a Moravian, and is converted on 24 May. George Whitefield undertakes missionary work in America.

1739   Wesley follows Whitefield's example of preaching in the open air. Methodist Society meets in Old Foundry, Moorfields, London.

1740   Wesley severs his connection with the Moravians. Begins to employ lay preachers and build chapels. Controversy with Whitefield over Calvinist doctrine of predestination.

1742   Dodwell's *Christianity Not Founded on Argument* attacks both Deists and Christians for belief in the harmony of reason and revelation.

1743   Methodists produce rules for 'classes'.   Welsh Calvinistic Methodist body founded by Whitefield.

1744   First Methodist Conference held at Foundry Chapel, London, consisting of John and Charles Wesley, four clergy and four lay preachers. Resolves that bishops are to be obeyed 'in all things indifferent', canons to be observed 'as far as can be done with a safe conscience' and 'societies to be formed wherever the preachers go'.

1746   Persecution of Scottish episcopal clergy for Jacobitism. Meetings of more than five banned and clergy forbidden to act as private chaplains.

1747   Methodist societies grouped into circuits.

1749   Calvinists under Whitefield desert Wesley; Whitefield becomes chaplain to Lady Huntingdon.

1756   Wesley's *Twelve Reasons Against a Separation from the Church* attempts to restrain breakaway tendencies among his followers.

1760   Wesley's lay preachers take out licences as dissenting teachers and administer the sacraments. Condemned by Charles Wesley.

1762   Warburton attacks Wesley and 'Enthusiasm'.

1768   Lady Huntingdon founds a seminary at Trefecca.

1770   Wesley denounces Calvinism at conference; General Baptist New Communion established.

1771   Feathers Tavern petition against subscription to the Thirty-nine Articles; rejected by 217 to 17 in parliament. Several clergy leave Established Church and become Unitarians.

1777   City Road Chapel, London, founded by Methodists.

1778   Sir George Savile obtains Catholic Relief Act. Roman Catholic worship permitted. New oath of allegiance. Protestant Association founded.

1779   Dissenting ministers and schoolmasters relieved from subscription to the Thirty-nine Articles.

1780   Gordon riots following campaign by Protestant Association against Catholic Relief Act of 1778. Mass petition of parliament leads to riots in London with attacks on houses, chapels and embassies of Catholics.   Raikes founds Sunday schools at Gloucester.

1781   Lady Huntingdon's Connexion separates from Church of England.

1782   Charles Simeon ordained curate of Trinity Church, Cambridge; introduces evangelical movement into the University.

1784   Wesley ordains Coke and Asbury as 'Superintendents' in America.

1787   Beaufoy's motion for repeal of the Test and Corporation Acts is defeated in the House of Commons.   Beilby Porteus becomes Bishop of London and leads the Evangelical Revival within the Church of England, assisted by Hannah More, William Wilberforce and other members of what became known as the 'Clapham Sect'.

1789   Dr Richard Price, Unitarian preacher and theologian, preaches sermon at the annual dinner of the London Revolution Society (4 November), welcoming the French Revolution for its stimulus to reform in civil and ecclesiastical affairs.

1790   Motions for repeal of Test and Corporation Acts withdrawn from parliament without a division.

1791   Attacks on Dissenters at Birmingham, Priestley's house destroyed by mob.   Death of Wesley.

1794   Paley's *Evidence of Christianity* assumes the existence of a Personal God and infers the probability of revelation. Paine's *Age of Reason* attacks Christianity from a Deistic standpoint. Stonyhurst College founded for Roman Catholic students.

1795   Separation of Methodist and Anglican Churches made final as a result of breakdown of plans for reconciliation.   Maynooth College founded in Ireland to provide seminary for Catholic priests other than in France.

1797   Methodist New Connexion secedes from main Wesleyan body.

1799   Church Missionary Society agreed on in principle by evangelical group (fully established in 1801).

1801   Pitt's proposals for Catholic relief blocked by opposition of the King.

1804   British and Foreign Bible Society founded.

1807   William Wilberforce, Henry Thornton, Sir James Stephen, Lord Teignmouth, Granville Sharp and John Venn form the 'Clapham Sect' and campaign for various philanthropic causes, including the end of the slave trade.

1808   Expulsion of Hugh Bourne from Wesleyan Methodist Conference for open-air preaching.

1811   Welsh Calvinistic Methodists leave Church of England. Sidmouth's Bill to limit itinerant preaching defeated after protests from dissenting groups.

1812   Gratton's proposal for Catholic relief defeated. Unitarian Relief Act passed; Conventicle and Five-Mile Acts repealed. Primitive Methodist Connexion formed by Hugh Bourne and William Clowes.

1814   Wesleyan Missionary Society organised.   Death of prophetess Joanna Southcott; followers, known as the New Israelites, found chapel in London.

1815   Bryanites or 'Bible Christians' separate from Methodists.

1816   Motion for Catholic relief defeated in the Lords.

1817   Military and Naval Officers' Oath Bill opens all ranks in the army and navy to Catholics.

1818   Church Building Society founded. At its instigation parliament grants £1 million for church building and appoints a Commission to superintend its distribution.

1820   Revd Darby leaves Church of England and founds Plymouth Brethren, teaching a rigid Calvinism and the priesthood of all believers.

1826   Rose preaches at Cambridge on duties of the clergy and founds modern High Churchmanship.

1828   Repeal of Test and Corporation Acts, hence admitting Nonconformists to Parliament.   Church Building Act passed.

1829   Catholic Emancipation passed; Catholics permitted to sit in parliament.

1831   Formation of Congregational Union of England and Wales.

1832   Palmer's *Origines Liturgicae* prepare the way for the Oxford Movement and Rose founds *British Magazine* for defence of High Church principles.   Church Inquiry: Commissioners appointed.

1833   Keble's Assize Sermon on 'National Apostasy' denounces suppression of 10 Irish bishoprics and is later declared by Newman to have inaugurated the Oxford Movement.   *Tracts for the Times* begin to appear.   Nonconformists allowed to celebrate marriages in their chapels.

1834   Lords defeat admission of Nonconformists to university degrees.   Wesleyan Methodist Association founded.

1835   Wiseman returns to England to lecture on the beliefs and system of catholicism. Pusey joins the High Church movement.

1836   Tithes paid in kind commuted into a rent charge to vary with the price of corn.   Ecclesiastical Commissioners incorporated.   Newman's *Prophetical Office of the Church* defines the theory of the Oxford Movement.   Church Pastoral Aid Society founded.   Solemnisation of Marriages Act permitted licences to be issued for marriage in register offices and Nonconformist chapels.

1837   Additional Curates Society founded to provide extra clergy.

1838   Pluralities Act and Acts for building and enlarging churches passed.   Froude's *Remains*, edited by Newman and Keble, condemns the Reformation.

1840   New Church Discipline Act.

1841   Tait and three other Oxford tutors issue protest against Tract 90, in which Newman explained the Thirty-nine Articles in a Catholic sense. Newman censured and persuaded to end the Tracts.   Miall founds *The Nonconformist*.

1843   Newman resigns as vicar of St Mary's. Pusey forbidden to preach for two years.   New Parishes Act.   'Disruption' in Scotland and formation of Free Church of Scotland.

1844   Ward's *Ideal of a Christian Church* condemned by Oxford authorities.   Nonconformists found Liberation Society.

1845   Ward joins the Roman Catholic Church; Newman follows. Pusey, Marriott and Mozley lead the Anglo-Catholic Party.

1846   The Evangelical Alliance formed to oppose Romanism, Puseyism and rationalism.

1847   United Presbyterian Church of Scotland formed.

1849   Wesleyan Methodist Reformers formed after 'Fly-sheets' controversy leads to expulsion from main body.

1850   Re-establishment of Catholic hierarchy to English sees.   Manning (later Cardinal) joins Roman Catholic Church.   Pusey censured for use of Catholic devotional literature.   Beginning of 'papal aggression' scare in England.

1851   Census of church attendance reveals only half the population regularly attend Sunday worship (see p. 167).

1852   Convocation recommences.

1854   Act for extending licences of dissenting places of worship.

1859   Darwin publishes the *Origin of Species by Natural Selection*, starting controversy about the literal truth of the Bible.

1860   At meeting of British Association in Oxford, Bishop Wilberforce attacks and Huxley defends Darwin's theory of evolution.   English Church Union founded to organise High Church movement.   *Essays and Reviews* published and arouse considerable controversy over their 'broad church' views, attaching little importance to nicety of dogma but stressing Christian virtues.   Act for opening grammar schools to Dissenters.

1861   Convocation condemns *Essays and Reviews*.

1862   *The Pentateuch*, by Dr Colenso, Bishop of Natal, asserts the Bible contains 'unhistorical parts'. Condemned by convocation and excommunicated.

1863   Bishop of London's fund for remedying spiritual destitution founded.

1864   Newman publishes his spiritual autobiography, *Apologia pro Vita Sua*.

1865   'General' William Booth assumes leadership of a Christian Mission for the 'evangelization of the very lowest classes', later called the Salvation Army.   Church Association formed to oppose ritualism.   Manning appointed Catholic Archbishop of Westminster.

1866   Pope condemns efforts to promote Anglican and Catholic reunion.   Act for removing religious oaths for public offices.

1868   Compulsory church rates abolished by Gladstone.   Irish Church Disestablishment Bill introduced by Gladstone.

1869   Irish Church Disestablishment passed, effective from 1 January 1871

1870   Suffragan bishops appointed.   Keble College, Oxford founded.   Declaration of Papal Infallibility by Vatican Council.

1871   Motion for disestablishment of English Church obtains 96 votes.   Act for abolition of religious tests at the universities.

1874   Gladstone's pamphlets on Vaticanism declare Papal decree of 1870 inconsistent with civil allegiance.

1876   Presbyterian Church of England formed.

1877   Methodist Conference admits laity.

1878   General William Booth formally constituted as superintendent of Salvation Army with control over funds, property and the power to nominate successor.   Catholic hierarchy restored in Scotland.

1880   Burials Act allows Christian Dissenters to hold services in the churchyard of the parish.

1881   Revised version of the New Testament appears.

1882   General Booth sets forth his principles in the *Contemporary Review*, upholding the gospel, opposing sectarianism and requiring implicit obedience from his 'soldiers', aiming at the reformation of 'drunkards and other reprobates'.

1888   *Lux Mundi*, a collection of essays, defines the position of the new Oxford Movement.

1889   Mansfield Congregational College, Oxford, founded.

1890   General Booth publishes *In Darkest England, and the Way Out*, an exposé of destitution and poverty among the 'submerged tenth'.   Bishop of Lincoln prosecuted in the Archbishop's Court for High Church practices.

1891   Church's *History of the Oxford Movement* published.

1892   Conference held at Grindelwald discusses reunion of Established Church and Nonconformist bodies.

1894   Informal discussions begin about Catholic and Anglican reunion.

Bill for disestablishment of Anglican Church in Wales fails to reach second reading in parliament.

1895   Construction of Catholic Cathedral at Westminster begun.

1896   Pope condemns Anglican Orders and attempt at reconciliation comes to an end.

1898   Benefices Act forbids the public sale of advowsons and increases the power of bishops.   Renewed attacks by Low Church Anglicans upon the ritualist party.

1899   Protestant agitation continues and archbishops pronounce against use of incense and processional lights.   Balfour declares in favour of a Catholic university in Ireland.

1900   Free Church of Scotland and United Presbyterian Church of Scotland unite.

1904–5   Great Welsh revival. Large increases in membership of Nonconformist churches.

1906   Royal Commission appointed to consider Welsh Disestablishment.

1907   United Methodist Church formed from several of existing separate Methodist churches.

1914   Disestablishment of the Anglican Church in Wales.

1921   Church of Scotland Act confirms its complete independence in all spiritual matters.

1924   Inter-denominational conference at Birmingham urges churchmen to pay greater attention to social questions.

1927–8   Revised Prayer Book controversy. House of Commons rejects attempt by Church of England to modernise the Prayer Book.

1932   Following a conference at the Albert Hall in London, the Wesleyan Methodists, the Primitive Methodists and the United Methodists joined to become the Methodist Church.

1942   William Temple becomes Archbishop of Canterbury.

1958   Death of Pius XII; Pope John XXIII elected.

1959   Second Vatican Council convened, the first since 1870; begins reappraisal of Roman Catholic liturgy and policy.

1960   Lord Fisher became first Archbishop of Canterbury to visit the Pope since the Reformation.

1962   Consecration of new Coventry Cathedral.

1963   Controversy aroused by the radical theology of the Bishop of Woolwich's (John Robinson) *Honest to God*. Sales reach 300,000 copies.

1964   Dr Coggan, Archbishop of York, advocates 'marriage' between Anglican and Methodist churches.

1965   Dr Heenan, Roman Catholic Archbishop of Westminster, created cardinal.

1969   The Sharing of Church Buildings Act enables agreements to be made by two or more churches for the sharing of church buildings.

1970   Translation of the New English Bible completed.

1972   United Reformed Church formed from the merger of the Congregational Church of England and Wales and the English Presbyterian Church. General Synod of the Church of England failed to approve a scheme for Anglican–Methodist unity, already approved by Methodists.

1979   Revised Prayer Book introduced for Anglican services.

1982   Pope John Paul II visits Britain.

The Church of England: clergy and Easter Day communicants, 1801–1966

	Clergy	Easter Day communicants (000s)		Clergy	Easter Day communicants (000s)
1801	—	535	1891	22,753	1,490
1811	14,531	550	1901	23,670	1,945
1821	—	570	1911	23,193	2,293
1831	14,933	605	1921	22,579	2,236
1841	15,730	755	1931	21,309	2,311
1851	16,194	875	1941	n.a.	2,018
1861	17,966	995	1951	18,196	1,867
1871	19,411	1,110	1961	18,749	2,159
1881	20,341	1,225	1966	20,008	1,899

(*Source*: A. D. Gilbert, *Religion and Society in Industrial England: Church, Chapel and Social Change, 1740–1914*, London, Longman, 1976, p. 28; A. H. Halsey (ed.), *Trends in British Society since 1900*, London, Macmillan, 1972, p. 424.)

Nonconformist church membership in England, 1750–1900

	Congregationalists (000s)	Baptists (000s)	Presbyterians (000s)
1750	15	10	—
1790	26	20	—

	Congregationalists (000s)	Baptists (000s)	Presbyterians (000s)
1838	127	100	10
1850	165	140	15
1880	190	200	56
1900	257	239	78

(*Source*: A. D. Gilbert, *Religion and Society in Industrial England: Church, Chapel and Social Change, 1740–1914*, London, Longman, 1976, p. 37.)

Nonconformist church membership in Wales, 1815–1900

	Congregationalist (000s)	Baptist (000s)	Presbyterians (000s)
1815	23	—	—
1838	43	25	110
1851	60	35	—
1870	—	60	245
1880	116	80	275
1890	130	91	288
1900	150	107	324

(*Source*: C. Cook and B. Keith, *British Historical Facts, 1830–1900*, London, Macmillan, 1975, pp. 226–9.)

Church membership in Scotland, 1831–1901

	Episcopal Church (000s)	Presbyterian Church of Scotland (000s)	Free Church (000s)	United Presbyterian Church (000s)	Wesleyan Methodist (000s)	Baptist (000s)
1831	—	—	—	—	4	—
1841	—	—	—	—	4	—
1851	14	—	199	—	4	—
1861	—	—	243	154	4	—

	Episcopal Church (000s)	Presbyterian Church of Scotland (000s)	Free Church (000s)	United Presbyterian Church (000s)	Wesleyan Methodist (000s)	Baptist (000s)
1871	—	436	—	163	5	9
1881	—	528	312	175	5	10
1891	36	600	337	185	7	12
1901	47	662	288	194	8	17

(*Source*: C. Cook and B. Keith, *British Historical Facts, 1830–1900*, London, Macmillan, 1975, pp. 222–30.)

Nonconformist church membership in the United Kingdom, 1900–1977

	Baptist Union (000s)	Congregational Union (000s)	United Reformed (000s)	Presbyterian Church of England (000s)	Presbyterian Church of Scotland (000s)
1900	366	436	—	76	1,164
1910	419	494	—	87	1,220
1920	405	—	—	84	1,278
1930	406	390	—	84	1,281
1940	382	459	—	82	1,269
1950	338	387	—	82	1,273
1960	318	212	—	71	1,293
1970	293	165	—	57	1,134
1975	256	—	—	—	—
1977	—	—	175	—	1,003

Note: Figures for Baptist Union relate to the whole of the British Isles. In 1972 the Congregational Union and the Presbyterian Church in England merged to form the United Reformed Church.

(*Source*: D. Butler and A. Sloman, *British Political Facts, 1900–1979*, London, Macmillan, 5th edn, 1980, pp. 470–2.)

Methodist membership in England and Wales, 1767–1914, and Great Britain, 1921–1976

1767	22,410	1819	194,670	1871	570,936	1926	839,797
1771	26,119	1821	215,466	1876	610,846	1932	838,019
1776	30,875	1826	267,652	1881	630,575	1936	818,480
1781	37,131	1831	288,182	1886	676,542	1941	778,712
1786	46,559	1836	364,641	1891	690,022	1946	746,757
1791	56,605	1841	435,591	1896	702,411	1951	741,596
1796	77,402	1846	452,238	1901	732,668	1956	742,444
1801	91,825	1851	490,000	1906	800,234	1961	723,529
1806	109,135	1856	443,493	1911	783,723	1966	678,776
1811	143,311	1861	513,628	1914	777,886	1968	651,139
1816	189,777	1866	547,613	1921	801,861	1976	567,400

(*Source*: A. D. Gilbert, *Religion and Society in Industrial England: Church, Chapel and Social Change, 1740–1914*, London, Longman, 1976, p. 31; A. H. Halsey (ed.), *Trends in British Society since 1900*, London, Macmillan, 1972, p. 433.)

The Roman Catholic Church, 1720–1976

	Estimated Catholic population	Churches and chapels	Actual mass attendants
1720	115,000	—	61,600
1780	69,376	—	37,200
1840	700,000	469	371,500
1851	900,000	597	482,000
1891	1,357,000	1,387	726,000
1911	1,710,000	1,773	915,000
1921	1,915,475	1,932	—
1941	2,414,002	2,580	—
1961	3,553,500	4,222	2,018,000

	Estimated Catholic population	Churches and chapels	Actual mass attendants
1969	4,143,854	4,770	—
1976	5,004,000	—	—

(*Source*: A. D. Gilbert, *Religion and Society in Industrial England: Church, Chapel and Social Change, 1740–1914*, London, Longman, 1976, p. 46; A. H. Halsey (ed.), *Trends in British Society since 1900*, London, Macmillan, 1972, p. 421.)

The 1851 Religious Census of England and Wales

	Persons present at church on census Sunday	% of total population	% 'at church' on census Sunday
Church of England	2,971,268	17	47
Nonconformist	3,110,782	17	49
Roman Catholic	249,389	1	4
Other	24,793	0.1	0.4
Total	6,356,222	35	100

Note: The government's Census of Religious Worship was a unique attempt to enumerate religious attendance in the nineteenth century. It was based on a return of all those attending places of worship for morning, afternoon or evening services on a given Sunday in 1851. For further details see, K. S. Inglis, 'Patterns of religious worship in 1851', *Journal of Ecclesiastical History*, ii, No. 1, 1960.

(*Source*: G. Best, *Mid-Victorian Britain, 1851–75*, London, Weidenfeld and Nicolson, 1971, p. 179.)

169

Section III: Economic history

Agriculture

Percentage area of each county enclosed by Act of parliament in the eighteenth and nineteenth centuries

County	%	County	%	County	%
Northampton	51.5	Warwick	25.0	Hereford	3.6
Huntingdon	46.5	Wiltshire	24.1	Somerset	3.5
Rutland	46.5	Gloucester	22.5	Stafford	2.8
Bedford	46.0	Middlesex	19.7	Essex	2.2
Oxford	45.6	Worcester	16.5	Sussex	1.9
Yorkshire, East Riding	40.1	Derby	15.9	Northumberland	1.7
Leicester	38.2	Hertford	13.1	Cumberland	1.1
Cambridge	36.3	Yorkshire, North Riding	11.6	Durham	0.7
Buckingham	34.2	Dorset	8.7	Westmorland	0.6
Nottingham	32.5	Suffolk	7.5	Cheshire	0.5
Norfolk	32.3	Hampshire	6.4	Monmouth	0.4
Lincoln	29.3	Surrey	6.4	Shropshire	0.3
Berkshire	26.0	Yorkshire, West Riding	6.3	Lancashire, Kent, Devon, Cornwall	0.0

(*Source*: G. Slater, *The English Peasantry and the Enclosure of Common Fields*, London, Constable, 1907, pp. 140–7.)

Number of parliamentary Enclosure Acts per decade

Decade	Acts	Decade	Acts	Decade	Acts
1720–9	25	1760–9	385	1800–9	847
1730–9	39	1770–9	660	1810–9	853
1740–9	36	1780–9	246	1820–9	205
1750–9	137	1790–9	469		

The pace of enclosure by Act of parliament accelerated during the eighteenth century, reaching a peak during the Napoleonic Wars. Although enclosure continued after 1830 it was on a smaller scale than in the preceding decades.

(*Source*: G. R. Porter, *The Progress of the Nation*, Vol. I, London, C. Knight, 1836, pp. 155–6.)

The corn trade: imports and exports of wheat and flour by Great Britain (annual average per decade)

	Imports	Exports		Imports	Exports
	(000s of quarters)			(000s of hundredweights)	
1700–9	n	104.8	1800–9	1,989.0	n
1710–19	n	108.8	1810–19	2,617.0	n
1720–9	11.5	116.0	1820–9	1,631.0	n
1730–9	n	296.9	1830–9	3,743	n
1740–9	1.3	290.7	1840–9	10,676	n
1750–9	16.2	329.0	1850–9	19,326	n
1760–9	97.0	235.0	1860–9	33,692	n
1770–9	130.0	87.0	1870–9	50,406	n
1780–9	153.0	129.0	1880–9	70,282	n
1790–9	405.0	83.0	1890–9	85,890	n
			1900–9	102,551	n
			1910–19	104,502	n
			1920–9	108,699	n
			1930–9	110,422	n
			1940–9	94,775	n
			1950–9	82,625	n

(n = negligible)

(*Source*: B. R. Mitchell and P. Deane, *Abstract of British Historical Statistics*, Cambridge University Press, 1962, pp. 94–5, 97–9; B. R. Mitchell and H. G. Jones, *Second Abstract of British Historical Statistics*, Cambridge, University Press, 1971, p. 61)

Trade

Major trade and tariff agreements, 1760–1980

1786 Commercial treaty signed with France. France reduced duties on British exports of manufactured goods in return for preferential treatment for French wines and luxury goods.

1807–12 Orders in Council issued by Britain in retaliation for Napoleon's 'Continental System'. All neutral ships trading with Europe compelled to proceed via British ports and pay duties.

1812 Orders in Council revoked after widespread protests by commercial community and unrest in the manufacturing districts.

1815 Corn Law passed prohibiting import of wheat into Britain until price of wheat on the domestic market reached 80s per quarter. Passed in order to protect the interests of British farmers who had invested heavily in agricultural production during the Napoleonic Wars, the Act aroused considerable opposition from commercial interests led by the Anti-Corn Law League.

1822–5 Revision of mercantilist Navigation Acts begun by Thomas Wallace, vice-president of the board of trade, and continued by William Huskisson as secretary to the Board of Trade. Obsolete penalties on Dutch shipping were removed; restrictions on shipping of other European nations considerably eased; but imperial trade was still reserved to British or colonial shipping.

1823 Huskisson obtains Reciprocity of Duties Act in order to permit reduction of duties with individual countries on a reciprocal basis. By 1830 such treaties concluded with most European states.

1824–5 Huskisson reduces tariffs on imports and exports to an average of 20 per cent (maximum of 30 per cent). Over 1,000 Customs Acts repealed and remaining tariffs codified.

1826 Consolidated tariff brought into operation for the whole of the United Kingdom.

1828 'Sliding scale' introduced to modify operation of Corn Law of 1815. High duties on imports now only payable when domestic price of corn low, and progressively reduced as price rose. Though a step towards Free Trade in line with the other commercial legislation of the 1820s, it failed to satisfy manufacturers and consumers.

1842–5 Sir Robert Peel reduces or abolishes duties on a wide range of raw materials, food and manufactured goods.

1846   Repeal of the Corn Laws. Free trade in corn established apart from minor registration dues (removed in 1869).

1853   Gladstone halves duties on fruit and dairy produce, cotton yarn.

1860   Gladstone abolishes all duties on fruit, dairy produce, and on all manufactured goods.   Free Trade treaty signed with France.

1914–18   Temporary duties imposed on a wide range of luxury goods to restrict home consumption and economise on the use of merchant shipping in wartime.

1921   Safeguarding of Industries Act placed duties on goods from countries with depreciated currencies. Preference given to products from the Empire.

1925   Duties imposed on imports of motor vehicles, musical instruments and films. Imperial preferences (reduced duties) for trade with British colonies and Dominions.

1932   Import Duties Act passed in wake of financial crisis of 1931. General duties of 10 per cent placed on most manufactured goods, and committee appointed to revise duties as necessary. Ottawa Agreement signed with Dominions for limited scheme of imperial preference.   Wheat Act imposes levy on foreign wheat and guaranteed domestic price to help agriculture.

1944   Britain signs Bretton Woods Agreement setting up International Monetary Fund (IMF). Member states bound themselves not to devalue currencies except under certain conditions, not to discriminate against other member states by tariffs and not to restrict international payments. The agreement came into force in 1947.

1947   Britain signatory to General Agreement on Trade and Tariffs (GATT), lowering tariff and trade restrictions.

1959   Britain organises European Free Trade Association (EFTA) as a customs union.

1973   Britain becomes a member of the European Economic Community (EEC) and accepts programme of gradual adjustment of tariffs and customs to bring her into line with existing members and curtail imperial preferences.

Imports and exports, 1700–1850 (annual averages per decade in £m.)

	Imports	Exports	Re-exports
1700–9	4.8	4.4	1.7
1710–19	5.6	4.8	2.2
1720–9	6.8	4.9	2.8

	Imports	Exports	Re-exports
1730–9	7.8	5.9	3.2
1740–9	7.3	6.6	3.6
1750–9	8.3	8.8	3.5
1760–9	10.7	10.0	4.8
1770–9	12.1	9.3	5.1
1780–9	13.8	10.2	4.3
1790–9	21.8	17.5	9.4
1800–9	28.7	25.4	12.2
1810–19	31.6	35.0	11.7
1820–9	38.3	46.1	10.0
1830–9	52.0	76.0	11.6
1840–9	79.4	124.5	17.0

Note: Figures for England and Wales to 1790; for Great Britain 1790–1850. Official values throughout. Figures rounded up to nearest £100,000.

(*Source*: B. R. Mitchell and P. Deane, *Abstract of British Historical Statistics*, Cambridge University Press, 1962, pp. 279–83.)

Imports and exports, 1860–1980 (annual averages per decade in £m.)

	Imports	Exports
1860–9	260.9	159.7
1870–9	360.6	218.1
1880–9	393.6	230.3
1890–9	435.8	237.1
1900–9	570.4	333.3
1910–19	937.5	504.6
1920–9	1,259.2	791.4
1930–9	841.0	438.9
1940–9	1,672.1	768.5
1950–9	3,615.8	2,835.2
1960–9	5,433.4	4,817.7
1970–9	23,408.2	21,058.2

Note: Figures for imports based on computed values 1860–9; declared values 1871–1939; current values 1940–80. Exports at current prices. Figures 1940–5 include munitions.

(Source: B. R. Mitchell and P. Deane, Abstract of British Historical Statistics, Cambridge University Press, 1962, pp. 283–4.)

Exports of manufactures (England), 1700–1800 (% of total exports)

	Woollens	Linen	Cotton	Iron
1700	57.3	—	0.5	1.6
1750	45.9	2.1	—	4.4
1772	42.2	7.3	2.3	8.0
1790	34.8	4.2	10.0	6.3
1800	28.5	3.3	24.2	6.1

(Source: B. R. Mitchell and P. Deane, Abstract of British Historical Statistics, Cambridge University Press, 1962, pp. 293–5.)

Principal components of British imports, 1760–1830 (% of total value)

	Corn	Other foods	Textile raw materials	Other raw materials	Other
1760–9	2	36	16	6	40
1770–9	3	32	16	6	43
1780–9	3	31	18	5	43
1790–9	5	35	15	4	41
1800–9	5	42	19	6	28
1810–19	5	41	26	8	20
1820–9	3	35	33	10	19

(Source: B. R. Mitchell and P. Deane, Abstract of British Historical Statistics, Cambridge University Press, 1962, pp. 285–9.)

Principal components of British exports, 1760–1830 (% of total value)

	Cotton	Woollen goods	Iron and steel	Other materials	Other
1760–9	2	44	6	6	42
1770–9	3	43	7	7	40
1780–9	7	35	6	7	45
1790–9	15	30	7	7	41
1800–9	39	24	5	4	28
1810–19	53	16	4	3	24
1820–9	62	12	4	2	20

(*Source*: B. R. Mitchell and P. Deane, *Abstract of British Historical Statistics*, Cambridge University Press, 1962, pp. 293–5.)

Principal components of British imports, 1860–1939 (% of total value)

	Foodstuffs	Textile raw materials	Other raw materials	Manufactured goods	Other
1860–9	30	30	16	2	22
1870–9	30	35	12	2	21
1880–9	35	27	12	3	23
1890–9	35	21	12	4	28
1900–9	32	19	14	6	29
1910–19	31	19	16	6	28
1920–9	30	17	16	5	32
1930–9	29	11	18	7	35

(*Source*: B. R. Mitchell and P. Deane, *Abstract of British Historical Statistics*, Cambridge University Press, 1962, pp. 298–301.)

Principal components of British exports, 1830–1938 (% of total value)

	Cottons	Other textiles	Iron and steel	Machinery	Coal	Vehicles
1830–9	48	24	11	1	1	—
1840–9	45	25	15	1	2	—
1850–9	36	24	18	2	2	—
1860–9	36	26	15	3	3	—
1870–9	33	22	16	4	4	—
1880–9	32	17	15	5	5	—
1890–9	28	16	14	7	7	—
1900–9	26	12	14	7	10	3
1910–19	25	15	12	5	10	2
1920–9	24	12	12	7	8	4
1930–8	14	10	12	10	9	5

(*Source*: B. R. Mitchell and P. Deane, *Abstract of British Historical Statistics*, Cambridge University Press, 1962, pp. 302–6.)

Principal components of British imports, 1954–1976 (% of total value)

	Food, drink and tobacco	Basic raw materials	Fuels and lubricants	Semi-manufactures	Finished manufactures
1954	39	30	10	15	5
1964	32	20	11	21	15
1976	16	10	18	26	28

(*Source: Pears Cyclopaedia, 1980–81*, London, Pelham Books, 1980.)

Principal components of British exports, 1954–1976 (% of total value)

	Food, drink and tobacco	Basic raw materials	Fuels and lubricants	Metals	Engineering products	Textiles	Other manuf. goods
1954	6	4	6	13	38	12	18
1964	7	4	3	12	45	6	20
1976	7	3	5	9	39	4	31

(*Source: Pears Cyclopaedia, 1980–81*, London, Pelham Books, 1980.)

Geographical distribution of British exports, 1701–1798 (official values, £m.)

	Europe	North America	West Indies
1701	3.7	0.3	0.2
1731	3.9	0.4	0.4
1751	6.3	1.0	0.4
1773	3.8	2.5	1.2
1781	3.3	1.4	1.3
1790	5.3	3.3	1.7
1798	3.8	5.7	4.6

(*Source*: B. R. Mitchell and P. Deane, *Abstract of British Historical Statistics*, Cambridge University Press, 1962, p. 312.)

Geographical distribution of British trade, 1760–1970 (% of total)

	1760	1800	1850	1900	1938	1970
South America	15	18	16	8	10	5
Africa	1½	15	3	3	7	10
North America	15	1½	15	25	17	20
Asia	12	12	12	12	12	12

	1760	1800	1850	1900	1938	1970
Europe	43	35	33	44	32	25
Others	13½	18½	21	8	22	28

(*Source*: B. R. Mitchell and P. Deane, *Abstract of British Historical Statistics*, Cambridge University Press, pp. 312–26; *Facts in Focus*, Harmondsworth, Penguin, 1972, p. 150.)

The balance of payments of the United Kingdom, 1816–1978 (annual averages in £m., all figures rounded)

	Balance of visible trade	Balance of invisible trade	Net balance
1816–20	−11	+18	+7
1821–5	− 8	+18	+10
1826–30	−15	+17	+3
1831–5	−13	+19	+6
1836–40	−23	+26	+3
1841–5	−19	+25	+6
1846–50	−26	+30	+5
1851–5	−33	+41	+8
1856–60	−34	+60	+26
1861–5	−59	+81	+22
1866–70	−65	+106	+41
1871–5	−64	+139	+75
1876–80	−124	+149	+25
1881–5	−99	+161	+61
1886–90	−89	+177	+88
1891–5	−134	+186	+52
1896–1900	−159	+199	+40
1901–5	−177	+226	+49
1906–10	−144	+290	+146
1911–13	−140	+346	+206
1920–4	−258	+419	+161
1925–9	−398	+481	+83

	Balance of visible trade	Balance of invisible trade	Net balance
1930–4	−328	+301	−27
1935–8	−356	+332	−24
1946–50	−160	+104	−56
1951–5	−345	+326	−19
1956–60	−94	+226	+132
1961–5	−218	+176	−42
1966–70	−297	+441	+144
1971–5	−2,263	+1,219	−1,044
1976–8	−2,158	+1,959	−199

(*Source*: P. Deane and W. A. Cole, *British Economic Growth, 1688–1959*, 2nd edn, Cambridge University Press, 1967, p. 36; B. R. Mitchell and H. G. Jones, *Second Abstract of British Historical Statistics*, Cambridge University Press, 1971, p. 142; Central Statistical Office, *United Kingdom Balance of Payments 1967–78*, London, HMSO, 1978.)

Prices and wages

The Schumpeter – Gilboy price index, 1714 – 1823 (index of consumer goods including cereals; 1701 = 100)

1714	103	1736	87	1758	106	1780	110	1802	174
1715	104	1737	93	1759	100	1781	115	1803	156
1716	99	1738	91	1760	98	1782	116	1804	161
1717	95	1739	89	1761	94	1783	129	1805	187
1718	93	1740	100	1762	94	1784	126	1806	184
1719	97	1741	108	1763	100	1785	120	1807	186
1720	102	1742	99	1764	102	1786	119	1808	204
1721	100	1743	94	1765	106	1787	117	1809	212
1722	92	1744	84	1766	107	1788	121	1810	207
1723	89	1745	85	1767	109	1789	117	1811	206
1724	94	1746	93	1768	108	1790	124	1812	237
1725	97	1747	90	1769	99	1791	121	1813	243
1726	102	1748	94	1770	100	1792	122	1814	209
1727	96	1749	96	1771	107	1793	129	1815	191
1728	99	1750	95	1772	117	1794	136	1816	172
1729	104	1751	90	1773	119	1795	147	1817	189
1730	95	1752	93	1774	116	1796	154	1818	194
1731	88	1753	90	1775	113	1797	148	1819	192
1732	89	1754	90	1776	114	1798	148	1820	162
1733	85	1755	92	1777	108	1799	160	1821	139
1734	88	1756	92	1778	117	1800	212	1822	125
1735	89	1757	109	1779	111	1801	228	1823	128

(*Source*: B. R. Mitchell and P. Deane, *Abstract of British Historical Statistics*, Cambridge University Press, 1962, pp. 468 – 9.)

The Rousseaux price index, 1800–1913 (Index of total agricultural and principal industrial products; average of 1865 and 1885 = 100)

1800	175	1823	120	1846	109	1869	107	1892	82
1801	188	1824	122	1847	115	1870	110	1893	82
1802	152	1825	133	1848	100	1871	115	1894	74
1803	161	1826	117	1849	95	1872	128	1895	72
1804	159	1827	117	1850	95	1873	127	1896	73
1805	170	1828	112	1851	91	1874	121	1897	74
1806	166	1829	110	1852	94	1875	117	1898	78
1807	161	1830	109	1853	112	1876	115	1899	84
1808	189	1831	112	1854	125	1877	110	1900	91
1809	206	1832	109	1855	125	1878	101	1901	86
1810	193	1833	107	1856	124	1879	98	1902	86
1811	178	1834	112	1857	127	1880	102	1903	86
1812	196	1835	112	1858	111	1881	99	1904	83
1813	203	1836	123	1859	115	1882	101	1905	86
1814	202	1837	118	1860	120	1883	101	1906	93
1815	164	1838	119	1861	115	1884	95	1907	97
1816	144	1839	130	1862	120	1885	88	1908	87
1817	161	1840	128	1863	121	1886	83	1909	91
1818	160	1841	121	1864	119	1887	81	1910	97
1819	147	1842	111	1865	117	1888	84	1911	102
1820	132	1843	105	1866	120	1889	84	1912	104
1821	121	1844	108	1867	118	1890	87	1913	106
1822	116	1845	110	1868	115	1891	86		

(*Source*: B. R. Mitchell and P. Deane, *Abstract of British Historical Statistics*, Cambridge University Press, 1962, pp. 471–3.)

The Sauerbeck– *Statist* price index, 1900–1965
(overall index of consumer goods, raw materials and food; average of 1866–77 = 100)

1900	75	1914	85	1928	120	1942	151	1956	384
1901	70	1915	108	1929	115	1943	155	1957	376
1902	69	1916	136	1930	97	1944	160	1958	355
1903	69	1917	179	1931	83	1945	164	1959	356
1904	70	1918	192	1932	80	1946	186	1960	359
1905	72	1919	206	1933	79	1947	230	1961	354
1906	77	1920	251	1934	82	1948	260	1962	360
1907	80	1921	155	1935	84	1949	274	1963	374
1908	73	1922	131	1936	89	1950	324	1964	401
1909	74	1923	129	1937	102	1951	401	1965	404
1910	78	1924	139	1938	91	1952	380		
1911	80	1925	136	1939	94	1953	366		
1912	85	1926	126	1940	128	1954	361		
1913	85	1927	122	1941	142	1955	370		

(*Source*: B. R. Mitchell and P. Deane, *Abstract of British Historical Statistics*, Cambridge University Press, 1962, pp. 474–5; B. R. Mitchell and H. G. Jones, *Second Abstract of British Historical Statistics*, Cambridge University Press, 1971, p. 187.)

Average price of wheat, 1771–1914 (by calendar year; per imperial quarter)

	s.	d.		s.	d.		s.	d.
1771	48	7	1780	36	9	1789	52	9
1772	52	3	1781	46	0	1790	54	9
1773	52	7	1782	49	3	1791	48	7
1774	54	3	1783	54	3	1792	43	0
1775	49	10	1784	50	4	1793	49	3
1776	39	4	1785	43	1	1794	52	3
1777	46	11	1786	40	0	1795	75	2
1778	43	3	1787	42	5	1796	78	7
1779	34	8	1788	46	4	1797	53	9

	s.	d.		s.	d.		s.	d.
1798	51	10	1833	52	11	1868	63	9
1799	69	0	1834	46	2	1869	48	2
1800	113	10	1835	39	4	1870	46	11
1801	119	6	1836	48	6	1871	56	8
1802	69	10	1837	55	10	1872	57	0
1803	58	10	1838	64	7	1873	58	8
1804	62	3	1839	70	8	1874	55	9
1805	89	9	1840	66	4	1875	45	2
1806	79	1	1841	64	4	1876	46	2
1807	75	4	1842	57	3	1877	56	9
1808	81	4	1843	50	1	1878	46	5
1809	97	4	1844	51	3	1879	43	10
1810	106	5	1845	50	10	1880	44	4
1811	95	3	1846	54	8	1881	45	4
1812	126	6	1847	69	9	1882	45	1
1813	109	9	1848	50	6	1883	41	7
1814	74	4	1849	44	3	1884	35	8
1815	65	7	1850	40	3	1885	32	10
1816	78	6	1851	38	6	1886	31	0
1817	96	11	1852	40	9	1887	32	6
1818	86	3	1853	53	3	1888	31	10
1819	74	6	1854	72	5	1889	29	9
1820	67	10	1855	74	8	1890	31	11
1821	56	1	1856	69	2	1891	37	0
1822	44	7	1857	56	4	1892	30	3
1823	53	4	1858	44	2	1893	26	4
1824	63	11	1859	43	9	1894	22	10
1825	68	6	1860	53	3	1895	23	1
1826	58	8	1861	55	4	1896	26	2
1827	58	6	1862	55	5	1897	30	2
1828	60	5	1863	44	9	1898	34	0
1829	66	3	1864	40	2	1899	25	8
1830	64	3	1865	41	10	1900	26	11
1831	66	4	1866	49	11	1901	26	9
1832	58	8	1867	64	5	1902	28	1

	s.	d.		s.	d.		s.	d.
1903	26	9	1907	30	7	1911	31	8
1904	28	4	1908	32	0	1912	34	9
1905	29	8	1909	36	11	1913	31	8
1906	28	3	1910	31	8	1914	34	11

(*Source*: B. R. Mitchell and P. Deane, *Abstract of British Historical
Statistics*, Cambridge University Press, 1962, pp. 487–9.)

Real wages in London and Lancashire, 1700–1796 (1700 = 100)

	London wages	Lancashire wages
1700	100	100
1710	74	71
1720	108	130
1730	122	149
1740	97	112
1750	129	143
1760	122	127
1770	103	169
1780	98	160
1790	n.a.	175
1796	n.a.	152

(*n.a.* = not available)

Note: Wages relate to wages of men in full employment.

(*Source*: E. W. Gilboy, 'The cost of living and real wages in
eighteenth-century England', *Review of Economic Statistics*, Vol. 18,
1936.)

Money wages in Great Britain, 1790–1860
(1840 = 100)

1790	70	1816	117	1845	98
1795	82	1820	110	1850	100
1800	95	1824	105	1855	117
1805	109	1831	101	1860	115
1810	124	1840	100		

(*Source*: P. Deane and W. A. Cole, *British Economic Growth, 1688–1959*, Cambridge University Press, 1969, p. 23.)

Money wages and real wages in the United Kingdom, 1850–1906 (1850 = 100)

	Money wages	Real wages
1850	100	100
1855	116	94
1860	114	105
1866	132	117
1871	137	125
1874	155	136
1877	152	132
1880	147	132
1883	150	142
1886	148	142
1891	162	166
1896	162	177
1900	179	184
1906	181	194

(*Source*: P. Deane and W. A. Cole, *British Economic Growth, 1688–1959*, Cambridge University Press, 1969, p. 25.)

Money wages, the cost of living and real wages, 1880–1914 (1914 = 100)

	Money wages	Cost of living	Real wages		Money wages	Cost of living	Real wages
1880	72	105	69	1898	87	88	99
1881	72	103	71	1899	89	86	104
1882	75	102	73	1900	94	91	103
1883	75	102	73	1901	93	90	102
1884	75	97	77	1902	91	90	102
1885	73	91	81	1903	91	91	99
1886	72	89	81	1904	89	92	97
1887	73	88	84	1905	89	92	97
1888	75	88	86	1906	91	93	98
1889	80	89	90	1907	96	95	101
1890	83	89	93	1908	94	93	101
1891	83	89	92	1909	94	94	100
1893	83	89	94	1910	94	96	98
1892	83	90	92	1911	95	97	97
1894	83	85	98	1912	98	100	97
1895	83	83	100	1913	99	102	97
1896	83	83	100	1914	100	100	100
1897	84	85	98				

(*Source*: E. C. Ramsbottom, 'The course of wage rates in the United Kingdom,' *Journal of the Royal Statistical Society*, vol. 98, 1935.

Average money wages and real wages, 1913, 1920–1938 (1930 = 100)

	Annual money wages	Annual real wages		Annual money wages	Annual real wages
1913	52.4	82.8	1923	100.0	90.8
1920	143.7	91.2	1924	101.5	91.6
1921	134.6	94.1	1925	102.2	91.7
1922	107.9	93.2	1926	99.3	91.2

	Annual money wages	Annual real wages		Annual money wages	Annual real wages
1927	101.5	95.8	1933	95.3	107.6
1928	100.1	95.2	1934	96.4	108.1
1929	100.4	96.7	1935	98.0	108.3
1930	100.0	100.0	1936	100.2	107.7
1931	98.2	105.1	1937	102.8	105.4
1932	96.3	105.7	1938	106.3	107.7

Note: Figures cover most manufacturing and service industries, but exclude salary-earners.

(*Source*: D. H. Aldcroft, *The Inter-war Economy: Britain, 1919–1939*, 2nd edn, Batsford, 1973, pp. 352, 364.)

Prices and wages, 1950–1979 (1955 = 100)

	Retail price index	Weekly wage rates	Weekly earnings	Real wage rates	Real earnings
1950	77	73	68	96	91
1955	100	100	100	100	100
1960	114	124	130	109	114
1965	136	151	175	112	129
1970	170	202	250	119	147
1977	407	579	661	142	162
1979	499	759	844	152	169

(*Source: Pears Cyclopaedia, 1980–81*, London Pelham Books, 1980.)

Production

Coal output, 1800–1978

	Total UK output (m. tons)	% exported		Total UK output (m. tons)	% exported
1800	11.0	2.0	1895	189.7	22.6
1816	15.9	2.5	1900	225.2	25.9
1820	17.4	1.4	1905	236.1	20.1
1825	21.9	1.4	1910	264.4	23.5
1830	22.4	2.2	1915	253.2	17.2
1835	27.7	2.7	1920	229.5	10.8
1840	33.7	4.8	1925	243.2	20.9
1845	45.9	5.5	1930	243.9	22.5
1850	49.4	6.8	1935	222.3	17.4
1855	61.5	8.1	1940	224.3	8.8
1860	80.0	9.2	1945	182.2	1.8
1865	98.2	9.3	1950	216.3	6.2
1870	110.4	13.4	1955	221.6	5.5
1875	131.9	13.5	1960	193.6	2.6
1880	146.8	16.3	1965	187.5	2.0
1885	159.4	19.3	1970	133.4	1.0
1890	181.6	21.3	1978	122.0	1.4

(*Source*: B. R. Mitchell and P. Deane, *Abstract of British Historical Statistics*, Cambridge University Press, 1962, pp. 115–19, 120–1; B. R. Mitchell and H. G. Jones, *Second Abstract of British Historical Statistics*, Cambridge University Press, 1971, pp. 66, 68; *Britain 1979*, London, HMSO, 1979, p. 252.)

Coal statistics, 1967–1978

	1967–8	1975–6	1976–7	1977–8
Output (m. tons)	170.9	123.8	118.9	119.0
Labour force (000s)	391.9	247.1	242.0	240.5
Number of collieries	376	241	238	231

(*Source: Britain 1979,* London, HMSO , 1979, p. 252.)

Energy consumption, 1967–1977 (m. tonnes coal equivalent)

	1967	1972	1975	1977
Oil	122.6	162.2	136.5	136.6
Coal	165.8	122.4	120.0	122.7
Natural gas	2.1	40.9	55.4	62.8
Nuclear energy	9.0	10.6	10.9	14.3
Hydro-electric	2.7	1.9	2.0	2.0
Total	302.2	338.0	324.8	338.4

(*Source: Britain 1979*, London, HMSO, 1979, p. 243.)

Iron production, 1720–1976 (000 tons)

1720	25	1900	9,000
1788	70	1925	10,000
1820	450	1950	12,000
1850	2,000	1970	18,000
1875	6,500	1976	14,000

(*Source*: B. R. Mitchell and P. Deane, *Abstract of British Historical Statistics*, Cambridge University Press, 1962, pp. 129–32; *Facts in Focus*, Harmondsworth, Penguin Books, 1972, p. 109.)

Steel production, 1870–1978 (000 tons)

1870	300	1930	7,000
1880	1,250	1940	12,000
1890	3,500	1950	16,000
1900	5,000	1960	24,000
1910	6,500	1970	28,000
1920	9,000	1978	20,000

(*Source*: B. R. Mitchell and P. Deane, *Abstract of British Historical Statistics*, Cambridge University Press, 1962, pp. 136–7; *Britain, 1979*. London, HMSO, 1979, p. 218.)

Cotton production and exports, 1750–1977
(annual average per decade)

	Raw cotton (retained imports, 000 lb)	Exports of piece goods (m. yd)
1750–9	2,820	—
1760–9	3,531	—
1770–9	4,797	—
1780–9	14,824	—
1790–9	28,645	—
1800–9	59,554	—
1810–19	96,339	227
1820–9	173,000	320
1830–9	302,000	553
1840–9	550,000	978
1850–9	795,000	1,855
1860–9	803,000	2,375
1870–9	1,244,000	3,573
1880–9	1,473,000	4,575
1890–9	1,556,000	5,057
1900–9	1,723,000	5,649
1910–19	1,864,000	5,460
1920–9	1,498,000	4,239

	Raw cotton (retained imports, 000 lb)	Exports of piece goods (m. yd)
1930–9	1,360,000	1,970
1940–9	1,074,000	621
1950–9	928,000	596
1960–9	469,000	—
1970–7	311,000	—

(*Source*: B. R. Mitchell and P. Deane, *Abstract of British Historical Statistics*, Cambridge University Press, 1962, pp. 177–81; B. R. Mitchell and H. G. Jones, *Second Abstract of British Historical Statistics*, Cambridge University Press, 1971, pp. 90–1; *Economic Trends*, London, HMSO, 1972–8.)

Ships built and registered in the United Kingdom, 1790–1913 (000 tons)

1790	68.7	1840	211.3	1890	652.0
1800	134.2	1850	133.7	1900	739.0
1810	84.9	1860	212.0	1910	601.0
1820	66.7	1870	342.7	1913	975.2
1830	75.5	1880	403.8		

(*Source*: B. R. Mitchell and P. Deane, *Abstract of British Historical Statistics*, Cambridge University Press, 1962, pp. 221–2.)

Total shipping completed in the United Kingdom, 1900–1970 (000 tons)

1900	1,440	1925	800	1950	1,400
1905	1,625	1930	950	1955	1,350
1910	1,150	1935	680	1960	1,303
1913	1,950	1939	1,000	1965	1,204
1920	2,400	1945	1,250	1970	1,297

(*Source*: B.R. Mitchell and P. Deane, *Abstract of British Historical Statistics*, Cambridge University Press, 1962, pp. 221–2; *Facts in Focus*, Harmondsworth, Penguin Books, 1972, p. 114.)

Motor vehicles produced, 1908–1979 (000s)

1908	10	1933	286	1965	1,722
1913	34	1938	445	1970	1,641
1923	95	1948	500	1975	1,648
1928	212	1960	1,353	1979	1,479

(*Source: The Motor Industry of Great Britain*, annual reports; M. Jenkins, *Daily Mail Year Book, 1981*, Harmsworth Publications, 1980, p. 290.)

Finance

Major legislation concerning finance and banking

1694 Bank of England founded (Bank of Scotland, 1695).

1716 'Sinking Fund' established to redeem National Debt.

1720 South Sea Bubble. A spate of speculation in the shares of the South Sea Company, promoted by members of the government, is followed by a collapse, causing financial and political crisis. Walpole eventually restores public credit.

1733 Walpole introduces excise scheme to discourage smuggling and reduce land tax. Widespread opposition forces him to withdraw.

1773 Stock Exchange founded.

1799 Income tax introduced to pay for the war with France. Abolished 1802, reimposed 1803.

1816 Income tax abolished.

1826 Legalisation of joint-stock banks outside a 65-mile radius of London.

1831 Land tax ceases to be collected.

1833 Bank Act, making Bank of England notes the legal tender.

1842 Income tax reimposed at 7d. in the £.

1844 Bank Charter Act. Note issue and central banking functions of the Bank of England regularised.

1855 Limited Liability Act limits responsibility of investors in the event of bankruptcy of the company.

1890 Bank of England becomes responsible for foreign exchange and gold reserves.

1894 Estate, or "death', duties introduced.

1909 Supertax or 'surtax', on incomes over £2,000 per year introduced.

1914 Britain goes off Gold Standard as a result of First World War.

1925 Britain goes back on to Gold Standard.

1931 Financial crisis; Britain leaves Gold Standard.

1940 Purchase tax introduced to reduce spending on luxury goods; essential items exempt. Tax added to the price paid by the customer.

1946   Bank of England nationalised.

1949   Devaluation of the pound by 30.5 per cent.

1965   Capital gains tax and corporation tax introduced.

1966   Selective employment tax (SET) introduced.

1967   Devaluation of the pound by 14.3 per cent

1972   Pound allowed to 'float'.

1973   Purchase tax and selective employment tax abolished; value added tax (VAT) introduced, levied on all goods and services, bringing British taxation into line with the European Economic Community.

1975   Capital transfer tax introduced to replace estate duty.

1980   Controls on international movement of currency and property abolished.

National income, 1855–1977 Income (at factor cost)

	Total (£m.)		Total (£m.)		Total (£m.)
1855	636	1900	1,750	1950	10,784
1860	694	1905	1,776	1955	15,511
1865	822	1910	1,984	1960	20,809
1870	936	1915	2,591	1965	28,807
1875	1,113	1920	3,664	1970	39,567
1880	1,076	1925	3,980	1975	82,179
1885	1,115	1930	3,957	1977	107,990
1890	1,385	1935	4,109		
1895	1,447	1938	4,671		

(*Source*: B. R. Mitchell and P. Deane, *Abstract of British Historical Statistics*, Cambridge University Press, 1962, pp. 367–8; *National Income and Expenditure*, annual Blue Books.)

Unemployment

Total numbers registered unemployed, Great Britain, 1922–1980 ('000s; average for 12 months)

1922	1,543	1937	1,484	1952	414	1967	556
1923	1,275	1938	1,791	1953	342	1968	554
1924	1,130	1939	1,514	1954	285	1969	534
1925	1,226	1940	963	1955	232	1970	579
1926	1,385	1941	350	1956	257	1971	724
1927	1,088	1942	123	1957	312	1972	899
1928	1,217	1943	82	1958	457	1973	575
1929	1,216	1944	75	1959	475	1974	542
1930	1,917	1945	137	1960	360	1975	866
1931	2,630	1946	374	1961	341	1976	1,332
1932	2,745	1947	480	1962	463	1977	1,450
1933	2,521	1948	310	1963	573	1978	1,381
1934	2,159	1949	308	1964	380	1980	1,668
1935	2,036	1950	314	1965	329		
1936	1,755	1951	253	1966	353		

(*Source*: B. R. Mitchell and P. Deane, *Abstract of British Historical Statistics*, Cambridge University Press, 1962, p. 66; B. R. Mitchell and H. G. Jones, *Second Abstract of British Historical Statistics*, Cambridge University Press, 1971, p. 43; *Britain, 1979*, London HMSO, 1979, p. 310.)

Transport

Turnpike Acts by period, 1663–1839 (England)

	Number of Acts passed		Number of Acts passed
1663–1719	37	1761–72	205
1720–9	46	1773–91	65
1730–9	24	1792–1815	173
1740–50	39	1816–39	139
1751–60	184		

Turnpike Acts by area, 1663–1839

	Number of Acts passed
Home counties	73
Southern counties	134
East Anglia	61
Western counties	102
Far West	68
Northants, Cambs., Hunts., and Beds.	45
South Midlands	58
North Midlands	84
East Midlands	75
Yorkshire and Lancashire	148
Far North	64

(*Source*: W. Albert, *The Turnpike Road System of England, 1663–1844*, Cambridge University Press, 1972.)

Major canal developments

1757   Sankey canal completed from St Helens to the Mersey.

1761   Bridgewater canal completed from Worsley to Manchester.

1769   Birmingham canal completed from Wednesbury to Birmingham.

1772   Bridgewater canal extended to the Mersey at Runcorn.
Staffordshire and Worcestershire canal completed.

1774   Bradford canal completed.

1776   Chesterfield canal completed.

1777   Trent and Mersey canal completed.

1778   Oxford canal opened from Banbury to Coventry.

1779   Stroudwater canal opened.

1789   Thames and Severn canal completed.

1790   Forth and Clyde canal completed. Oxford canal reaches Oxford.

1792   Shropshire canal completed.

1794   Glamorgan canal opened from Merthyr Tydfil to Cardiff.

1796   Lune aqueduct completed.

1797   Ashton and Shrewsbury canals completed.

1798   Huddersfield, Ashton to Stalybridge, and Hereford to Gloucester
canals completed.

1799   Barnsley canal completed.

1800   Peak Forest canal completed.

1801   Grand Junction (London–Buckingham) canal completed.

1802   Nottingham canal completed.

1804   Rochdale canal completed.

1810   Kennet and Avon trunk canal completed.

1813   Aylesbury branch of Grand Junction canal completed.

1814   Grand Western canal (Loudwell–Tiverton) completed.

1815   Grand Junction (Northampton branch) completed.

1816   Leeds and Liverpool canal completed.

1819   North Wiltshire and Sheffield canals completed.

1822   Caledonian canal completed; Edinburgh and Glasgow Union
canal completed.

1824   Thames and Medway canal completed.

1826   Lancaster canal completed.

1827   Harecastle New Tunnel completed and Gloucester and Berkeley
canal completed.

1830   Hereford Union canal completed.

1831   Liskeard and Looe, Portsmouth and Arundel, and Macclesfield canals completed.

1833   Glastonbury canal completed.

1835   Birmingham and Liverpool canal completed.

1839   Manchester and Salford canal completed.

1842   Chard canal completed.

1847   Par canal opened.

1853   Droitwich junction canal completed.

1894   Manchester ship canal completed.

Shipping registered in English ports in the eighteenth century

	(000 tons)	
	1702	1788
London	140.0	315.3
Newcastle	11.0	106.1
Liverpool	8.6	76.1
Sunderland	3.9	53.6
Whitehaven	7.2	52.3
Hull	7.6	52.1
Whitby	8.3	47.9
Bristol	17.3	37.8
Yarmouth	9.9	36.3

(Source: R. Davis, The Rise of the English Shipping Industry, London, Macmillan, 1962, p. 35.)

Shipping registered in the United Kingdom, 1790–1978

	(000 tons)		(000 tons)		(000 tons)
1790	1,383	1860	4,659	1930	20,322
1800	1,699	1870	5,691	1940	17,891
1810	2,211	1880	6,575	1950	18,219
1820	2,439	1890	7,979	1960	21,131
1830	2,202	1900	11,514	1970	25,825
1840	2,768	1910	16,768	1978	30,896
1850	3,565	1920	18,111		

(*Source*: B. R. Mitchell and P. Deane, *Abstract of British Historical Statistics*, Cambridge University Press, 1962, pp. 217–19; *Lloyd's Register of Shipping*, annual statistical tables.)

Tonnage cleared by major ports, 1880, 1937, 1970

		(000 tons)			
1880		1937		1970	
London	12,900	London	62,600	London	84,900
Liverpool	10,300	Liverpool	35,000	Southampton	51,100
Cardiff	8,000	Southampton	27,500	Liverpool	43,000
Newcastle	5,200	Tyne ports	18,300	Milford Haven	28,900
Hull	3,400	Cowes	16,100	Belfast	20,000
Glasgow	2,500	Cardiff	15,400	Grimsby	15,400
Newport	2,400	Belfast	15,200	Tyne ports	11,300
South Shields	1,900	Glasgow	13,000	Hull	10,000
Southampton	1,700	Hull	12,300	Manchester	9,600
Sunderland	1,600	Plymouth	12,200	Glasgow	7,000
Middlesbrough	1,200	Dover	8,200	Bristol	5,100
Grimsby	1,200	Manchester	7,700	Swansea	4,800

(*Source*: C. Cook and J. Stevenson, *Longman Atlas of Modern British History*, London, Longman, 1978, p. 54; *Facts in Focus*, Harmondsworth, Penguin Books, 1972, p. 145.)

Railway mileage and passengers carried in the United Kingdom, 1845–1977

	Miles open	Passengers carried (m.)		Miles open	Passengers carried (m.)
1845	2,441	30.4	1915	—	—
1850	6,084	67.4	1920	20,312	1,579.0
1855	7,293	111.4	1925	20,400	1,232.6
1860	9,069	153.5	1930	20,265	844.3
1865	11,451	238.7	1935	20,152	856.2
1870	13,562	322.2	1940	19,931	691.1
1875	14,510	490.1	1945	19,863	1,055.7
1880	15,563	596.6	1950	19,471	704.0
1885	16,594	678.1	1955	19,061	730.2
1890	17,281	796.3	1960	18,369	721.3
1895	18,001	903.5	1965	14,920	580.5
1900	18,680	1,114.6	1970	11,799	823.9
1905	19,535	1,170.0	1977	11,169	702.0
1910	19,986	1,276.0			

(*Source*: B. R. Mitchell and P. Deane, *Abstract of British Historical Statistics*, Cambridge University Press, 1962, pp. 225–7; B. R. Mitchell and H. G. Jones, *Second Abstract of British Historical Statistics*, Cambridge University Press, 1971, p. 104; *Britain 1979*, London, HMSO, 1979, p. 292.)

Motor Vehicles in use, 1905–1970

	Private cars ('000s)	Goods vehicles ('000s)	All vehicles* ('000s)
1905	16	9	—
1910	53	30	144
1915	139	85	407
1920	187	101	650
1925	580	224	1,510
1930	1,056	348	2,274
1935	1,477	435	2,570

	Private cars ('000s)	Goods vehicles ('000s)	All vehicles* ('000s)
1939	2,034	488	3,149
1945	1,487	473	2,553
1950	2,258	895	4,409
1955	3,526	1,109	6,465
1960	5,526	1,397	9,439
1965	8,917	1,602	12,940
1970	11,515	1,622	14,950
1978	14,069	2,216	17,654

* 'All vehicles' includes buses, trams, taxis and motor-cycles, as well as cars and goods vehicles.

(*Source*: B. R. Mitchell and P. Deane, *Abstract of British Historical Statistics*, Cambridge University Press, 1962, p. 230; B. R. Mitchell and H. G. Jones, *Second Abstract of British Historical Statistics*, Cambridge University Press, 1971, p. 106.)

Section IV: Foreign affairs and defence

Military and naval

British wars and campaigns
Jacobite rebellions 1715 and 1745

The '15
The Earl of Mar raised the Stuart standard at Braemar on 6 September
1715. The rebellion faltered when Mar failed to dislodge the royal army
under Argyll from Sheriffmuir, north of Stirling, on 13 November, and on
the same day a Jacobite army surrendered at Preston. The Pretender
landed in Scotland on 22 December, but as Argyll advanced the Jacobite
army dispersed, and James sailed again for France on 5 February 1716.

The '45
Prince Charles Edward, the Young Pretender, raised his standard at
Glenfinnan on 19 August 1745. He occupied Edinburgh on 17 September
and defeated a royalist army under Sir John Cope at Prestonpans on 20
September. On 31 October Charles led an army of 5,000 men south into
England. The Jacobites reached Derby on 4 December, but their hopes of
an English uprising were disappointed, and the decision to retreat was
taken the following day. The rebellion had its last success with a victory
at Falkirk on 17 January 1746, but on 16 April the Duke of Cumberland
decisively defeated the Jacobites at Culloden, near Inverness. After
several months as a fugitive, Charles Edward escaped to France in
September 1746.

War of the Quadruple Alliance 1718–20

Following the Spanish occupation of Sardinia in November 1717 and
Sicily in July 1718, the Quadruple Alliance was formed by France,
Austria, England and Holland on 2 August 1718 to oppose Philip of
Spain's designs on Italy and France. On 11 August 1718 Admiral Byng
destroyed the Spanish fleet off Cape Passaro. The English fleet then
supported Austrian operations in Sicily and carried out raids on the
Galician coast in October 1719. The war was ended by the treaty of the
Hague on 17 February 1720, by which Philip gave up his claims. Fighting
took place briefly between Spain and France and England in 1727 over
the implementation of the terms of the treaty of the Hague. The dispute
over Philip's son's succession to the Italian duchies was resolved by the
treaty of Seville in November 1729.

War of the Austrian Succession 1740–8

Colonial conflicts, and particularly the incident in which Captain Jenkins
claimed to have had his ear cut off by a Spanish official, led Britain to

declare war on Spain on 19 October 1739. This war became part of a
wider European conflict when Frederick the Great of Prussia launched his
campaign to seize Silesia from Maria Theresa of Austria on 16 December
1740. King George II, commanding in person an army of British,
Hanoverian and Dutch troops in support of Maria Theresa, defeated the
French at Dettingen on 27 June 1743. In May 1745 the French began an
advance into the Austrian Netherlands, defeated the Duke of Cumberland
at Fontenoy on 10 May and completed their conquest of Flanders. In 1747
the French invaded Holland and defeated the allies at Lauffeld on 2 July.
At sea, Admiral Anson, who had carried out a circumnavigation and
raided Spanish possessions, 1740–4, defeated the French at the first
battle of Finisterre on 3 May 1747. Admiral Hawke achieved a similar
victory over a convoy escort in a second battle in October. In North
America, Louisburg was captured from the French in June 1745, but in
India, Madras was lost in September 1746. They were exchanged by the
treaty of Aix-la-Chapelle signed on 18 October 1748, which brought the
war in Europe to a close.

Seven Years War 1756–63

Britain and France declared war on 17 May 1756, but the war in Europe
began when Frederick the Great invaded Saxony in August. In 1757 a
French army invaded Hanover and defeated the allies at Hastenbeck on
26 July. The Duke of Cumberland signed the Convention of
Kloster-Seven on 8 September, disbanding his army, but this was
repudiated after Frederick the Great's victory at Rossbach on 5 November
1757. Ferdinand of Brunswick took command of the allied army and Pitt
began the payment of subsidies to Frederick the Great. On 1 August 1759
Ferdinand routed the French at Minden, and on 31 July 1760 saved
Hanover by a victory at Warburg. While Prussia bore the brunt of the
fighting in Europe, in North America Britain mounted a fourfold attack on
the French in 1758. This culminated in Wolfe's victory before Quebec on
13 September 1759 and the capture of the city. On 8 September 1760 the
Marquis de Vaudreuil surrendered Montreal and with it French Canada.
French plans to invade England were disrupted by Admiral Boscawen's
victory at Lagos Bay on 18 August 1759 and Hawke's victory at Quiberon
Bay on 20 November. A French expedition to Ireland surrendered at
Kinsale in February 1760. Following the outbreak of war with Spain in
January 1762, Britain seized Havana and Manila. The death of Empress
Elizabeth of Russia on 5 January 1762 led to a peace treaty between
Prussia and Russia on 5 May 1762. Britain, France, Spain and Portugal
signed the treaty of Paris on 10 February 1763, and Prussia, Austria and
Saxony concluded the treaty of Hubertusburg on 15 February.

War of American Independence 1775–83

The first shots of the war were fired on 19 April 1775 when British troops
sent from Boston to destroy stores of the Massachusetts Militia at
Concord were opposed at Lexington. George Washington was appointed
commander-in-chief of the rebels' Continental Army on 15 June 1775. An
American attack on Canada failed, but in March 1776 the British were
forced to evacuate Boston. The Americans issued their Declaration of

Independence on 4 July 1776. In September 1776 the British occupied
New York, and Washington retreated across the Delaware river into
Pennsylvania. However, on 26 December 1776 he recrossed the river and
defeated an army of Hessian auxiliaries at Trenton. In 1777 a British plan
to divide the rebels by a threefold attack, with Burgoyne advancing from
Canada, in cooperation with St Leger from Lake Ontario and Howe from
New York, was a complete failure and resulted in Burgoyne's surrender
at Saratoga on 17 October 1777. In 1778 the scope of the conflict widened
as France declared war on Britain on 17 June. Spain declared war on 21
June 1779, and Britain declared war on Holland on 20 December 1780.
British command of the seas was further challenged by the Armed
Neutrality of the North formed by Russia, Sweden and Denmark in 1780.
In 1781 General Cornwallis was besieged at Yorktown by Washington
and Rochambeau on land and by the French fleet under de Grasse, and
forced to surrender on 19 October. This ended any chance of a British
suppression of the rebellion, but command of the seas was restored by
Admiral Rodney's victory over de Grasse at the battle of the Saints in the
West Indies on 12 April 1782. Peace was concluded and the
independence of the United States recognised by the treaty of Versailles
signed on 3 September 1783.

Expeditions and naval operations 1793–1814

1793	France, already at war with Austria, Prussia and Piedmont, declared war on Britain and Holland on 1 February, and on Spain on 7 March. In August Admiral Hood occupied Toulon after a royalist uprising, but French successes on land forced him to evacuate on 19 December. In December a British expedition arrived too late to aid royalist rebels in La Vendée.
1793–5	Campaign in the Low Countries: the Duke of York was sent to the Low Countries at the head of a force of British, Dutch, Hanoverians and Hessians. He was defeated at Hondschoote in September 1793 and Tourcoing in May 1794. In July 1794 the French reoccupied Brussels and the Austrians retreated towards the Rhine, while the British fell back into Holland. The British forces were evacuated from Bremen in April 1795.
1793–8	Campaign in the West Indies: in November 1793, 7,000 men under Grey sailed with a squadron under Jervis to the West Indies. By 1796 military action, particularly involving slave revolts, and disease, had resulted in 40,000 dead and 40,000 incapacitated. The campaign was brought to a close by the evacuation of San Domingo in October 1798.
1794	Howe defeated the French fleet off Ushant (1 June), but a vital French food convoy was able to reach Brest safely. British forces occupied Corsica (August).
1795	In June *emigrés* landed from British ships at Quiberon Bay. They were defeated by Hoche, 16–20 July, and a small British force was evacuated, 20–21 July. In November an expedition of 2,500 men sailed to La Vendée but did not disembark.

1797	Jervis defeated Spanish fleet at Cape St Vincent, 14 February. Duncan defeated Dutch fleet at Camperdown, 11 October.
1798	In June rebels in Ireland were defeated at Vinegar Hill. A force of 1,200 French under General Humbert landed in Killala Bay on 22 August, but Cornwallis forced their surrender on 8 September. Nelson destroyed the French fleet at the battle of the Nile, 1 August. In November the British captured Minorca.
1798–1800	British forces supported uprising by Maltese against the French who surrendered on 5 September 1800.
1799	Expedition to Holland: on 27 August British troops under Abercromby landed at the Helder; the Dutch navy in the Texel surrendered. Russo-British forces, now under the Duke of York, planned to advance on Amsterdam, but were checked in the battle of Bergen-op-Zoom on 19 September. Further attacks on 2 October and 6 October made little progress. By the Convention of Alkmaar on 18 October the allies agreed to evacuate Holland.
1801	Campaign against the French in Egypt: on 8 March British troops under Abercromby landed at Aboukir Bay. An attack on Alexandria failed on 13 March, but a French counter-attack was beaten off on 21 March, though Abercromby was fatally wounded. His successor, General Hutchinson, advanced on Cairo, which the French agreed to evacuate in June. The French forces remaining in Alexandria surrendered on 31 August. Nelson, second-in-command to Sir Hyde Parker, defeated the Danes in the battle of Copenhagen, 2 April.
1805	Nelson defeated Franco-Spanish fleet in the battle of Trafalgar, 21 October, but was himself fatally wounded.
1806	In June an expedition of 6,000 men under General Sir David Baird captured the Cape of Good Hope from the Dutch.
1806–7	Expeditions to South America: in June 1806, Home Popham, who had escorted Baird to Cape Town, took 1,500 men under Beresford to Buenos Aires. Beresford was forced to surrender by a local uprising in August 1806. In 1807 General Whitelocke led a second expedition to South America. He occupied Montevideo, but his attack on Buenos Aires failed and he was forced to evacuate the country.
1807	Danish fleet captured in the second battle of Copenhagen, 2–7 September.
1809	Walcheren expedition: in July 40,000 men under Chatham sailed for the Scheldt estuary to take Antwerp. They were delayed by the resistance of Flushing and suffered heavy losses when fever broke out. Half the force returned to England in September; the rest remained to garrison Walcheren, but were evacuated in December.
1810	Mauritius and Réunion captured.

1811   Java captured.

1813   Graham sent to Holland with 6,000 men to support an
              Orangeist revolt. But the Prussians failed to take part in an
              intended attack on Antwerp, and after an unsuccessful attack
              on Bergen-op-Zoom, Graham's force remained largely
              inactive until the end of the war.

Peninsular War 1808–14

The French conquest of Portugal in 1807 was followed by the invasion of
Spain in March 1808 and the imposition of Napoleon's brother, Joseph,
as King of Spain. To encourage resistance to the French, a British army
under Sir Arthur Wellesley reached Lisbon on 1 August 1808. The French
were defeated at Roliça (17 August) and Vimeiro (21 August), but were
allowed to evacuate Portugal by the Convention of Cintra (30 August). Sir
John Moore took command in Portugal and advanced into Spain. He was
forced to retreat before Napoleon and was killed evacuating his army
from Corunna on 16 January 1809. In April 1809 Wellesley landed with a
British army at Lisbon and defeated the French at Talavera on 28 July, for
which he was created Viscount Wellington. When the French invaded
Portugal in 1810, Wellington took shelter behind the fortified lines of the
Torres Vedras, and in 1811 Masséna was forced to retreat. In 1812
Wellington defeated the French at Salamanca (22 July) and entered
Madrid. In 1813 he won another victory at Victoria (21 June) and invaded
southern France. Before hostilities were suspended in 1814, Wellington
defeated Soult at Orthez (27 February) and Toulouse (10 April).

War of 1812

Grievances, arising from British conduct of the maritime war against the
French, led the United States to declare war on Britain on 19 June 1812.
An American plan for a threefold attack on Canada failed, and a British
force under General Brock forced the surrender of Detroit on 16 August
1812. In April 1813 the Americans captured and burnt Toronto, and in
September defeated the British in the battle of Lake Erie and recaptured
Detroit. In August 1814 a force of 4,000 British veterans landed in
Chesapeake Bay, defeated the Americans at Bladensburg and burnt parts
of Washington. A peace treaty was signed at Ghent in Belgium on 24
December 1812, largely restoring the pre-war situation. Before news of
the peace reached America, General Pakenham was killed on 8 January
1815 leading an unsuccessful British attack on New Orleans.

Waterloo Campaign 1815

Following Wellington's advance from Spain, and allied attacks on Paris,
the capital fell on 30 March 1814 and Napoleon went into exile. Napoleon
returned to France from Elba on 1 March 1815 and resumed power.
Faced by the renewal of the victorious coalition against him, he planned
to take the allied armies in Belgium by surprise. On 16 June Napoleon
attacked Blücher's Prussians at Ligny, while engaging the Anglo-Dutch
Army at Quatre Bras. Both allied armies were able to conduct orderly

retreats. On 17 June Napoleon sent Grouchy to prevent Blücher joining Wellington, but Blücher had retreated towards Wavre and not Liège as he imagined. Thus, Grouchy was absent when the battle of Waterloo was fought on 18 June. French attacks failed to drive Wellington from his defensive positions, and the arrival of Blücher in the late afternoon ensured the total defeat of the French. Napoleon abdicated on 22 June.

Chronology of conflicts in India 1744–1818

First Carnatic War
25 July 1746, Count de la Bourdonnais defeated British fleet at Negapatam, and with Dupleix, the French governor-general, captured Madras in September.   1746–8, unsuccessful attempts by the French to capture Fort St George and Pondicherry from the British.
18 October 1748, treaty of Aix-la-Chapelle. Madras returned to Britain, in exchange for Louisburg.

1749–54 Second Carnatic War
Conflict between British and French East India Companies supporting rival native forces. In 1751 Robert Clive captured Arcot, capital of the pro-French Nawab of the Carnatic, Chanda Sahib, who was besieging the English garrison at Trichinopoly. Clive successfully withstood a siege of over 50 days.   1754, Dupleix recalled to France.

1756 20 June, Surajah Dowlah, Nawab of Bengal, captured Calcutta and imprisoned 146 Europeans in the 'Black Hole' where 123 died.

1757 2 January, Robert Clive and Admiral Watson recaptured Calcutta. 23 June, Clive routed Surajah Dowlah at Plassey.

1758 French force under Comte de Lally-Tollendal reached Pondicherry, and captured Fort St David in June.

1758 December 1758–February 1759, Lally unsuccessfully besieged Madras.

1760 22 January, Eyre Coote defeated Lally at Wandewash.

1761 15 January, Lally's surrender at Pondicherry marked the end of the French bid for power in India.

1764 23 October, mutiny in Bengal army crushed by Major Munro at Buxar.

1766–9 First Mysore War
Ended when Hyder Ali concluded a defensive alliance with East India Company.

1779–82 First Maratha War
Gwalior stormed by Captain Popham in 1780. Peace by the treaty of Salbai.

1780–4 Second Mysore War
1780, Hyder Ali invaded the Carnatic, but was defeated by Coote at Porto Novo in June, Pollilur in August and Sholingarh in September.
August 1782, French under Admiral de Suffren captured Trincomalee, and sent aid to Hyder Ali.   1784, Ali's son, Tippoo Sahib, made peace by the treaty of Mangaloore.

1789–92 Third Mysore War
Tippoo Sahib attacked the ruler of Travancore, an ally of Britain.
Cornwallis invaded Mysore, stormed the capital Bangalore and besieged
Tippoo in Seringapatam. Tippoo made peace in March 1792.
1795–6 Ceylon captured from the Dutch.

1799 Fourth Mysore War
After a small French force had landed in Mysore, Wellesley declared war,
and Tippoo Sahib was killed when Seringapatam was stormed in May
1799.

1803–05 Second Maratha War
In 1803 Arthur Wellesley defeated Sindhia of Gwalior at Assaye, 23
September, and Argaum, 29 November. General Lake stormed Aligarh, 4
September, and defeated the Marathas at Delhi, 16 September, and
Laswari, 1 November. Sindhia submitted 20 December. Further uprisings
by Marathas suppressed, 1804–5.
1814 In November Britain invaded Nepal. The Gurkhas were forced to
     make peace in 1816.

1817 Third Maratha War
Attacks by Marathas and bands of marauding robbers called Pindaris.
On 21 December 1817 Sir Thomas Hyslop crushed the army of Maratha
leader, Holkar, at Mahidput.   In 1818, Lord Rawdon-Hastings hunted
down the Pindaris; the ruler of the Marathas, the Peshwa, surrendered
on 2 June.

Wars with Burma 1824–6, 1852–3, 1885–92

The threat of a Burmese invasion of India led to a British declaration of
war on 5 March 1824. An expedition under Sir Archibald Campbell
imposed the treaty of Yandabo on 24 February 1826. An appeal for
protection by British merchants at Rangoon in 1852 resulted in a further
expedition which captured Rangoon. South Burma was annexed in
December 1852. In 1885, as a result of King Thibaw's confiscation of the
property of the Bombay-Burma Company, a British amphibious force
invaded Burma and on 1 January 1886 it was annexed as a province of
the Indian Empire. Guerrilla warfare continued until 1892.

Battle of Navarino 1827

By the treaty of London signed on 6 July 1827 France, Russia and
England threatened action in support of the Greeks who were fighting for
their independence from the Ottoman Empire, unless the Turks agreed to
an armistice. On 8 September 1827 the Egyptian fleet landed fresh troops
at Navarino to suppress the Greek rebellion. On 20 October the
Egyptian–Turkish fleet was destroyed by the action of British, French and
Russian squadrons. Russia subsequently declared war on Turkey on 26
April 1828, and Greek independence was recognised by the treaty of
London of 7 May 1832.

Wars with China 1839–42, 1856–60

The 'Opium War' of 1839–42 originated in drastic action taken by the Chinese against British merchants in an attempt to curb the opium trade. An expedition under Sir Hugh Gough captured Canton on 24 May 1841. Shanghai was captured on 19 June 1842, and peace was concluded by the treaty of Nanking on 29 August 1842. Chinese seizure of the British ship, the *Arrow*, at Canton in October 1856 led to renewed fighting. Canton was taken and the Taku forts near Tientsin were silenced. The treaty of Tientsin was signed on 26 June 1858. However, in 1859 a naval force under Admiral James Hope was repulsed at the Taku forts on the way to obtain ratification of the treaty. A British and French expedition led by Sir Hope Grant captured the Taku forts and occupied Peking on 9 October 1860. The treaty of Peking, ending the war, was signed on 24 October 1860.

Afghan wars 1839–42, 1878–81

Fears regarding the threat to India posed by Russian activity in Afghanistan led to a British invasion which captured Kabul on 7 August 1839. Following an uprising, General Elphinstone's force was massacred at Gardamak on 13 January 1842, while attempting to withdraw. Parts of Kabul were destroyed by a punitive expedition in September 1842, but the country was then evacuated. A further British invasion was mounted in 1878. A British force was defeated at Maiwand on 27 July 1880, but Sir Frederick Roberts relieved Kandahar on 1 September. A pro-British government was established and the evacuation of Afghanistan completed by April 1881.

Conquest of Sind (India), 1843

Following friction between the rulers of Sind and the British, the British Residency in the capital, Hyderabad, was attacked. Sir Charles Napier marched to its relief, defeated the enemy at Miari on 17 February 1843 and proceeded to conquer the territory. He summed up his campaign in a one-word message to the governor-general: 'Peccavi' ('I have sinned').

Maori Wars 1843–8, 1860–70

The Maoris' resentment of encroachment by British settlers in New Zealand led to periods of guerrilla warfare. The uprisings were suppressed by a combination of the local militia, helped by troops from Britain and Australia, and diplomacy.

Sikh Wars, 1845–6, 1848–9

On 11 December 1845 a Sikh army crossed the Sutlej into British Indian territory. Sir Hugh Gough beat off an attack at Mudki on 18 December, and then defeated the Sikhs at the battle of Ferozeshah on 21–22 December. Further defeats were inflicted by the British at Aliwal (29 January 1846) and Sobraon (10 February 1846), and by the treaty of

Lahore, signed on 11 March 1846, the Punjab became a British protectorate. A mutiny at Multan on 20 April 1848 sparked off a Sikh uprising. Gough invaded the Punjab and fought inconclusive battles at Ramnagar (22 November 1848) and Chilianwala (13 January 1849), before finally defeating the Sikhs at Gujerat on 21 February 1849. The Punjab was subsequently annexed.

Crimean War 1854–5

Turkey declared war on Russia on 23 September 1853. The Turkish fleet was destroyed at Sinope on 30 November 1853, and a Franco-British fleet entered the Black Sea to protect the Turkish coast. France and Britain declared war on Russia on 28 March 1854. In September 1854 an allied force landed on the Crimean Peninsula and besieged Sebastopol. Major battles fought were Alma (20 September), Balaclava (25 October) and Inkerman (5 November). The French capture of the Malakoff strongpoint on 8 September 1855 led to the Russian evacuation of Sebastopol. The Russians accepted a preliminary peace on 1 February 1856 and the treaty of Paris was signed in March 1856. British losses were 4,600 killed and 13,000 wounded; a further 17,500 died of disease.

Persian War 1856–7

On 1 November 1856 Britain declared war on Persia, which had occupied Herat in Afghanistan. Sir James Outram led an invasion of Persia, and by a peace treaty signed in March 1857 the Shah agreed to evacuate Afghanistan.

Indian Mutiny 1857–8

The mutiny broke out at Meerut on 10 May 1857. From there the mutineers marched on Delhi and seized the city. The mutiny spread rapidly and the British were besieged at Cawnpore and Lucknow. At Cawnpore they surrendered on 26 June to Nana Sahib, who then massacred his prisoners. In September 1857 the British recaptured Delhi. Sir Henry Havelock reached Lucknow, but was himself besieged there until relieved in November by Sir Colin Campbell, who evacuated the defenders. Lucknow was finally recaptured in March 1858. In Central India Sir Hugh Rose defeated Tantia Topi at Gwalior on 19 June 1858. Peace was proclaimed on 8 July 1858.

Abyssinian War 1867–8

An expedition of British and Indian troops led by Sir Robert Napier was sent to rescue diplomats and Europeans held by King Theodore of Abyssinia in his capital, Magdala. Theodore's army was defeated at Arogee and he committed suicide on 10 April 1868. Magdala was stormed and the hostages rescued on 13 April.

Ashanti campaign 1873–4

After initial fighting, Sir Garnet Wolseley, the administrator and commander-in-chief on the Gold Coast, mounted an expedition against Kumasi, the capital of the Ashanti, who were threatening British settlements. Kumasi fell in February 1874 and peace was imposed. Further expeditions took place against the Ashanti in 1896 and 1900, the latter leading to the annexation of the territory.

Zulu War 1878–9

The Zulus under Chief Cetewayo ignored a British demand on 11 December 1878 for the establishment of a British protectorate over Zululand. Lord Chelmsford invaded Zululand on 11 January 1879, but part of his army was annihilated at Isandhlwana on 22 January. The defence of Rorke's Drift during the following night saved Natal from being overrun. After the arrival of reinforcements, Chelmsford defeated Cetewayo in the battle of Ulundi on 4 July 1879.

First South African War 1880–1

Great Britain annexed the Transvaal Boer Republic in 1877. In December 1880 the Boers proclaimed their independence. General Sir George Colley, leading British troops from Natal, was defeated and killed at Majuba Hill on 27 February 1881. The British government decided on withdrawal. An armistice was signed on 6 March 1881, and peace made by the Convention of Pretoria on 5 April 1881. The Boers were granted their independence under British suzerainty.

Egyptian War 1882

A nationalist uprising led by Colonel Arabi against the growth of European influence in Egypt resulted in June 1882 in the deaths of many Europeans in riots in Alexandria. As a result British forces bombarded and occupied Alexandria and Colonel Arabi's revolt was crushed at the battle of Tel-el-Kebir on 13 September 1882.

The Sudan 1884–5, 1896–9

In October 1883 an Egyptian army led by Colonel Hicks was defeated at El Obeid by the Sudanese forces of the Mahdi. In January 1884 General Gordon was sent to Khartoum to bring back the Egyptian garrison, but he remained and was cut off. A relief expedition under Sir Garnet Wolseley arrived on 28 January 1885, two days after Khartoum had fallen and Gordon killed. The British government undertook the reconquest of the Sudan in 1896. The Sudanese were defeated on 2 September 1898 at the battle of Omdurman, and on 19 January 1899 an Anglo-Egyptian condominium was established over the Sudan.

Second South African War 1899–1902

The war began in October 1899 following the rejection of a Boer ultimatum to the British government to disband military preparations. In the first phase of the war British troops were defeated and forced on the defensive; Mafeking, Kimberley and Ladysmith were besieged. In February 1900 the British counter-offensive relieved Kimberley and Ladysmith. After further fighting, Mafeking was relieved in May and the Boer capital, Pretoria, was captured on 5 June 1900. Eighteen months of guerrilla warfare then followed before peace was brought about by the treaty of Vereeniging, signed on 31 May 1902. British casualties were 5,774 killed and 22,829 wounded; the Boers lost an estimated 4,000 killed.

Expedition to Tibet 1903–4

A British expedition led by Colonel Younghusband invaded Tibet to force the Dalai Lama to enter into negotiations about the frontier with India. After fierce fighting, Younghusband reached Lhasa on 3 August 1904, and a treaty was signed on 7 September.

First World War 1914–18

Britain declared war on Germany on 4 August 1914 after the German invasion of Belgium. Pre-war military planning had committed the British Expeditionary Force to fighting alongside the French. The Germans, advancing according to the Schlieffen Plan, were halted at the battle of the Marne in September 1914. The defensive power of modern weapons led to the development of trench warfare on the Western Front. Despite the use of poison gas and tanks, the major British attacks on the Somme (1916) and at Ypres (1917) failed to achieve a breakthrough. The German offensive in March 1918 was initially successful, but the allies were able to counter-attack as German morale weakened. The Armistice was signed on 11 November 1918. The Western Front was the crucial theatre in the First World War, and British campaigns against the Turks at Gallipoli in 1915 and in the Middle East were very much sideshows. At sea the greatest naval battle of the war was fought at Jutland (31 May to 1 June 1916) between the British and German fleets. More important as regards the final outcome of the war was the defeat of the German U-boats (which had brought Britain close to starvation in 1917) by the adoption of the convoy system. Casualties suffered by the British Empire in the conflict were 908,000 killed and 2,090,000 wounded.

Anglo-Irish conflict 1916–21

Rebellion broke out in Dublin on Easter Monday, 24 April 1916. The rebellion was suppressed by 1 May, and Sir Roger Casement and leaders of the risings were tried and executed. Open warfare began again in 1919, and atrocities by the Irish Republican Army were matched by those committed by a special force brought in by the British, the Black and Tans. Peace was formally established by a treaty recognising the dominion status of the Irish Free State signed on 6 December 1921.

British intervention in Russia 1918–19

In 1918 small expeditions composed of British, French and American troops seized Murmansk and occupied Archangel, in order to aid the White Russian forces against the Bolsheviks. Sporadic operations were conducted for over a year until the final evacuation of allied troops in September 1919.

Amritsar 'massacre' 1919

Fears of a revolt in the Punjab led Brigadier-General Dyer, commander of the garrison at Amritsar, to order his men to open fire on an unarmed mob which had refused to disperse. Three hundred and seventy-nine Indians were killed and 1,208 wounded. A commission of enquiry heavily censured Dyer and the shootings embittered Anglo-Indian relations.

Third Afghan War 1919

In May 1919 Amir Amanullah declared a holy war (Jihad) against Britain, crossed the border and occupied Bagh. While Jalalabad and Kabul were bombarded by the RAF, a British expedition drove the Afghans out of Bagh and forced the Khyber Pass into Afghanistan. An armistice was agreed on 31 May and the treaty of Rawalpindi was signed on 8 August.

Second World War 1939–45

German forces invaded Poland on 1 September 1939, which led to declarations of war by Britain and France on 3 September. The Germans invaded the Low Countries on 10 May 1940, and France was compelled to sign an armistice on 22 June. The British army was evacuated from Dunkirk, while in the 'Battle of Britain' the German Luftwaffe failed to defeat the RAF and establish air superiority which would have made an attempted invasion of Britain possible. Italy declared war on 10 June 1940, and Britain attacked Italian forces in North Africa. Allied forces eventually drove the Germans and Italians out of North Africa, captured Sicily and invaded the Italian mainland, forcing the Italians to make a separate peace on 3 September 1943. The British and American air forces conducted a costly strategic bombing offensive against Germany in 1942 and 1943, but it was mainly German losses in Russia which paved the way for the success of the allied invasion of Europe, launched on D-Day, 6 June 1944. The allies linked up with the Russians on the Elbe on 28 April 1945 and the Germans accepted unconditional surrender terms on 7 May. In the Far East Japan attacked the American base at Pearl Harbor on 7 December 1941, and within six months the Japanese were masters of South-East Asia and Burma. The allied counter-offensive culminated in the dropping of the first atomic bombs on Hiroshima and Nagasaki in August 1945. The Japanese surrendered on 14 August 1945. Casualties suffered by the British Empire in the conflict were 486,000 killed and 590,000 wounded.

Palestine 1945–8

A period of guerrilla warfare was waged by Jewish Zionists against British mandate forces and the Arab population, to achieve an independent Jewish nation. On 22 July 1946 the King David Hotel in Jerusalem, housing the British headquarters, was blown up, with the loss of 91 lives. With the proclamation of the independence of Israel on 14 May 1948, Britain surrendered her League of Nations mandate over Palestine and withdrew her armed forces.

Malayan emergency 1948–60

The Federation of Malaya was proclaimed on 1 February 1948. Communist guerrilla activity began, and on 16 June a state of emergency was declared. In April 1950 General Sir Harold Briggs was appointed to coordinate anti-Communist operations by Commonwealth forces. He inaugurated the Briggs Plan for resettling Chinese squatters in new villages to cut them off from the guerrillas. After the murder of the British high commissioner, Sir Henry Gurney, on 6 October 1951, General Sir Gerald Templer was appointed high commissioner and director of military operations on 15 January 1952, and on 7 February a new offensive was launched. On 8 February 1954 British authorities announced that the Communist Party's high command in Malaya had withdrawn to Sumatra. The emergency was officially ended on 31 July 1960.

Korean War 1950–3

The invasion of South Korea by North Korea on 25 June 1950 led to intervention by United Nations forces, following an emergency session of the Security Council. The advance of United Nations forces into North Korea on 1 October 1950 led to the entry of the Chinese into the war on 25 November on the side of the North. An armistice was signed at Panmunjon on 27 July 1953. Casualties suffered by the British contribution to the United Nations force were 686 killed, 2,498 wounded and 1,102 missing.

Cyprus emergency 1952–9

Agitation for union with Greece ('enosis') by the Greek population of Cyprus led to terrorism and guerrilla warfare against British forces and the Turkish minority by EOKA, the militant wing of the enosis movement. It was led by Colonel Grivas, and supported by Archbishop Makarios, who was deported to the Seychelles in March 1956. A cease-fire came into effect on 13 March 1959, prior to the establishment of the independent republic of Cyprus on 16 August 1960.

Mau Mau revolt 1952–60

Violence by the Mau Mau, an African secret society in Kenya, led to a British declaration of a state of emergency on 20 October 1952. Leading Kikuyu nationalists were arrested and Jomo Kenyatta was given a seven-year prison sentence in October 1953. A separate East African command consisting of Kenya, Uganda and Tanganyika was set up under General Sir George Erskine. In campaigns in the first half of 1955 some 4,000 terrorists in the Mount Kenya and Aberdare regions were dispersed. Britain began to reduce her forces in September 1955; the state of emergency in Kenya ended on 12 January 1960.

Suez 1956

Following Egyptian nationalisation of the Suez Canal on 26 July 1956, Israel invaded Sinai on 29 October. When Egypt rejected a cease-fire ultimatum by France and Britain, their air forces began to attack Egyptian air bases on 31 October. On 5 November Franco-British forces invaded the Canal Zone, capturing Port Said. Hostilities ended at midnight on 6–7 November, following a cease-fire call by the United Nations. Allied losses were 33 killed and 129 wounded.

'Confrontation' between Indonesia and Malaysia 1963–6

When the Federation of Malaysia was established on 16 September 1963, President Sukarno of Indonesia announced a policy of 'confrontation', on the grounds that it was 'neo-colonialist'. There followed a campaign of propaganda, sabotage and guerrilla raids into Sarawak and Sabah. An agreement ending 'confrontation' was signed in Bangkok on 1 June 1966 (ratified 11 August). In the conflict Commonwealth forces lost 114 killed and 181 wounded, and the Indonesians 590 killed, 222 wounded and 771 captured.

Aden 1964–7

On 18 January 1963 Aden acceded to the South Arabian Federation. British troops were involved in frontier fighting with the Yemen, and in suppressing internal disorders in Aden. A large-scale security operation was launched in January 1964 in the Radfan region, north of Aden. On 26 November 1967 the People's Republic of South Yemen was proclaimed, and the British military withdrawal from Aden was completed on 29 November. In the period 1964–7 British security forces lost 57 killed and 651 wounded in Aden.

Northern Ireland 1969–80

As a result of a request by the government of Northern Ireland, facing severe rioting, British troops moved into Londonderry on 14 August 1969 and into Belfast on 15 August. The first British soldier was killed by a sniper in Belfast on 6 February 1971. Internment without trial was introduced on 9 August 1971; it was ended on 7 December 1975. Direct rule from London was imposed from 30 March 1972. At the peak in August 1972 there were 21,500 British soldiers in Northern Ireland. Sporadic outbreaks of terrorism by the IRA occur, while the search for a political solution to the problems of Northern Ireland continues.

Major military legislation and administrative reforms

1757   Militia Act creates county-based force raised by ballot for use in emergencies under the command of lord-lieutenants and responsible to the home secretary.

1792   Barrack-building programme begun to provide accommodation for troops in ports and major manufacturing areas.

1794   First secretary for state for war appointed. Volunteer regiments formed to resist a French invasion.

1797   In aftermath of the naval mutinies, Mutiny Act makes it treasonable to incite disaffection among the armed forces. Pay rises awarded to both army and navy.

1832   All naval business consolidated under the Board of Admiralty.

1847   Life service in the army abolished; replaced by a minimum term of 10 years.

1852   Militia Act reorganises militia and places it under the control of the secretary at war.

1853   Continuous Service Act re-organises naval service with fixed terms of enlistment.

1854–5   Secretary of state for war takes overall control of the armed forces, though discipline and command of the army reserved to the commander-in-chief at the Horse Guards. Board of Ordnance abolished and duties of secretary at war combined with secretary of state for war.

1858   Creation of the Indian Army. Army of the East India Company transferred to the control of the Crown.

1856   Staff college set up at Sandhurst.

1859   Volunteer force created to protect against threat of French invasion.

1862   Fixed terms of enlistment made compulsory in the navy.

1867   Army of Reserve Act plans formation of a trained reserve of 80,000 men.

1868   Edward Cardwell becomes secretary for war and begins period of reform.

1870   War Office Act reorganises War Office, incorporating the Horse Guards. Army Enlistment Act fixes terms of enlistment at 12 years, part on active service, part with the reserve.

1871   Purchase of commissions abolished.   Flogging suspended in the navy in peacetime.

1872   Cardwell reorganises regimental structure on basis of linked battalions, one to serve abroad, one to remain at home. Regiments to have local attachment for recruiting.

1879   Flogging in navy suspended in wartime.

1881   Flogging abolished in the army.   Regular and militia battalions of the army amalgamated into territorial regiments with local designation and depot.

1902   Committee of Imperial Defence created.

1904   Office of commander-in-chief abolished; Army Council established and General Staff created.

1906   Richard Haldane becomes secretary for war and begins series of 'Haldane reforms'.

1907   British Expeditionary Force created for commitment to the Continent in the event of European war.   Territorial Reserve Forces Act abolishes militia and volunteers and replaces them with Territorial regiments organised by county associations.

1914–15   Kitchener's 'New Army' raised from volunteers.

1916   Conscription introduced by Military Service Acts.

1918   Royal Air Force formed from British Royal Flying Corps. Air Board, later Air Ministry, established.

1923   Royal Tank Corps formed.

1931   Pay cuts in the armed forces provoke mutiny among naval units at Invergordon.

1939   Territorial Army doubled from 13 to 26 divisions. Compulsory Training Act calls reservists up for six months' training. Conscription introduced some months before Second World War (May).

1940   'Local Defence Volunteers' or 'Home Guard' formed for defence against invasion.

1946   Ministry of Defence created.

1947   National Service Act provides for continuation of compulsory military service; at first for 12 months; extended to two years in 1950.

1948   Britain signs Brussels treaty with France and Benelux countries, committing herself to military assistance in the event of an attack on Europe; confirmed in NATO treaty of 1949. British army of the Rhine henceforth to be part of the NATO forces in Germany.

1957   Defence White Paper envisages reduction in conventional armed forces and greater reliance upon nuclear deterrence and a strategic reserve stationed in the United Kingdom.

1958–61   Large-scale amalgamation of existing regiments.

1960   National Service abolished.

1963   War Office, Admiralty and Air Ministry brought under the control of the Ministry of Defence. Defence Council set up under the secretary of state to exercise the powers previously wielded by each service.

1966   Territorial Army greatly reduced and replaced by smaller Territorial and Army Volunteer Reserve (TAVR).

1967   Further amalgamations of regiments and brigades.

1968   Announcement of withdrawal of British forces from East of Suez
by 1971

Strengths of army, navy and air force 1714–1979

	Army	Navy	Air force
1714	16,347	10,000	–
1745	74,187	n.a	–
1756	49,749	50,000	–
1761	67,776	88,355	–
1762	17,536	89,061	–
1777	90,734	45,000	–
1783	54,678	110,000	–
1793	17,013	45,000	–
1802	84,445	94,461	–
1815	204,386	85,384	–
1820	92,586	23,000	–
1830	88,848	29,000	–
1850	99,128	39,000	–
1855	223,224	70,000	–
1870	113,221	61,000	–
1880	131,859	58,800	–
1890	153,483	68,800	–
1900	430,000	114,880	–
1914*	733,514	147,667	–
1918†	3,759,500	n.a	290,743
1920	435,000	133,000	28,000
1930	333,000	97,000	33,000
1939	1,128,000	214,000	215,000
1945	3,007,300	852,600	1,124,400
1950	377,600	140,000	202,000
1960	264,300	97,800	163,500

	Army	Navy	Air force
1970	173,000	87,000	113,000
1979	163,681	72,900	86,310

* January   ‡December   † November   §January

(*Source*: C. Cook and B. Keith, *British Historical Facts 1830–1900*, London, Macmillan, 1975, p. 185;. *Parliamentary Papers*, 1868–69, XXXV, pp. 693–5)

222

Treaties

Key British defence treaties and alliances

1717   Triple Alliance between Britain, France and The Netherlands signed at the Hague to oppose Philip V's ambitions in France and Italy, 4 January. This became the Quadruple Alliance after the accession of Austria on 2 August 1718.

1720   Treaty of the Hague ended the War of the Quadruple Alliance, 17 February.

1725   Treaty of Hanover, 3 September, created defensive league between Britain, France and Prussia to counterbalance alliance between Austria and Spain signed earlier in the year.

1727   Treaty of Paris, 31 May, between Austria and Britain, France and Prussia ended brief conflict. A peace treaty with Spain was signed at the Pardo on 6 March 1728.

1729   Treaty of Seville for peace and friendship between Britain, France and Spain was concluded on 9 November.

1731   Treaty of Vienna between Britain, Spain, The Netherlands and Austria, 22 July. Britain and The Netherlands guaranteed the Pragmatic Sanction in return for which the Emperor suspended the Ostend East India Company.

1741   Treaty of Hanover, 24 June: Britain offered Maria Theresa support against Prussia and France.   George II concluded treaty with France for the neutrality of Hanover, 7 September.

1745   Quadruple Alliance against Prussia signed at Warsaw by Austria, England, The Netherlands and Saxony, 8 January.   Convention of Hanover between Britain and Prussia, 26 August.

1748   Treaty of Aix-la-Chapelle ending War of the Austrian Succession signed on 18 October by Britain, France and The Netherlands (also accepted by Spain, Austria, Madeira, Genoa and Sardinia by December). Maria Theresa recognised, but Silesia ceded to Prussia. Succession of House of Hanover in its German states and Great Britain confirmed.

1750   Treaty of alliance with Austria and Bavaria signed at Hanover, 22 August.   Treaty of alliance with Austria and Russia signed at St Petersburg, 30 October.

1755   Treaty with Russia for defence of Hanover, 30 September.

1756   Treaty of London with Prussia to oppose attacks in Germany, 16 January.

1758   Subsidy treaty with Prussia, 11 April.

1762 Preliminary articles of peace signed by Britain, France and Spain, 3 November.

1763 Peace of Paris, 10 February between France, Spain and Britain ended Seven Years War. France ceded to England Canada, Cape Breton Island, Granada and Senegal; the Mississippi recognised as the frontier between Louisiana and the British colonies. England restored to France Goree in Africa, and all conquests in India. Spain ceded Florida to England, but received back all conquests in Cuba.

1782 Provisional articles of peace signed by Britain and the United States at Paris, 30 November.

1783 Preliminaries of peace signed with France and Spain, 20 January.   Treaty of Versailles signed by Britain, France, Spain and the United States, 3 September. Recognition of the independence of the United States and establishment of its boundaries. United States' fishing rights established on Grand Bank, Newfoundland coast, and in the Gulf of St Lawrence. Navigation of the Mississippi to be open to both Great Britain and the United States. Great Britain ceded Tobago and Senegal to France and Florida to Spain.

1784 Treaty of peace and friendship with The Netherlands signed in Paris, 20 May.

1786 Treaty of commerce and navigation with France 26 September.

1788 Defensive alliance with The Netherlands to maintain the peace of Europe, 15 April.   Defensive alliance with Prussia to maintain the peace of Europe, 13 August.

1790 Alliance with Prussia and The Netherlands, 9 January. Convention with The Netherlands, Empire and Prussia concerning the Austrian Netherlands, 10 December.

1793 Convention with Russia for concerted action against France, 25 March.   Treaty of alliance with Sardinia against France, 25 April.   Convention with Spain against France, 25 May.   Convention with Sicily against France, 12 July.   Convention with Prussia against France, 14 July.   Convention with the Emperor against France, 30 August.   Treaty with Portugal against France, 26 September.

1794 Agreement with Spain against France, 11 January.   Subsidy treaty between Britain and The Netherlands, and Prussia, 19 April.

1795 Defensive alliance with Russia, 18 February.   Loan convention with the Emperor, 4 May.   Defensive alliance with the Emperor, 20 May.

1796 Loan convention with the Emperor, 16 May.

1798 Treaty of alliance against France with the King of the Two Sicilies, 1 December.   Provisional treaty with Russia to act against France, 29 December.

1799   Treaty of alliance with Turkey against France, 5
        January.   Convention with Russia against France, 22 June.

1800   Subsidy treaty with Bavaria, 16 March.   Convention with the
        Emperor, 20 June.   Preliminary convention with Denmark, 29
        August.

1801   Convention with Russia, 17 June (accessions: Denmark, 23
        October 1801, Sweden, 30 March 1802); grants British right to
        search vessels.   Preliminary articles of peace with France, 1
        October.

1802   Treaty of Amiens 27 March: peace with France, Spain and the
        Bavarian Republic. Surrender of all conquests made by England to
        France and her allies except Ceylon and Trinidad. Malta restored
        to the Knights of St John and Minorca to Spain. France
        recognised Ionian Republic and evacuated the Sicilies, the Papal
        States, Portugal and Egypt.

1805   Treaty with Russia, 11 April, for the purpose of restoring the
        balance of power in Europe (accessions: Austria, 9 August;
        Sweden, 3 October).

1807   Convention of friendship and amity with Portugal, 22 October.

1808   Convention of Cintra permits evacuation of defeated French Army
        from Portugal on British ships, 30 August.

1809   Treaty of alliance with Austria against France, 24 April.

1812   Treaties of peace, union and friendship with Russia and Sweden,
        18 July.

1813   Treaty of subsidy and concert with Sweden against France, 3
        March.   Convention with Prussia signed at Reichenbach, 14
        June, to provide subsidies for war with France.   Convention
        with Russia signed at Reichenbach, 27 June, to provide subsidies
        for war with France.   Preliminary treaty of alliance with Austria
        signed at Toplitz, 3 October.

1814   Treaties of union, concert and subsidy signed with Austria,
        Prussia and Russia at Chaumont, 1 March.   Convention for
        suspension of hostilities with France, 23 April.   Treaty of peace
        with France signed at Paris, 30 May. France restricted to her
        boundaries in 1792 and forced to recognise the independence of
        The Netherlands, the German and Italian states and Switzerland.
        England restored all French colonies except Tobago, St Lucia and
        the Ile de France (Mauritius), and also retained Malta, Heligoland
        and the Cape of Good Hope.   Treaty of peace with United
        States signed at Ghent, 24 December.

1815   Treaty of alliance with Austria, Prussia and Russia against
        Napoleon signed at Vienna, 25 March, each power engaging to
        furnish 180,000 men.   Act of the Congress of Vienna signed by
        Britain, Austria, France, Portugal, Prussia, Russia and Sweden, 9
        June.   Treaty of peace with France signed at Paris, 20
        November.

1827   Treaty with France and Russia for pacification of Greece signed at
        London, 6 July.

1830   Protocol signed with France and Russia concerning Greek independence, 3 February.

1831   Protocol of conference regarding the separation of Belgium and the Netherlands signed by Britain, Austria, France, Prussia and Russia, 20 January.

1832   Convention regarding the sovereignty of Greece signed by Britain, France, Russia and Bavaria, 7 May.

1834   Treaty of Quadruple Alliance with France, Spain and Portugal for the pacification of the Iberian Peninsula, 22 April.   Agreement with Russia to respect the integrity and independence of Persia, 5 September.

1839   Treaty between Britain, Austria, France, Prussia, Russia and Belgium regarding Belgium and The Netherlands, 19 April.

1840   Convention between Britain, Austria, Prussia, Russia and Turkey for the pacification of the Levant, 15 July.

1841   Convention between Austria, France, Prussia, Russia and Turkey regarding the Dardanelles, 13 July.

1842   Treaty of Nanking between Britain and China ending the Opium War, 29 August; Hong Kong was ceded to Britain and the five treaty ports were opened to foreign trade.

1846   Treaty with the United States settling the Oregon boundary with Canada, 15 June.

1854   Treaty of alliance with Austria and France, 2 December.

1855   Treaty with France and Sweden and Norway regarding the integrity of the United Kingdoms of Sweden and Norway, 21 November.

1856   Peace of Paris ending the Crimean War signed by Britain, Austria, France, Prussia, Russia, Sardinia and Turkey, 30 March.
       Treaty between Britain, Austria and France guaranteeing the independence and integrity of the Ottoman Empire, 15 April.

1864   Geneva Convention regarding the amelioration of the condition of the wounded in armies in the field, 22 August.

1871   Treaty concerning the navigation of the Black Sea and the Danube between Britain, Austria, France, Germany, Italy, Russia and Turkey, 13 March.   Treaty between Britain and the United States regarding the amicable settlement of disputes, 8 May.

1878   Treaty arising out of the Congress of Berlin signed by Britain, Austria-Hungary, France, Germany, Italy, Russia and Turkey for the settlement of Balkan problems, 13 July.   Agreement between Britain and Turkey regarding British government of Cyprus, 14 August.

1881   Final Act for the settlement of the frontier between Greece and Turkey agreed between Britain, Austria-Hungary, France, Germany, Italy and Russia, 18 September.

1885   General Act of the 15-nation conference at Berlin regarding affairs of Central Africa, 26 February.   Declaration regarding Egyptian finances and the free navigation of the Suez Canal by Britain, Austria-Hungary, France, Germany, Italy and Russia, 17 March.   Agreement between Britain and Germany regarding spheres of action in Africa, 29 April.   Protocol between Britain and Russia regarding the Afghan frontier, 10 September.

1888   Convention respecting the free navigation of the Suez Canal, 29 October.

1889   Final Act of the conference on the affairs of Samoa, 14 June.

1890   Convention with China relating to Sikkim and Tibet, 17 March.   Agreement with Zanzibar placing Zanzibar under the protection of Britain, 14 June.   Agreement between Britain and Germany regarding Zanzibar, Heligoland and spheres of influence in Africa, 1 July.   Declarations exchanged with France respecting territories in Africa, 5 August.

1891   Agreement with France regarding spheres of influence in Africa, 26 June.

1893   Protocol with Germany respecting the delimitation of the Anglo-German boundary in East Equatorial Africa. 8 July.   Arrangements with France fixing boundary between British and French possessions on the Gold Coast, 12 July.   Protocol with France respecting territories in the region of the Upper Mekong, 31 July.   Agreement with Afghanistan respecting frontier between India and Afghanistan, 12 November.   Agreement with Germany respecting boundaries in Africa, 15 November.

1894   Protocol between Britain and Italy regarding spheres of influence in eastern Africa, 5 May.

1897   Convention with France concerning Tunis, 18 September.

1898   Convention with France concerning spheres of influence east and west of the Niger, 14 June.   Convention with Germany regarding Portuguese Africa and Timor, 30 August.

1899   International conventions for the pacific settlement of international disputes; for adapting to maritime warfare the principles of the Geneva Convention; and with respect to the laws and customs of war by land, 29 July.   Conventions with Germany and the United States relating to Samoa, 7 November–2 December.   Exchange of notes with the United States accepting the commercial policy of the 'open door' in China, September–December.

1900   Agreement with Germany, regarding China, 16 October. Both parties agree to restrain foreign territorial aggression in China and maintain the 'open door' for trade.

1902   Anglo-Japanese Alliance signed, 30 January. Concluded initially for five years, both powers recognised the special interests of each other in China, and Japan's interests in Korea. Agreement to remain neutral in the event of war with a third power, or provide assistance in the event of war with two other powers. Renewed in

August 1905 and modified to provide for mutual support in the
event of attack by another power.

1904   Anglo-French *Entente* (*Entente Cordiale*) signed, 8 April. Although
no formal military alliance was arranged, there was an unwritten
understanding of mutual assistance if required. Agreed that Egypt
and Morocco to be under British and French influence
respectively. Disputes over Newfoundland, Madagascar and Siam
settled.

1907   Anglo-Russian *Entente* signed, 31 August. Settled outstanding
differences over Afghanistan, Tibet and Persia, paving the way
for Russia to side with Britain and France against Germany in
1914.

1914   Triple *Entente* signed between Britain, France and Russia, 3
September, agreeing not to make a separate peace with Germany.

1915   Secret Anglo-Russian treaty signed, 12 March. Agreed that
Constantinople and the Straits to go to Russia after the conclusion
of the war. Britain obtained concessions in Persia and Asiatic
Turkey in return.   Secret treaty of London signed, 25 April. Italy
agreed to declare war on the central powers in return for
territorial concessions from the Austro-Hungarian Empire,
including the Tyrol, Istria, and North Dalmatia.

1916   Sykes–Picot agreement between Britain and France reached in
January to partition Turkish Empire in Asia. Syria allotted to
France and Mesopotamia to Britain, with British outlet to the
Mediterranean at Haifa. The agreement was subject to Russian
consent, obtained in May 1916 when Turkish Armenia was
allotted to Russia.

1919   Peace treaty signed between Germany and the allied powers at
Versailles, 28 June. Germany surrendered Alsace-Lorraine to
France; the Rhineland was declared a demilitarised zone to be
occupied by the allies for 15 years; territory was ceded to
Belgium, Denmark, Poland and Czechoslovakia; the German Army
was limited to 100,000 men and denied tanks or aircraft; and
Germany was stripped of all overseas colonies which were placed
under League of Nations control or 'mandate'. The treaty declared
German responsibility for the war and made her liable for the
payment of reparations. The treaty also contained the Covenant of
the League of Nations.   Peace treaty of St Germain with Austria
signed, 10 September. Austrian territory ceded to Italy,
Yugoslavia, Poland, Czechoslovakia and Romania. Hungary
became a separate state; union of Austria and Germany
forbidden; Austrian Army reduced to 30,000 men and the state
made liable for reparations.   Peace treaty of Neuilly with
Bulgaria signed, 27 November. Territory ceded to Greece and
Yugoslavia and army reduced to 20,000 men.

1920   Peace treaty between Hungary and the allied powers, 4 June.
Hungary reduced to two-thirds pre-war size and army limited to
35,000 men.   Treaty of Sèvres with Turkey, 10 August; never
ratified by the Turks.

1921   Articles of agreement for a treaty between Great Britain and
        Ireland signed, 6 December. Irish Free State created with
        Dominion status; six counties of Ulster excluded.   Washington
        Four Power treaty signed, 13 December. Britain, Japan, France
        and United States agree not to strengthen their island
        possessions in the Pacific.

1922   Washington Nine Power treaty signed, 6 February. Naval limits
        agreed; Britain, America and Japan to have battleships in ratio
        5 : 5 : 3; no battleships over 35,000 tons to be constructed and
        no battleships or cruisers built for 10 years.

1923   Treaty of Lausanne with Turkey signed, 23 August. Treaty made
        necessary by Turkey's refusal to accept the treaty of Sèvres.
        Turkey surrendered parts of the Ottoman Empire occupied by
        non-Turks, but retained Constantinople and eastern Thrace in
        Europe. Smyrna ceded by Greece, but all other Aegean Islands
        excepts Imbros and Tenedos ceded by Turkey. Turkey recognised
        annexation of Cyprus by Britain and Dodecanese by Italy.
        Bosporus and Dardanelles demilitarised.

1925   Locarno treaties, 15 October: France, Germany and Belgium
        agreed to the inviolability of the Franco-German and
        Belgo-German frontiers and the existence of the demilitarised
        zone of the Rhineland; this was guaranteed by Britain and Italy.
        Franco-Polish and Franco-Czech treaties of mutual guarantee
        were also signed.

1928   Kellogg–Briand Pact signed by Britain, France, Germany, Italy,
        Japan and the United States renouncing aggressive war, 27
        August.

1930   London Naval treaty signed by Britain, France, Italy, Japan and
        the United States limiting naval armaments, 22 April. Building of
        capital ships suspended for six years and existing numbers
        reduced.

1935   Anglo-German Naval Agreement 18 June, limiting the German
        Navy to 35 per cent of the British, with submarines at 45 per cent
        or equality in the event of danger from Russia.

1936   London Naval treaty, 25 March. Warships limited to 14-inch guns
        and size of aircraft-carriers reduced. Not implemented by Japan,
        Italy or France.   Montreux Convention by which Turkey was
        permitted to refortify the Straits, July.   Non-intervention
        Agreement with regard to Spanish Civil War signed by major
        powers, 7 August. Abrogated by Germany and Italy.

1937   Anglo-Italian 'Gentleman's Agreement' to maintain the status quo
        in the Mediterranean, 2 January.

1938   Munich Agreement: agreement reached by Britain, France, Italy
        and Germany, by which territorial concessions were made to
        Germany, Poland, and Hungary at the expense of Czechoslovakia
        29 September. The rump of Czechoslovakia was to be guaranteed
        against unprovoked aggression, but German control was
        extended to the rest of Czechoslovakia in March 1939.

1939   Franco-British guarantee to Poland, 31 March. Agree to lend
       support if independence threatened.   British guarantee to
       Romania and Greece, 13 April. Offered support in the event of
       external threat.

1941   Atlantic Charter published by Britain and United States pledging
       preservation of world freedom, 14 August.

1942   'United Nations' (principally United States, Great Britain, Soviet
       Union, China) declare will not make separate peace, 1
       January.   Anglo-American Mutual Aid Agreement, 23 February.
       Confirmed 'lend-lease' arrangements between Britain and United
       States and pledged reduction of trade barriers after the
       war.   Anglo-Soviet treaty, 26 May.

1945   Yalta Agreement between leaders of Britain, Russia and the
       United States, 11 February. Agreement to split Germany into
       zones of occupation after the war, try war criminals and set up
       United Nations.   United Nations Charter signed, 26
       June.   Potsdam Agreement, 2 August. Leaders of Russia and
       United States arrange regular meetings to settle problems; trials
       of war criminals arranged; reparations to be taken from war zones
       by occupiers.

1947   Peace treaties with Italy, Bulgaria, Finland, Hungary and Romania,
       10 February.   Treaty of Dunkirk: 50-year alliance with France, 4
       March.   Defence agreement with Burma 29 August; ended by
       Burma, 3 January 1953.   Defence agreement with Ceylon, 11
       November.

1948   Twenty-year mutual defence treaty with Jordan, 15 March; ended
       14 March 1957.   Treaty of Brussels, 17 March, signed by
       Britain, Belgium, France, Luxembourg and the Netherlands for
       collective military aid and economic and social cooperation;
       amended and expanded by Paris agreements of 23 October 1954,
       when the Brussels Treaty Organisation was renamed Western
       European Union.

1949   North Atlantic treaty signed in Washington by Britain, Belgium,
       Canada, Denmark, France, Iceland, Italy, Luxembourg, the
       Netherlands, Norway, Portugal and the United States; joined later
       by Greece, Turkey and the German Federal Republic.

1951   Peace treaty with Japan, 8 September.

1953   Treaty of friendship and alliance with Libya 29 July: in 1967 Libya
       requested the withdrawal of all British forces and liquidation of
       bases.

1954   Geneva Conventions on Indo-China, 20 July. Laos and Cambodia
       become independent; Vietnam divided at 17th
       parallel.   South-East Asia collective defence treaty signed in
       Manila, 8 September, by Britain, Australia, France, New Zealand,
       Pakistan, the Philippines, Thailand and the United States. Pakistan
       left the South-East Asia Treaty Organisation (SEATO) on 7
       November 1973. On 24 September 1975 the SEATO Council
       agreed to disband the organisation, but not to abrogate the treaty.

1955   Britain joined Turkey and Iraq in the Baghdad Pact, 4 April; later joined by Pakistan and Iran. The name was changed to the Central Treaty Organisation (CENTO) on 21 August 1959.   Austrian State treaty signed by Britain, France, Soviet Union, United States and Austria re-establishing Austria as a sovereign, independent and neutral state, 15 May.   Simonstown naval cooperation agreement with South Africa, 4 July; revised January 1967; ended 16 June 1975.

1957   Treaty of defence and mutual assistance with Malaysia, 12 October.

1959   Britain joins European Free Trade Association (EFTA), 20 November.
Britain signs treaty for the demilitarisation of Antarctica, 1 December.

1960   Defence agreement with Nigeria, November; abrogated by joint decision 21 January 1962.

1963   Britain signs the Partial Test Ban treaty prohibiting nuclear tests in the atmosphere, in outer space and under water, 5 August.

1967   Britain signs the Outer Space treaty banning the development of weapons of mass destruction in outer space, 27 January.

1968   Britain signs Non-Proliferation treaty intended to prevent the spread of nuclear weapons, 1 July.

1971   Britain signs Sea-Bed treaty banning the installation of weapons of mass destruction on the ocean floor, 11 February.

1972   Treaty of Accession to European Economic Community and European Atomic Energy Community, 22 January. Effective from 1 January 1973.   Britain signs the Chemical and Bacteriological Convention, prohibiting the development, production and stockpiling of bacteriological and toxic weapons, 10 April.

1975   Helsinki Agreement on Security and Cooperation in Europe, 1 August.

1976   International (UN) Convention on Economic and Social Rights and on Civil and Political Rights, 20 May.

Ireland

Major events in Irish history, 1714–1980

1720   6 Geo 1: formal assertion of British parliament's right to legislate for Ireland.

1722   William Wood, an Englishman, granted a patent to coin money for Ireland.

1724   Swift publishes his *Drapier's Letters*.

1756   Money Bill defeated in Irish parliament because preamble states surplus revenue belongs to the Crown not to the nation.

1778   Widespread volunteer movement to repel French invasion and assert Irish rights. Gardiner's Relief Act permitted Catholics to lease land if they took oath of allegiance.

1779   4 November: demonstration of armed volunteers in Dublin.

1780   Grattan's 'declaration of independence' by Irish parliament adjourned as inexpedient; Irish magistrates refuse to operate the Mutiny Act. Perpetual Mutiny Act passed by British parliament.

1782   15 February: Ulster Volunteers meet at Dungannon and pass a patriot programme.   16 April: Grattan's motion, postponed for a second time in February, passed unanimously. 'The Constitution of 1782' repeals the legislative authority of the British parliament and alters Poyning's Law, to end the power of the chief governor, and Council of Ireland to originate or alter Bills; only Bills enacted by the Irish parliament were to be transmitted to the King. Perpetual Mutiny Act replaced by a Biennial Act. Irish judges granted same security of tenure as their English counterparts.

1783   Renunciation Act confirms the legislative and judicial independence of Ireland.

1791   Society of United Irishmen founded by Theobald Wolfe Tone and others in Belfast for religious equality and radical reform. Similar societies set up elsewhere.

1792   Catholic Relief Act removes restrictions on Roman Catholics in education, marriage and the professions they could follow. Provisions for granting political rights defeated.   December: Catholic Convention in Dublin; petitions for further concessions.

1793   Catholic Relief Act admits Roman Catholics to municipal and parliamentary franchise on the same terms as Protestants with the right to bear arms and hold most civil and military offices except in parliament.

1794–5   Earl Fitzwilliam becomes viceroy of Ireland and commits the government to Catholic relief.   May: Grattan's Bill to admit Roman Catholics to parliament rejected.   First 'Orange Society' founded in response to sectarian fighting.

1796–7   Insurrection Act passed giving government repressive powers to deal with the disturbances. United Irishmen take up arms and are suppressed by the military.

1798   23 May: outbreak of rebellion; initially successful in Wexford, but eventually suppressed.   22 August: General Humbert lands at Killala Bay. Forced to surrender at Ballinamuch, and the rising in Connaught ended within a month with the recapture of Killala.   October: Hardy's expedition to Lough Swilly fails; Wolfe Tone is captured.

1799   Act establishes virtual martial law in Ireland.

1800   1 August: Act of Union receives Royal Assent. It establishes 'The United Kingdom of Great Britain and Ireland'; succession of the Crown to be governed by the same provisions as the union with Scotland; Irish parliament abolished; 32 Irish peers (28 temporal, 4 spiritual) to sit in the House of Lords and 100 members (64 county, 35 borough and 1 university) in the House of Commons. The churches were united, but the financial systems remained distinct. Ireland was to provide 2/17 of United Kingdom expenditure.

1803   Emmett's 'rising' suppressed. He and 21 others executed.

1816–17   Partial failure of potato crop produces famine conditions in several areas; relief committees set up.

1822   Further failure of potato crop; major public works programme started to provide employment.

1823   Catholic Association founded by O'Connell to campaign for political and other rights.

1828   Election of O'Connell for Co. Clare, forces consideration of granting Catholics right to sit in parliament.

1829   Catholic Emancipation Act. Roman Catholics made eligible for all offices of state except Regent, lord lieutenant and lord chancellor. No oath of supremacy required to sit in either House of Parliament.

1832   Irish Reform Act receives Royal Assent, 7 August.

1833   Irish Church Temporalities Act suppresses 10 sees and reduces the revenues of the rest. Surplus revenues to be administered for purely ecclesiastical purposes.

1836   Potato famine.

1838   Tithe Act removes a popular source of grievances.

1840   Irish Municipal Corporations Act enfranchises £10 householder, abolishes 58 corporations, establishes 10 new ones, and overhauls municipal administration. 'Young Ireland' Party formed.

1842   *The Nation* magazine founded by group of 'Young Ireland' journalists to promote nationalism.

1843   O'Connell begins programme of mass meetings to promote repeal of the union at Trim (16 March), but forced to cancel monster meeting at Clontarf (October) when government declared it illegal. O'Connell arrested, tried for sedition and conspiracy and sentenced to a year's imprisonment and a fine, but judgment reversed in the House of Lords.

1845   Grant to Irish Catholic college at Maynooth increased in spite of bitter opposition in parliament. Irish National Education Board formed.

1845–50   Great famine due to successive failures of potato crop as a result of blight. Irish population fell from 8,178,124 in 1841 to 6,552,386 in 1851 as a result of deaths and emigration.

1847   'Young Ireland' set up the Irish Confederation under William Smith O'Brien.   O'Connell's death at Genoa, 15 May.   Thirty-nine repealers returned in the general election.   John Mitchell begins publication of *United Irishman* newspaper, promoting radical agrarian reform.

1848   Arrest of Mitchell, 13 May; 'Young Ireland' rising in Tipperary easily suppressed and leaders transported (July).   Encumbered Estates Act passed.

1849   Serious affray between Catholics and Protestants at Dolly's Brae.

1850   Establishment of Queen's University, Belfast. Irish Franchise Act increased voters from 61,000 to 165,000.

1851   First meeting of Catholic Defence Association.

1852   Warrenstown Tenant Right demonstration.

1853   Income tax extended to Ireland.

1858   Fenian Brotherhood started by John O'Mahoney and James Stephens, directed at achieving nationhood 'soon or never'.

1862   Catholic University College founded in Dublin.

1867   Failure of Fenian insurrection.

1868   Election of Gladstone as prime minister.

1869   Disestablishment and Disendowment of the Irish Church. From January 1871 the Church of Ireland was disestablished; all property except churches in use was vested in a body of commissioners for Irish Church temporalities. Compensation set at £16 million, half of the capital of confiscated property, the remainder to be used for public benefit.

1870   Land Act designed to protect the tenant. The Ulster custom was established by law where it already existed; elsewhere greater compensation was to be given for improvements and for disturbance. Agrarian disorder continued.   Home Government Association formed by Irish Protestant Conservative lawyer, Isaac Butt. In 1873 re-formed as Home Rule League.

1872   Six Home Rulers in parliament commit themselves to land reform and denominational education.

1873   Home Rule League founded in Dublin.

1874   Home Rule League led by Isaac Butt wins 59 seats in general election and initiates policy of 'obstruction'.

1879   Death of Isaac Butt; Land League formed by Michael Davitt (Parnell as president), for fair rents to be fixed by arbitration, fixity of tenure while rent was paid and freedom of tenant to sell his right of occupancy.

1880   Parnell becomes the new leader of the 61 Home Rulers returned in the general election. 'Boycotts' organised against whose who offended against the Land League's code. Troops used to harvest crops on Lord Erne's land managed by Captain C. C. Boycott, who gave his name to the tactic used against him.

1881   New Coercion Act passed in March. But in April Gladstone introduced a new Land Act conceding many of the basic demands of the Land League. Its reception was hostile and in October Parnell was imprisoned in Kilmainham Gaol, and was not released until April 1882. A 'No Rent' movement was launched in protest at the imprisonment.

1882   By the so-called 'Kilmainham treaty' Parnell promised to use his influence to end crime and disorder, while the government promised a new policy of conciliation. Spencer became new viceroy and Lord Frederick Cavendish, chief secretary. On 6 May, Cavendish and T. H. Burke, the under-secretary, were murdered in Phoenix Park by 'the Invincibles'; New Crimes Bill introduced. National League founded by Parnell, closely linked to Irish parliamentary party.

1884   Franchise Act gave the counties (outside Ulster) to the Home Rulers.

1885   Redistribution Act. Number of Irish MPs unchanged despite the fall in population.   Ashburne's Act: provides the advance to the tenant of the whole sum needed to buy his land, to be repaid over 49 years at 4 per cent. In three years the £5 million grant was exhausted.   Eighty-five Home Rulers returned for Irish seats in the general election. They held the balance in the House of Commons and chose to support Gladstone because of a press rumour that he was in favour of Home Rule.   Home Rule Bill defeated in Commons, 343–313 (93 Liberals voted against).

1886   General election: 85 Home Rulers returned, but in England Home Rule was heavily rejected.   National League organises a plan of campaign by tenants against landlords.

1887   Parnell accused of complicity in agrarian outrages in letter in *The Times*; cleared by committee of enquiry, who discovered the forgery.

1890   Parnell cited in Mrs O'Shea's divorce, which made continued alliance with the Liberals impossible. The Home Rulers split, 26 supporting Parnell, the majority disavowing him.

1891   Death of Parnell (October).   Chief Secretary Balfour encourages
        land purchase; £30 million made available.   Congested Districts
        Board set up to assist poorest areas.

1892   June: Duke of Abercorn declares in Belfast, 'We will not have
        Home Rule.'

1893   Second Home Rule Bill; this would continue Irish representation
        at Westminster. Defeated in House of Lords.   Edward
        Saunderson, MP for North Armagh, helps establish the Ulster
        Defence Union.   Gaelic League founded.

1898   William O'Brien puts new life into the Home Rule movement with
        the United Ireland League, begun in Connaught with a policy of
        agrarian reform. Doctrine of 'Sinn Fein' ('ourselves alone')
        preached by *United Irishman*, a weekly paper published in Dublin
        by A. Griffith.   James Connolly founds the Irish Socialist
        Republican Party.

1900   Irish Nationalists reunited under Redmond; 82 returned in general
        election.

1902   Sinn Fein founded by Arthur Griffith.

1903   'Wyndham's Act' went far to making sale of estates universal;
        £100 million made available for land purchase by tenants.

1904   Negotiations for a scheme for devolution between government
        and Irish Nationalists.

1905   Ulster Unionist Council established; a large representative body
        with a permanent executive committee.

1906   Eight-three Irish Nationalists returned at the general
        election.   Bill to introduce devolution rejected by Redmond, but
        no alternative offered by government.

1907   Augustine Birrell becomes Chief Secretary.   Sinn Fein League
        organised for 'the re-establishment of the independence of
        Ireland'.

1908   Sinn Fein contests North Leitrim election; violence, but Redmond
        wins.   Universities' Act founded Queen's University, Belfast,
        and National University of Ireland.

1909   Birrell Act to encourage land purchase eases financial clauses of
        Wyndham's Act.

1910   At the January general election, 70 followers of Redmond and 11
        independent Irish Nationalists returned.   Sir Edward Carson
        leads the Ulster Unionists in opposition to plans for Home Rule.

1911   Carson declares in Belfast: 'We will yet defeat the most nefarious
        conspiracy that has ever been hatched against a free people.'
        Unionist Council prepares plans to take over civil administration
        in Ulster in event of Home Rule.

1912   Bonar Law, the Conservative leader, espouses Unionist cause 'as
        the cause of the Empire'. At Blenheim supports plans for Ulster
        resistance.   Liberal government introduces a Home Rule Bill for

the whole of Ireland. Ulster Volunteers formed as a military force to resist Home Rule. Ulster's 'Solemn League and Covenant' signed by over 200,000 Protestants.

1913   Home Rule Bill defeated in the House of Lords, but awaits automatic implementation under provisions of Parliament Act; idea of excluding Ulster from its provisions raised by Liberal government.   Citizen Army, later known as the 'Irish Volunteers', formed in the South.

1914   Asquith persuades Redmond to accept exclusion of Ulster from operation of Home Rule for six years, but Carson rejects compromise.   'Mutiny' at the Curragh (headquarters of the British Army in Ireland), following rumours of unwillingness of army officers to coerce the Ulster Protestants.   Gun-running into Ulster and Dublin arms the two 'volunteer' forces.   Conference at Buckingham Palace in July fails to reach agreement on Ulster's exclusion from Home Rule.   Outbreak of First World War defers implementation of Home Rule.

1916   Easter rising in Dublin by members of the Irish Republican Brotherhood crushed by British troops. Execution of leaders sparks off bitter anti-British feeling.

1917   'Irish Convention' organised by Lloyd George to discuss future government of Ireland.   Two Sinn Fein candidates elected in by-elections at Roscommon and Longford.   De Valera assumes leadership of Sinn Fein.

1918   Attempt to extend conscription to Ireland provokes widespread protest.   Sinn Fein and Irish Volunteers declared illegal and leaders detained, but in December general election 73 Sinn Fein candidates elected.

1919   Sinn Fein members refuse to sit at Westminster and set up provisional government; unofficial parliament of the Irish Republic, Dail Eireann, meets in Dublin in January. De Valera escapes from Lincoln gaol and is elected president. Sinn Fein and Dail declared illegal. Clashes between republican 'flying columns' and British forces. Irish Volunteers reconstituted as Irish Republican Army (IRA).

1920   Virtual guerrilla war between IRA and British forces. Black-and-Tans and auxiliaries recruited to assist Royal Irish Constabulary carry out reprisals.   Government of Ireland Act passed in December; dividing Ireland into two: 'Northern Ireland', based on the 6 Ulster counties, and 'Southern Ireland', consisting of the remaining 26. Each part to have its own parliament, but accept the supremacy of Westminster where both to retain representatives. A Council of Ireland to be set up to coordinate matters relating to the whole of Ireland.   Ulster politicians accept the Act, but Republicans refuse to agree to it and continue attacks on British forces.

1921   Southern elections return 124 Sinn Fein candidates out of 128, but members refuse to sit and parliament adjourned.   Treaty signed with southern Irish, giving southern Ireland dominion status as Irish Free State.

1922   Dail approves treaty with Britain, by 64 votes to 57. De Valera leads anti-treaty 'Republican' faction and resigns as president. General election confirms majority support for pro-treaty group. Split in IRA, and anti-treaty group begin raids against Ulster and arms raids in South. Four Courts in Dublin occupied by anti-treaty forces; besieged by Free State forces and Republicans forced to surrender.   Michael Collins assassinated in Republican ambush at Cork and widespread fighting between Free State and Republican forces. Executions of Republican leaders.

1923   Cease-fire accepted by de Valera and Republican group. Free Staters set up political party, *Cumann na nGaedheal*.

1925   Tripartite agreement signed in London confirming existing boundary between Northern Ireland and Irish Free State relieving Irish Free State of responsibilities for any share of British national debt and transferring powers of Council of Ireland relating to Northern Ireland to Northern Irish government.

1927   De Valera splits from Sinn Fein and founds Fianna Fail Party.

1932   Republican electoral victory in the South followed by hostility to Great Britain and tariff war. New constitution; name of Southern Ireland now 'Eire'.

1933   Cumann na nGaedheal changes name to Fine Gael.

1939   Irish proclaim neutrality in Second World War.

1949   The Republic of Ireland was proclaimed in April 1949, the British government formally accepting the complete independence of Southern Ireland, which leaves the Commonwealth.

1952   Revival of IRA activity; attacks on customs posts and police barracks on Ulster border.

1957   Southern Irish government acts against IRA in conjunction with Ulster government.

1962   'Terrorist' campaign against Ulster officially abandoned by IRA.

1972   Ireland signs treaty of accession to the European Economic Community.

1979   Visit of Pope John Paul II to Ireland.

1980   Meeting of Irish premier, Charles Haughey and Mrs Thatcher in London, followed by visit of Mrs Thatcher and Lord Carrington to Dublin to discuss Northern Ireland.

Major events in Northern Ireland, 1920–1980

1920   Government of Ireland Act sets up Northern Ireland parliament with a Senate and House of Commons elected by proportional representation. Special constabulary created to assist in peacekeeping.

1921   Northern Ireland parliament opened and elections held, producing a large Unionist majority. Continuing guerrilla war by IRA against Ulster and British forces.

1922 Civil Authorities Act gives extensive powers to the Northern Irish home secretary to preserve public order in face of IRA attacks from the South.

1925 Tripartite agreement with Irish Free State and British government confirms existing boundary between Northern Ireland and the Irish Free State; Northern Ireland released from its share of the British national debt; powers of the Council of Ireland relating to Northern Ireland under the Government of Ireland Act of 1920 transferred to the Northern Ireland government. Full-time special constabulary dissolved but part-time 'B specials' retained for use in emergencies.

1926 Unemployment insurance agreement provides for payments to be made by British Treasury to assist social expenditure in Northern Ireland.

1929 Proportional representation in parliamentary elections withdrawn in favour of single-member constituencies.

1932 Two people killed after unemployment workers' demonstration in Belfast leads to rioting.

1933 De Valera elected MP for constituency of South Down, but refuses to take seat.

1935 Serious sectarian rioting in Belfast; 11 killed and 600 injured.

1937 New Southern Irish constitution lays claim to 'the whole island of Ireland'. Beginning of renewed IRA campaign against Ulster.

1938 British government agrees to fund deficits in Northern Ireland budget, provided that the levels of social expenditure and taxation remain comparable with Britain.

1941 Major air raids on Belfast; 700 people killed and 1,500 wounded.

1946 Agreement that future Northern Irish budgets to be arranged in consultation with British government and that parity in services and taxation to be maintained with Britain.

1949 Social Services Agreement arranges for Britain to pay four-fifths of the excess cost of Northern Irish social services.

1951 National Insurance funds of Britain and Ulster merged and agreement reached for transfer of funds in case of need.

1956 Beginning of renewed IRA campaign against Ulster.

1962 Campaign against Ulster called off by IRA.

1963 Prime Minister Terence O'Neill begins attempt to develop amicable relations with the South.

1965 Exchange of visits between Prime Minister Terence O'Neill and Irish premier, Sean Lemass.

1966 Revd. Ian Paisley imprisoned for militant anti-Catholic activities. Secret Protestant Ulster Volunteer Force declared illegal after spate of attacks on Catholics.

1967   Northern Ireland Civil Rights Association set up.

1968   Civil Rights march in Dungannon. Rioting in Londonderry
following Civil Rights march (October). Cameron Commission set
up to investigate disturbances.

1969   People's Democracy march from Belfast to Londonderry broken
up (January). General election weakens O'Neill's position at
Stormont. Further rioting leads to call-up of 'B specials'. O'Neill
resigns and replaced by Chicester-Clark (April). British Army sent
into Belfast and Londonderry following sectarian fighting. IRA
splits into 'Official' and 'Provisional' wings. Following report of
Hunt Advisory Committee, Royal Ulster Constabulary disarmed
and 'B specials' disbanded, the latter replaced by non-sectarian
Ulster Defence Regiment, Housing allocation transferred from
local government to Stormont.

1970   Growing violence leads to ban on parades. Army uses rubber
bullets and CS gas to combat rioters.

1971   First British soldier killed in Northern Ireland (February).
Chichester-Clark resigns as Northern Ireland premier and replaced
by Brian Faulkner (March). Bombing campaign of IRA intensifies,
followed by introduction of internment without trial.

1972   'Bloody Sunday' (30 January): holding of banned Civil Rights
march in Londonderry leads to 13 people being shot by British
soldiers. Stormont suspended and direct rule introduced (March).

1973   Northern Ireland Assembly elected on proportional representation
set up to replace Stormont. 'Bloody Friday' (21 July): Bomb
explosions in Belfast. Operation 'Motorman': troops occupy
Catholic 'no-go' areas in Belfast and Londonderry. Consultative
document on 'power-sharing' in Northern Ireland agreed.
Sunningdale talks between London and Dublin agree to setting up
of a Council of Ireland and to preserve status of Northern Ireland
as part of the United Kingdom (December).

1974   Direct rule ended and beginning of 'power-sharing' experiment
(January). General Strike called by Protestant Ulster Workers'
Council leads to resignation of Brian Faulkner and Northern
Ireland executive (May). Direct rule reimposed. IRA extend
bombing campaign to Great Britain.

1975   Elections held for a Constitutional Convention on Northern Ireland
result in landslide victory for United Ulster Unionist Council.
Majority report of Constitutional Convention recommends end of
direct rule and re-establishment of a Northern Irish Assembly.

1976   Breakdown of talks between British government and Ulster
representatives (March). Direct rule continued. British
ambassador in Dublin, Christopher Ewart-Biggs assassinated by
IRA. European Commission for Human Rights finds Britain guilty
of torture in Northern Ireland. Peace Movement launched by Betty
Williams and Mairead Corrigan.

1977   Ten-day strike (May) by Ulster Unionist Action Council in support
of tougher action against the IRA and the implementation of the
Constitutional Convention's Report ends in failure.

1978   European Court of Human Rights clears Britain of torture in Northern Ireland, but convicts it of 'inhuman and degrading treatment'.

1979   Airey Neave assassinated at the House of Commons by Irish National Liberation Army (March). Earl Mountbatten assassinated by IRA in Irish Republic (August). Devolution Conference of Northern Ireland political parties fails to reach agreement.

1980   Charles Haughey, Irish prime minister, visits Mrs Thatcher in London. New political initiative in Ulster fails to achieve common support. Visit of Mrs Thatcher and Lord Carrington to Dublin to discuss Northern Irish situation.

Religious affiliations in nineteenth-century Ireland

	1834		1881	
	000s	%	000s	%
Roman Catholic	6,436	81	3,952	77
Anglican Church	853	11	636	12
Presbyterians	643	7	486	9
Others	40	1	86	2

(*Source*: figures compiled from R. Dudley Edwards, *An Atlas of Irish History*, London, Methuen, 1973, p. 127, and G. Best, *Mid-Victorian Britain, 1851–75*, London, Weidenfeld and Nicolson, 1971, p. 193)

Religious affiliations in Irish provinces in 1861

	Roman Catholics (%)	All Protestants (%)
Ulster	50.5	49.47
Leinster	85.9	14.01
Munster	93.8	6.07
Connaught	94.84	5.13

(*Source*: R. Dudley Edwards, *An Atlas of Irish History*, London, Methuen, 1973, p. 129.)

Religious affiliations in Ulster, 1911 and 1961

1911

	Protestant		Catholic	
	No	%	No	%
Belfast	293,704	75.9	93,243	24.1
Co. Antrim	154,113	79.5	39,751	20.5
Co. Armagh	65,765	54.7	54,526	45.3
Derry City	17,857	43.8	22,923	56.2
Derry County	58,367	58.5	41,478	41.5
Co. Down	139,818	68.4	64,485	31.6
Co. Fermanagh	27,096	43.8	34,740	56.2
Co. Tyrone	63,650	44.6	79,015	55.4

1961

	Protestant		Catholic	
	No	%	No	%
Belfast	301,520	72.5	114,336	27.5
Co.Antrim	206,976	75.6	66,929	24.4
Co. Armagh	61,977	52.7	55,617	47.3
Derry City	17,689	32.9	36,073	67.1
Derry County	64,027	57.4	47,509	42.6
Co. Down	190,676	71.4	76,263	28.6
Co. Fermanagh	24,109	46.8	27,422	53.2
Co. Tyrone	60,521	45.2	73,398	54.8

(*Source: Census of Ireland*, 1911, Vol. 3, *Ulster*, Cd. 6051–1, London, HMSO, 1912, and General Register Office, Northern Ireland, *Census of Population 1961*, County volumes, Tables XVI, Belfast, HMSO, 1964.)

242

Imperial

Empire chronology, 1714–1980

1713   Treaty of Utrecht: Britain gains Gibraltar, Minorca, Hudson Bay, Nova Scotia and Newfoundland.

1729   Dispute over government of Carolina resolved and divided into North and South Carolina by Act of parliament.

1733   Settlement of Georgia, the last of the 13 colonies, under the auspices of James Oglethorpe and associates.

1740   Unsuccessful expedition of Oglethorpe and colonists against Florida.

1744   French attack on Nova Scotia heralds beginning of Anglo-French struggle over colonies.

1745   Siege and capture of Louisburg in Canada by British colonial forces.

1748   Treaty of Aix-la-Chapelle between England, France and Spain. In reciprocal surrender of conquests, Cape Breton restored to the French. Formation of Ohio Company under Crown charter.

1750   Settlement begins on the Gold Coast.

1754   Benjamin Franklin proposes a union of all the American colonies under a president appointed by the Crown. Proposal rejected by Connecticut and later by the colonies and the Crown.

1755   War between England and France. Defeat of General Braddock at battle of Fort Duquesne in Canada.

1756   Capture of Forts Oswego and George by Marquis of Montcalm, commander of French armies in Canada, led to temporary abandonment of British attacks on French positions in North America.   Imprisonment of 146 British persons in 'Black Hole of Calcutta' by the Nabob of Bengal.

1757   Battle of Plessey; Clive is victorious in Bengal.

1759   General Wolfe captures Quebec after battle of the Plains of Abraham.

1760   Battle of Wandewash breaks French power in India.

1763   Treaty of Paris: all French possessions in North America east of the Mississippi ceded to Great Britain; also Grenada, St Vincent, Tobago and the Windward Islands; Florida gained from Spain.

1765   Clive becomes governor of Bengal.   Treaty of Allahabad restores the Nabobs.   The East India Company's privileges are confirmed by the Mogul and extended to revenue collection.

1766   First Mysore War

1768   Separate secretary of state for the colonies established.

1769   Cook's first Pacific voyage.

1773   Lord North's Regulating Act: British rule in India to be carried on in the name of the Crown.

1774   Warren Hastings becomes governor-general of Bengal. Quebec Act: Canada becomes a Crown colony.

1776   American colonies declare independence.

1777   General Burgoyne surrenders at Saratoga (see also p. 206). France enters the war against Britain.

1779   First Maratha War. (see p. 209).

1780   Second Mysore War. (see p. 209).

1783   Treaty of Versailles recognises American independence. France recovered her trading stations in India, Senegal, St Lucia and Tobago.   Britain retained Gibraltar.

1784   Pitt's India Act separates the commercial and political functions of the East India Company; the latter to be supervised by a Board of Control in London.

1787   Freetown, Sierra Leone, established as settlement for freed slaves.

1788   First convict settlement at Port Jackson (Sydney). Norfolk Island settled.   Impeachment of Warren Hastings.

1789   Third Mysore War (see p. 209).

1791   Canada Act: Canada was divided into two provinces (Upper and Lower Canada) each with its own government subject to a joint governor-general.

1794   Seychelles captured.

1800   Malta captured.

1802   Ceylon ceded.

1803   Second Maratha War (see p. 210).

1807   Slave trade abolished by Britain.

1808   Crown takes over Sierra Leone.

1813   East India Company loses its monopoly of Indian trade.

1814   St Lucia, Malta, Mauritius, British Guiana, Windward Islands and Cape of Good Hope ceded to Great Britain as colonies, after the defeat of Napoleon.

1817–18   Third Maratha War destroys Maratha power (see p. 210).

1821   North West Company and the Hudson's Bay Company amalgamate. Royal African Company abolished and forts taken over by the Crown as part of its West African settlements.

1823   New South Wales becomes a Crown colony.

1824   Burmese War (see p. 210). Singapore ceded to Britain.

1827   Western Australia explored by Captain Stirling.

1830   Edward Gibbon Wakefield forms the Colonisation Society.

1833   East India Company ceases to trade; governor-general of Bengal becomes governor-general of India. Indian Legislative Council established. Slavery abolished in the British Empire. Falkland Islands annexed.

1834   South Australia Act authorises the establishment of a colony.

1835   Great Trek of Boer colonists from the Cape.

1837   Aborigines Protection Society founded. New Zealand Association begun by Wakefield.   Rebellion of Papineau and Mackenzie in Canada.

1838   Earl of Durham becomes governor-general of Canada. Apprenticeship system in West Indies abolished.

1839   Aden annexed. First Afghan War (see p. 211).   First China 'Opium' War (see p. 000). Republic of Natal founded. Durham Report published. It suggests process of granting greater autonomy to colonies.

1840   Canada Act reunites Upper and Lower Canada in a single administration and legislature.   New Zealand annexed: treaty of Waitangi aims to protect Maoris by forbidding private sale and purchase of land.   Transportation to New South Wales discontinued.

1841   Retreat from Kabul.

1842   Treaty of Nanking ends the war with China (see p. 225). Hong Kong is ceded to Britain, and five treaty ports (Amoy, Canton, Foochow, Ningpo and Shanghai) opened to British trade. Ashburton treaty settles the Maine boundary. Representative government established in New South Wales.   Conquest of Burma and Assam begins.

1843   Maori Wars begin.   Sind conquered.   Natal annexed.

1845   First Sikh War (see p. 211).

1846   Oregon treaty fixes the boundary of Canada at the 49th Parallel.   Earl Grey's Act establishes two provinces in New Zealand, each with executive and legislative councils under the governor.

1847   Elgin becomes governor-general of a united Canada. Governor of Cape Colony becomes high commissioner for South Africa.

1848   Orange Free State becomes a Crown colony.   Second Sikh War: Punjab annexed.   Nova Scotia becomes the first colony with a responsible ministry.

1849   Navigation Acts repealed.

1851   Australian gold rush. Victoria becomes a separate colony.

1852   Rangoon annexed in Second Burmese War (see p. 210). By the
        Sand River Convention, Britain abandons attempts to control the
        Boer trekkers.   Responsible government attained in New
        Zealand.

1853   Cape Colony gains representative government.

1854   Bloemfontein Convention: Orange Free State gained
        self-rule.   Separate Colonial Office established.

1855   New South Wales, Victoria and Newfoundland granted
        responsible government.

1856   Oudh annexed.   War with China renewed.   South
        Australia and Tasmania gain responsible government.

1857   Indian Mutiny begins in Meerut in May, quickly spreading
        across northern India (see p. 212). When the revolt was quelled
        the Crown assumed direct control of India. A secretary of state
        for India was established with a Council of India to advise him.
        The East India Company's rule was abolished.

1858   Treaty of Tientsin secured, when Anglo-French forces defeated
        the Chinese. China repudiated the treaty in 1859.   British
        Columbia becomes a Crown colony.

1859   Queensland becomes a separate colony with responsible
        government.   Sir George Grey, governor of Cape Colony
        proposes a plan for South African federation.

1860   Britain attained full Free Trade.   Maori Wars recur when the
        New Zealand Company broke the treaty of Waitangi (see p. 211).

1861   Lagos annexed. India Councils Act.   Parliamentary committee
        agreed territories enjoying responsible government should make
        a greater contribution to their own defence.

1864   Quebec Conference laid the foundation for the Dominion of
        Canada.

1865   Colonial Laws Validity Act: colonial legislatures could pass laws
        contrary to the common law of England, but not contrary to Acts
        of the imperial parliament applying to the colony.   Governor
        Eyre suppresses Morant rising in Jamaica.

1867   British North America Act creates the Dominion of Canada as a
        self-governing federation of four provinces.   Straits
        Settlements becomes a Crown colony.

1869   Suez Canal opened.   Hudson's Bay Company cedes its
        territorial rights to the Dominion of Canada.   Rebellion led by
        Louis Riel in Canada.

1870   Manitoba admitted to Dominion of Canada.

1871   British Columbia joins the Dominion of Canada.   Griqualand
        West annexed (diamond fields discovered there).   Protectorate
        proclaimed in Basutoland.   Dutch cede Gold Coast forts to
        Britain.

1872   Responsible government implemented in Cape Colony.

1873   Ashanti War (see p. 213).   Prince Edward Island joins the
        Dominion of Canada.

1874   Fiji Islands annexed.   Treaties with chiefs of Perak and
        Selangor by which British Residents were to give advice to the
        Malay rulers.

1875   Suez Canal shares purchased giving United Kingdom a majority
        holding.   Lord Carnarvon launches plan for South African
        Confederation.

1876   Victoria created Empress of India. Lord Lytton became viceroy.

1877   Transvaal annexed.

1878   Cyprus occupied under the treaty of Berlin.   Dual control
        established in Egypt (Britain and France).   Walvis Bay, South
        Africa, annexed.   Second Afghan War begins.

1879   British Resident at Kabul murdered. Peace restored when
        Afghanistan independence was recognised, 1880.   Zulu War;
        British defeated at Isandhlwana, victorious at Ulundi (see p. 213).

1880   First Boer War began (see p. 213).

1881   British defeated at Majuba Hill. Convention of Pretoria recognises
        the Transvaal as an independent republic subject to the suzerainty
        of the Queen.   Revolt of the Mahdi in the Sudan (see p. 213).

1882   British North Borneo Company chartered.   Four territories
        organised from the Canadian prairies, Alberta, Athabasca,
        Assiniboine and Saskatchewan.   Revolt of Arabi Pasha,
        defeated at Tel-el-kebir (see p. 213). Britain occupies Egypt and
        assumes control of Egyptian finance.

1883   British force under Hicks Pasha defeated in the Sudan.   Sir
        Evelyn Baring (Lord Cromer) appointed British agent and
        consul-general in Egypt.   Sir J. R. Seeley's *Expansion of
        England* published.

1884   Imperial Federation League founded.   Transvaal recognised as
        the South African Republic, when Britain abandoned her
        suzerainty.   Berlin Conference opens. It established
        ground-rules for partition of Africa.   Britain takes possession of
        remainder of New Guinea after German annexations.

1885   Death of General Gordon at Khartoum.   Crisis in Penjdeh, the
        disputed boundary area between Afghanistan and Russian
        Turkestan. Indian National Congress founded.   Upper Burma
        invaded (see p. 210).   Protectorate established in
        Bechuanaland.   Federation of the Windward Islands.

1886   Royal Niger Company chartered for trade and government.
        Anglo-German treaties partition East Africa and the Pacific.
        Gold discovered in the Transvaal; Johannesburg founded.
        Annexation of Burma.

1887   First Colonial Conference.   Protectorate proclaimed in British
        Somaliland.

1888   Imperial British East Africa Company chartered. Zululand
        annexed.   Protectorates in Matabeleland, British North Borneo
        and Sarawak.

1889   British South Africa Company chartered; begins colonisation in
        what became Rhodesia.   Federation of Australia proposed by
        Sir Henry Parkes at Tenterfield.

1890   Anglo-German treaties concerning East Africa.   Rhodes
        becomes prime minister of Cape Colony.   Responsible
        government in Western Australia.

1891   Anglo-Portuguese colonial treaty recognises British protectorate
        in Nyasaland.

1892   India Councils Act introduces first Indian members to the viceroy's
        legislative council. Gold discovered in Western Australia.

1893   Responsible government in Natal.   Durand Line fixed the
        frontier between Afghanistan and British India.

1894   L. S. Jameson appointed administrator of Southern Rhodesia.
        Protectorate established in Uganda.

1895   Joseph Chamberlain appointed colonial secretary.   British East
        Africa protectorate established.   Jameson leads an
        unsuccessful raid into the Transvaal.

1896   Kitchener advances into the Sudan.   Second Ashanti War: the
        monarchy was abolished and a protectorate established.

1897   Milner became high commissioner of the Cape.   Second
        Colonial Conference on Queen's Diamond Jubilee.   Royal
        Commission on the West Indies.   Convention at Adelaide to
        prepare terms for Australian Federation.

1898   Niger convention with France.   Wei-hai-wei leased.
        Confrontation with France at Fashoda on Upper Nile.
        Anglo-Egyptian condominium proclaimed over the Sudan after
        the defeat of the Mahdi at Omdurman.   Curzon appointed
        viceroy of India.

1899   Anglo-French agreement concerning the Nile Valley.   Royal
        Niger Company loses its powers to the Crown. Second Boer War
        begins. Britain defeated at Magersfontein, Stormberg and
        Colenso.

1900   Ladysmith, Kimberley and Mafeking relieved.   Boxer Rising in
        China.   First Pan-African Congress in London.   Cook Islands
        annexed. Protectorate established in Tobago.

1901   Commonwealth of Australia established.   North West Frontier
        Province created.

1902   Peace of Vereeniging: Transvaal and Orange Free State annexed.
        Colonial Conference decides to meet again every four years.

1904   Anglo-French *entente*: acceptance of mutual spheres of influence
        in Africa.

1905   Partition of Bengal alienates Hindu nationalists.   Alberta and
        Saskatchewan created as provinces of Canada.

1906   Transvaal gains responsible government.   All India Muslim League formed: British promise Muslims separate electorates.

1907   Australia and New Zealand gain dominion status. Imperial Conference: Dominions division established in the Colonial Office.   Orange Free State gains responsible government.   Gorst becomes British agent in Egypt and increases the powers of provincial councils.

1909   Morley – Minto constitutional reforms in India. India Councils Act.

1910   Union of South Africa formed.

1911   Coronation Durbar: Indian capital transferred from Calcutta to Delhi; division of Bengal abandoned.

1914   Protectorate proclaimed in Egypt.   Cyprus annexed. Northern and Southern Nigeria protectorates joined together. France and Britain conquer German colonies except German East Africa.

1917   Balfour declaration promises the Jews a national home in Palestine. Montagu declaration states the eventual aim of full responsible government in India.   Imperial War Conference includes India.

1918   Rhodesian Native National Congress formed.

1919   Nationalist revolt in Egypt.   Massacre at Amritsar. Government of India Act enacts the Montagu – Chelmsford reforms. Dyarchy introduced – responsible government in certain departments.

1920   Gandhi wins control of Congress, and leads the non-cooperation movement in India.   East African protectorate becomes colony of Kenya.

1921   Southern Ireland granted dominion status as the Irish Free State.   Responsible government introduced in Malta.   League of Nations mandate for Iraq accepted. National congress in British West Africa formed.

1922   Palestine and Transjordan administered by Britain under League of Nations.   Egyptian independence recognised with reservations.   Increasing violence leads Gandhi to call off non-cooperation.

1923   Southern Rhodesia becomes a self-governing colony.

1924   Protectorate of Northern Rhodesia established.   Irish Free State is the first dominion to establish a separate diplomatic representative abroad.

1925   Cyprus becomes a colony.

1926   Imperial Conference declares Great Britain and the dominions autonomous and equal though 'freely associated as members of the British Commonwealth of Nations'.

1927   Simon Commission sent to investigate the Montagu – Chelmsford system.

1929   Separate secretary of state for the Dominions established.

1930   Nehru proclaims independence of India. Gandhi begins second civil disobedience campaign. Round Table Conference begins

1931   Statute of Westminster embodies the decisions of the 1926 Imperial Conference.

1932   Imperial Economic Conference at Ottawa establishes limited preferential duties.

1935   Government of India Act; establishes responsible government in the provinces.

1942   Cripps mission to India offers dominion status after the war; rejected by Indian nationalists.

1942   Japanese capture Singapore – a major blow to Britain's imperial prestige in Asia.

1946   North Borneo becomes a colony. Sarawak ceded. Full independence granted to Transjordan.

1947   Independence granted to India and Pakistan (the latter in Muslim majority areas).

1948   Ceylon and Burma become independent. State of Israel formed.   Beginning of a conflict with communist guerrillas in Malaya.

1949   Ireland withdraws from the Commonwealth.

1950   India becomes the first republic to belong to the Commonwealth.

1952   Beginning of Mau Mau rebellion in Kenya (see pp. 216–7).

1953   Southern Rhodesia, Nyasaland and Northern Rhodesia are united in the Federation of Rhodesia and Nyasaland.

1956   Suez expedition.   Mau Mau rebellion in Kenya suppressed.

1957   Ghana and the Malay states gain independence.

1958   West Indies Federation formed.

1960   Harold Macmillan's 'wind of change' speech presages African decolonisation.   Cyprus, Nigeria and British Somaliland gain independence.

1961   South Africa withdraws from the Commonwealth. Tanganyika, Sierra Leone and British Cameroons gain independence.

1962   West Indies Federation breaks up when Jamaica and Trinidad and Tobago become independent. Western Samoa and Uganda gain independence.

1963   Zanzibar and Kenya gain independence.

1964   Commonwealth Secretariat established. Malta gains independence. The Federation of Rhodesia and Nyasaland is dissolved; Nyasaland becomes the independent state of Malawi; Northern Rhodesia becomes Zambia.

1965   Southern Rhodesia unilaterally proclaims independence. Gambia and the Maldive Islands gain independence.

250   Foreign affairs and defence

1966   Basutoland (Lesotho), Bechuanaland (Botswana), British Guiana
        (Guyana) and Barbados become independent.

1967   Aden gains independence.

1968   Mauritius and Swaziland gain independence.

1970   Fiji and Tonga gain independence.

1973   Bahamas gains independence.

1979   Rhodesian settlement reached; Britain and Patriotic Front
        conclude a ceasefire agreement.

1980   Elections in Rhodesia, under supervision of monitoring force.
        Zimbabwe independent (April).

Section V
Biographies

Aberdeen, 4th Earl of, George Hamilton-Gordon (1784–1860):
Hamilton-Gordon became Earl of Aberdeen in 1801. From 1806 to 1814
he was a Scottish representative peer, and served as ambassador
extraordinary at Vienna in 1813. In 1814 he represented Britain in the
negotiation of the treaty of Paris. Later that year he was created a peer of
the United Kingdom. He held office as chancellor of the duchy of
Lancaster, January to June 1828, as foreign secretary, 1828–30, as
secretary for war and the colonies, 1834–5 and as foreign secretary
again from 1841 to 1846. After 1846 he was leader of the Peelite faction in
the House of Lords. Between 1852 and 1855 he presided as prime
minister over a coalition of Whigs and Peelites. In 1855 he resigned when
Roebuck's motion for a committee of enquiry into the conduct of the
Crimean War was carried.

Addington, Henry, *see* Sidmouth

Applegarth, Robert (1833–1925): Secretary of Amalgamated Society of
Carpenters and Joiners (1862), and dominating figure in London Trades
Council which advocated industrial conciliation and arbitration of
disputes; he and four other union leaders assumed title 'Conference of
Amalgamated Trades' in attempt to influence 1867 Royal Commission
into unionism; cautious attitude of 'Junta' leaders helped disarm
criticism of unionism.

Arch, Joseph (1826–1919): Liberal MP 1885–6, 1892–1902; pioneer of
agricultural trade unionism, forming first agricultural labourers' union,
1872; puritan and Primitive Methodist lay preacher.

Asquith, Herbert Henry, 1st Earl of Oxford and Asquith (1852–1928):
Asquith was Liberal MP for East Fife from 1886 to 1918 and for Paisley
from 1920 to 1924. In 1925 he was created Earl of Oxford and Asquith. He
was home secretary, 1892–5, chancellor of the exchequer, 1905–8 and
prime minister 1908–16. During 1914 he was also secretary for war. He
resigned the premiership in 1916 and became leader of the opposition. In
1926 he resigned the leadership of the Liberal Party when it failed to
endorse his censuring of Lloyd George for refusing to attend a shadow
cabinet. Asquith's term as P.M. was a troubled one, embracing the
budget, House of Lords and Ulster crises, suffragette militancy and the
outbreak of the First World War. His replacement by Lloyd George and
their subsequent feuds did great harm to the Liberal Party.

Attlee, Clement Richard, 1st Earl Attlee (1883–1967): Attlee was Labour
MP for Limehouse Stepney from 1922 to 1950, and for West
Walthamstow from 1950 to 1955. He served as parliamentary private
secretary to Ramsay MacDonald, 1922–4 and as under-secretary for war
in 1924. He was chancellor of the duchy of Lancaster, 1930 to 1931 and
postmaster-general in 1931. He was elected leader of the Labour Party in
1935. In the wartime coalition government he took office as lord privy
seal, 1940–2, secretary for the dominions 1942–3 and as lord president
of the council 1943–5. He was deputy prime minister, 1942–5 and prime
minister from 1945 to 1951. During 1945–6 he was also minister of
defence. He was leader of the opposition, 1951 to 1955 and was created
an earl in 1955. Attlee's rise to the leadership of the Labour Party was

facilitated by the disruption of the party in 1931. As Labour prime minister he presided over an active and able cabinet which introduced the National Health Service, comprehensive social welfare and nationalised many basic industries.

Attwood, Thomas (1783–1856): MP for Birmingham from 1832. Founder of the Birmingham Political Union which conducted a vigorous campaign for parliamentary reform in the early 1830s; fanatical believer in currency reform; became closely associated with Chartists and in July 1839 presented Chartist 'monster petition' to House of Commons.

Baldwin, Stanley, 1st Earl Baldwin of Bewdley (1867–1947): Baldwin was Conservative MP for his father's old constituency of Bewdley, Worcs., from 1908 to 1937. In 1917 he became joint financial secretary to the Treasury and held that post until 1921. He was president of the Board of Trade, 1921–2 and chancellor of the Exchequer, 1922–3. He served as prime minister, 1923–4 and 1924–9. From 1931 to 1935 he sat in the National government as lord president of the council, and in 1932–3 was also lord privy seal. His final term as prime minister ran from 1935 to 1937, when he resigned. In 1937 he was created an earl. In many ways Baldwin's achievements as P.M. were considerable. He succeeded in uniting a divided party and in pursuing a conciliatory course through the difficult inter-war years. However, his handling of the questions of rearmament and mass unemployment has tended to obscure his more successful endeavours.

Balfour, Arthur James, 1st Earl of Balfour (1848–1930): Balfour was Conservative MP for Hertford, 1874–85, for Manchester East, 1885–1906, and for the City of London, 1906–22. He was created an earl in 1922. Balfour served as parliamentary private secretary to his uncle, Lord Salisbury, 1878–80. In 1885 he was president of the Local Government Board and in 1886 was secretary for Scotland. He was chief secretary for Ireland between 1887 and 1891, and leader of the Commons and first lord of the Treasury, 1891–2 and 1895–1902. He became prime minister in 1902, resigning in 1905. He resigned the leadership of the Conservative Party in 1911. In 1914 he was made a member of the Committee of Imperial Defence and attended meetings of the war cabinet, 1914–15. He served as first lord of the Admiralty, 1915–16 and as foreign secretary, 1916–19. He was lord president of the council, 1919–22 and 1925–9. A well-connected Conservative, Balfour proved a highly intelligent and able administrator in most offices. But as P.M. and party leader he gave an impression of indecision and indifference on the question of Tariff Reform which split the party. After the Liberal government's reform of the House of Lords, accusations of ineffectuality and nepotism helped persuade Balfour to resign the leadership.

Bath, 1st Earl, William Pulteney, (1684–1764): MP 1705–42; secretary of war, 1714–17; Whig politician prominent in opposition to Walpole; joined with Bolingbroke (*q.v.*) in attempt to form united party of opposition, and encouraged alliance between Whig and Tory factions opposed to Walpole; declined two invitations from George II to form ministry after Walpole's fall, 1742; failed to organise government with Granville (*q.v.*) in 1746.

Beaconsfield, 1st Earl of, *see* Disraeli.

Bentham, Jeremy (1748–1832): Jurist and utilitarian philosopher who expounded doctrine of 'the greatest happiness of the greatest number'; publications included *A Fragment on Government* (1776) attacking form of law in England, and *Introduction to Principles of Morals and Legislation* (1789); advocated reform and codification of criminal law and more logical poor law; formative influence on Edwin Chadwick, Francis Place, Henry Brougham and Robert Peel (*qq.v.*)

Bevan, Aneurin (1897–1960): Labour MP for Ebbw Vale, 1929–60; minister of health, 1945–51; minister of labour, 1951; deputy leader of Labour Party 1959–60; emerged from Welsh coal-mining background to become spokesman for South Wales miners in General Strike of 1926; pioneered National Health Service, resigning in protest at Gaitskell's (*q.v.*) proposals to introduce Health Service charges to meet defence expenditure. Led unilateral wing of party.

Beveridge, William Henry, 1st Baron Beveridge of Tuggal (1879–1963): Economist and author of Beveridge Report on *Social Insurance and Allied Services* (1942), which became blueprint for Britain's welfare state policies and institutions; particularly interested in unemployment; director of labour exchanges 1909–16; director of London School of Economics, 1919–37; master of University College Oxford from 1937; Liberal MP, Berwick-on-Tweed, 1944–5.

Bevin, Ernest (1881–1951): Labour MP Central Wandsworth, 1940–50 and East Woolwich, 1950–1; chairman TUC General Council, 1937; minister of labour 1940–5; foreign secretary, 1945–51 lord privy seal, 1951. Rose through Dockers' Union to unite 50 unions into Transport and General Workers' Union in 1921, the largest union in world; prominent in TUC. General Council service, 1925–40; supported creation of NATO in April 1949; summoned Commonwealth Foreign Ministers' Conference, February 1950.

Bolingbroke, Henry St John, 1st Viscount (1678–1751): MP 1701–8; secretary of state for northern Department, 1710; prominent in reign of Queen Anne (1702–14), when he became major political propagandist opposing Whig Party; attempts to advance Tory cause led to dismissal by George I; fled to France 1715, where he supported Jacobites; returned to England 1725, and attempted to renew literary and political career. Leader of opposition to Walpole and author of *The Idea of a Patriot King*.

Booth, Charles (1840–1916): shipowner and social investigator. Privy councillor 1904; member of Royal Commission on Poor Law, 1905–9; contributed greatly to knowledge of social problems and statistical methodology in 17-volume *Life and Labour of The People in London* (1891–1903); advocate of old-age pensions for all.

Booth, William (1829–1912): Founder and first general of Salvation Army, which began as Christian Mission intended to evangelise and serve London poor; originally ordained minister of Methodist New Connexion, 1852; resigned 1861 to become itinerant evangelist and

social worker; particularly interested in problems of alcoholics and
released prisoners.

Bright, John (1811– 1889): Radical MP 1840; Liberal MP 1843– 89;
president of Board of Trade, 1868– 70; chancellor of duchy of Lancaster,
1873– 4 and 1880– 82; first entered politics in 1840s and became
associated with Cobden (*q.v.*) in leading Anti-Corn Law League; ardent
supporter of Free Trade; supported admission of Jews to House of
Commons, 1858, and campaign leading to 1867 Reform Act; opposed
Crimean War, Irish Home Rule and Gladstone government's Egyptian
venture of 1882.

Brougham, Henry Peter, 1st Baron Brougham and Vaux (1778– 1868):
Politician, barrister and writer. Founder of *Edinburgh Review*, 1802;
associated himself with cause of Queen Caroline in 1820; helped found
London University in 1828; lord chancellor, 1830– 4; as lord chancellor,
introduced rational reforms in legal system and supervised passage of
1832 Reform Bill through Lords; gave his name to the carriage
henceforth known as 'brougham'.

Burdett, Sir Francis (1770– 1844): Radical politician. MP for Westminster,
1807– 37; MP for Wiltshire, 1837– 44; became mouthpiece of discontent
with wartime taxation and repression in early nineteenth century; first
chairman of Hampden Club; defence of radical orator John Gale Jones
led to arrest and committal to Tower; release marked by demonstrations
in London; became Tory Democrat in 1830s.

Burgoyne, John (1723– 1792): soldier, MP and playwright, Burgoyne
began his army career in 1740. He took part in raids on Cherbourg, 1758
and St Malo, 1759, and raised and commanded a light cavalry regiment
in Portugal, 1762. He was sent to Boston in 1774, then to Canada as
second-in-command to Carleton. He proposed a plan for a threefold
attack on the rebel Americans, but due to bungling in London, the plan
went awry. Advancing from Canada, Burgoyne found himself cut off and
surrounded, and was forced to surrender his army to General Gates at
Saratoga on 17 October 1777. A storm of controversy broke out in
England over responsibility for this fiasco, which did much to secure
foreign aid for the rebel colonists. Burgoyne was commander-in-chief in
Ireland, 1782– 3.

Burke, Edmund (1729– 1797); Whig polemicist and conservative thinker;
MP from 1766; first established reputation through opposition to duties
on American trade; 1770 published attack on power of Crown under
George III entitled *Thoughts on the Causes of our Present Discontents*;
advocated economical reform during 1780s and attacked corruption of
Indian administration of Warren Hastings; *Reflections on the Revolution
in France* (1790) initiated years of debate on the subject, and estranged
Burke from Foxite Whigs.

Bute, 3rd Earl of, John Stuart (1713– 1792): Stuart succeeded as Earl of
Bute in 1723. A favourite of George III he was a secretary of state,
1761– 2, and followed Newcastle as first lord of the Treasury in 1762. He
resigned office in 1763.

Callaghan (Leonard) James (1912–): Labour politician. Labour MP for South Cardiff, 1945–50 and for South East Cardiff from 1950. He was parliamentary secretary to the Ministry of Transport, 1947 to 1950, parliamentary secretary and financial secretary to the Admiralty, 1950–1. From 1964 to 1967 he was chancellor of the exchequer and from 1967 to 1970, home secretary. In 1974 he became foreign secretary, relinquishing the post when he was elected leader of the Labour Party and made prime minister in 1976. He remained prime minister until Labour's general election defeat of May 1979. Although an experienced Labour politician, Callaghan faced a difficult task in trying to secure continuing trade union support for his government's counter-inflation policy. He also had to shore up his party's weak parliamentary position by the Lib–Lab pact, two factors which severely hindered his freedom of manoeuvre as premier.

Campbell-Bannerman, Sir Henry (1836–1908): Liberal MP for Stirling Burghs from 1868 to 1908. He was financial secretary to the War Office, 1871–4 and 1880–2. Between 1882 and 1884 he was financial secretary to the Admiralty and chief secretary for Ireland 1884–5. He served as secretary for war in 1886 and 1892–5. He led the Liberal Party in the Commons between 1899 and 1908, and was prime minister, 1905–8, when he retired through ill-health. Campbell-Bannerman was the last Liberal P.M. to win office with a Liberal majority, and succeeded in uniting a party previously divided on imperial questions.

Canning, George (1770–1827): MP for Newport, 1794–6 and 1806–7, for Wendover from 1796 to 1802, for Tralee from 1802 to 1806, for Hastings, 1807–12, for Liverpool 1812–22, for Warwick 1823–6, for Newport 1826–7 and for Seaford in 1827. He held the offices of under-secretary for foreign affairs, 1796–9, president of the India Board, 1799–1800, paymaster-general, 1800–1, treasurer of the navy, 1804–6, foreign secretary, 1807–9 and 1822–7 and president of the India Board, 1816–21. He became prime minister and chancellor of the exchequer in 1827, shortly before his death. Better known for his liberal views on foreign policy, Canning was also able to hold together a Tory–Whig coalition in 1827. After his death the government was unable to continue for long.

Cardwell, Edward (1813–1886): Conservative MP 1842–6; Peelite and Liberal MP 1847–74; president of Board of Trade, 1852–5; secretary for Ireland, 1859–61; secretary for colonies, 1864–6; secretary for war, 1868–74; prepared ground for colonial military campaigns during imperialist period by expansion and modernisation of army to meet challenge of Prussian unification and militarisation.

Carson, Sir Edward (1854–1935): Unionist MP, Dublin University, 1892–1918; Belfast, 1918–21. Appointed solicitor-general, 1900–5. Leader of the anti-Home Rule movement. Founded the Ulster Volunteer Force in 1913. Attorney-general, 1915–16; first lord of Admiralty, 1916–17.

Castlereagh, Viscount, Robert Stewart, 2nd Marquess of Londonderry (1769–1822): Secretary for Ireland, 1798–1801; secretary for war and colonies, 1805–6, 1807–9; foreign secretary, 1812–22. Advocate of union of Britain and Ireland; resigned when George III vetoed Catholic Emancipation; quarrel with Canning led to duel and resignation of both men in 1809; very influential at Congress of Vienna in implementing ideas regarding European balance of power, but rapidly disillusioned with functioning of Congress System. Committed suicide, 1822.

Cartwright, John (1740–1824): Radical who began political career in Society for Constitutional Information; pamphlet *Take Your Choice* (1776) outlined reform programme including annual parliaments, payment of MPs, secret ballot and adult manhood suffrage for which he campaigned throughout latter decades of eighteenth century and Napoleonic Wars of early nineteenth century; founder of Hampden Clubs which sought enfranchisement of all taxpayers and abolition of income tax.

Chamberlain, (Arthur) Neville (1868–1940): Conservative politician, Lord Mayor of Birmingham, 1915–16, and director-general of National Service, 1916–17. He entered parliament as MP for Birmingham Ladywood in 1918, a seat he held until 1929. From 1929 to 1940 he was MP for Birmingham Edgbaston. Chamberlain held office as postmaster-general, 1922–3, paymaster-general, 1923, minister of health, 1923, chancellor of the exchequer, 1923–4, minister of health, 1924–9 and in 1931. From 1931 to 1937 he was again chancellor of the exchequer, and was prime minister from 1937 to 1940. In 1940 he resigned the premiership and became lord president of the council in Churchill's war cabinet. That same year he retired from politics completely on health grounds. Chamberlain proved a dynamic and efficient administrator at the ministry of health and the exchequer, but as P.M. displayed a less sure touch in foreign affairs and has been much criticised for his attempts to appease the Axis powers. His apparent complacency in the face of wartime defeats brought forth the pressure both within and without the Conservative Party that resulted in his resignation as P.M.

Chamberlain, Joseph (1836–1914): Politician. Mayor of Birmingham, 1873–5; MP for Birmingham, 1876–1910 first as a Liberal, later as a Unionist; president of Board of Trade, 1880–5; colonial secretary, 1895–1903; Unitarian and reformer who pioneered slum clearance in Birmingham; broke away from Gladstone to form Liberal Unionists in 1886 in opposition to Irish Home Rule; joined Salisbury's Conservative–Unionist government, and as colonial secretary became great exponent of tariff reform and imperial federation.

Chamberlain, Sir (Joseph) Austen (1863–1937): Conservative politician. Unionist MP for Worcestershire East, 1892–1914; Birmingham West from 1914; chancellor of the exchequer, 1903–5, 1919–21; secretary of state for India, 1915–17; lord privy seal, 1921–2, when also Conservative leader; foreign secretary, 1925–9; first lord of Admiralty, 1931. Son of Joseph Chamberlain (*q.v.*) whose parliamentary seat he took over in 1914. Won Nobel Peace Prize for prominence in discussions leading to Locarno treaties of 1925.

Chatham, 1st Earl of, William Pitt ('the Elder') (1708–1778): MP for Old Sarum, 1735–47, for Seaford 1747–54, for Aldborough, 1754–6, for Okehampton 1756–7, and for Bath 1757–66. He became vice-treasurer of

Ireland in 1746, paymaster-general, 1746 to 1755, secretary of state from 1756 to 1757 and 1757 to 1761. He was lord privy seal, acting as prime minister, between 1766 and 1768. He was leader of the Commons from 1756 to 1761. Pitt was created Earl of Chatham in 1766. A major opponent of Walpole (*q.v.*), Pitt earned a great reputation for his parliamentary speeches. During the 1750s Pitt came increasingly to represent the voice of the country against maladministration, but the disfavour of the King and his lack of parliamentary connections kept him from high office until 1756. His aggressive war policy helped Britain to victory in the Seven Years War, but he was forced to resign shortly after the accession of George III. Though prime minister again in 1766, ill-health and cabinet divisions prompted his resignation. He supported the claims of the American Colonists, but could not prevent the drift to war.

Churchill, Lord Randolph Henry Spencer (1849– 1894): Conservative MP 1874– 94; secretary for India, 1885– 6; leader of the House and chancellor of the exchequer 1886; during 1880s, became leader of Tory Democracy, which sought a core working-class support by maintaining Disraeli's policy of social reform; resigned from government in response to increased expenditure, thus prematurely ending his political career.

Churchill, Sir Winston Leonard Spencer (1874– 1965): Churchill entered parliament as Conservative MP for Oldham in 1900. In 1904 he became a Liberal in protest at the Conservative policy on Tariff Reform, but remained member for Oldham until 1906. He was Liberal MP for Manchester North West from 1906 to 1908 and for Dundee from 1908 to 1922. He represented Epping from 1924 to 1945, originally as a Constitutionalist, but later as a Conservative. He was Conservative MP for Woodford from 1945 to 1964. Churchill held office as under-secretary for the Colonial Office 1906– 8, president of the Board of Trade, 1908– 10, home secretary, 1910– 11, first lord of the Admiralty, 1911– 15, chancellor of the duchy of Lancaster, 1915, minister of munitions, 1917– 19, secretary for war and air, 1919– 21, secretary for air and colonies, 1921, colonial secretary, 1921– 2, chancellor of the exchequer, 1924– 9, first lord of the Admiralty, 1939– 40, minister of defence and prime minister, 1940– 5. He was leader of the opposition 1945– 51, prime minister, 1951– 5, and minister of defence, 1951– 2. In 1953 Churchill was appointed Knight of the Garter. Churchill's career was long and varied. After leaving the Conservative Party he became a radical and reforming minister. In the First World War disputes at the Admiralty and the failure of the Gallipoli expedition led to a temporary fall from grace, but he returned to office and served in the post-war coalition. He returned to the Conservative Party as chancellor of the exchequer and presided over Britain's return to the Gold Standard. During the inter-war period suspicions that he was at heart a reactionary appeared confirmed by his militant attitude against the General Strike and his opposition to the movement for Indian independence. But India and the question of rearmament also distanced him from his leaders in the 1930s and allowed his return as an alternative to Chamberlain. His natural dynamism inspired the country during the Second World War, but he was less in tune with the electorate's desire for post-war reform, and led his party to defeat in 1945. By 1951 he had come to terms with the demands of post-war Britain and led his party back to power.

Citrine, Walter McLennan, 1st Baron (1887–   ): General secretary of TUC 1926–46; chairman, Central Electricity Authority, 1947–57; Merseyside trade union leader; assistant general secretary of Electrical Trades Union 1920–3; led moderate wing of TUC after 1931, and worked with Bevin (*q.v.*) in support of moderation and against fascism; organised Second World War production policies, and presided over nationalisation of electricity.

Clive, Robert, 1st Baron (1725–1774): Clive was posted to Madras in the service of the East India Company in 1743. In the 1750s his actions established British supremacy over the French in India. In 1751 he seized Arcot to distract Chanda Sahib from the siege of Trichinopoly, and followed this up with victories at Arni and Covrepauk. In 1757 he led the expedition which recaptured Calcutta and defeated Surajah Dowlah at Plessey on 23 June 1757. Clive served as governor of Bengal, 1757–60 and 1765–7. He was acquitted of corruption in India before parliamentary committees in 1772–3, but committed suicide on 22 November 1774.

Cobbett, William (1763–1835): Radical journalist and politician. MP for Oldham from 1832; began publication in 1802 of weekly *Political Register* which became organ for his highly individualistic radical criticism; published *Parliamentary Debates* in 1804; imprisoned in 1810 following his attack on flogging in army; zealous parliamentary reformer; published *Rural Rides*, account of tours through England, in 1830; successfully defended case of inciting violence in reform agitation of 1831.

Cobden, Richard (1804–1865): Liberal MP 1841–65; active after 1835 as pamphleteer, chiefly concerned with issues of Free Trade and disarmament; together with Bright (*q.v.*) led Anti-Corn Law League; responsible for commercial treaty with France in 1860, reducing tariffs; helped maintain relations between Lincoln and Palmerston administrations during American Civil War.

Cole, George Douglas Howard (1889–1958): British socialist writer who published over 50 volumes in field of economics, socialist theory and working-class history; socialist and pacifist during First World War; became prominent in Labour politics as a leading Fabian; during Second World War he made important contributions to social policy through organising Nuffield College's Social Reconstruction Survey.

Cook, Arthur James (1885–1931): Trade union leader prominent in General Strike of 1926; active after 1905 in syndicalist and pacifist causes; led Miners' Federation of Great Britain after First World War, and built up alliance with road, railway and engineering workers to resist anticipated attempt to cut miners' wages.

Cornwallis, Charles, 1st Marquess (1738–1805): Cornwallis joined the Grenadier Guards in 1756, and distinguished himself in the Seven Years War. He was sent to America as a major-general in 1776, and made second-in-command of the forces there in 1778. In 1780 he was given the task of stamping out resistance in the southern states, defeating the Americans at Camden, 1780, and Guilford Courthouse, 1781. However, at a time when Britain had temporarily lost command of the seas, he was surrounded at Yorktown and forced to surrender on 19 October 1781. Cornwallis was governor-general and commander-in-chief in India, 1786–93, and defeated Tippoo Sahib in the Third Mysore War. On his return to England he was master-general of the ordnance, 1795–1801, and viceroy and commander-in-chief in Ireland, 1798–1801. He was again appointed to command in India in 1805, but died there on 5 October.

Cripps, Sir Richard Stafford (1889–1952): Labour MP Bristol East, later South East 1931–50; solicitor-general, 1930–1; lord privy seal and leader of House of Commons, 1942; president of Board of Trade, 1945–7; chancellor of the exchequer, 1947–50; expelled from Labour Party 1939 for advocating Popular Front; readmitted 1945; as chancellor advocated policy of 'austerity', but strict taxation and voluntary wage freeze failed to check inflation, and pound was devalued September 1949.

Davitt, Michael (1846–1906): Irish nationalist leader. Son of an Irish Roman Catholic peasant; joined the Fenians in 1865; founded Land League, 1879; Irish Nationalist MP 1892–3, 1895–9; endured several spells of imprisonment. Supporter of democratic nationalism, land nationalisation and anti-clericalism.

Derby, 14th Earl of, Edward George Geoffrey Smith Stanley (1799–1869): Stanley was Whig MP for Stockbridge 1820–6, for Preston 1826–30, for Windsor 1831–2 and for Lancashire North 1832–44. In 1844 he was elevated to the House of Lords as Lord Stanley of Bickerstaffe. Stanley served as under-secretary to the Colonial Office, 1827–28, chief secretary for Ireland 1830–3 and colonial secretary, 1833–4. In 1834 he resigned office in protest at the proposed lay appropriation of surplus Irish Church revenue. He served in Peel's government as colonial secretary, 1841–5. In 1845 he resigned in protest at proposals to repeal the Corn Laws. He became prime minister of Conservative governments 1852, 1858–9 and 1866–8. The major aim of Stanley and his colleagues in repeatedly agreeing to form minority governments was to establish the Conservative Party as a credible governing force. It was probably the desire to achieve this which prompted his 1866–8 government to extend the franchise.

Devonshire, 4th Duke of, William Cavendish (1720–1764): Styled the Marquess of Hartington, Cavendish was MP for Derbyshire, 1741–51. In 1751 he became Lord Cavendish of Hardwicke. He was made master of the horse and a privy councillor in 1751. In 1755 he became lord treasurer of Ireland, and later the same year lord lieutenant and chief governor of Ireland. He also succeeded as Duke of Devonshire in 1755. He became first lord of the Treasury (prime minister) in 1756, serving until 1757. In 1756 he was made lord lieutenant of Derbyshire and in 1757 a Knight of the Garter. His period as prime minister was the result of Pitt's refusal to serve with Newcastle and the Whigs' success in keeping Pitt out of office. Devonshire was a reluctant and unsuccessful prime minister and when Pitt and Newcastle came to terms he was soon replaced. In 1757 he became lord chamberlain of the household and held that post until 1762.

Disraeli, Benjamin, 1st Earl of Beaconsfield (1805– 1881): Disraeli was Conservative MP for Maidstone, 1837– 41, for Shrewsbury, 1841– 7 and for Buckinghamshire, 1847– 76. He served as leader of the Commons and chancellor of the exchequer in 1852, in 1858– 9 and 1866– 8. He was prime minister in 1868 and again from 1874 to 1880, also holding the office of lord privy seal, 1876– 8. Disraeli was created Earl of Beaconsfield in 1876. He led the Conservative Party until shortly before his death in 1881. Disraeli was a leading Conservative opponent of repeal of the Corn Laws. In 1867 he was responsible for a large extension of the franchise and as Conservative prime minister sought to emphasise Tory interest in social reform and the benefits of the Empire to the working class. As a novelist he dramatised the themes of his Toryism, in particular attacking the existence of 'two Englands'.

Douglas-Home, Sir Alec (Alexander Frederick), Lord Home of the Hirsel (1903–   ): Home was styled Lord Dunglass from 1918 to 1951. He was Conservative MP for South Lanark from 1931 to 1945, for Lanark, 1950– 1. In 1951 he succeeded as the 14th Earl of Home. He renounced his title in 1963 and between 1963 and 1974 was Conservative MP for Kinross and West Perthshire. In 1974 he was made a life peer. Home was parliamentary private secretary to Neville Chamberlain, 1937– 40, joint under-secretary to the Foreign Office, 1945, minister of state at the Scottish Office, 1951– 5, secretary for Commonwealth relations, 1955– 60, and deputy leader of the Lords, 1956– 7. He was lord president of the council in 1957 and 1959– 60, and leader of the Lords, 1957– 60. Between 1960 and 1963 he was foreign secretary. In 1963 he was chosen as leader of the Conservative Party and was prime minister, 1963– 64. From 1970 to 1974 he was foreign secretary. Although an experienced politician and diplomat, Home was a somewhat surprising choice as Macmillan's successor. Effectively in the position of 'caretaker' P.M. until the 1964 general election, Home was successful in preventing the expected large Labour victory.

Dowding, Hugh Caswell Tremenheere, Baron (1882– 1970): Air force leader. He joined the army in 1900 but served in the Royal Flying Corps during the First World War and stayed in the RAF when that was founded. From 1930 to 1936 he was air member for research and development on the Air Council where he encouraged development of Spitfire and Hurricane planes and authorised expenditure for experiments on building up a radar chain. He was appointed head of Fighter Command in 1936. He opposed the sending of fighter squadrons from England to France in 1940. He directed the British victory in the Battle of Britain. He was retired in 1942. Nicknamed 'Stuffy'.

Eden, Sir Robert Anthony, 1st Earl of Avon (1897– 1977): Conservative politician. Eden sat as Conservative MP for Warwick and Leamington from 1925 until he retired in 1957. He acted as parliamentary private secretary to Sir Austen Chamberlain (foreign secretary), 1926– 9, was under-secretary at the Foreign Office 1931– 3, lord privy seal, 1934– 5, minister without portfolio for League of Nations Affairs, 1935 and foreign secretary 1935– 8. In 1938 he resigned in protest at the government's policy of appeasement. He was secretary for the Dominions, 1939– 40, secretary for war, 1940 and foreign secretary, 1940– 5. Between 1942 and

1945 he was also leader of the Commons. He returned to the Foreign Office in 1951 and remained there until 1955. In 1954 he was made a Knight of the Garter. He was prime minister from 1955 to 1957, resigning in 1957 because of ill health. In 1961 he was created Earl of Avon. Eden was an extremely experienced diplomat but he miscalculated domestic and world opinion when authorising the ill-fated invasion of Suez in 1956.

Fisher, 1st Baron, John Arbuthnot Fisher (1841–1920): Naval leader. Fisher joined the navy in 1854 and served in the Crimean War. He had great energy and enthusiasm for new developments in naval warfare. As commander-in-chief in the Mediterranean, 1899–1902, he introduced new techniques in training and tactics, and as first sea lord, 1904–10, he pushed through the creation of a British battlefleet of big-gun ships. The first, the *Dreadnought*, with 10 12-inch guns, was launched in 1906. He retired in 1910, but returned as first sea lord in October 1914 when Battenberg resigned. Fisher resigned in 1915 after clashes with Churchill, the first lord of the Admiralty, over the wisdom of the Dardanelles expedition.

Fox, Charles James (1749–1806): MP for Midhurst, 1768–74; Malmesbury, 1774–80; Westminster, 1780–1806. Secretary of state for foreign affairs in Fox–North coalition 1782–3; foreign secretary again in 1806 during 'Ministry of All the Talents'. Joined Rockingham Whigs to oppose the government's American policy in 1774; thereafter remained in opposition except for two brief periods of office. Sympathetic to reform, religious toleration and other liberal causes, he welcomed the French Revolution and opposed the war with Revolutionary France. During the 1790s he emerged as a champion of English liberties in the face of Pitt's repressive measures, but his continued support for Revolutionary France split the Whig party, reducing his followers to a small group in the House of Commons.

Fry, Elizabeth (1750–1845): Social reformer and Quaker; visit to Newgate prison prompted her to become a champion of prison reform, especially regarding the treatment of women prisoners. Her activities were largely directed towards improving prison conditions in order to 'reform' prisoners. She became a European authority on prison reform.

Gaitskell, Hugh Todd Naylor (1906–1963): Labour MP in Leeds, 1945–63; chancellor of the exchequer, 1950–1; Labour Party leader from 1955 to 1963; considered by some the outstanding representative of the social democratic tradition within Labour Party; clashed with Bevanites over Health Service charges, but later united with Bevan (*q.v.*) to denounce Eden's Suez policy: sought unsuccessfully after 1959 election defeat to persuade party to drop socialist commitments. Died shortly after reuniting party on Common Market issue and defeating unilateralists.

George, David Lloyd, 1st Earl Lloyd George of Dwŷfor (1863–1945): Lloyd George was Liberal MP for Caernarvon Boroughs from 1890 to 1945. He served as president of the Board of Trade from 1905 to 1908, chancellor of the exchequer from 1908 to 1915, minister of munitions from 1915 to 1916, secretary for war, 1916 and was prime minister from 1916 to 1922. He led the Liberal Party from 1926 to 1931. In 1945 he was created Earl Lloyd George. As chancellor Lloyd George proved a radical social reformer, and as minister of munitions and wartime P.M. an efficient and dynamic administrator and leader. Seeking to thwart the ambitions of socialists and the Labour Party, he was often a keen advocate of Liberal–Conservative fusion or coalition, and it was Conservative backbench unrest at such a possibility that caused them to rebel against his government in 1922. His decision to oust Asquith from the premiership in 1916, and then to continue the wartime coalition after 1918, also did irreparable harm to the Liberal Party.

Goderich, 1st Viscount, *see* Ripon

Gordon, Charles George (1833–1885): Military leader. Gordon joined the Royal Engineers in 1852, and took part in the Crimean War and the capture of Peking in 1860. He then took command of the Chinese forces, the 'Ever Victorious Army', which crushed the Taiping Rebellion, earning him the nickname of 'Chinese' Gordon. He then entered the service of the Khedive of Egypt and administered the Sudan, 1877–80. As a devout evangelical Christian, one of his main concerns was the suppression of the slave trade. In 1884 he accepted the commission to organise the evacuation of the Sudan in the face of the rebellion led by the Mahdi. However, he remained in Khartoum. A relief expedition was sent too late, and Gordon was killed when Khartoum fell to the Mahdi's forces on 26 January 1885. In England the prime minister, Gladstone, the 'Grand Old Man', was renamed the 'MOG' ('Murderer of Gordon').

Grafton, 3rd Duke of, Augustus Henry Fitzroy (1735–1811): Fitzroy was MP for Bury St Edmunds in 1756, succeeding as the Duke of Grafton in 1757. He was secretary of state for the Northern Department, 1765–6 and nominal head of the 1766 Chatham administration. When Chatham (*q.v.*) resigned in 1768 he became prime minister and held the office until 1770. He was lord privy seal, 1771–5 and again in 1782.

Graham, Sir James Robert George (1792–1861): MP from 1818, first at Hull, then St Ives and Carlisle; first lord of the Admiralty, 1830; home secretary 1841–6; first lord of the Admiralty, 1852; Canningite in 1820s, Graham joined Grey between 1830 and 1834 when he and Stanley seceded from the Whigs on the question of Irish Church Reform; as Peelite home secretary was responsible for public order during Chartist disturbances.

Granville, 1st Earl, John Carteret, (1690–1763): Secretary of state for Northern Department, 1742–4; as ambassador to Sweden, contributed to negotiations ending Great Northern War in 1721; protégé of Stanhope (*q.v.*); pursued energetic foreign policy aimed at isolating French; supporter of Hanoverian succession; became violent critic of government as result of struggle with Walpole and Townshend (*qq.v.*); later incurred hostility of Pelham–Hardwicke faction; failed in attempt to form ministry, 1746.

Grenville, George (1712–1770): Grenville was MP for Buckingham, 1741–70. He became treasurer of the navy in 1756 and held that office until 1762. In 1762 he became secretary of state. He was first lord of the

Admiralty, 1762–3, chancellor of the exchequer, 1763–5, and first lord of the Treasury, 1763–5.

Grenville, 1st Baron, William Wyndham Grenville (1759–1834): Grenville was MP for Buckingham, 1782–4, and for Buckinghamshire 1784–90. In 1790 he was created 1st Baron Grenville. Grenville was chief secretary for Ireland 1782–3, paymaster and joint paymaster, 1783–9, vice-president of the Board of Trade, 1786–9, speaker in 1789, home secretary, 1789–90 president of the Board of Control, 1790–3, foreign secretary, 1791–1801 and prime minister, 1806–7.

Grey, 2nd Earl, Charles Grey, Viscount Howick (1764–1845): Grey was MP for Northumberland, 1786–1807, for Appleby in 1807. He was styled Viscount Howick in 1806 on his father's elevation in the peerage and succeeded as 2nd Earl Grey in 1807. He held office as first lord of the Admiralty in 1806, and as foreign secretary 1806–7. He was prime minister from 1830 to 1834. Grey was a conservative Whig, and although he accepted the need for franchise reform, and was P.M. when the 1832 Reform Bill was passed, he saw the 1832 Act as a final concession to popular opinion and not as the start of a continuous process of reform.

Grey, 1st Viscount, Sir Edward Grey (1862–1933): Liberal MP Berwick-on-Tweed, 1885–1916; foreign secretary, 1905–16. His support of Britain's obligation to help Belgium in 1914 took Britain into the First World War; believed in international arbitration, used successfully in Balkan Wars; later a champion of the League of Nations.

Guildford, 2nd Earl of, *see* North

Haig, 1st Earl, Sir Douglas Haig (1861–1928): Military leader. The son of a Scottish distiller, Haig was commissioned in the 7th Hussars in 1885, and distinguished himself in the Boer War. He was principal military adviser to the reforming war minister, Haldane, from 1906 to 1908. He led the 1st Army Corps of the British Expeditionary Force to France in 1914, and fought at Mons, on the Meuse and at Ypres. In 1915 he succeeded French as British commander-in-chief on the Western Front. Haig has been fiercely criticised for the way in which he conducted the battles of attrition of the Somme, 1916, and Ypres, 1917, but his determination and confidence in 1918 overcame the shock of defeat in March and led to final victory in November.

Halifax, 1st Earl of, Edward Frederick Lindley Wood, 1st Baron Irwin (1881–1959): Conservative MP for Ripon, 1910–25; viceroy of India, 1926–31; lord president of the council, 1937–8; foreign secretary 1938–40; ambassador to USA, 1941–6. As Indian viceroy, he dealt with unrest on the North West Frontier and Gandhi's campaign of civil disobedience; reached agreement with Gandhi, March 1931. As foreign secretary he was one of the major exponents of policy of 'appeasement'.

Harcourt, Sir William George Granville Venables Vernon- (1827–1904): Liberal MP for Derby then West Monmouthshire 1868–1904; home secretary, 1880–5; chancellor of the exchequer, 1886 and 1892–5;

Liberal leader in the House of Commons, 1894–8; influential
parliamentarian; introduced single graduated estate duty in 1894.

Hardie, James Keir (1856–1915): Labour leader. Independent Labour MP
for West Ham 1892–5; Chairman ILP 1893–1900, 1913–15; Labour MP
for Merthyr Tydfil 1900–15; chairman, Labour Party, 1906, Coal-miner
who became foremost British socialist, establishing Scottish Labour
Party in 1888 and helping to establish the ILP in 1893; crucial influence
in shaping political history of British Labour movement, and directing it
into independence of existing major parties.

Harris, Sir Arthur (1892–   ): A major advocate of offensive air power
before 1939; Harris became head of Bomber Command in February 1942,
and remained there until the end of the war where he gained fame as
'Bomber Harris'. Concluding that selective bombing was impossible, he
began the campaign of area bombing, which he believed would destroy
Germany's war-making capacity and morale.

Heath, Edward Richard George (1916–   ): Conservative politician.
Heath was Conservative MP for Bexley from 1950 to 1974, and MP for
Sidcup from 1974. He was a whip from 1951 to 1955 and chief whip from
1955 to 1959. He was minister of labour from 1959 to 1960, lord privy seal
from 1960 to 1963 and secretary for trade and industry between 1963 and
1964. In 1965 he became the first leader of the Conservative Party to be
elected by ballot. He was prime minister from 1970 to 1974. In 1975 he
withdrew from the contest for party leadership after being beaten by Mrs
Thatcher in the first ballot. As prime minister Heath never succeeded in
coming to terms with the trade unions and could not solve the problem
of inflation. The fuel crisis and the miners' strike forced him to call the
February 1974 election. Two electoral defeats led the party to opt for
fresh leadership in 1975.

Henderson, Arthur (1863–1935): Labour politician. Labour MP for
Barnard Castle, 1903–18; Widnes, 1919–22; Newcastle, 1923; Burnley,
1929–31; Clay Cross, 1933–5; Labour chief whip 1906–14; president of
Board of Education, 1915–16; minister for labour as paymaster-general,
1916; member of war cabinet, 1916–17; home secretary, 1924; foreign
secretary, 1929–31. Wesleyan lay preacher and trade union official who
believed in necessity of Labour Party as means of representing
working-class interests; an architect of the 1918 Labour Party
Constitution; helped Labour recovery from 1931 election debacle.

Home of the Hirsel, Lord, *see* Douglas-Home

Howard, John (1726–1790): Quaker philanthropist, notable for efforts to
improve prison conditions, especially bad sanitation and system of
paying gaolers out of fees extracted from prisoners.

Hunt, Henry (1773–1835): MP for Preston, 1830–2; radical political
reformer known popularly as 'Orator Hunt'; advocate of universal
suffrage and annual parliaments; presided over meeting at St Peter's
Fields, Manchester, in August 1819 which culminated in notorious

Peterloo Massacre. Tried and convicted for radical views in 1820, Hunt wrote exposé of prison conditions. Won parliamentary seat on reform platform, but lost it in 1832 election following Reform Act.

Huskisson, William (1770–1830): MP for Morpeth 1796–1802; for Liskeard 1802–7; Hawick, 1807–12; Chichester, 1812–23; Liverpool, 1823–30; president of Board of Trade 1823–7; secretary for war and colonies, 1827–8; Tory reformer and protégé of Pitt, who continued Pitt's work of fiscal reform; resigned as secretary for war following clash with Wellington; killed by locomotive while attending opening of Liverpool and Manchester Railway.

Hyndman, Henry Mayers (1842–1921): British Marxist; author of *England for All*, 1881, and many other works of socialist propaganda; founder of Social Democratic Federation; important influence on many early socialists; failed to recognise the importance of trade unions and working-class liberals as potential supporters of working-class political party.

Jones, Ernest (1819–1869): Advocate of socialist ideas. Son of a wealthy cavalry officer who became a barrister. Joined O'Connorite chartists in 1846. Stood as Chartist candidate for parliament. Imprisoned in 1848 for advocating 'physical force'; he wrote *Chartist Songs*, 1846, and edited the *People's Paper*, 1852–8.

Keble, John (1792–1866): Anglican theologian. Professor of Poetry at Oxford, 1831; became leading member of Oxford Movement following sermon in 1833 against proposed suppression of 10 Irish bishoprics; contributed to *Tracts for the Times*; friend and adviser of Newman (*q.v.*) and later worked closely with Pusey (*q.v.*) to keep High Church movement attached to Church of England; Keble College, Oxford, was founded in his memory.

Kitchener, 1st Earl, Horatio Herbert Kitchener (1850–1916): Military leader. Kitchener joined the Royal Engineers in 1870. He served in the Sudan and Egypt, 1882–5, and was governor-general of East Sudan, 1886–8. As commander-in-chief ('Sirdar') of the Anglo-Egyptian Army in the 1890s he undertook the reconquest of the Sudan, defeating the dervishes at Omdurman on 2 September 1898. In the Boer War he acted as chief of staff to Roberts until November 1900. On becoming commander-in-chief in South Africa he broke the resistance of the Boers by the use of blockhouses and concentration camps. As commander-in-chief in India, 1902–9 he quarrelled over control of the Indian Army with the viceroy, Lord Curzon, who resigned in 1905. Kitchener was British agent and consul-general in Egypt, 1911–14, then on 5 August 1914 he was appointed war minister. He had enormous success in raising new volunteer armies for the Western Front, but the habits of military command did not fit him to work well with his political colleagues. He was drowned on a mission to Russia on 5 June 1916, when the cruiser HMS Hampshire struck a mine off the Orkney Islands.

Lansbury, George (1859–1940): Labour leader. Labour MP for Poplar,

Bow and Bromley, 1910–12, 1922–40; member of Labour government
1929–31 as first commissioner of works; Labour Party leader, 1932–5;
pacifist and Christian socialist; influential propagandist as editor of *Daily
Herald*.

Lansdowne, 1st Marquess, *see* Shelburne

Law, Andrew Bonar (1858–1923): Conservative politician. Law was
Conservative MP for Glasgow Blackfriars from 1900 to 1906, for Dulwich
from 1906 to 1910, for Bootle from 1911 to 1918, for Glasgow Central
from 1918 to 1923. He was parliamentary secretary to the Board of Trade
from 1902 to 1905. In 1911 he became leader of the Conservative Party.
He took office in the wartime coalition as colonial secretary, 1915 to 1916,
and chancellor of the exchequer from 1916 to 1918. In the post-war
coalition he was lord privy seal and leader of the House of Commons
from 1919 to 1921. In 1921 he resigned. In 1922 he became leader of the
Conservative Party again following the revolt of the Conservative
backbenchers and prime minister. He retired in 1923 and died the same
year. The main significance of Law's premiership was that it proved the
Conservatives could form a government without the Liberal Lloyd
George being necessary to lead them.

Liverpool, 2nd Earl of, Robert Banks Jenkinson (1770–1828): Jenkinson
was MP for Appleby, 1790–6, and for Rye, 1796–1803. In 1803 he
became Baron Hawkesbury. He was master of the Mint, 1799 to 1801,
foreign secretary 1801–4, home secretary, 1804–6 and 1807–9. He
succeeded as 2nd Earl of Liverpool in 1808. From 1809 to 1812 he held
the office of secretary for war and the colonies, and became first lord of
the Treasury (and prime minister) in 1812, a post he held until 1827.
Liverpool's ministry was perhaps more impressive than that of the more
famous Pitt, and was based both on Liverpool's own political skill and on
the collective talents of his ministers.

Lloyd George, David *see* George

MacDonald, James Ramsay (1866–1937): Labour politician. MacDonald
was Labour MP (National Labour, 1931–7) for Leicester 1906–18, for
Aberavon 1922–9, for Seaham 1929–35, and for Scottish Universities,
1936–7. He was secretary of the Labour Representation Committee and
the Labour Party, 1900–12, treasurer of the party, 1912–24 and
chairman, 1911–14. He was chairman of the Independent Labour Party,
1906–9, and of the Parliamentary Labour Party in 1922. He was leader of
the Labour Party, 1922–31. MacDonald was prime minister and foreign
secretary in 1924, prime minister of the 1929–31 Labour government and
of the National Government, 1931–5. From 1935 to 1937 he was lord
president of the council. A servant of the Labour Party from its early days
MacDonald helped make Labour appear a plausible and competent
governing force, particularly in foreign affairs. But his desire to make
Labour a 'responsible' party of government led to the cabinet split of
1931 on the reduction of unemployment benefits; and his decision to
form a 'National' government and to campaign against the Labour Party
in the ensuing election earned his expulsion from the party.

Macmillan, (Maurice) Harold (1894–   ): Conservative politician. Macmillan was Conservative MP for Stockton-on-Tees from 1924 to 1929 and 1931 to 1945, and for Bromley from 1945 to 1964. He served as parliamentary secretary to the Ministry of Supply, 1940 to 1942, under secretary to the Colonial Office in 1942, minister resident at Allied HQ in NW Africa, 1942–5, secretary for air, 1945, minister of housing and local government, 1951–4, minister of defence 1954–5, Foreign Secretary, 1955, chancellor of the exchequer, 1955–7 and prime minister, 1957–63. As early as the 1930s Macmillan revealed himself as an advocate of the Tory paternalist tradition in the Conservative Party, a stance which suited the mood of the 1950s and facilitated his rise to the premiership. His term in Downing Street was seen as something of a high point of post-war prosperity. But by the time of his resignation in 1963 it appeared to many people that Macmillan's style of leadership was dated and out of touch with the new decade. He retired due to ill health.

Mann, Tom (1856–1941): Trade union leader and socialist propagandist. Miner and artisan who came to London from Birmingham, and joined trade union movement in 1881; joined Hyndman's (q.v.) Social Democratic Federation in 1885, and supported the movement to establish eight hour working day; involved in dockworkers' strike 1889. A leader of the militant industrial struggles before the First World War, he became general secretary of the Amalgamated Society of Engineers, 1918–21, and a leading member of the Communist Party.

Manning, Henry Edward (1808–1892): Religious leader, an evangelical who swung to Tractarian side in 1840s and became one of leaders of the Oxford Movement after Newman's (q.v.) secession in 1845; received into Roman Catholic Church in 1851 and reordained; Roman Catholic archbishop of Westminster from 1865 he became a cardinal; gave support to doctrine of Papal Infallibility at Vatican Council (1869–70); prominent in social work of all kinds and in 1889 successfully mediated in London dock strike.

Martineau, Harriet (1802–1876): Philanthropist. Author of *Illustrations of Political Economy*, 1832, moral tales designed to explain workings of economic laws, and of *Forest and Game Law Tales* and the novel *Deerbrook*; visited USA between 1834 and 1836 and became advocate of abolition of slavery; *Positive Philosophy*, 1853, was popularisation and condensation of Comte's philosophy.

Mayhew, Henry (1812–1887): Pioneer of systematic social investigation; in 1849–50, published 76 letters about London poor (*London Labour and the London Poor*) as part of *Morning Chronicle*'s nationwide survey of poverty; republished 1861–2, but then discontinued following reaction to vigour of its attack on political economy of day; joint first editor of *Punch*, 1841.

Melbourne, 2nd Viscount, William Lamb (1779–1848): Politician. Lamb was Whig MP for Leominster in 1806, for Portarlington, 1807–12, for Northampton, 1816–19 and for Hertfordshire, 1819–29. In 1829 he became Viscount Melbourne. He held office as secretary for Ireland, 1827–8 and home secretary, 1830–40. Melbourne was prime minister in

1834 and again from 1835 to 1841. A Whig, and disliked as such by the
King, Melbourne's outdated view of the constitution helped result (in
1834) in his being the last P.M. to be dismissed by the monarch. Between
1835 and 1841 Melbourne proved reluctant to respond to the Chartist and
Anti-Corn Law movements.

Mill, James (1773–1836): Scottish philosopher who became early
exponent of utilitarianism in government and the centre of a group of
philosophic liberals including his son J. S. Mill (*q.v.*), Bentham (*q.v.*) and
Ricardo; his articles on prisons in *Encyclopaedia Britannica*, 1823,
advocated reform through industry rather than mere punishment;
supported foundation of London University, 1828.

Mill, John Stuart (1806–1873): Liberal MP for Westminster, 1865–8;
influenced by Bentham (*q.v.*) and utilitarian philosophy of James Mill
(*q.v.*), became leading philosopher of nineteenth-century liberalism;
advocate of equal rights for women and respect for minorities; author of
On Liberty, 1859; humanist who saw need for state intervention to
prevent abuses of *laissez-faire*; later regarded himself as socialist.

Montgomery, 1st Viscount, Sir Bernard Law Montgomery (1887–1976):
Military leader. Son of a bishop, he joined the Royal Warwickshire
Regiment from Sandhurst in 1908. Although wounded in the chest in
1914 he returned to France in 1916. He rose to the rank of
lieutenant-colonel and battalion commander by the end of the war. In
1940 he was evacuated from Dunkirk with the 3rd Division which he was
commanding. By December 1941 he was head of South-eastern
Command and a lieutenant-general. Montgomery was chosen to
command the 8th Army in North Africa in 1942. He transformed the army
so that it was able to halt Rommel's advance on Cairo at Alam Halfa (31
August–7 September) and counter-attack at El Alamein beginning 23
October. The battle, well planned and methodically accomplished, was a
British victory. He led the invasion of Sicily and Italy, then was appointed
land commander for the invasion of Europe (Overlord). He came into
conflict over personal and strategic matters with American allies. After
the war he was chief of the imperial general staff and deputy commander
of NATO.

Moore, Sir John (1761–1809): Military leader. The son of a Glasgow
doctor, Moore joined the 51st Foot in 1776 and saw action in Nova Scotia
during the American War of Independence. In the following years he
served in many campaigns – Corsica 1794–5, West Indies 1796–7,
Ireland 1797–9, Holland 1799, the Mediterranean and Egypt, 1800–1,
Sicily 1806 and Sweden 1808. His reputation as a military reformer was
enhanced by his period at Shorncliffe Camp, 1803–6, where he
successfully experimented with light infantry tactics and the training of
troops. He took command of the British force in the Peninsula in 1808. He
advanced into Spain, but was forced to retreat to Corunna. He was fatally
wounded as his army evacuated on 16 January 1809.

Morris, William (1834–1896): Idealist socialist, poet, painter, designer;
founder of Arts and Crafts movement; established close association
between art and political beliefs; involved in creation of Socialist League,

1884, and Hammersmith Socialist Society, 1890; lasting artistic influence, and a major influence on later socialists.

Mosley, Sir Oswald Ernald (1896–1980): Conservative MP for Harrow, 1918–22; Independent MP, 1922–4; Labour MP for Smethwick, 1926–31; chancellor of the duchy of Lancaster, 1929–30; founder of progressive socialist New Party which unsuccessfully contested 21 seats in 1931 general election; formed British Union of Fascists in 1932, which engaged in anti-Semitic and Hitlerite activities until 1936 Public Order Act banned political uniforms and street marches; interned 1940–3.

Mountbatten, 1st Earl, Lord Louis Mountbatten (1900–1979): Naval commander. At the outbreak of the Second World War Mountbatten was commanding the Fifth Destroyer Flotilla. In 1941 his ship, HMS *Kelly*, was sunk in the Mediterranean and he was nearly drowned. He was then appointed adviser on combined operations. His largest operation was the Dieppe Raid in August 1942, which though a failure, taught valuable lessons. Mountbatten was then appointed supreme commander in South-East Asia, arriving in India in October 1943 to find a diversity of problems. After the war he was viceroy of India and presided over the partition of the subcontinent and the independence of India and Pakistan. He later returned to a naval career. In 1955 he was first sea lord and in 1959 chief of the defence staff. He was assassinated by Irish extremists in 1979.

Newcastle, 1st Duke of, Thomas Pelham-Holles (1695–1768): Newcastle was secretary of state for the Southern Department, 1724–54. He held the office of first lord of the Treasury twice, 1754–6 and 1757–62. Between July 1765 and August 1766 he was lord privy seal. Pelham-Holles was created Earl of Clare in 1714 and Duke of Newcastle in 1715. Newcastle was a skilled and efficient manipulator of parliamentary patronage, but as prime minister found that, although he had the confidence of George II, he needed the support of Pitt to secure the confidence of the Commons. When Chatham left office in 1761, Newcastle found it increasingly difficult to hold his ministry together and was replaced by George III's favourite, Bute, in May 1762.

Newman, John Henry (1801–1890): Theologian. Brought up in Church of England under evangelical influence, in 1833 he became leading spirit of the Oxford Movement; he wrote 24 *Tracts for the Times* between 1833 and 1841; he believed the Church of England should hold an intermediate position between Romanism and Protestantism; he withdrew from Oxford following controversy over interpretation of the Thirty-nine Articles in 1841, and was received into the Roman Catholic Church in 1845; he became a cardinal and had considerable influence on the revival of Catholicism in England.

Nelson, 1st Viscount, Horatio Nelson (1758–1805): Naval leader. The son of a Norfolk parson, Nelson entered the navy in 1770 and saw service in the Arctic, the East Indies and the West Indies. In 1793 he was sent to the Mediterranean, where he lost an eye the following year in the occupation of Corsica. In 1797 he played a leading role in the victorious battle of Cape St Vincent in February, but in July lost his right arm in the unsuccessful attack on Santa Cruz. In 1798 he failed to intercept the French expedition to Egypt while blockading Toulon, but destroyed the French fleet at the battle of the Nile on 1 August. A brilliant tactician, Nelson had the ability to inspire his subordinates to display courage and initiative. In 1801 he destroyed the Danish fleet in Copenhagen harbour, putting his telescope to his blind eye to avoid seeing his superior's order to disengage. Nelson was appointed to the Mediterranean command in 1803. The French admiral, Villeneuve, eluded his blockade of Toulon in spring 1805, but after a pursuit, Nelson defeated the Franco-Spanish fleet at Trafalgar on 21 October. During the battle Nelson was mortally wounded by a sniper.

North, Frederick, 2nd Earl of Guildford (1732–1792): North was styled Lord North from 1752 to 1790. He was MP for Banbury, 1754–90. In 1790 he succeeded as Earl of Guildford. He served as lord of the treasury, 1759 to 1765, joint paymaster-general from 1766 to 1767, chancellor of the exchequer, 1767–82 and first lord of the Treasury (prime minister), 1770–82. He was secretary of state for colonial affairs, April–December 1783 in the Fox–North coalition. North has been held by many historians to have been an able domestic politician, but whose handling of the American crisis and conduct of the war led to his downfall.

O'Brien, James Bronterre (1805–1864): Irish radical and advocate of land nationalisation and extension to workers of credit based on it; member of Working Men's Association; Chartist who advocated violence, but after 1839 stressed need for middle-class support and thereafter advised moderation.

O'Connell, Daniel (1775–1847): Irish nationalist; known as 'The Liberator'. Born in County Kerry, he founded the Catholic Association in 1823 as a mass movement to campaign for Catholic Emancipation. Elected for County Clare in 1828, but as a Catholic not allowed to take his seat. His efforts helped to secure the passing of the Roman Catholic Relief Act, 1829. Subsequently, took seat as MP for County Clare, 1830, and for Waterford, 1832. Organised mass meetings in 1842 and 1843 to secure repeal of the 1800 Act of Union. His cancellation of the Clontarf meeting in October 1843 discredited him with many Irish extremists. He died at Genoa.

O'Connor, Feargus (1794–1855): Chartist leader. MP for Cork, 1832–35; MP for Nottingham from 1847; leading Chartist who owned and edited Chartist periodical *Northern Star* and dominated militant northern section of movement; organised Chartist demonstration, 1848.

Orford, 1st Earl of, *see* Walpole.

Owen, Robert (1771–1858): Utopian socialist propagandist. Scottish millowner who attempted at New Lanark to create model factory employing no young children, educating older children and limiting adult hours; used term 'socialist' to describe experiment; *New View of Society*, 1813, expounded value of cooperative ideal; unsuccessful in attempt to establish socialistic community in USA, 1825–9; helped found Grand National Consolidated Trades Union, 1834.

Oxford and Asquith, 1st Earl of, *see* Asquith

Paine, Thomas (1737–1809): Excise officer who emigrated to America following conflict over pay claim; published *Common Sense* in 1776 demanding complete independence for the American colonies; served with Washington, but returned to England, 1787; published Parts I and II of *The Rights of Man* between 1791 and 1792 in response to Burke's (*q.v.*) criticisms of French Revolution; fled to France, 1792 and was convicted of seditious libel *in absentia*; died in exile in America.

Palmerston, 3rd Viscount, Henry John Temple (1784–1865): Temple was Tory MP for Newport, 1807–11, for Cambridge University 1811–31, Whig member for Bletchingly, 1831–2, for Hampshire South, 1832–4, and for Tiverton, 1835–65. Temple succeeded as Viscount Palmerston in 1802. He was a lord of the Admiralty, 1807–09. In 1809 he declined the chancellorship of the exchequer and became secretary for war, 1809 to 1828. He was foreign secretary, 1830–4, 1835–41, 1846–51, and home secretary, 1852–5. He was prime minister from 1855 to 1858 and 1859 to 1865. Palmerston captured the imagination of mid-Victorian Britain by his aggressive nationalism, and his popularity was such that he was returned as prime minister in 1859 despite his known hostility to the growing demand for electoral reform.

Pankhurst, Emmeline (1858–1928): Feminist leader. Joint founder and leader after 1898 of Women's Franchise League, and with daughter Christabel of more militant Women's Social and Political Union, 1903; talks with prime minister in 1906 led to disillusionment with Liberals and resort to more violent tactics; engaged in arson and hunger strikes while imprisoned; encouraged women to join armed forces and work in industry during First World War.

Parnell, Charles Stewart (1846–91): Irish nationalist leader. Son of Anglican gentry family, educated at Cambridge. Nationalist MP for Co. Meath, 1875–80, Cork 1880–91, leading Irish Nationalist Party in parliament from 1878. Led agitation for Home Rule, skilfully coordinating political bargaining at Westminster with more radical movements in Ireland. Career ruined when cited in O'Shea divorce case of 1890.

Passfield, 1st Baron, *see* Webb

Peel, Sir Robert, 2nd Bt (1788–1850): Conservative politician. Peel was Tory MP for Cashel, 1809–17, for Oxford University, 1817–28, for Westbury, 1829, and for Tamworth, 1830–50. He was under-secretary at the Colonial Office, 1810–12, chief secretary for Ireland, 1812–18, home secretary, 1822–7 and 1828–30, leader of the Commons, 1828–30 and prime minister and chancellor of the exchequer, 1834–5. He again became prime minister in 1841, resigning in 1845, but resuming office when the Whigs could not form a government. He retained the premiership until 1846. Peel is best remembered for his financial reforms and for his endeavours to prove that Conservatism was compatible with cautious reform. His repeal of the Corn Duties in 1846 split his party and left him at the head of a band of Free Trade 'Peelites' until his death in a riding accident in 1850.

Pelham, Henry (1695–1754): He was MP for Seaford, 1717–22, Sussex, 1722–54, secretary at war from 1724, and paymaster of the Forces from 1730, first lord of the Treasury and chancellor of the exchequer, 1743–54. An able administrator, Pelham sought to re-establish the country's finances and pursue a peaceful foreign policy. His position was substantially assisted by his brother's (the Duke of Newcastle) control of parliamentary patronage.

Perceval, Spencer (1762–1812): Perceval was MP for Northampton, 1796–1812. He was attorney-general from 1802 to 1806, and chancellor of the exchequer and the duchy of Lancaster from 1807 to 1809. He was prime minister and chancellor of the exchequer from 1809 to 1812 when he became the only British prime minister to have been assassinated, by one John Bellingham, who had nurtured a grievance against the government.

Pitt, William, 'the Elder', *see* Chatham

Pitt, William (1759–1806): Son of William Pitt 'the Elder', he was MP for Appleby, 1781–4; Cambridge University, 1784–1806. He was chancellor of the exchequer, 1782–3 and prime minister and chancellor of the exchequer, 1783–1801 and 1804–6. The youngest ever prime minister, Pitt was chosen by the King as an alternative to the Fox–North (*q.v.*) coalition, but emerged as a powerful leader in the House of Commons. He carried out sweeping administrative reforms in the 1780s and was sympathetic to parliamentary reform. From 1793 he led Britain in the war against Revolutionary France, repressing radicalism at home and initiating new financial measures, such as the income tax. He resigned when George III refused to allow Catholic Emancipation in 1801, but returned to office in 1804.

Place, Francis (1771–1854): Radical reformer. London journeyman breeches-maker prominent in London Corresponding Society and reform agitation of 1790s; later led campaign against 'Sinking Fund' and Combination Laws, repeal of the latter being secured in 1824. Helped 'Political Unions' formulate demands for parliamentary reform, 1832; helped draft 'People's Charter'.

Portland, 3rd Duke of, William Henry Cavendish-Bentinck (1738–1809): Cavendish-Bentinck, styled Marquess of Titchfield, was MP for Weobley, 1761–2. In 1762 he succeeded as Duke of Portland. He was viceroy of Ireland in 1782, prime minister in 1783 and again from 1807 to 1809. He was home secretary from 1794 to 1801 and lord president of the council from 1801 to 1805.

Potter, George (1832–1893): Trade union leader. He was a carpenter prominent in London builders' strike of 1859; he ran an influential labour paper in London, *Beehive*, to encourage strikes in provinces; and was an aggressive unionist who saw the vote as a necessity for members to secure legislation safeguarding union funds and protecting rights; in the summer of 1864 he organised Conference of Trades; as president of London Working Men's Association, opened Trade Union Congress in 1868.

Pulteney, William, *see* Bath

Pusey, Edward Bouverie (1800–1882): Regius Professor of Hebrew and Canon of Christ Church, Oxford; leading member of Oxford Movement; became leader following Newman's withdrawal, 1841; assisted in establishment of first Anglican sisterhood; sermon on absolution in 1846 led to practice of private confession in Anglican Church.

Redmond, John Edward (1856–1918): Irish nationalist leader. Son of an Irish Catholic gentry family, he was Irish Nationalist MP for New Ross, 1881–5; N. Wexford, 1885–91, Waterford, 1891–1918, and leader of reunited Nationalist Party from 1900. Worked for Home Rule by constitutional means up to Easter rising of 1916, but the rise of Sinn Fein made his approach seem redundant.

Rhodes, Cecil John (1853–1902): Champion of the British imperial cause in southern Africa. Went to Africa in 1870 where he earned a fortune from diamond-mining. Founded De Beers Company in 1880 at Kimberley and acquired interests in the Transvaal gold-fields. In 1887 founded the British South Africa Company to develop the region north of the Transvaal, later know as Rhodesia, and in 1890 mounted an expedition which established a settlement in Salisbury and secured the rest of the country. Made premier of Cape Colony in 1890, but was forced to resign in 1896 because of his connection with the Jameson raid. He left most of his fortune to Oxford University.

Ripon, 1st Earl of, Frederick John Robinson, 1st Viscount Goderich (1782–1859): Robinson was MP for Carlow Borough, 1806–7, and for Ripon from 1807 to 1827. In 1827 he was created 1st Viscount Goderich. In 1833 he was created Earl of Ripon. Robinson was president of the Board of Trade and treasurer of the navy from 1818 to 1823, chancellor of the exchequer, 1823 to 1827, secretary for war and colonies, April–August 1827 and 1830–3. He served as prime minister from August 1827 to January 1828, as lord privy seal, April 1833 to May 1834, as president of the Board of Trade, 1841–3 and as president of the Board of Control 1843–6. Goderich was asked to serve as prime minister following the death of his friend, Canning. He proved unable to control his ministry and resigned following the refusal of Huskisson and Herries to serve together.

Roberts, 1st Earl, Frederick Sleigh Roberts (1832–1914): Military leader. The son of a general, Roberts was born in India and joined the Bengal Artillery in 1851. He won the Victoria Cross during the Indian Mutiny, in January 1858. As commander of the Punjab Frontier Force, he defeated the Afghans and imposed the treaty of Gardamak in May 1879. After a British force had been defeated by the Afghans at Maiwand, Roberts became a national hero by marching his army 300 miles in 22 days to relieve Kandahar on 1 September 1880. He was commander-in-chief in India, 1885–93 and in Ireland, 1895–9. After the initial British disasters in the Boer War, Roberts was sent to command in South Africa. He returned to England in 1901 to be commander-in-chief (until 1904). His last years were devoted to advocating conscription through the National Service

League. He died on 14 November 1914 after contracting pneumonia during a visit to Indian troops in France.

Robinson, Frederick John, *see* Ripon

Rockingham, 2nd Marquess of, Charles Watson-Wentworth (1730–1782): Watson-Wentworth succeeded as Marquess of Rockingham in 1750. He was lord lieutenant of the North and West Ridings of Yorkshire from July 1751 to December 1762, and lord of the bedchamber, 1751–62. He held the office of first lord of the Treasury from July 1765 to July 1766, and again from March 1782 until his death.

Rodney, 1st Baron, George Brydges Rodney (1718–1792): Naval leader. Rodney joined the navy in 1732. He served in the War of the Austrian Succession and the Seven Years War, and was governor of Newfoundland, 1749–52. Promoted to admiral in 1778, he led a fleet to relieve Gibraltar in 1780, then sailed for the West Indies. At the battle of the Saints on 12 April 1782, he defeated the French fleet under the Comte de Grasse, restoring English naval supremacy and helping to ensure a more favourable peace settlement at the end of the American War of Independence.

Rosebery, 5th Earl of, Archibald Philip Primrose, 1st Earl of Midlothian (1847–1929): Created earl in 1868, Rosebery held first the office of under-secretary to the Home Office, 1881–3. In 1885 he became first commissioner of works and later in the year lord privy seal. He served as foreign secretary in 1886 and from 1892 to 1894. He was prime minister and lord president of the council, 1894–5. In 1889 and 1890 and again in 1892 he was chairman of the London County Council. After internal party squabbles he resigned the leadership of the Liberal Party in 1896. An exceptionally gifted individual, Rosebery proved a surprisingly inept premier, and through hesitancy and indecision failed to return to office after resigning the party leadership.

Rowntree, Seebohm (1871–1954): British manufacturer and philanthropist; son of Quaker reformer and chocolate manufacturer, Joseph Rowntree, he spent a considerable time in the study and alleviation of poverty, and was involved in organisations such as the Nuffield Trust for Special Areas, the Outward Bound Trust and the War on Want Committee. Publications include studies of urban poverty and *Poverty and the Welfare State*.

Russell, 1st Earl, Lord John Russell (1792–1878): Liberal politician. Russell was MP for Huntingdonshire from 1820 to 1826, for Bandon Bridge 1826–30, for Tavistock in 1831, for Devon, 1831–2, for Devon South, 1832–5, for Stroud, 1835–41 and for the City of London, 1841–61. In 1861 he was created Earl Russell. He was postmaster-general, 1830–4, obtaining a seat in the cabinet in 1831, home secretary, 1835–9 and colonial secretary, 1839–41. He served as prime minister between 1846 and 1852. After resigning the premiership he held office as foreign secretary, 1852–3, minister without portfolio, 1853–4, lord president of the council, 1854–5, colonial secretary, 1855; and foreign secretary,

1859–65. In 1865 he again became prime minister, leaving office in 1866. Russell failed to achieve the union of Whigs and Peelites which he desired during his first premiership, and was unable to establish the control he would have wished over his cabinet and the Commons. During his second administration he proved a bold advocate of electoral reform and alarmed some of his colleagues by his 'rapidity'.

Salisbury, 3rd Marquess of, Robert Arthur Talbot Gascoyne-Cecil (1830–1903): Cecil was Conservative MP for Stamford, 1853–68. In 1865 he became Viscount Cranbourne. He served as secretary for India in 1866, resigning in protest at the 1867 Reform Bill. In 1868 he succeeded as Marquess of Salisbury. He returned as secretary for India, 1874–76, and as foreign secretary, 1878–80. He was leader of the opposition in the House of Lords and joint Leader of the Conservative Party, 1881–5. In 1885 he became prime minister and sole party leader. He acted as prime minister and foreign secretary, 1885–6, prime minister in 1886, prime minister and foreign secretary, 1887–92 and 1895–1900. He was prime minister and lord privy seal, 1900–2. Salisbury was a remarkably able diplomat, while in the domestic sphere he had an incisive knowledge of the Conservative Party. As a Tory and a High Church Anglican he was able to control an unruly party, and by moderate social reform and opposition to Home Rule he succeeded in forging the Unionist alliance which dominated British politics between 1886 and 1906.

Shaftesbury, 7th Earl, Anthony Ashley Cooper, Baron Ashley (1805–1885): MP for Woodstock, 1826–30; Dorchester, 1830–1; Dorset, 1833–46; champion of measures to improve factory conditions, including various Factory Acts between 1833 and 1850, and Owners Act of 1842; he was a noted philanthropist and evangelist, interested in bible society movements at home and abroad.

Shelburne, 2nd Earl of, William Petty, 1st Marquess of Lansdowne (1737–1805): Petty was MP for Wycombe, 1760–1. In 1761 he succeeded as Earl of Shelburne. He was president of the Board of Trade, April – September 1763, secretary of state for the Southern Department, 1766–8, home secretary, March – July 1782 and first lord of the Treasury (prime minister), July 1782 to April 1783. He was created Marquess of Lansdowne in 1784.

Sidmouth, 1st Viscount, Henry Addington (1757–1844): Addington was MP for Devizes from 1784 to 1805. In 1805 he was created Viscount Sidmouth. Addington was speaker of the House of Commons, 1789–1801, prime minister and chancellor of the exchequer, 1801–4, lord president of the council, 1805, lord privy seal, 1806, lord president of the council, 1806–7 and 1812. From 1812 to 1822 he was home secretary and from 1822 to 1824 was a member of the cabinet without ministerial office. Although an able administrator, Sidmouth proved a mediocre prime minister. He proved an efficient but repressive home secretary.

Slim, 1st Viscount, William Joseph Slim (1891–1970): Military leader. Commissioned from the ranks in the First World War into the Royal Warwickshire Regiment, he took a regular commission in the Indian Army. In March 1942 he was sent to Burma to take command of 1 Corps and from March to May retreated from Rangoon to Imphal where he took up a defensive position. In December 1943 he was given command of the Fourteenth Army. In February 1944 he halted a Japanese attack in the Arakan. This was a turning-point in the Burmese War, a boost to morale. He repulsed the Japanese attacks at Imphal and Kohima, March – July 1944, then mounted a counter-offensive, defeating the Japanese at Meiktila, March 1945. By 3 May he had captured Rangoon. He was worshipped by all who knew him. There was no serious criticism of Slim during or after the war. He restored the army's offensive spirit and developed new techniques of jungle fighting.

Smith, William Henry (1825–1891): Conservative MP 1868–91; first lord of the Admiralty 1877–80; first lord of the Treasury and leader of the House 1887–91; founder of W. H. Smith Booksellers; opposed Lord Randolph Churchill's (q.v.) budgetary proposals for economies and succeeded him as leader of House.

Snowden, 1st Viscount, Philip Snowden (1864–1937): Labour MP for Blackburn, 1906–18, and for Colne Valley 1922–31; chancellor of the exchequer 1924 and 1929–31; lord privy seal, 1931–2. He came into the Labour Party through the Independent Labour Party, of which he was chairman, 1903–6, 1917–20. He became an expert on national finance and temperance questions and a champion of Free Trade. He opposed the First World War and championed conscientious objectors; he was a vigorous opponent of Bolshevism. In 1931, with the break-up of the Labour government, he followed MacDonald (q.v.) into the National government, but resigned the following year over the adoption of Imperial Preference.

Stanhope, 1st Earl, James Stanhope (1673–1721): First lord of the Treasury and chancellor of exchequer 1717–18; secretary of state for Northern Department, 1716–17, 1718–21. British soldier and diplomat who aimed to build up a system of European alliances and gain continental support for the Hanoverian succession; he negotiated the Triple Alliance, 1717, and Quadruple Alliance, 1718; a champion of one-party government and Whig supremacy.

Stephens, James (1824–1901): Irish revolutionary. Member of the Young Ireland movement. Founded the Fenians in 1858.

Tawney, Richard Henry (1880–1962): Christian socialist, social critic, reformer and historian; the economic history of England from 1540 to 1640 became known as 'Tawney's Century'; Professor of Economic History at the London School of Economics from 1931, and Professor Emeritus, 1949; adviser to numerous government bodies; critic of capitalism as corrupter of rich and poor alike. His book, *Religion and the Rise of Capitalism*, 1926, was an important study of the sixteenth-and seventeenth-century development of capitalism and its relationship to Protestantism.

Thatcher, Margaret Hilda (née Roberts) (1925–   ): Mrs Thatcher has been Conservative MP for Finchley since 1959. She was parliamentary secretary to the Ministry of Pensions and National Insurance 1961–4, and secretary of state for education and science 1970–4. In 1975 she was elected leader of the Conservative Party. Between 1975 and 1979 she led the party away from the centrist policies of Heath (q.v.) and it adopted a monetarist stance on economic problems and a 'hard line' on law and order, defence and immigration. In May 1979 she became Britain's first woman prime minister.

Thistlewood, Arthur (1770–1820): Imbibed revolutionary ideas while serving in army during American and French Wars; organised Spa Fields meetings 1816; led group of London extremists arrested for conspiring to murder Castlereagh and cabinet in 1820; convicted of high treason for Cato Street conspiracy and hanged.

Thomas, James Henry (1874–1949): Labour MP for Derby, 1910–36. Colonial secretary, 1924; lord privy seal and minister responsible for unemployment issues, 1929–30; Dominions secretary, 1930–5; colonial secretary 1935–6. Railwayman who became active in Amalgamated Society of Railway Servants; later general secretary of the National Union of Railwaymen (NUR), 1918–31; urged support for Labour Party, but later expelled from party and NUR for staying with MacDonald in National government of 1931. His political career was ended by alleged budget leak, 1936.

Tillett, Benjamin (1866–1943): Trade Union leader. Labour MP for N. Salford, 1917–24, 1929–31; chairman TUC General Council 1928–9; helped organise unionisation of dockworkers; secretary of Dock, Wharf, Riverside and General Workers' Union, 1887–1922; one of leaders of 1889 London dock strike; initiative led to formation of National Transport Workers' Federation; alderman of London County Council, 1892–8; a founder of the Independent Labour Party and Labour Party; member TUC General Council, 1921–31.

Townshend, 2nd Viscount, Charles Townshend (1674–1738): Secretary of state, 1714–16; lord president of the council, 1720; secretary of state, 1721; Whig statesman who directed foreign policy between 1721 and 1730. His conflict with Stanhope (q.v.) over pro-French policy led to Townshend's dismissal in 1716, and formation with Walpole of effective opposition movement within Whig Party; reconciled 1720; resigned 1730 because Walpole prevented aggressive policy towards Austria; his nickname 'Turnip Townshend' resulted from the crop rotation system he devised.

Townshend, Charles (1725–1767): Lord of the Admiralty, 1754; secretary for war 1761–2; president of Board of Trade, 1763; chancellor of the exchequer and leader of the House of Commons, 1766–7. His fiscal policies, notably the Townshend duties on certain goods imported from America, contributed to revolt of American colonists in 1776.

Walpole, Sir Robert, 1st Earl of Orford (1676–1745): Walpole was MP for Castle Rising, 1700–1 and for King's Lynn 1702–12, 1713–42. In 1701 he served on the Committee for Privileges and Elections and in 1705 he became a member of the council to Prince George of Denmark. From 1708 to 1711 he was secretary at war and from 1714 to 1717 he was paymaster of the Forces. In 1714 he became a privy councillor and in

1715 was charged with the conduct of Bolingbroke's (*q.v.*) impeachment.
He was appointed first lord of the Treasury and chancellor of the
exchequer by Townshend (*q.v.*) in 1715, but resigned in 1717 when
Townshend was dismissed from the lord lieutenancy of Ireland. In 1720
he became paymaster of the forces again and in 1721 again became first
lord of the Treasury and chancellor of the exchequer. In 1725 he was
awarded the Order of the Bath, and in 1726 was made a Knight of the
Garter. He was reappointed to his offices by George II in 1727. He
resigned in 1742 and was created Earl of Orford. Walpole is usually
considered to be the first prime minister, being left with a clearly
dominant position in the government when Townshend resigned in 1730.
He was able to establish a disciplined control over office-holders and
parliamentary groups which had not previously been achieved, and
transferred the centre of power from the House of Lords to the
Commons.

Webb, Beatrice (née Potter) (1858–1943) *see* Webb, Sidney.

Webb, Sidney James, 1st Baron Passfield (1859–1947); With his wife
Beatrice (*q.v.*), a pioneer of British social and economic reform; they
were joint authors of numerous influential works on labour history,
including *The History of Trade Unionism* 1894, and *Industrial Democracy*,
1897; and were founders of the London School of Economics and of the
New Statesman; Sidney Webb helped in reorganisation of University of
London and provision of public education legislation, and held various
offices: MP Seaham, 1922–9; president of Board of Trade, 1924,
secretary of state for dominion affairs 1929–30 and for colonies, 1930–1;
elevated to peerage as 1st Baron Passfield, 1929.

Wellington, 1st Duke of, Arthur Wellesley (1769–1852): Military leader
and politician. Wellesley was MP for Trim, 1790–5, for Rye in 1806, for
Mitchel in 1807 and for Newport from 1807 to 1809. In 1812 he was
created Earl Wellington and then Marquess. In 1814 he was created Duke
of Wellington. Between 1807 and 1809 he acted as chief secretary for
Ireland. From 1819 to 1827 he was master-general of the ordnance. He
was prime minister from 1828 to 1830 and during November and
December 1834 was secretary of state of all departments and prime
minister. He served as foreign secretary, 1834–5, and minister without
portfolio, 1841–6. After rising to pre-eminence as a military leader during
the Napoleonic Wars, culminating in his victory at Waterloo in 1815,
Wellington found it difficult to adapt to the necessities of compromise
and expediency concomitant on political life. He viewed
his premiership simply as fulfilling the duty of carrying on the King's
government and was on uneasy terms with many of his cabinet. His
reluctance to countenance franchise reform led to the break-up of his
government in 1830.

Wesley, John (1703–1791): Central figure in the rise of Methodism. A
fellow and tutor at Lincoln College, Oxford, he founded the 'Methodist'
Society in 1729 for stricter religious observance and undertook
missionary work in America. In 1738 he underwent a personal
'conversion' and began to devote himself to evangelistic work in
England. He formed a 'United Society' for weekday meetings in 1739 and
founded chapels in Bristol and London. The conference of lay preachers

held in 1744, later became an annual event. Though pressures for separation built up between Methodists and Anglicans, Wesley maintained his desire to remain an Anglican. The conferring of orders in 1784 and the increasing organisation of 'circuits' and classes made separation virtually certain by the time of his death.

Whitefield, George (1714–1770): Methodist evangelist; came under influence of Wesley (*q.v.*) while at Oxford and accompanied him on mission to America where he founded orphanage in Georgia; began publication of *Journal*, 1739; obtained patronage of Countess of Huntingdon and opened Tabernacle in Tottenham Court Road; a rigid theologian, his oratory was influential in awakening eighteenth-century religious consciousness.

Wilberforce, William (1759–1833): MP for Hull 1780–4; for Yorkshire, 1784–1812; for Bramber, 1812–25; a famous advocate of the abolition of the slave trade, he introduced a Bill to this end into the House of Commons in 1791; the legislation eventually passed in 1804 and became law in 1807; he later supported total abolition of slavery; a Pittite and an evangelical Christian, he was associated with the 'Clapham Sect'.

Wilkes, John (1727–97): MP for Aylesbury, 1757–64, Middlesex, 1768–9 and 1774–90. The slogan of 'Wilkes and Liberty' became the battle-cry of popular radicalism in the 1760s, after Wilkes was arrested in 1763 for an alleged libel on the King in issue No. 45 of the *North Briton*. Elected for Middlesex in 1768, he was not allowed to take his seat, although re-elected three times in succession. His supporters founded the Bill of Rights Society in 1769 to support his cause and he was elected without opposition for Middlesex in 1774. He spoke in favour of reform in 1776, but thereafter concentrated on London politics.

Wilmington, 1st Earl of, Spencer Compton (1673–1743): Wilmington was Tory MP for Eye, 1698–1710. In 1705 he became Whig chairman of the Committee of Privileges and Elections. He lost his seat in 1710, but in 1713 was elected for East Grinstead. He was MP for Sussex from 1715 until 1728 when he was created Baron Wilmington. In 1707 he was appointed treasurer and receiver to George, Prince of Denmark and paymaster of the Queen's Pensioners. In 1709 he was on the committee which drew up the impeachment of Sacheverell. He served as speaker in 1715 and became a privy councillor in 1716. From 1722 to 1730 he was paymaster-general. In 1730 he became lord privy seal and the same year was created Earl of Wilmington. He also became lord president of the council. From 1741 to 1743 he was first lord of the Treasury, but with Carteret and Newcastle in the offices of secretaries of state was prime minister in a nominal sense only.

Wilson, Sir (James) Harold (1916–   ): Labour politician. Wilson was director of economics and statistics at the Ministry of Fuel and Power from 1943 to 1944. He was Labour MP for Ormskirk, 1945–50, and for Huyton from 1950. He served as parliamentary secretary to the Ministry of Works, 1945–7, secretary of overseas trade, 1947, and president of the Board of Trade, 1947–51. In 1951 he resigned in protest at the government's decision to impose National Health prescription charges.

In 1963 he was elected leader of the Labour Party. He was prime minister, 1964–70 and 1974–76 when he resigned office. In 1976 he was appointed a Knight of the Garter. Perhaps Wilson's greatest achievement was in keeping an inexperienced government in power with a precarious majority from 1964 to 1966, and in steering a minority government through the months from February to October 1974. Wilson led the Labour Party to office in four out of five consecutive elections and became the longest serving peacetime prime minister this century.

Wolfe, James (1727–59): Military leader. Wolfe joined the Marines in 1741, but transferred to the 12th Foot in 1742. He fought at Dettingen in 1743, against the Jacobites at Falkirk and Culloden, 1745–6 and was wounded at Lauffeld in 1747. In 1758 he served under Amherst in the expedition which captured Louisburg, and this led Pitt to give him command of the attempt against Quebec the following year. After the British force had scaled the Heights of Abraham, the French under Montcalm were drawn out of the Quebec defences. In the ensuing battle on 13 September 1759, the French were defeated, but both Wolfe and Montcalm were killed.

Wyvill, Christopher (1740–1822): Landowner and cleric who advocated parliamentary reform and religious toleration. Leader of Yorkshire Association, founded in 1779, which initiated petitioning campaign for reform; after collapse of movement, Wyvill supported the Foxite Whig attacks on the French Wars, and advocated Catholic Emancipation; also encouraged Hampden clubs (see Cartwright).

Section VI
Glossary of terms

Adullamites   Old Testament reference used by John Bright to describe group of Liberals, led by Robert Lowe, who revolted in 1866 against the Gladstone government's proposals for parliamentary reform, thus precipitating its downfall in spring 1867.

Anglo-Catholic, *see* High Church

Appeasement   Foreign policy seeking to avert war by making concessions, typified by attempts of British and French governments between 1936 and 1939 to propitiate Germany. The Chamberlain government acquiesced in Hitler's violation of Rhineland demilitarisation, 1936, the *Anschluss*, 1938 and the acquisition of Czech Sudetenland, September 1938.

Aristocracy of labour   Collective term for members of skilled trades whose earnings and superior status gave them a distinctive political stance in Victorian Britain and later, and made them often more inclined to reformist and labourist (*q.v.*) policies.

Artisan   Term applied to skilled craft workers, traditionally associated with independence, higher earnings, superior status and greater political involvement than the general mass of labourers.

Asiento   As a consequence of the treaty of Utrecht 1713, the Spanish government granted *Asiento*, or a contract to ship African slaves to America to the English South Sea Company, which was authorised to provide 4,800 slaves per annum for 30 years.

Balance of power   Doctrine of maintaining a European system in which no single power was dominant. Britain was traditionally concerned to support coalitions opposing one power gaining hegemony over Europe.

Bevanite   Follower of Aneurin Bevan, who led left-wing group of Labour Party from 1951 to 1956–7. Particularly critical of high defence expenditure, especially on nuclear arms. Opposed proposals for dropping commitment to nationalisation (revisionism) advocated by Gaitskellites (*q.v.*) and appealed for more all-embracing doctrines of socialism.

Blackshirts   Members of British Union of Fascists, founded by Sir Oswald Mosley in 1932, and wearing black shirts and uniforms on the Italian fascist model. The Public Order Act of 1936 banned the wearing of uniforms in public.

Blanketeers   Lancashire textile workers, mainly handloom weavers, who attempted to march on London in March 1817 to petition the Prince Regent and highlight distress resulting from post-war economic crises. The military arrested 200, and stopped the march.

Blitz   Sustained night-bombing attacks by German air force (Luftwaffe) on London and other British cities from 7 September 1940 to May 1941.

Blitzkrieg   Literally 'lightning war'. Term originally applied to technique of attack perfected by German generals in France in 1940. The essential elements were speed and surprise of attack, resulting in shock and disorganisation among enemy forces.

Boers   Literally 'farmers' (Afrikaans). Descendants of Dutch settlers in South Africa. Two wars fought between British and Boers in 1881 and 1899–1902 known as First and Second Boer Wars.

Bourgeoisie   Marxist term for the middle and upper classes who own and profit from capital; the class who will destroy feudalism, but themselves be displaced by the proletariat (*q.v.*).

Boxers   Young Chinese provoked in 1900 to engage in anti-foreign violence by the expansion of European commerce and territorial acquisitions in China by Germany, Russia and Britain. Major Boxer disturbances occurred in Peking and the provinces of Shensi and Manchuria.

Boycott   Organised refusal to buy goods and services. Originated by Parnell during Irish land agitation of 1880, when peasants effectively ostracised an estate manager, Captain C. C. Boycott, to protest against land evictions.

Butskellism   Term which refers to a broad consensus between the two major parties in the years after 1945 on progressive social policies and the maintenance of a mixed economy with both public and private sectors. The word is a conflation of the names of R. A. Butler, author of the 1944 Education Act and Conservative chancellor of the exchequer from 1951 to 1956, and Hugh Gaitskell (*q.v.*), Labour chancellor of the exchequer from 1950 to 1951 and later leader of the Labour Party.

Catholic Emancipation (or Relief)   Issue of freeing Catholics from disabilities which prevented them holding offices, voting and serving in parliament. Not finally secured until 1829.

Chartist   One who advocated fulfilment of People's Charter of 1838, cardinal aims of which were universal male suffrage, annual parliaments, vote by ballot, payment for MPs, equal electoral districts, and abolition of property qualifications for MPs. From 1839 to 1848 the Chartists engaged in petitioning parliament and demonstrations. The entire phase of activity is referred to as Chartism.

Chequers   Official country residence of British prime ministers. The property was acquired by Viscount Lee of Fareham in 1909, and in 1917 he made provision for it to become a weekend retreat for the prime minister. Lloyd George was the first to occupy it in 1921.

Chiltern Hundreds   Ancient royal sinecure office. Members of parliament are disbarred from holding it as it is technically an 'office of profit' under the Crown. Used as a device to circumvent MPs' inability to resign from the House of Commons. An MP wishing to vacate a seat asks for Chiltern Hundreds, and once the appointment is notified, the seat automatically becomes vacant.

Clapham Sect   Formed from leading evangelicals (*q.v.*) within the Church of England, who lived in the village of Clapham in South London. Believing in personal salvation through good works, they campaigned on behalf of the abolition of the slave trade and were involved in a number of humanitarian causes, including Sunday schools, penal reform and promoting a high standard of public morality. Leading members included William Wilberforce (1759–1833), Hannah More (1743–1833), Henry Thornton (1760–1815), James Stephen (1758–1832), and Zachery Macaulay (1768–1838).

Clydesiders   Militant trade union and socialist group led by shop stewards in the engineering industry around Glasgow during and after the First World War. Formed a Clyde Workers Committee to campaign against dilution (*q.v.*) and organised series of strikes and demonstrations in 1915–19. See also dilution, 'Red' Clydeside, and shop stewards' movement.

CND   Campaign for Nuclear Disarmament. Movement launched in February 1958 by Bertrand Russell and Canon Collins to abandon nuclear weapons and reduce British defence spending. At its peak in 1960–61, it had more active supporters than any mass movement in Britain since the Anti-Corn Law League. See also Unilateralism.

Collectivism   Name applied to policies or philosophy of the pursuit of the common good and social equality, even at the expense of limiting individual liberty or traditional privilege. Usually associated with welfare legislation and government intervention of the twentieth century.

Condition of England Question   Phrase used to describe concern for social conditions in the manufacturing districts in the 1830s and 1840s and fears of social unrest, reflected in the novels of Charles Dickens, Mrs Gaskell and Benjamin Disraeli and major parliamentary enquiries into social problems such as child and female labour.

Corn Laws   Used to describe Corn Law of 1815, which prevented the import of foreign grain until the domestic price reached 80*s*. per quarter, and its successor of 1828 which introduced a sliding scale of tariffs.

Country gentlemen, *see* Independents.

County movement   Late eighteenth-century movement for moderate parliamentary reform led by prominent country gentlemen such as Christopher Wyvill (*q.v.*). Led to formation of Yorkshire Association in 1779 and petitioning movement for reform. See also economical reform.

Court and Treasury Party   Group of office-holders or placemen who could generally be relied upon to support an eighteenth-century administration. Perhaps numbering as many as 100–120 MPs by 1760, their numbers were reduced by economical reform (*q.v.*) and administrative reorganisation from the 1780s onwards.

Dilution   Use of unapprenticed labour, especially women, to do skilled work previously reserved to craftsmen. It was used to increase munitions production in the First World War and was the subject of agreements between government and unions, but continued to cause strikes and unrest in some areas, such as Clydeside. See also Clydesiders and Shop stewards' movement.

Disestablishment   Process of separation of church and state, implying end of state support for the Anglican Church and of any attempt by the state to enforce religious duties or discriminate in its favour. Usually adopted in relation to the moves to disestablish the Anglican Church in Ireland, completed in 1871, and later moves to disestablish the Anglican Church in Wales, passed in 1914 and coming into effect after the First World War.

Dreadnought   An 'all-big-gun' battleship class deriving its name from HMS *Dreadnought*, launched in February 1906. It represented a revolution in naval shipbuilding, and inaugurated naval armaments race.

Durbar   Hindustani word signifying ceremonial court of audience. Used to refer to formal assemblies such as that on the occasion of Queen Victoria's proclamation as Empress of India (1876), and the famous Delhi Durbar of December 1911 when King George V announced restitution of Bengal as united province.

Eastern Question   Nineteenth-century term, reflecting concern about the future of the Balkan territories belonging to the declining Ottoman Empire. Britain was fearful of the expansion of Russian influence over the Balkans, Constantinople, the Dardanelles and the eastern Mediterranean and the consequent threat to the route to India. Britain often supported Turkey against Russian 'aggression' and sought arbitration of the disputes in the area.

Economical reform   Late eighteenth-century movement led by Edmund Burke (*q.v.*), among others, aiming to reduce the number of sinecurists and placeholders in parliament. Economical reform legislation was passed in 1782. See also county movement and Christopher Wyvill.

Eire   Name by which Southern Ireland (now Republic of Ireland) was known from 1937 to 1948 when it was a dominion within the British Commonwealth.

Emancipation, *see* Catholic Emancipation

Entente Cordiale   French: 'cordial understanding'. Description of relationship between Britain and France following Anglo-French *entente* reached in 1904, and continuing in spite of foreign policy differences until 1940.

Evangelicals   Group within Church of England who in the late eighteenth century sought to combat clerical apathy, while accepting Anglican discipline. Emphasised importance of moral earnestness and proclaimed salvation by faith. They gave rise to important philanthropic movements in the nineteenth century. See also Clapham Sect.

Fabian Follower of a largely middle-class group established in January 1884 to spread socialist ideas in Britain. Early Fabians included Bernard Shaw and Sidney and Beatrice Webb. The society played an important role in founding the Labour Party, and subsequently acted as a research body attached to it. As a term, it came to be applied to a supporter of gradual social reform.

Fellow-traveller Term used, usually in derogatory fashion, to describe one who accepts much of communism, but is not or denies being a member of the Communist Party. Sometimes used by politicians to describe left-wingers generally.

Fenian Supporters of an Irish revolutionary movement which was formed in the USA in 1858 and spread to Ireland in 1865. Fenian disturbances in Chester (February 1867) and bomb attacks on Clerkenwell prison and other places helped make Gladstone aware of the urgency of the Irish problem.

Force, physical and moral Phrases used in the nineteenth century to describe methods of popular agitation; moral force denoting peaceful agitation, physical the resort to arms.

Free Trade, *see Laissez-faire*

Gaitskellite Supporter of Hugh Gaitskell's social democratic view of Labour Party principles. As chancellor of the exchequer (October 1950) Gaitskell and followers clashed with Bevanites (*q.v.*) on introduction of Health Service charges to finance rearmament programme. Believed in need for nuclear weapons and for reforming the Labour Party constitution, removing commitment to nationalisation.

General Unions Phase of trade union activity in the 1830s marked by attempts to achieve a 'General Union of Trades', under the influence of the ideas of Robert Owen (*q.v.*) and the leader of the Lancashire cotton spinners, John Doherty. Early attempts in 1810, 1818 and 1829 culminated with the formation of the Grand National Consolidated Trades' Union of Great Britain and Ireland in February 1834. Achieving a maximum of 50,000 members drawn mainly from London and Lancashire, the scheme collapsed after a series of strikes in spring and summer 1834.

Great Depression Phrase applied to the period of low agricultural prices, slower industrial growth and cyclical economic depressions in the late nineteenth century, contrasting with the rapid and almost continuous expansion of the mid-Victorian period. Some historians doubt the validity of the term for a period which continued to show overall growth in the economy.

Gunboat diplomacy Conduct of foreign policy by use of naval power, usually associated with Palmerston's (*q.v.*) time as foreign secretary.

Hansard Colloquial term for official report of debates in Houses of Parliament. From 1812 Hansard family published parliamentary debates, and even after the family sold the undertaking it continued to be known as Hansard.

High Church   Section within the Church of England upholding belief in sacraments and ritual, the authority of the church hierarchy, and the close relationship between church and state. In the seventeenth and early eighteenth centuries associated with political support for the monarch as head of church and state, and later with opposition to the removal of civil disabilities on dissenters and Roman Catholics and to disestablishment (*q.v.*). In the nineteenth century, the 'Anglo-Catholic' movement represented High Churchmen nearest to Roman Catholic doctrine and liturgy.

High Farming   Period of great agricultural prosperity in the interval between the repeal of the Corn Laws and the flood of cheap agricultural produce from abroad which began in the 1870s, characterised by heavy investment in new techniques, including the large-scale application of machinery.

High Politics School   View of politics which places emphasis upon the relationships between the top politicians as the crucial determinants of policy-making and action.

Holland House   Holland House in Kensington, London, became a fashionable *salon* during the early nineteenth century, patronised by leading Whig politicians, as well as writers, painters and actors. Hence, sometimes used as a term to describe Whig opinion generally.

Home Rule   Policy of granting partial self-government to Ireland, including the re-creation of an Irish parliament. Home Rule Bills were introduced in 1886, 1893 and 1914.

Hunger marches   During the depression of the inter-war years, groups of unemployed men were organised by the communist-run National Unemployed Workers' Movement to march on London and provincial centres to protest about unemployment. Major marches occurred in 1922, 1929, 1930, 1932, 1934 and 1936. However, the most famous of the hunger marches was the 'Jarrow Crusade' when the town council of the shipbuilding town of Jarrow organised a march of 200 unemployed men to London led by the local MP, Ellen Wilkinson, to seek aid for the town in 1936.

Hungry Forties   The 1840s, so described not only because of famine in Ireland, 1845–9, but because of depression and unemployment in Britain which provoked widespread discontent, including the Chartist and Anti-Corn Law movements. Widespread concern with the 'Condition of England' question (*q.v.*) was reflected in contemporary literature.

Hustings   Booths where votes were taken at parliamentary elections, or platforms from which candidates spoke. Synonymous with electioneering and political campaigns.

Independents   Backbench MPs not directly dependent upon the administration or opposition. Regarded as the 'floating vote' in the eighteenth- and nineteenth-century House of Commons before party discipline became more effective. Variously estimated at no more than 80 members (L. Namier) and up to 300–350 (J. Owen), the independents could usually be counted upon to support an administration unless its credibility was seriously undermined by the opposition.

Jacobins   Radical faction of the French revolutionaries of 1789 led by Robespierre. In Britain, a derogatory term applied by loyalists to French sympathisers and reformers in general. Used by historians to denote British radicals with similar aims and ideology as their French counterparts.

Jacobites   Supporters of hereditary succession of House of Stuart following dethronement of James II in 1689. Jacobite risings took place after the death of Queen Anne in 1715, and again in 1745–6. Sympathy was strongest in the Scottish Highlands, but many Tories supported the Jacobite cause in England. It was crushed as a political force after 1746.

Jingoism   Chauvinistic patriotism. Derives from music-hall song of 1878 threatening Russia; a spirit prominent during the Boer and First World Wars.

King's Friends, *see* Court and Treasury Party

Labourism   Phase of working-class activity after 1850 characterised by pursuit of limited objectives of wage bargaining and strengthening trade union organisation. More generally, a phrase used to characterise the more cautious traditions of the Labour movement.

Laissez-faire   Doctrine of non-interference of state in economic affairs derived from teachings of classical political economists like Adam Smith, Malthus and Ricardo, and from Benthamite tradition (Utilitarians *q.v.*) It was a fundamental tenet of British liberalism for most of the nineteenth century.

Leicester House, *see* Reversionary interest

Liberal Toryism   Reforming Toryism associated with the later years of Lord Liverpool's (*q.v.*) administration and his leading ministers, Canning, Peel and Huskisson (*qq.v.*).

Lib–Lab   Prior to formation of Labour Party, trade unionists and working men looked to Liberals to support their interests and a number of trade union MPs were known by this label. The 1977 Lib–Lab Pact was a published agreement reached between James Callaghan's (*q.v.*) Labour government and the Liberal Party, allowing Callaghan to continue his administration with the backing of Liberal MPs.

Luddism   Phase of widespread machine-breaking in the North and Midland counties of England between 1811 and 1817. Machine-breaking was said to be carried out on the orders of a mythical 'Ned Ludd' or 'General Ludd'. Machine-breaking began in Nottinghamshire as part of the campaign of the framework-knitters for greater regulation of their trade and higher wages for work in a period of high prices and unemployment. Disturbances spread to Yorkshire where shearing-frames were destroyed by the wool-croppers and to Lancashire where power looms were attacked. The main disturbances were over by the end of 1812 when some 10,000 troops were deployed in the manufacturing districts.

Marxist history   Interpretation of history which follows the ideas of Karl Marx (1818–83) and Friedrich Engels (1820–95) and implied by their writings. Although many variations of Marxist theory exist, they follow broadly the view of Marx and Engels that 'all history is the history of class struggle', giving primacy to the economic forces which mould society and determine its divisions into bourgeoisie (*q.v.*) and proletariat (*q.v.*). This 'materialist conception of history' assumes inevitable progression from feudalism, through capitalism, to communism.

Model unionism, *see* 'New Model' unionism

Multilateralism, *see* Unilateralism

Namierite   Method of analysing political action and membership of political parties which stresses the role of individuals and their interests rather than beliefs and ideologies; after Sir Lewis Namier, author of *The Structure of Politics at the Accession of George III* (1929) and other studies in eighteenth- and twentieth-century politics.

New imperialism   Term applied to the renewed phase of imperial expansion in the latter part of the nineteenth century, to distinguish it from the eighteenth-century colonial expansion.

New Liberalism   Term applied to the philosophy and phase of progressive social reform undertaken by Liberal governments after 1908 and associated with Lloyd George and Winston Churchill, distinguished from traditional Liberalism (*q.v.*) by the greater readiness to countenance state intervention and increased government spending.

'New Model' unionism   Phase of trade union organisation in the mid-Victorian period marked by the formation of the Amalgamated Society of Engineers in 1851. It set a pattern of high fees and exclusiveness, national organisation and restriction to skilled craft workers. The 'New Model' unions pursued moderate, craft interests in contrast to the more ambitious aims of the General Unions (*q.v.*) and had greater permanence than the purely local trade societies.

'Nomination' boroughs, *see* 'Pocket' boroughs

Old Corruption   Term used to describe the unreformed political and ecclesiastical system before the 1832 Reform Act and the beginning of reform in the Church of England, characterised by patronage and influence.

'Open door' policy   Term describing principle of equal trading opportunities for great powers in parts of Africa, as adopted by the Berlin Conference, 1884–5; a policy later used by the USA towards China.

Orange card, playing the   Support for Ulster Protestants by British politicians in order to preserve the Act of Union (*see* Unionist) and frustrate Home Rule (*q.v.*). Normally associated with the Conservative opposition to Home Rule for Ireland in the period 1880–1914.

Oxford Movement   Group within Church of England from the 1830s seeking to restore the High Church (*q.v.*) traditions of the seventeenth century. The movement arose out of anxiety over the implications of Catholic Emancipation (*q.v.*) and the Parliamentary Reform Act of 1832. It was led by three Fellows of Oriel College, Oxford, and led to a strong Anglo-Catholic revival. Though Keble and Pusey (*qq.v.*) remained in the Church of England, Newman (*q.v.*) became a Roman Catholic.

Parnellites   Followers of Charles Stewart Parnell (*q.v.*), the Irish politician who launched a campaign to secure Home Rule for Ireland. Parnell lost influence in 1890s following involvement in divorce case.

Pax Britannica   Period of Britain's maritime and diplomatic supremacy (and hence 'peace') in the nineteenth century, associated particularly with Palmerston's (*q.v.*) periods as foreign secretary.

Peelite   Policies associated with Sir Robert Peel (*q.v.*) of sound, efficient government dominated by concern for national rather than party interests.

Peterloo 'Massacre'   Name for the break-up of a peaceful reform demonstration in St Peter's Fields, Manchester, on 16 August 1819, when the local magistrates sent in troops to arrest the radical orator, Henry Hunt (*q.v.*). Eleven people were killed and over 400 injured. 'Peterloo' was a pun on Waterloo.

'Pocket' boroughs   Boroughs directly controlled by a patron, sometimes the government, who could dominate representation and 'nominate' its MPs. See also 'Rotten' boroughs.

Poplarism   Support for local control over welfare payments and for fairer distribution of resources to poor areas. The term derives from the struggles of the borough of Poplar, London, led by George Lansbury (*q.v.*) to maintain higher benefits for the unemployed than were allowed by the economy measures of governments in the 1920s. Similar conflicts were exposed in the early 1930s over the operation of the 'Means Test' and in the 1970s against the imposition of higher council house rents by the Conservative government of 1970–4.

Potwalloper   Franchise qualification prior to Reform Act of 1832. In some boroughs, every man who had a family and boiled a pot there qualified for the franchise, if resident for six months, and not in receipt of poor rates. Such voters were considered susceptible to bribery and instructions from borough patrons.

Powellite Advocate of coloured repatriation and ending of Commonwealth immigration, as suggested by Enoch Powell (b. 1912). A former right-wing Tory MP and minister of health in the Macmillan government from 1960 to 1963, Powell became an Ulster Unionist MP in 1974.

Pretender, Old James Edward Stuart (1688–1766) son of dethroned King James II. Known as 'Old Pretender' to throne of England and backed by Jacobite (*q.v.*) support in Britain. Unsuccessful in attempt to prevent succession of Elector of Hanover in 1714 and in rising of following year.

Pretender, Young Charles Edward Stuart, known as 'Bonny Prince Charlie'. Son of James Edward Stuart, led rising in Scotland in 1745–6; aimed to place his father on the throne. Defeat at battle of Culloden in 1746 effectively ended danger of Stuart restoration.

Proletariat Economic and social class of industrial workers deriving income solely from sale of labour power. Identified by Marxist analysis as group which would become conscious of class difference from bourgeoisie, and would organise to promote communist revolution.

Protestant ascendancy Term for the political and religious dominance by the Protestant minority in Ireland from the seventeenth to the nineteenth centuries.

Puseyite Follower of Edward Pusey (*q.v.*), English theologian and leader of Oxford Movement (*q.v.*). In 1865 Pusey declared his belief in possiblity of union of Church of England and Church of Rome.

Radical First used to describe the supporters of universal suffrage, annual parliaments and secret ballot. Major Cartwright contrasted 'radical' and 'moderate' parliamentary reform as early as 1776 in *Take Your Choice*, and in 1792 the London Corresponding Society promulgated a 'Plan of Radical Reform'. Proposals for 'radical' reform were taken up by MPs such as Sir Francis Burdett (q.v.) and popular writers and speakers such as William Cobbett and Henry Hunt (*qq.v.*). The campaign for 'radical' reform continued after 1832 in the Chartist movement. In the later nineteenth century the term became associated more broadly with sweeping social and economic reform.

Raj Literally 'rule' or 'sovereignty'. Refers to period of British rule in India.

'Red' Clydeside Period of strikes and socialist unrest in the Glasgow area from 1915 to 1919. Strikes organised by the Clyde Workers' Committee against dilution (*q.v.*) in 1915–16 led to arrests and suppression of left-wing journals by government. Attempts to form a Workers' and Soldiers' 'Soviet' in 1918 prohibited by government. Forty Hours' strike in January–February 1919 led to disturbances and the placing of troops and tanks in the streets. See also shop stewards' movement and Clydesiders.

Referendum Reference of political issue to electorate for direct decision by popular vote. Unknown in Great Britain until 1973 when used in

Northern Ireland, followed in 1975 by a referendum which endorsed membership of the EEC (European Economic Community), and two in 1979 which rejected devolution of government in Scotland and Wales.

Reversionary interest   Name given to politicians who clustered about the Prince of Wales in the eighteenth and early nineteenth centuries. In 1718 the Prince of Wales (later George II) bought Leicester House in London, hence sometimes called the Leicester House interest (*q.v.*).

'Robinocracy'   Collective name for supporters of Sir Robert Walpole (*q.v.*).

'Rotten' boroughs   Boroughs where, prior to the 1832 Reform Act, the electorate had shrunk almost to nothing. Among the most notorious were Gatton and Old Sarum. They were a source of political influence for borough owners. See also 'Pocket' boroughs.

Scot and Lot   Franchise based on ability to pay poor rate; paying rates was deemed to be equivalent of being obliged in the Middle Ages to pay Scot and bear Lot.

Shop steward's movement   Term for the growth of shop-floor trade union organisation, particularly in the engineering industry, before, during and after the First World War. Committees of shop stewards were active in opposition to dilution (*q.v.*) and on the Clyde Workers' Committee. See 'Red' Clydeside.

Six Acts   Repressive legislation passed by Lord Sidmouth (*q.v.*) in 1819 in the aftermath of Peterloo (*q.v.*), prohibiting meetings of more than 50 people, preventing military drilling, increasing newspaper duties, permitting magistrates to search for arms and seditious writings, and to speed up judicial proceedings.

Speenhamland system   Method of outdoor relief (i.e. given to people who remained outside the workhouse) announced by the Berkshire JPs at Speenhamland in Berkshire in May 1795 by which parochial rates were used to supplement wages on a sliding scale according to the price of bread.

Splendid isolation   Phrase used to describe period of British foreign policy prior to entering the system of alliances in 1902 when a treaty was concluded with Japan.

Standard-of-living debate   Debate over the course of living standards during the Industrial Revolution between 'optimists' who see a general real rise in living standards and the 'pessimists' who see a fall. Main protagonists include J. H. Clapham, T. S. Ashton and R. M. Hartwell ('optimists'), and J. L. and B. Hammond, E. Hobsbawm and E. P. Thompson ('pessimists').

Storming the closet   Eighteenth-century term for seizure of major positions in government by winning the support of the monarch and forcing expulsion of existing administration.

Suffragette   Supporter of Women's Social and Political Union, founded in 1903, and dominated by Emmeline and Christabel Pankhurst. Between 1906 and 1914 it undertook militant action to further the cause of women's enfranchisement. Women over 30 were enfranchised in 1918, and women between 21 and 30 in 1928.

Suffragist   Supporter of National Union of Women's Suffrage Societies. Believed in constitutional methods to obtain women's suffrage, and adult suffrage in general. Mrs Millicent Fawcett was the best-known suffragist leader.

'Sweated' trades   Refers to the domestic trades such as tailoring, hat-making and flower-making where child, female and foreign labour were often grossly underpaid for work in poor conditions. The conditions of 'sweated' workers became a major cause for concern in the late nineteenth and early twentieth centuries, leading to government legislation in 1909, the Trade Boards Act, which set minimum wages.

'Swing'   Term used by psephologists (investigators of voting patterns) to express percentage change in votes between major parties at election, particularly in the years since 1945 when the operation of a virtual two-party system made its calculation much more straightforward and relevant.

Syndicalist   Supporter of principle of ownership and running of industry by workers directly. Syndicalism was influenced by writings of Proudhon and Sorel, and obtained some following in Britain between 1910 and 1914, for which Tom Mann was a spokesman.

Tariff Reform   Campaign for introduction of protective tariffs associated with Joseph Chamberlain (*q.v.*) in 1903–5.

Taxes on knowledge   Newspaper and stamp duties were attacked by radicals in the early nineteenth century as 'taxes on knowledge'. The 'unstamped' or 'pauper' press were those publications which avoided or evaded such duties. Stamp duties were abolished in 1855.

Temperance movement   Movement to restrict or ban the consumption of alcohol. Temperance societies were started as early as the 1820s, soon achieving strong support from Nonconformist and Methodist churches. Temperance became a major feature of the Liberal Party's programme in the latter half of the nineteenth century and resulted in Licensing Acts in 1872 and 1902.

Tory   Name which became current in the Exclusion Crisis of the early 1680s for a supporter of hereditary succession, the royal prerogative, divine right and loyalty to the Church of England. After the deposition of James II many became Jacobites (*q.v.*), and the taint of Jacobitism excluded them from office for 30 years after 1715. By the end of the eighteenth century, the term was being applied to those who upheld the prerogatives of George III, resisted the removal of disabilities from Dissenters and Roman Catholics, and opposed parliamentary reform. The name 'Tory' was revived by Canning (*q.v.*) in the early nineteenth century for the natural party of government which was opposed by the Whigs (*q.v.*). In the mid-nineteenth century, the Tories also came to be called the Conservative Party.

Tory democracy   Description of policies advocated by Disraeli (*q.v.*) and Lord Randolph Churchill (*q.v.*), combining maintenance of established institutions with cautious social reform in an attempt to win working-class support for the Conservative Party.

Tractarians   Name applied to supporters of the Oxford Movement (*q.v.*), following J. H. Newman's *Tracts for the Times*. The revived liturgical ceremonial and the emphasis on the social obligations of the church led to the introduction of religious communities within the Church of England. Many Tractarians became Roman Catholics, including Newman who became a cardinal in 1879.

Tribunites   Group within the Labour Party, named after the left-wing weekly, *Tribune*, founded in 1937. In the years after 1945 the group advocated a programme of further nationalisation, unilateral nuclear disarmament and, later, opposition to membership of the European Economic Community. During the early 1950s the Tribune group included Aneurin Bevan (*q.v.*), Harold Wilson (*q.v.*), Ian Mikardo and Richard Crossman and was highly critical of official Labour Party policy, especially on nuclear weapons. The group remains an active force within the Labour Party.

Triple Alliance   Agreement for mutual support between the three most powerful unions, the miners, transport workers and railwaymen. Negotiations were opened in 1914 and agreement reached in 1915, but not put into operation until after the First World War. In April 1921 the Triple Alliance broke down when the other two unions failed to call sympathetic strikes in support of a miners' stoppage.

'Troubles, the'   Period of unrest in Ireland from 1918 to 1921, characterised by virtual guerrilla war between the Irish Republican Army (IRA) and the British forces, continuing after 1921 in the civil war between the Irish government and the IRA over the terms of the truce with Britain and the exclusion of Ulster.

UDI   Unilateral Declaration of Independence in Southern Rhodesia by the Rhodesian Front Government of Ian Smith on 11 November 1965. The British government rejected the Declaration, which was also condemned by the United Nations, because of Smith's opposition to sharing power with the African majority and his rejection of majority rule. Britain imposed trade sanctions and an oil embargo on Rhodesia, but failed to reach an agreement with Ian Smith. The rebellion came to an end in 1980 following a protracted guerrilla war in Rhodesia which led to a settlement at Lancaster House, London, and the holding of elections which returned an African majority government led by Robert Mugabe.

Ultra-Tories   Section of the Tory Party active from the 1820s through to the 1850s which opposed Catholic Emancipation (*q.v.*) and supported the Corn Laws (*q.v.*). Their opposition contributed to the downfall of the Tory government in 1830, precipitating the Reform Crisis of 1830–2, and they subsequently opposed Peel over the Maynooth grant in 1845 and voted against repeal of the Corn Laws in 1846.

'Unauthorised programme'   Radical programme adopted by Joseph Chamberlain (*q.v.*) during the 1885 election campaign which called for free education, housing reform and a programme of smallholdings to relieve unemployment. Although Chamberlain campaigned as a Liberal the programme was not official party policy.

Unilateralism   Policy of surrendering use and deployment of nuclear weapons without obtaining similar assurances from other governments, adopted by sections of C.N.D. and the Labour Party from the 1950s. Contrasted with multilateralism, insisting on mutual nuclear disarmament as only basis for peace and security. *See also* C.N.D.

Unionist   Supporter of the constitutional union between Britain and Ireland, dating from the Act of Union of 1800, and by implication an opponent of Home Rule or Irish independence. In 1886 used by Lord Randolph Churchill (*q.v.*) to describe opponents in Ireland and Britain of attempts to include Ulster in Home Rule proposals. In 1912, the Conservative Party adopted the title Conservative and Unionist Party when it formally absorbed those Liberals opposed to Home Rule. The Protestant majority in Ulster formed an Ulster Unionist Council in 1905, the forerunner of the Ulster Unionist Party which controlled the province from 1921. See also Liberal Unionists.

United Irishmen   Society established in Belfast in 1791 by Theobald Wolfe Tone (1763–98) to seek removal of religious and political grievances. After the outbreak of war with France, many United Irishmen looked to French aid and adopted republicanism. From 1796 repression of its activities drove the movement underground, but its members conspired with the French to mount an invasion of Ireland and formed links with radicals in England. The movement was largely destroyed by the abortive 1798 rebellion, the break-up of the Despard conspiracy in 1802 and the defeat of Robert Emmet's rising in 1803.

Utilitarians   Upholders of Jeremy Bentham's (1748–1832) belief that government policy should be based on the need to secure the 'greatest happiness of the greatest number'. His views were very influential in the field of social policy between the 1820s and 1850s.

'Wee Frees'   Group of 'independent' Liberals, supporters of Herbert Asquith (*q.v.*) who resisted reunion with the Coalition Liberals led by Lloyd George (*q.v.*) after 1918. Led in the House of Commons by Sir Donald Maclean, they eventually reunited with the Lloyd George Liberals in 1923.

Whig   Parliamentary party which emerged in the late seventeenth century, dominated British politics in the first half of the eighteenth century and evolved into the Liberal Party in the middle of the nineteenth century. Whigs were defenders of parliamentary government, ministerial responsibility and Protestantism. The 'Glorious Revolution' of 1688–9 was regarded as a triumph of Whig principles and the Whigs monopolised power following the Hanoverian succession in 1714, but in the later eighteenth century fell from favour under George III and became associated with religious toleration, economical reform (q.v.) and opposition to the revival of monarchical authority. Divided by the French Revolution, they became supporters of moderate parliamentary reform in the 1820s and passed the Reform Act of 1832. The Liberal Party was formed in the mid-nineteenth century out of a fusion of Whigs, radicals and Peelites. More generally, the term has been used to refer to a paternalist, but moderately reforming, approach to politics.

Whig history   Interpretation of history as a process of improvement from earliest times to the present, and involving viewing the past from contemporary moral assumptions. Thomas Macaulay (1800–59) and Lord Acton (1834–1902) are considered principal exponents of the Whig interpretation of history.

Whiteboys   Association of Irish peasants, first formed in about 1761 in Co. Tipperary to redress grievances. They wore white shirts and committed agrarian outrages at night.

Young England   Movement led by younger Tories including Disraeli (q.v.) in the late 1830s and 1840s in opposition to Peel's reforming tendencies; sometimes known as 'Throne and Altar' conservatism from its professed attachment to the monarchy and the established church. Other members included George Smythe (1818–57) and John Manners (1818–1906).

Section VII
Topic Bibliography

Topics

1. The reign of Queen Anne and the Hanoverian succession.
2. Jacobitism.
3. Walpole and the Whig supremacy.
4. The Church of England and the rise of Methodism.
5. The Agricultural Revolution.
6. Eighteenth-century society.
7. The Elder Pitt.
8. British colonial policy and the American War of Independence.
9. George III, the constitution and the parliamentary reform movement, 1770–89.
10. The impact of the French Revolution on Britain.
11. Pitt and Fox.
12. The Industrial Revolution.
13. Reform, radicalism and the Tory Party in Regency England.
14. The Great Reform Act.
15. Peel, the Tory Party and the repeal of the Corn Laws.
16. Chartism.
17. Social reform in nineteenth-century Britain.
18. Trade unionism.
19. Victorian religion.
20. British foreign policy in the nineteenth century.
21. Gladstone and Liberalism.
22. Disraeli and the late nineteenth-century Conservative Party.
23. The Irish Question.
24. British imperialism.
25. The rise of the Labour Party.
26. The Liberal Party in the age of Asquith and Lloyd George.
27. The causes and consequences of the First World War.
28. Britain in the 1920s.
29. Britain and the slump.
30. Appeasement and British foreign policy in the 1930s.
31. Britain and the Second World War.
32. Decolonisation and foreign policy since 1945.
33. Britain since 1951.

List of abbreviations

Ag. H.	*Agricultural History*
Am. H.R.	*American Historical Review*
B.I.H.R.	*Bulletin of the Institute of Historical Research*
C.H.J.	*Cambridge Historical Journal*
D.U.J.	*Durham University Journal*
E.	*Economica*
E.H.	*Economic History*
Econ. H.R.	*Economic History Review*
E.H.R.	*English Historical Review*
H.	*History*
H.J.	*Historical Journal*
H.L.Q.	*Huntingdon Library Quarterly*
H.T.	*History Today*
I.H.S.	*Irish Historical Studies*
I.R.S.H.	*International Review of Social History*
J.B.S.	*Journal of British Studies*
J.C.H.	*Journal of Contemporary History*
J. Eccl. H.	*Journal of Ecclesiastical History*
J. Econ. H.	*Journal of Economic History*
J.H.I.	*Journal of the History of Ideas*
J.M.H.	*Journal of Modern History*
L.H.S.B.	*Labour History Society Bulletin*
L.J.	*The London Journal*
N.H.	*Northern History*
P.A.	*Public Affairs*
P.B.A.	*Proceedings of the British Academy*
P.P.	*Past and Present*
P.S.	*Population Studies*
S.H.	*Social History*
T.H.A.S.	*Transactions of the Hunter Archaeological Society*
T.R.H.S.	*Transactions of the Royal Historical Society*
W.H.R.	*Welsh History Review*
W.M.Q.	*William and Mary Quarterly*
V.S.	*Victorian Studies*

Introductory note

This bibliography is arranged in rough chronological order and is intended to represent a fair selection of the major topics in modern British history. The essay titles are merely intended to focus attention on some of the most commonly raised issues, but by no means exhaust the range of possibilities on each subject. The reading is deliberately greater than would be required for an average essay, but does reflect the wealth of bibliographical material now available for most of these subjects and allows a degree of specialisation on particular aspects of a topic. Similarly, the article literature mentioned, while not an exhaustive list, is intended as a guide to some of the most important material from which a selection can be made according to preference. A selection of source material is also provided for each topic.

General texts
(*not yet published*)

Those seeking an introduction to the period are advised to consult the various general texts that are available. Perhaps the most succinct one-volume study is R. K. Webb, *Modern England: From the Eighteenth Century to the Present* (1969).

In the Longman History of England (General Editor W. N. Medlicott), the relevant volumes are D. Marshall, *Eighteenth Century England, 1714–1784* (2nd edn, 1975); A Briggs, *The Age of Improvement 1783–1867* (1959); D. Read, *England 1868–1914: The Age of Urban Democracy* (1979); W. N. Medlicott, *Contemporary England, 1914–1964: with Epilogue, 1964–1974* (rev. edn, 1976). Five volumes of the *Oxford History of England* cover this period: B. Williams, *The Whig Supremacy, 1714–60* (2nd edn, 1962), J. Steven Watson, *The Reign of George III, 1760–1815* (1960); Llewellyn Woodward, *The Age of Reform, 1815–70* (2nd edn, 1962); R. Ensor, *England, 1870–1914* (1936); A. J. P. Taylor, *English History, 1914–1945* (1965). The relevant volumes of the Pelican History of England (General Editor, J. E. Morpurgo) are: J. H. Plumb, *England in the Eighteenth Century 1714–1815* (1950); D. Thomson, *England in the Nineteenth Century, 1815–1914* (1950) and *England in the Twentieth Century, 1914–63* (1964).

In the Nelson History of England (General Editors, C. Brooke and D. Mack Smith), see J. B. Owen, *The Eighteenth Century, 1714–1815* (1974); D. Beales, *From Castlereagh to Gladstone, 1815–1885* (1969); H. Pelling, *Modern Britain, 1885–1955* (1960). In the Edward Arnold New History of England (General Editors, A. G. Dickens and N. Gash), see W. A. Speck, *Stability and Strife, England 1714–1760* (1977); I. R. Christie, *Wars and Revolutions, Britain 1760–1815;** N. Gash, *Aristocracy and People, Britain 1815–1865* (1980); H. J. Hanham, *Industry and Ascendency, Britain 1865–1914;** M. Beloff, *Wars and Welfare, Britain 1914–1952.** The Paladin History of England (General Editor, Robert Blake) contains S. Baxter, *England's Rise to Power 1660–1760;** F. B. Smith, *England Transformed, 1760–1865;** R. Shannon, *The Crisis of Imperialism, 1865–1915* (1974); R. Blake, *The Decline of Power, 1915–1970.**

Reference
(*not yet published)

Detailed statistics on this period can be found in B. R. Mitchell and P. Deane, *Abstract of British Historical Statistics* (1962), while a wide selection of factual information is presented in diagrammatic form in C. Cook and J. Stevenson, *Longman Atlas of Modern British History: a visual guide to British society and politics, 1700–1970* (1978). For maps on economic history see also H. C. Derby (ed.), *A New Historical Geography of England after 1600* (1976).

Detailed reference works for this period are C. Cook and J. Stevenson, *British Historical Facts 1760–1830*; C. Cook and B. Keith, *British Historical Facts, 1830–1900* (1975) and D. Butler and A. Sloman, *British Political Facts, 1900–79* (5th edn, 1980).

1. The reign of Queen Anne and the Hanoverian succession

The reign of Queen Anne and the 'rage of party' has been reinterpreted in recent years. The relevance and meaning of 'party' have been subjected to examination and studies of constituency politics, particular elections and the electorate have added a new dimension to our study of politics, carrying the discussion of political attitudes beyond the confines of Westminster. The place of religious strife requires consideration and the bitter conflict over foreign policy involves some understanding of the war and the financial and political issues it involved. The 'inevitability' of the Hanoverian succession also demands critical scrutiny.

Essay topics

What were the causes of political conflict in England during the reign of Queen Anne?

Was the increasing bitterness of politics in the reign of Queen Anne due primarily to a conflict between 'land' and 'money'?

Sources and documents

G. S. Holmes and W. A. Speck (eds), *The Divided Society, 1694–1716* (1967) is a short, lively collection of documents. A. Browning (ed.), *English Historical Documents, 1660–1714* (1953) has the usual wide selection of documents for the series. Dean Swift, *The Conduct of the Allies* (1711) is a brilliant tract on foreign policy. Equally interesting is Gregory King, 'Natural and political observations...upon the state of England', reprinted in G. E. Barnett (ed.), *Two Tracts by Gregory King* (1936).

Secondary works

The most straightforward account remains the latter part of G. M. Trevelyan, *England under the Stuarts* (1904 and 1960). The essential modern interpretation is G. S. Holmes, *British Politics in the Age of Anne* (1967), while *Religion and Party in Late Stuart England* (Historical Association pamphlet, 1975) is a briefer version of some of his views. J. H. Plumb, *The Growth of Political Stability in England, 1675–1725* (1967) and B. W. Hill, *The Growth of Parliamentary Parties, 1689–1742* (1977) are also important contributions. These largely supersede R. Walcott, *English Politics in the Early Eighteenth Century* (1956) which analysed politics primarily in terms of family groupings. B. Kemp, *King and Commons, 1660–1832* (1957) provides an admirably clear view of the constitutional position. The essential work on financial developments is P. G. Dickson, *The Financial Revolution in England: a study in the development of public credit, 1688–1756* (1967), especially chs 1–3. For local politics W. A. Speck, *Tory and Whig: the struggle in the constituencies 1701–1715* (1970) is valuable. The crucial period after 1709 is considered in G. S. Holmes, *The Trial of Dr. Sacheverell* (1973); H. T. Dickinson, *Bolingbroke* (1970), and S. Biddle, *Bolingbroke and Harley* (1975). G. S. Holmes (ed.), *Britain after the Glorious Revolution* (1969), also has essays bearing on several aspects of the period. Foreign policy background is considered in P. Langford, *Britain, 1688–1815: foreign policy in the eighteenth century* (1976). The most important detailed studies of foreign policy are D. B. Horn, *Great Britain and Europe in the Eighteenth Century* (1967) and J. McLachlan, *Trade and Peace with Old Spain, 1667–1739* (1940).

Articles

See H. Horwitz, 'Parties, connections, and parliamentary politics, 1689–1714: review and revision', *J.B.S.* (1966); H. N. Fieldhouse, 'Bolingbroke's share in the Jacobite intrigue of 1710–14', *E.H.R.* (1937); M. Ransome, 'Church and dissent in the election of 1710', *E.H.R.* (1941); M. A. Thomson, 'The safeguarding of the protestant succession', *H.* (1954); E. Gregg, 'Was Queen Anne a Jacobite?', *H.* (1972); J. H. Plumb, 'The organisation of the cabinet in the reign of Queen Anne', *T.R.H.S.* (1957); J. H. Plumb, 'The growth of the electorate in England from 1600 to 1715', *PP.* (1969); W. A. Speck, 'The General Election of 1715', *E.H.R.* (1975).

2. Jacobitism

Jacobitism is gradually being reclaimed from the realms of romantic fiction to reflect increasingly upon the insecurity of the Hanoverian succession and the many opportunities for division within the political nation which still existed after 1714. The role of Jacobitism as an ideology of opposition is important, especially for the way in which it shaded off into Toryism and the opposition to Walpole. The manipulation of the Jacobite issue by Walpole has also received attention.

Essay topics

At what point were conditions most propitious for Jacobite success?
What does the strength of Jacobite feeling suggest about the nature of political conflict in the reigns of George I and George II?

Secondary works

G. H. Jones, *The Mainstream of Jacobitism* (1954) is a good place to start, while G. Petrie, *The Jacobite Movement* (1959) is rather over-romantic. The last essay in G. S. Holmes (ed.), *Britain after the Glorious Revolution* (1969) discusses the political struggle preceding Anne's death. For the survival of Bolingbroke's influence, see I. Krammick, *Bolingbroke and his Circle: the politics of nostalgia* (1968). A. S. Foord, *His Majesty's Opposition 1714–1830* (1964) discusses the place of the Jacobites in the other factions aiming for the overthrow of Walpole, as does C. B. Realey, *The Early Opposition to Sir Robert Walpole* (1931). P. S. Fritz, *The English Ministers and Jacobitism between the Rebellions of 1715 and 1745* (1975) is an excellent study of the exploitation of the Jacobite 'threat' by Walpole, while for the risings themselves, see B. Lenman, *The Jacobite Risings in Britain, 1689–1746* (1980). R. C. Jarvis, *Collected Papers on the Jacobite Risings*, vols I and II (1971–2) are a powerful antidote to the view that Jacobitism was inevitably doomed to failure. The plot of 1722 is well analysed in G. V. Bennett, *The Tory Crisis in Church and State* (1975). Good biographical studies include, H. T. Dickinson, *Bolingbroke* (1970). and D. Daiches, *Charles Edward Stuart* (1973). The later phase of Tory/Jacobite activity is considered in E. Cruikshanks, *Political Untouchables* (1979).

Articles

N. Rogers, 'Popular disturbances in early Hanoverian London', *P.P.* (1978) gives a good account of pro-Tory and crypto-Jacobite feeling in London. P. D. G. Thomas, 'Jacobitism in Wales' *W.H.R.* (1963) is good on an often neglected area of British politics. H. N. Fieldhouse 'Bolingbroke and the idea of non-party government', *E.H.R.* (1937); E. Gregg, 'Was Queen Anne a Jacobite?' *H.* (1972) and M. A. Thomson, 'The safe-guarding of the Protestant succession?' *H.* (1954) are all relevant. See, too, N. Rogers, 'Popular disaffection in London during the forty-five', *L.J.* (1975).

3. Walpole and the Whig supremacy

Walpole's period of office dominated the first half of the eighteenth century. The nature of his power and its significance for the conduct of politics in this period provide a major theme. The relationship between Crown and parliament and the position of Walpole as *de facto* prime minister shed light on the working out of the constitutional implications of the Revolution Settlement. The weakening of party feeling from the 1720s provided an opportunity for a different style of politics in which patronage and 'influence' played a more crucial part than 'party'. As a result, much of the writing on this topic concerns the 'structure' of politics. Surprisingly little attention is paid to Walpole's policies, though there has been a revival of interest in the ideological basis of the 'Whig oligarchy' and that of Walpole's opponents.

Essay topics

Did Walpole govern by 'corruption'?

What did Walpole's long tenure of office reveal about the nature of politics in the first half of the eighteenth century?

Sources and documents

E. N. Williams (ed.), *The Eighteenth Century Constitution* (1960) has a good selection of contemporary documents, as has D. B. Horn and M. Ransome, *English Historical Documents, vol. X, 1714–83* (1957). Lord Hervey, *Memoirs* (3 vols, ed. R. Sedgewick, 1931) provides a fascinating account of court politics under Walpole. There is a vast amount of material on the structure of local politics in R. Sedgewick, *The House of Commons 1715–1754* (2 vols, 1970).

Secondary works

Good outlines exist in J. H. Plumb, *England in the Eighteenth Century, 1714–1815* (1950); W. A. Speck, *Stability and Strife: England 1714–1760* (1977); B. W. Hill, *The Growth of Parliamentary Parties, 1689–1742* (1977) and J. Owen, *The Eighteenth Century, 1714–1815* (1974). J. H. Plumb, *The Growth of Political Stability in England, 1675–1725* (1967) and B. Kemp, *King and Commons, 1660–1832* (1957) both have relevant material. J. H. Plumb, *Sir Robert Walpole* (2 vols, 1956 and 1960) is the standard iife, but does not go beyond 1734. H. T. Dickinson, *Walpole and the Whig Supremacy* (1973) and B. Kemp, *Sir Robert Walpole* (1976) are both useful shorter works. See also G. S. Holmes, 'Sir Robert Walpole' in H. Van Thal (ed.), *The Prime Ministers*, vol. I (1974). On the pattern of politics in this period, J. Owen, *The Eighteenth Century, 1714–1815* (1974), ch. 5 is the surest guide and his views are also stated in J. Owen, *The Pattern of Politics in Eighteenth Century England* (Historical Association Pamphlet, 1962). One of the most important episodes of Walpole's career is discussed in J. Carswell, *The South Sea Bubble* (1960), but see also P. G. M. Dickson, *The Financial Revolution* (1967). On other

issues, see P. Langford, *The Excise Crisis* (1975) and Walpole's concern
with Jacobitism in P.S. Fritz, *The English Ministers and Jacobitism
between the Rebellions of 1715 and 1745* (1975). The important foreign
policy background is discussed in P. Langford, *Britain, 1688–1815: foreign
policy in the eighteenth century* (1976) and the more detailed D. B. Horn,
Great Britain and Europe in the Eighteenth Century (1967) and J.
McLachlan, *Trade and Peace with Old Spain, 1667–1739* (1940).

The opposition to Walpole is considered in A. S. Foord, *His Majesty's
Opposition, 1714–1830* (1964) and C. B. Realey, *The Early Opposition to
Sir Robert Walpole* (1931). H. T. Dickinson, *Bolingbroke* (1970) and I.
Kramnick, *Bolingbroke and his Circle: the politics of nostalgia* (1968). The
important role of London is considered in L. S. Sutherland, 'The City of
London in eighteenth-century politics' in *Essays Presented to Sir Lewis
Namier* (eds R. Pares and A. J. P. Taylor, 1956); N. Rogers, 'Resistance to
oligarchy' in J. Stevenson (ed.) *London in the Age of Reform* (1977); A. J.
Henderson, *London and the National Government, 1721–1742: a study
of city politics and the Walpole administration* (1945). Rural protest is
considered in E. P. Thompson, *Whigs and Hunters* (1975).

Articles

See M. Ransome, 'Division lists in the House of Commons, 1715–1760',
B.I.H.R. (1942); E. A. Reitan, 'The Civil List in eighteenth-century British
politics', *H. J.* (1966); B. Williams, 'The Duke of Newcastle and the
general election of 1734', *E.H.R.* (1897); T. F. J. Kendrick, 'Sir Robert
Walpole, the old Whigs and the bishops, 1733–1736', *H. J.* (1968); E. R.
Turner, 'The excise scheme of 1733', *E.H.R.* (1927). On foreign policy see
C. Gibbs, 'Parliament and foreign policy in the age of Stanhope and
Walpole', *E.H.R.* (1962) and D. McKay, 'The struggle for control of George
I's northern policy', *J.M.H.* (1973).

4. The Church of England and the rise of Methodism

The rise of Methodism inevitably reflects upon the condition of the
Church of England in the eighteenth century and the problems posed by
population growth and economic change, but John Wesley is a
fascinating figure who would alone make this subject worth studying.
Three main topics emerge: what was the condition of the
eighteenth-century Church of England; why was it unable to harness
Methodism as a revival movement (as with the Evangelical Revival and
the Oxford Movement) and why did the two separate; and what effects
did Methodism have upon an industrialising England. It is worth
considering whether the Church of England was any worse than it ever
had been and why it found it difficult to adjust itself to meet the new
challenges. Elie Halévy's claim that Methodism prevented revolution in
England deserves some attention.

Essay topics

Why was the eighteenth-century Church of England unable to harness Wesley's reforming zeal?
    Was the rise of Methodism a condemnation of the Church of England?
    What were the political and social effects of Methodism before 1815?

Sources

John Wesley, *Journals*; even the smallest sample is valuable for the flavour of Methodism in its 'heroic' phase. E. N. Williams, *The Eighteenth Century Constitution* (1960) has a useful section on the church. John Wade, *The Extraordinary Black Book* (1820) is a scintillating exposé of corruption in the political and ecclesiastical establishment. Though biased, it provides a mine of information on the unreformed Anglican Church.

Secondary works

The most accessible one-volume treatment is A. Armstrong, *The Church of England, the Methodists and Society, 1700–1850* (1973), while A. D. Gilbert, *Religion and Society in Industrial England, 1740–1914* (1976) places Methodism within the context of religious adherence in general. W. G. Ward, *Religion and Society in England 1790–1850* (1972) is also relevant. N. Sykes, *Church and State in the Eighteenth Century* (1934) is the essential work on the Church of England, but see also G. V. Bennett and J. D. Walsh (eds), *Essays in Modern Church History in Memory of Norman Sykes* (1966). The older C. J. Abbey and J. H. Overton, *The English Church in the Eighteenth Century* (2 vols, 1878) is still useful, as are S. C. Carpenter, *Eighteenth-century Church and People* (1959) and *Church and People, 1789–1899* (1959).

For Methodism see R. Davies and E. G. Rupp (eds), *A History of the Methodist Church of Great Britain* (1965). On Wesley himself, F. Baker, *John Wesley and the Church of England* (1970) and V. H. H. Green, *John Wesley* (1964). For the period after Wesley's death, see M. L. Edwards, *After Wesley: a study in the social and political influence of Methodism in the Middle Period, 1791–1849* (1935). On Methodism's impact see R. F. Wearmouth, *Methodism and the Common People of the Eighteenth Century* (1945) and *Methodism and the Working-class Movements of England, 1800–1850* (1937) contain a lot of information, but are rather uncritical. E. R. Taylor, *Methodism and Politics, 1791–1850* (1935) is also useful. E. Halévy, *England in 1815* (1924) has an important section where he argues that Methodism prevented revolution in England. E. P. Thompson, *The Making of the English Working Class*, ch. 11 is polemical but interesting. J. D. Walsh, 'Methodism and the mob in the eighteenth century' in G. J. Cuming and D. Barker (eds), *Popular Belief and Practice, Studies in Church History*, vol. VIII (1972) throws light on the reception of Methodism.

On the intellectual background to eighteenth-century religious life see G. R. Cragg, *From Puritanism to the Age of Reason* (1966) and R. N. Stromberg, *Religious Liberalism in Eighteenth Century England* (1954).

The Evangelical Revival is considered in C. Smyth, *Simeon and Church*

Order (1940) which has important bearings on why the evangelicals could stay within the Church of England and Methodism could not. See also E. M. Howse, *Saints in Politics* (1953) for the 'Clapham Sect'.

Articles

E. Hobsbawm, 'Methodism and the threat of revolution in Britain', *H.T.* (1957), also reprinted in his collection *Labouring Men* (1964), is crucial on this issue. See also J. D. Walsh, 'Elie Halévy and the birth of Methodism', *T.R.H.S.* (1975). C. Smyth, 'The evangelical movement in perspective', *C.H.J.* (1941–3).

5. The Agricultural Revolution

Like the 'Industrial Revolution', the 'Agricultural Revolution' has been placed within the context of a more gradual and complex process of economic development. Explanations for the expansion of British agricultural output no longer concentrate upon the 'discovery' of a few techniques and inventions but upon the factors which stimulated a more enterprising approach to agriculture from the middle years of the eighteenth century. The Agricultural Revolution, and the enclosure movement, in particular, was seen as a social disaster by contemporaries such as Cobbett and by later historians, such as the Hammonds, but recent work has increasingly modified this picture. The story, however, remains complex and often repays study from a regional or local perspective.

Essay topics

Was there a 'revolution' in agriculture during the eighteenth and nineteenth centuries?
   Have the social and economic effects of enclosure been exaggerated?

Sources and documents

William Cobbett, *Rural Rides* (1830), immensely readable and prejudiced, is available in many modern editions. A. Young, *Tours in England and Wales* (reprinted 1932) is valuable for checking generalisations against contemporary facts. A. E. Bland, P. Brown and R. H. Tawney, *English Economic History* (1914), Pt III, section II has some useful documents on enclosure.

Secondary works

Many of the standard economic histories contain sections on agriculture; see especially D. C. Coleman, *The Economy of England, 1450–1750* (1977), ch. 7; C. Wilson, *England's Apprenticeship, 1603–1763* (1965), ch. 12; P. Mathias, *The First Industrial Nation: an economic history of Britain,*

1700–1914 (1969), ch. 3; P. Deane and W. A. Cole, *British Economic Growth, 1688–1959* (1969), ch. 2.

J. D. Chambers and G. E. Mingay, *The Agricultural Revolution, 1750–1880* (1966) is the major modern work, but see also E. Kerridge, *The Agricultural Revolution* (1967). J. Clapham, *An Economic History of Modern Britain* (3 vols 1926–38), chs 4 and 11 is still useful. E. L. Jones, *The Development of English Agriculture, 1815–1873* (1968) deals with the later stages. A. H. John, 'The course of agricultural change, 1660–1760' in L. S. Pressnell (ed.), *Studies in the Industrial Revolution* (1960) is important on the timing of change; see also the essays by E. L. Jones and A. H. John in E. L. Jones and G. E. Mingay (eds), *Land, Labour and Population in the Industrial Revolution* (1967). D. B. Grigg, *The Agricultural Revolution in South Lincolnshire* (1966) is a good regional study. J. L. and B. Hammond, *The Village Labourer* (1911) remains the classic 'pessimistic' view of the effects of agricultural change, but is now rather dated. E. Hobsbawm and G. Rudé, *Captain Swing* (1969) deals with agricultural protests of 1830–2 and sheds considerable light on early nineteenth-century conditions. R. A. C. Parker, *Coke of Norfolk* (1975) discusses one of the pioneers of agricultural improvement. The detailed regional progress of enclosure can be followed in G. Slater, *The English Peasantry and the Enclosure of Common Fields* (1907) and E. C. K. Gonner, *Common Land and Enclosure* (1912). See also G. E. Mingay, *Enclosure and the Small Farmer in the Age of the Industrial Revolution* (1968) and *The Gentry: the rise and fall of a ruling class* (1976).

Articles

G. E. Mingay's views are summarised in 'The Agricultural Revolution – a reconsideration', *Ag. H.* (1963); see also his 'The size of farms in the eighteenth century', *Econ.H.R.* (1962). E. L. Jones 'Agriculture and economic growth in England, 1600–1750', *J. Econ. H.* (1965) is important, while J. D. Chambers, 'The Vale of Trent, 1670–1800: a regional study of economic change', *Econ. H.R.* Supplement No. 3 (1957) is a useful case study. G. E. Mingay, 'The agricultural depression, 1730–1750', *Econ. H.R.* (1956); R. A. C. Parker, 'Coke of Norfolk and the agrarian revolution', *Econ. H.R.* (1955); T. H. Marshall, 'Jethro Tull and the new husbandry of the eighteenth century', *Econ. H.R.* (1929–30); J. D. Chambers, 'Enclosure and the small landowner', *Econ. H.R.* (1940) and 'Enclosure and labour supply in the Industrial Revolution', *Econ. H. R.* (1953) are also highly relevant. E. L. Jones, 'The agricultural labour market in England, 1793–1872', *Econ. H.R.* (1964–5) and F. M. L. Thompson, 'The second Agricultural Revolution, 1815–1880', *Econ. H. R.* (1968) deal with the later period.

6. Eighteenth-century society

The eighteenth century saw the beginnings of population growth, significant urbanisation and major developments in agriculture and industry. One of the main problems is how far Britain differed from other European societies and the extent to which social mobility increased with the rise of commerce and industry. Is the picture of a rigidly hierarchical society accurate, and how relevant is the concept of class to a society such as this? Considerable work in recent years has been done on the areas of riot, protest and crime.

Essay topics

What were the principal characteristics of eighteenth-century society?
   How relevant is the concept of 'class' to a discussion of eighteenth-century society?

Sources and documents

A portrait of village life can be found in J. Woodforde, *The Diary of a Country Parson* (ed. J. Beresford, in various editions). D. Defoe, *The Complete English Tradesman* (1735, and later editions) and James Boswell, *London Journal, 1762–1763* (ed. J. Pottle, 1950 and 1966) deal with urban life. See also T. Turner, *The Diary of a Georgian Shopkeeper* (1980), dealing with Sussex life in the 1750s. E. N. Williams, *The Eighteenth Century Constitution* (1960) has a section on social life.

Secondary works

J. D. Chambers, *Population, Economy and Society in Pre-Industrial England* (1972) and D. Marshall, *English People in the Eighteenth Century* (1956) are good starting-points. The landed classes are considered in G. E. Mingay, *English Landed Society in the Eighteenth Century* (1956) and *The Gentry: the rise and fall of a ruling class* (1976), especially chs 3–5. See also H. J. Habakkuk, 'England' in A. Goodwin (ed.), *The European Nobility in the Eighteenth Century* (1967). H. J. Perkin, *The Origins of Modern English Society, 1780–1880* (1969), ch. 2, and L. B. Namier's chapter 'The social foundations' in *England in the Age of the American Revolution* (2nd ed., 1961) are important sections of longer works.
   D. Marshall, *The English Poor in the Eighteenth Century* (1926) and M. D. George, *London Life in the Eighteenth Century* (1925) are mines of information on the lower classes. On London, see also G. Rudé, *Hanoverian London* (1971). P. Laslett, *The World We Have Lost* (1965) re-examines the nature of 'pre-industrial' society in the light of demographic and other evidence. J. L. and B. Hammond, *The Skilled Labourer, 1760–1832* (1919, 2nd edn republished 1978) and C. R. Dobson, *Masters and Journeymen* (1980) deal with industrial relations. E. P. Thompson, *Whigs and Hunters* (1975) presents a challenging view of the social conflicts over property rights, while the essays in D. Hay, P. Linebaugh, J. Rule, E. P. Thompson and C. Winslow, *Albion's Fatal Tree* (1975) throw light upon popular attitudes. On riots see J. Stevenson, *Popular Disturbances in England, 1700–1870* (1979) and on the law J. Brewer and J. Styles, *An Ungovernable People: the English and their law in the seventeenth and eighteenth centuries* (1980). Popular recreations are discussed in R. W. Malcolmson, *Popular Recreations in English Society, 1700–1850* (1973), and the press in G. A. Cranfield, *The Press and Society: from Caxton to Northcliffe* (1978). Family life and sexual

mores are discussed in L. Stone, *The Family, Sex and Marriage in England 1500–1800* (1977); see also P. Laslett (ed.), *Household and Family in Past Time* (1972).

The commercial middle classes and the important entrepreneurial role of religious minorities are discussed in R. B. Westerfield, *Middlemen in English Business, 1660–1760* (1915); E. Bebb, *Nonconformity and Social and Economic Life, 1660–1880* (1935); I. Grub, *Quakerism and Industry before 1800* (1930); C. Roth, *A History of the Jews in England* (1941). C. W. Chalkin, *The Provincial Towns of Georgian England* (1974) and C. W. Chalkin and M. A. Havinden (eds), *Rural Change and Urban Growth, 1500–1800* (1974) examine urban development outside London. E. Hughes, *North Country Life in the Eighteenth Century: the North-East, 1700–1750* (1952) and *Cumberland and Westmorland, 1700–1830* (1965); A. Temple Patterson, *A History of Southampton, 1700–1914, vol. I, 1700–1835* (1966); J. D. Chambers, *Nottinghamshire in the Eighteenth Century* (1966); J. Money, *Experience and Identity, Birmingham, 1770–1800* (1978); G. Jackson, *Hull in the Eighteenth Century* (1972); R. Wilson, *Gentlemen Merchants* (1971) (on Leeds), are among the most important local studies.

For cultural developments, see J. H. Plumb 'The public, literature and the arts' in P. Fritz and D. Williams (eds), *The Triumph of Culture: eighteenth-century perspectives* (1972). Country-house life is discussed in M. Girouard, *Life in the English Country House* (1978), especially chs 6, 7 and 8; see also J. Summerson, *Georgian London* (1962).

Articles

E. P. Thompson, 'Eighteenth-century English society: class struggle without class', *S. H.* (1978) raises some interesting general issues. On the ownership of property, see H. J. Habakkuk, 'English landownership, 1680–1740', *Econ. H. R.* (1940); C. Clay, 'Marriage inheritance and the rise of large estates in England, 1660–1815', *Econ. H.R.* (1968); B. Holdernesse, 'The English land market in the eighteenth century', *Econ. H.R.* (1974). E. Hughes, 'The professions in the eighteenth century', *D.U.J.* (1951) deals with an often neglected group. D. Rapp, 'Social mobility in the eighteenth century: the Whitbreads of Bedfordshire, 1720–1815', *Econ. H.R.* (1974) is an important case study. On the 'rise of the middle classes' generally, see A. Briggs, 'Middle class consciousness in English politics, 1780–1846', *P.P.* (1956) and H. J. Perkin, 'The social causes of the British Industrial Revolution', *T.R.H.S.* (1968). See also L. Stone, 'Literacy and education in England, 1640–1900', *P.P.* (1969) and J. H. Plumb, 'The new world of children in the eighteenth century', *P.P.* (1975). J. M. Beattie, 'The pattern of crime in England, 1660–1800', *P.P.* (1974) and E. P. Thompson, 'The moral economy of the English crowd in the eighteenth century' *P.P.* (1971) are among the most important articles on crime and protest.

7. The Elder Pitt

The Elder Pitt, Earl of Chatham, has, with his son, traditionally been seen as one of the 'great men' of British history. In large part this fame rests upon his leadership in the Seven Years War and his role in the development of Britain's overseas empire. Historians have also become increasingly interested in his domestic support which in some respects pre-figured the reform movement of George III's reign. Pitt's role in the early stages of the conflict with the American colonists also should not be ignored.

Essay topics

Assess the significance of the career of the Elder Pitt for the development of the British Empire.
 What social and political groups supported the Elder Pitt, and why?

Sources and documents

The Letters of Horace Walpole (various editions available) are valuable for the mood of the country in 1756–7 and Pitt's role generally. See also Lord Hervey, *Some Materials towards Memoirs of the Reign of George II* (3 vols, ed. R. Sedgwick, 1931). D. B. Horn and M. Ransome (eds), *English Historical Documents, Vol. X, 1714–1783* (1957), also has relevant material.

Secondary works

The chapters in H. van Thal, *The Prime Ministers*, vol. 1 (1974) and in P. Brown, *The Chathamites* (1967) are essential places to start. There are several biographies of which B. Williams, *Life of Chatham* is probably the best, if old (1913) and pro-Pitt. A. von Runville, *William Pitt, Earl of Chatham* is also elderly (1907), but massive, learned and anti-Pitt: a book to be quarried rather than read. J. H. Plumb, *Chatham* (1953) and B. Tunstall, *William Pitt, Earl of Chatham* (1938) are one-volume studies. Other biographies available include those by C. Grant Robertson, (1946), O. A. Sherrard (3 vols, 1952–8), P. D. Brown (1978), and S. Ayling (1976). There is a brief outline of foreign policy in P. Langford, *Great Britain, 1688–1815* (1976), but more detailed studies include D. B. Horn, *Great Britain and Europe in the Eighteenth Century* (1967); R. Pares, *War and Trade in the West Indies, 1739–1763* (1936); K. Hotblack, *Chatham's Colonial Policy* (1917). Britain's role in the Seven Years War is covered in J. Corbett, *England in the Seven Years War* (1907) and R. Savory, *His Britannic Majesty's Army in Germany during the Seven Years War* (1966). Pitt's domestic significance is reflected in Brown (1967), but also in R. Robson, *The Oxfordshire Election of 1754* (1949) which reveals some of the interplay of national and local politics in the 1750s. For the City of London's support for Pitt, see Dame Lucy Sutherland, 'The City of London in eighteenth century politics' in *Essays Presented to Sir Lewis Namier* (eds R. Pares and A. J. P. Taylor, 1956) and M. Peters, *Pitt and Popularity: the patriot minister and London opinion during the Seven Years War* (1981). For the struggle between Pitt and Henry Fox, see E. Eyck, *Pitt versus Fox* (1950). Chatham's career in the 1760s is discussed in L. Namier, *England in the Age of the American Revolution* (2nd edn, 1961) and J. Brooke, *The Chatham Administration, 1766–1768* (1956).

Articles

P. Langford, 'William Pitt and public opinion in 1757', *E.H.R.* (1973) is helpful. Good on the background to his war policy are C. M. Andrews, 'Anglo-French commercial rivalry, 1700–50', *A.M.H.R.* (1914–15) and R. Pares, 'American and continental warfare, 1739–63', *E.H.R.* (1936).

8. British colonial policy and the American War of Independence

A complex subject embracing political conflicts on both sides of the Atlantic and the general conduct of British imperial policy in the latter half of the eighteenth century. The view of American secession as inevitable needs to be carefully scrutinised and the divisions within America given full weight. Why there was a progress from resistance to taxation to 'revolution' needs to be examined carefully and the rhetoric of the colonists put in perspective. The impact of the American crisis on attitudes to the Empire is an important aspect of the topic.

Essay topics

How far was American independence the result of mistakes in British policy between 1763 and 1783?

What impact did the American War of Independence have upon the development of the British Empire?

Sources and documents

J. R. Pole (ed.), *The Revolution in America, 1754–1788* (1970) has a very useful selection of documents; see also R. C. Birch, *1776: the American challenge* (1977). E. Burke's speeches on American taxation can be read in B. W. Hill's collection of his works, *Edmund Burke on Government, Politics and Society* (1975). M. Beloff (ed.), *The Debate on the American Revolution* (1949) is also valuable.

Secondary works

I. R. Christie, *Crisis of Empire: Great Britain and the American Colonies, 1754–1783* (1966) is a brief introduction. B. Donoughue, *British Politics and the American Revolution: The path to war, 1773–75* (1964) is a more detailed account of the immediate crisis. J. C. Miller, *The Origins of the American Revolution* (2nd edn, 1959) is an alternative outline. P. Langford, *The Eighteenth Century, 1688–1815* (1976) chs 11 and 12 deals with foreign policy in general. His *The First Rockingham Administration, 1756–1766* (1973) is important on the Stamp Act crisis. C. R. Ritcheson, *British Politics and the American Revolution* (1954) and G. H. Guttridge, *English Whiggism and the American Revolution* (2nd edn, 1963) are both relevant. J. R. Pole, *Foundations of American Independence, 1763–1815* (1972) is important on the American background. Two useful collections are E. Wright (ed.), *Causes and Consequences of the American Revolution* (1966) and J. P. Greene (ed.), *The Reinterpretation of the American Revolution* (1968). An important historiographical essay is I. R. Christie, 'The historians' quest for the American Revolution', in A. Whiteman, J. S. Bromley and P. G. M. Dickson (eds), *Statesmen, Scholars and Merchants* (1973). P. Mackesy, *The War for America, 1775–1783* (1964) and J. R. Alden, *The American Revolution, 1775–1783* (1954) deal with military affairs. The wider issues of British imperial policy are considered in V. T. Harlow, *The Founding of the Second British Empire, 1763–1793, volume I: Discovery and Revolution* (1952); G. L. Bear, *British Colonial Policy, 1754–1765* (2nd edn, 1933); J. R. Alden, *A History of the American Revolution: Britain and the loss of the thirteen colonies* (1969). Two older studies C. H. Van Tyne, *The Causes of the War of Independence* (1922) and H. E. Egerton, *The Causes and Character of the American Revolution* (2nd edn, 1931) are still worth consulting. See also the important essay by J. G. A. Pocock '1776: the revolution against Parliament' in J. G. A. Pocock (ed.), *Three British Revolutions: 1641, 1688, 1776* (1980). The impact of the American crisis on the reform movement in England is discussed in J. Cannon, *Parliamentary Reform, 1640–1832* (1973) and I. R. Christie, *Wilkes, Wyvill and Reform* (1962). See also P. Langford, 'London and the American crisis' in J. Stevenson (ed.), *London in the Age of Reform* (1976). B. Bailyn, *The Ideological Origins of the American Revolution* (1967) and *The Origins of American Politics* (1969) are essential on the political ideology underlying the conflict.

Articles

R. W. van Alstyn, 'Europe, the Rockingham Whigs and the war for American independence: some documents', *H.L.Q.* (1961); P. Marshall, 'Radicals, Conservatives, and the American Revolution', *P.P.* (1962); G. H. Guttridge, 'The Whig Opposition in England during the American Revolution', *J.M.H.* (1934); E. S. Morgan, 'The American Revolution: revisions in need of revising', *W.M.Q.* (1957), are all useful.

9. George III, the constitution and the parliamentary reform movement, 1760–89

The latter years of the eighteenth century witnessed growing concern about the working of the constitution and in particular the power of the Crown. George III's attempts to exercise his right to choose his own ministers, the Wilkes affair and the conflict with America brought fresh issues into politics and led to the first widespread demands for parliamentary reform. It is important to understand why fears grew up about Crown influence and whether they were justified. The broader factors providing support for reform need to be considered and the different meanings given to 'reform'.

Essay topics

'The power of the Crown has increased, is increasing and ought to be diminished' (Dunning's motion, 1780). Discuss.

Why did the power of the Crown become an issue in British politics in the first 20 years of the reign of George III?

What groups supported parliamentary reform in Britain between 1760 and 1789, and why?

Sources and documents

E. Burke, *Thoughts on our Present Discontents* (1770 and later editions) is the classic statement of grievances against George III which provided the impetus for the 'economical reform' movement. E. N. Williams, *The Eighteenth Century Constitution, 1688–1815* (1960) has documents both on the role of the monarch and parliamentary reform.

Secondary works

The most balanced and lucid exposition of the constitutional developments after 1760 can be found in I. R. Christie, *Myth and Reality in later Eighteenth-Century British Politics, and Other Papers* (1970), especially the introduction and chs 1 and 2. See also R. Pares, *King George III and the Politicians* (1953). On the reform movement, J. Cannon, *Parliamentary Reform in England, 1640–1832* (1973), chs 3 and 4, is a good introduction. I. R. Christie, *Wilkes, Wyvill and Reform* (1962) has a full discussion of the various elements in reform. J. Brewer, *Party Ideology and Popular Politics at the Accession of George III* (1978) examines the political forces at work in the 1760s. An old but still useful study is G. S. Veitch, *The Genesis of Parliamentary Reform* (2nd edn, 1964). G. Rudé, *Wilkes and Liberty: A Social Study of 1763–1774* (1962) is essential on the metropolitan background and Wilkes' support, but see also L. S. Sutherland, *The City of London and the Opposition, 1768–74* (The Creighton Lecture, 1958), reprinted in J. Stevenson (ed.), *London in the Age of Reform* (1976). For the ideology of the English reformers see R. W. Harris, *Political Ideas in England, 1760–1792* (1963) and the latter sections of H. T. Dickinson, *Liberty and Property* (1978). C. Robbins, *The Eighteenth Century Commonwealthman* (1959) and C. Hill, 'The Norman yoke' in his essays *Puritanism and Revolution* (1958) trace continuities with earlier ideas. On leading personalities see J. W. Osborne, *John Cartwright* (1972); E. Foner, *Tom Paine and Revolutionary America* (1976); F. O'Gorman, *Edmund Burke* (1973).

Articles

I. R. Christie, 'Economical reform and the "influence of the Crown" 1780', *C.H.J.* (1956) explains the crucial link between fears of executive 'tyranny' and the demand for reform. His 'The Yorkshire Association, 1780–4', *H.J.* (1960) and H. Butterfield, 'The Yorkshire Association and the crisis of 1779–80' *T.R.H.S.* (1947) examine the 'County' movement. P. D. G. Thomas, 'The beginnings of parliamentary reporting in newspapers, 1768–74', *E.H.R.* (1959) discusses the growing influence of the press.

10. The impact of the French Revolution on Britain

Traditional interest focuses upon the effects of the French Revolution on party politics, especially on the Whigs, the rise of popular radicalism and its suppression, and the longer-term effects of the French Revolution on British politics. Much attention has focused in recent years on the popular political societies, E. P. Thompson seeing this as a crucial stage in the development of 'class consciousness' among working people. Goodwin is a recent reworking of the available evidence, especially strong on the provincial and dissenting origins of the early reform movement. The period after 1795 is beginning to receive more serious attention than it has hitherto.

Essay topics

What impact did the French Revolution have upon British politics between 1789 and 1815?
    Were there any British 'Jacobins'?

Sources and documents

The ideological debate can be followed in the various editions of T. Paine, *The Rights of Man* (1791–2) and E. Burke, *Reflections on the Revolution in France* (1790). A. Cobban (ed.), *The Debate on the French Revolution* (1950) contains selections from contemporary writers; see also G. D. H. Cole and A. W. Filson (eds), *British Working Class Movements: select documents, 1789–1875* (1951). M. Thale (ed.), *The Autobiography of Francis Place* (1972) gives an insider's account of one of the popular societies in the 1790s; see also T. Hardy, 'A memoir of Thomas Hardy', reprinted in D. Vincent (ed.) *Testaments of Radicalism* (1977).

Secondary works

P. A. Brown, *The French Revolution in English History* (1918) is still the best treatment, while G. S. Veitch, *The Genesis of Parliamentary Reform* (2nd edn, 1965) retains its value. J. Cannon, *Parliamentary Reform in England, 1640–1832* (1973) has some lucid chapters on the period. E. P. Thompson, *The Making of the English Working Class* (2nd edn, 1968), especially Pt I, chs 1–5, is a stimulating, if often controversial account of popular radicalism. On the London Corresponding Society see H. Collins in J. Saville (ed.), *Democracy and the Labour Movement* (1954); see also G. A. Williams, *Artisans and Sans-Culottes: popular movements in France and Britain during the French Revolution* (1968). A. Goodwin, *The Friends of Liberty* (1979) is a thorough discussion of reform and radical movements, while C. Emsley, *British Society and the French Wars, 1793–1815* (1979) ranges widely into both the political and social repercussions of the French Wars. F. O'Gorman, *The Whig Party and the French Revolution* (1967) and L. G. Mitchell, *Charles James Fox and the Disintegration of the Whig Party, 1782–1794* (1971) examine party developments, while D. G. Barnes, *George III and William Pitt, 1783–1806* (1939) is useful on the administration. E. N. C. Black, *The Association* (1963) has a section on loyalist organisations. A. D. Harvey, *Britain in the Early Nineteenth Century* (1978) is particularly helpful on the period 1800–12, but see also S. Maccoby, *English Radicalism, 1786–1832* (1955). The development of political ideology is admirably presented in H. T. Dickinson, *Liberty and Property* (1978). For the popular disturbances of the period, see J. Stevenson, *Popular Disturbances in England, 1700–1870* (1979) and R. Wells, *Dearth and Distress in Yorkshire, 1793–1801* (Borthwick Paper No. 52, 1977).

Articles

The fears of the government are discussed in C. Emsley, 'The London "insurrection" of December 1792: fact, fiction or fantasy', *J.B.S.* (1978). The reaction to the French Revolution is also dealt with in R. B. Rose, 'The Priestley riots of 1791', *P.P.* (1960); A. Mitchell, 'The Association Movement of 1792–3', *H.J.* (1961); D. E. Ginter, 'The Loyalist Association Movement of 1792–93 and British public opinion', *H.J.* (1966); J. R. Western, 'The Volunteer movement as an anti-revolutionary force, 1793–1800', *E.H.R.* (1956). For popular distress, see W. M. Stern, 'The bread crisis in Britain, 1795–96', *E.* (1964) and A. Booth, 'Food riots in North-West England, 1790–1801', *P.P.* (1977). Local movements are discussed in F. K. Donnelly and J. L. Baxter, 'Sheffield and the English revolutionary tradition, 1791–1820', *I.R.S.H.* (1974) and W. A. L. Seaman, 'Reform politics at Sheffield, 1791–1797', *T.H.A.S.* (1957). For the continuity of radical activity after 1795, see J. R. Dinwiddy 'The "Black Lamp" in Yorkshire, 1801–1802' and J. L. Baxter and F. K. Donnelly, 'The revolutionary "underground" in the West Riding: myth or reality?', *P.P.* (1974) and M. Elliott, 'The "Despard conspiracy" reconsidered', *P.P.* (1977).

11. Pitt and Fox

The two central characters of late eighteenth-century politics can be assessed together or separately. Pitt the Younger's career in the 1780s is now much clearer and it is important to assess the importance of the financial and administrative reforms he attempted. Discussions of his career often stop in the mid-1790s, and it is necessary to take in his conduct of the war and second administration for a full assessment. Fox remains a fascinating figure. It is equally important to see his *full* career in perspective (up to 1806) and in the context of the fortunes of his party as a whole. Some grasp of party developments and the continuing, but changing, role of the Crown is important to the careers of both men.

Essay topics

'A more effective prime minister than a war leader'. Discuss this view of Pitt the Younger.

Was the career of Charles James Fox a total failure?
How did the careers of *either* Pitt the Younger *or* Charles James Fox
reflect changes in the pattern of eighteenth-century politics?

Sources and documents

A. Aspinall and E. A. Smith (eds), *English Historical Documents, Vol. XI,
1783–1832* (1959) has a selection of documents on the period. A.
Aspinall (ed.), *The Later Correspondence of George III, December
1783–December 1810* (1962–70) also has relevant material. R. Coupland,
The War Speeches of William Pitt (1915) and W. Pitt, *Orations on the
French War* (1906) are useful for the war years. On Fox, see A. Bullock
and M. Shock (eds.) *The Liberal Tradition: From Fox to Keynes* (1956).

Secondary works

For Pitt, the basic study is J. Ehrman, *The Younger Pitt: the Years of
Acclaim* (1969), but this only goes up to 1789. D. G. Barnes, *George III
and William Pitt, 1783–1806* (1939) carries on the story to 1806. J. W.
Derry, *William Pitt* (1962) is a brief study, while the older J. Holland Rose,
William Pitt and National Revival (1911) and *William Pitt and the Great
War* (1911) is still valuable. Pitt's reaction to the French Revolution is
considered in P. A. Brown, *The French Revolution in English History*
(1918). P. Langford, *The Eighteenth Century, 1688–1815* (1976), chs 14
and 15, is useful on foreign affairs. See also C. Emsley, *British Society
and the French Wars, 1793–1815* (1979). J. Binney, *British Public Finance
and Administration, 1774–92* (1958) is relevant on Pitt's administrative
reforms. On the role of the Irish crisis, see G. C. Bolton, *The Passing of
the Act of Union* (1966).

On Fox, J. W. Derry, *Charles James Fox* (1973) is the best life, but
Loren Reid, *Charles James Fox: a man for the people* (1969) is useful on
Fox as an orator. An older alternative is E. C. P. Lascelles, *Charles James
Fox* (1936). The early part of his career is considered in J. Cannon, *The
Fox–North Coalition: crisis of the constitution* (1970). The effects of the
French Revolution are considered in F. O'Gorman, *The Whig Party and
the French Revolution* (1967), while L. G. Mitchell, *Charles James Fox and
the Disintegration of the Whig Party, 1782–94* (1970) deals more
generally with Fox's relationship with the Whig Party. The organisation
of the Whig Party is discussed in the introduction to D. E. Ginter, *Whig
Organisation in the General Election of 1790* (1967).

Of relevance to both careers are F. O'Gorman, *The Rise of Party in
England* (1975) and A. D. Harvey, *Britain in the Early Nineteenth Century*
(1978). See, too, R. Pares, *George III and the Politicians* (1953).

Articles

On Pitt, see R. J. White, 'The Younger Pitt', *H. T.* (1952); A. S. Foord, The
'Waning of the influence of the Crown, 1780–1832', *E.H.R.* (1947). For
Fox, see I. R. Christie, 'C.J. Fox', *H.T.* (1958); H. Butterfield, 'Charles
James Fox and the Whig Opposition in 1792', *C.H.J.* (1947–9); A. S.
Foord (above); J. R. Dinwiddy, 'Charles James Fox and the people', *H.*

(Oct. 1970); H. Butterfield, 'Sincerity and insincerity in C. J. Fox', *P.B.A.*, 57 (1971); M. D. George, 'Fox's Martyrs: the general election of 1784', *T.R.H.S.* (1939).

12. The Industrial Revolution

This is a huge subject which can be dealt with on several different levels. It is important to recognise that there are varying interpretations among economic historians of *how* industrialisation happens. The once-fashionable 'take-off' theory is now being modified by one which stresses a much broader and complex process of economic development. Some aspects, such as population growth, have almost become separate topics, raising a host of fresh questions. Traditional concerns are reflected in the debate over the effects of industrialisation on living standards and the quality of life. In general, research on the Industrial Revolution has tended to create a growing awareness of the sheer complexity of the changes taking place. A regional or one-industry approach is often the best way of tackling the question.

Essay topics

Why did Britain experience industrial development in the period 1750–1870?
   Have the social effects of industrialisation been exaggerated?

Sources and documents

A. E. Bland, P. A. Brown and R. H. Tawney (eds), *English Economic History: Select Documents* (1914) Pt III, sections I, III, IV, V. The collection edited by C. Harvie, A. Scharf *et al.* (eds), *Industrialisation and Culture, 1815– 1880* (1970) is also useful. There is a rich literature, mainly from the 1830s and 1840s, a few examples of which are C. Bronte, *Shirley* (1849) (Luddism features prominently here), T. Carlyle, *Past and Present* (1843), Mrs Gaskell, *Mary Barton* (1848) and *North and South* (1855).

Secondary works

R. M. Hartwell, *The Industrial Revolution in England* (Historical Association pamphlet, 1965) is a useful short guide to the sort of questions economic historians ask. P. Mathias, *The First Industrial Nation: an economic history of Britain, 1700– 1914* (1969) is the standard economic history. T. S. Ashton, *The Industrial Revolution, 1760 to 1830* (1948) is an older, brief outline. E. J. Hobsbawm, *Industry and Empire* (1968), P. Deane, *The First Industrial Revolution* (1965) and P. Deane and W. A. Cole, *British Economic Growth, 1688– 1959* (1962) are also valuable. R. M. Hartwell (ed.), *The Causes of the Industrial Revolution* (1967) has some interesting essays; see also the wide-ranging essay on 'continuity' and 'discontinuity' in R. M. Hartwell (ed.), *The Industrial Revolution and*

Economic Growth (1971). The origins of industrialisation are also discussed in M. W. Flinn, *Origins of the Industrial Revolution* (1966) and C. Wilson, *England's Apprenticeship, 1603–1763* (1966). Various aspects of industrialisation are dealt with in M. W. Flinn, *British Population Growth, 1700–1850* (1970); N. Tranter, *Population since the Industrial Revolution: the case of England and Wales* (1973); W. E. Minchington (ed.), *The Growth of English Overseas Trade in the Seventeenth and Eighteenth Centuries* (1969); A. E. Musson (ed.), *Science, Technology and Economic Growth in the Eighteenth Century* (1972); T. C. Barker and C. F. Savage, *An Economic History of Transport* (1959).

On the social effects of industrialisation, J. L. and B. Hammond, *The Town Labourer, 1760–1832: the new civilisation* (1917) is the classic 'pessimistic' case, but see also A. J. Taylor (ed.), *The Standard of Living in Britain in the Industrial Revolution* (1975) and M. I. Thomis, *The Town Labourer and the Industrial Revolution* (1974). E. P. Thompson, *The Making of the English Working Class* (2nd edn, 1968) and J. Foster, *Class Struggle and the Industrial Revolution* (1974) argue the case for the rise of a working class in the course of industrialisation; see also H. J. Perkin, *The Origins of Modern English Society 1780–1880* (1969); S. G. Checkland, *The Rise of Industrial Society in England, 1815–85* (1964); R. J. Morris, *Class and Class Consciousness in the Industrial Revolution* (1979).

Local histories of industrial development include J. D. Chambers, *Nottinghamshire in the Eighteenth Century* (2nd edn, 1966); N. H. Chaloner, *The Social and Economic Development of Crewe, 1780–1923* (1950); H. Hamilton, *An Economic History of Scotland in the Eighteenth Century* (1963) and *The Industrial Revolution in Scotland* (1966); A. H. John, *The Industrial Development of South Wales, 1750–1850* (1959); A. H. Dodd, *The Industrial Revolution in North Wales* (3rd edn, 1971); J. Rowe, *Cornwall in the Age of the Industrial Revolution* (1953); W. H. B. Court, *The Rise of the Midland Industries 1600–1838* (1953); B. Trinder, *The Industrial Revolution in Shropshire* (1973); T. C. Barker and J. R. Harris, *A Merseyside Town in the Industrial Revolution: St. Helens, 1750–1900* (1954); R. A. Church, *Economic and Social Change in a Midland Town: Victorian Nottingham, 1815–1900* (1966); J. C. Beckett and R. E. Glassock (eds) *Belfast: origin and growth of an industrial city* (1967).

For individual industries, see P. Mathias, *The Brewing Industry in England, 1700–1830* (1959); T. S. Ashton, *Iron and Steel in the Industrial Revolution* (1951); A. P. Wadsworth and J. Mann, *The Cotton Industry and the Rise of Industrial Lancashire to 1780* (1965); M. M. Edwards, *The Growth of the British Cotton Trade, 1780–1815* (1967); H. Heaton, *The Yorkshire Woollen and Worsted Industry* (1920); T. S. Ashton and J. Sykes, *The Coal Industry in the Eighteenth Century* (2nd edn, 1964); and A. and N. L. Clow, *The Chemical Revolution: a contribution to social technology* (1952).

Case studies of particular firms include J. R. Harris, *The Copper King: a biography of Thomas Williams of Llanidan* (1964); T. S. Ashton, *An Eighteenth Century Industrialist: Peter Stubs of Warrington, 1756–1806* (1939); G. Unwin, *Samuel Oldnow and the Arkwrights: the industrial revolution at Stockport and Marple* (1924); R. S. Fitton and A. P. Wadsworth, *The Strutts and the Arkwrights* (1964); A. Raistrick, *Dynasty of Ironfounders: the Darbys and Coalbrookdale* (1953); E. Roll, *An Early*

Experiment in Industrial Organisation, being a history of the firm of Boulton and Watt, 1775–1805 (1930); J. P. Addis, *The Crawshay Dynasty: a study in industrial organisation and development, 1765–1867* (1957); T. C. Barker, *Pilkington Brothers and the Glass Industry* (1960).

Articles

There is a large and specialised articles literature on this topic, much of which can be followed from the secondary sources mentioned above. Among the most important are D. C. Coleman, 'Industrial growth and industrial relations', *E.* (1956–7); A. H. John, 'Aspects of economic growth in the first half of the eighteenth century', *E.* (1961); E. A. Wrigley, 'Raw materials in the Industrial Revolution', *Econ. H.R.* (1962); C. H. Wilson. 'The entrepreneur in the Industrial Revolution', *H.* (1957); S. Pollard, 'Factory discipline in the Industrial Revolution', *Econ. H.R.* (1963); N. McKendrick, 'An eighteenth century entrepreneur in salesmanship and marketing techniques', *Econ. H.R.* (1960); K. Berrill, 'International trade and the rate of economic growth', *Econ. H.R.* (1960); T. S. Ashton, 'Changes in the standard of comfort in 18th century England', *P.B.A.* (1955); S. D. Chapman, 'The transition to the factory system in the Midlands cotton-spinning industry', *Econ. H.R.* (1965); J. D. Chambers, 'The Vale of Trent, 1760–1800', *Econ. H.R.* Supplement No. 3 (1957). For the 'standard of living' debate, see R. M. Hartwell, 'The rising standard of living in England, 1800–50', *Econ. H.R.* (1961); E. J. Hobsbawm, 'The British standard of living, 1790–1850', *Econ. H.R.* (1958); E. J. Hobsbawm and R. M. Hartwell, 'The standard of living during the Industrial Revolution – a discussion', *Econ. H.R.* (1963); R. S. Neale, 'The standard of living, 1780–1844: a regional and class study', *Econ. H.R.* (1966).

13. Reform, radicalism and the Tory Party in Regency England

The later years of the Napoleonic Wars and the period up to the early 1820s have frequently been viewed as ones in which the country faced agitations of almost revolutionary proportions. A combination of wartime and post-war distress, the effects of industrial development and a revival of reform activity led to a phase of widespread agitation and government repression. The nature and implications of the popular movements of these years need examining, especially the reasons for the failure of the reformers to achieve any legislative results in spite of periods of intense activity. The government of Lord Liverpool has frequently been criticised for its reactionary character, and some assessment of its strengths and weaknesses are necessary. Liverpool's reputation has been reassessed in recent years, some seeing the years 1820–2 as marking a turning-point from which a new 'liberal Toryism' emerged.

Essay topics

How near did Britain come to revolution in the years between 1810 and 1822?

Why were the Whigs so ineffective between 1810 and 1830?

Does the government of Lord Liverpool deserve more credit than it has received for its conduct of affairs between 1812 and 1827?

Sources and documents

G. D. H. Cole and A. W. Filson, *British Working Class Movements: select documents, 1789–1875* (1951) has documents on trade union and radical groups. S. Bamford, *Passages in the Life of a Radical* (1844, and later editions) is a famous account of radicalism in the post-war years, see especially the description of Peterloo. W. Reitzel (ed.), *The Autobiography of William Cobbett* (1967) is a compilation of Cobbett's writings on his life. See also A. Prentice, *Historical Sketches and Personal Recollections of Manchester: intended to illustrate the progress of public opinion from 1792–1832* (1851, new edn with introduction by D. Read, 1970). For ministerial politics see *The Croker Papers* (3 vols, ed. L. J. Jennings, 1884), vol. 1.

Secondary works

The latter sections of A. D. Harvey, *Britain in the Early Nineteenth Century* (1979) and C. Emsley, *British Society and the French Wars, 1793–1815* (1978) are relevant to this topic. R. J. White, *Waterloo to Peterloo* (1957) concentrates on the post-war years; see also his *Radicalism and its Results, 1760–1837* (Historical Association Pamphlet, 1965). On radicalism, see also E. P. Thompson, *The Making of the English Working Class* (2nd edn, 1968), Pt III, and S. Maccoby, *English Radicalism, 1786–1832: from Paine to Cobbett* (1955). Popular disturbances of the period are discussed in F. O. Darvell, *Popular Disturbances and Public Order in Regency England* (1934); M. I. Thomis, *The Luddites* (1970); A. J. Peacock, *Bread or Blood* (1965); M. I. Thomis and P. Holt, *Threats of Revolution in Britain, 1700–1870* (1977); J. Stevenson, *Popular Disturbances in England, 1700–1870* (1979). D. Read, *Peterloo: The 'Massacre' and its background* (1958) remains the best account of the famous event and its background. G. D. H. Cole, *The Life of William Cobbett* (3rd edn, 1947) or J. W. Osborne, *William Cobbett: his thought and his times* (1966) deal with the most important radical of the period. See also G. Wallas, *The Life of Francis Place, 1771–1854* (5th imp., 1951) and J. Dinwiddy, *Christopher Wyvill and Reform, 1790–1820* (Borthwick Paper No. 39, 1971). For the rise of public opinion, see D. Read, *The English Provinces, c. 1760–1960* (1964) and *Press and People, 1790–1850* (1960); R. K. Webb, *The British Working Class Reader, 1790–1848* (1955).

Ministerial politics are best treated in J. E. Cookson, *Lord Liverpool's Administration: the crucial years, 1815–1822* (1975); W. R. Brock, *Lord Liverpool and Liberal Toryism, 1820 to 1827* (2nd edn, 1967); and N. Gash, 'The Earl of Liverpool (1812–27)' in H. van Thal (ed.), *The Prime Ministers*, vol. I (1974). K. G. Feiling, *The Second Tory Party, 1714–1832*

(2nd imp., 1951) is also useful. Major political figures on the government side are considered in D. Gray, *Spencer Perceval: The evangelical prime minister, 1762–1812* (1963); N. Gash, *Mr. Secretary Peel: the life of Robert Peel to 1830* (1961); P. Ziegler, *Addington. a life of Henry Addington, first Viscount Sidmouth* (1965); C. J. Bartlett, *Castlereagh* (1966); C. R. Fay, *Huskisson and his Age* (1951).

The Whigs are treated in M. Roberts, *The Whig Party, 1807–1812* (1939) and A. Mitchell, *The Whigs in Opposition, 1815–1830* (1967). A. S. Foord, *His Majesty's Opposition, 1714–1830* (1964) is also relevant. The principal Whig personalities are discussed in G. M. Trevelyan, *Lord Grey of the Reform Bill: being the life of Charles, second Earl Grey* (1920) and C. W. New, *The Life of Henry Brougham to 1830* (1961).

Articles

A. S. Foord, 'The waning of the influence of the Crown, 1780–1832', *E.H.R.* (1947); A. Briggs, 'Middle class consciousness in English politics, 1780–1846', *P.P.* (1956); A. Aspinall, 'English party organisation in the early 19th C.', *E.H.R.* (1926) are useful on the conventional aspects of politics. J. Dinwiddy, 'Luddism and politics in the North,' *S.H.* (1979) is a judicious survey of the upheaval of those years. T. M. Parsinnen, 'The revolutionary party in London 1816–20', *B.I.H.R.* (1972) shows the genuine revolutionaries at work. For the North, see F. K. Donnelly and J. L. Baxter, 'Sheffield and the English revolutionary tradition, 1791–1820', *I.R.S.H.* (1974). Important radical personalities are discussed in J. R. Dinwiddy, 'Sir Francis Burdett and Burdettite Radicalism', *H.* (1980) and J. C. Belchem, 'Henry Hunt and the evolution of the mass platform', *E.H.R.* (1978).

14. The Great Reform Act

The Reform Act of 1832 occupies a central place in the history of nineteenth-century Britain, though in recent years historians have tended to stress how little rather than how much was changed by it. The passing of the Act falls into three main stages: the build-up of the reform movement in the period after 1815; the break-up of the Tory Party's dominance in the late 1820s; the reform crisis of the period 1830–2. The varying demands from radicals and reformers and how far they were met requires some attention. Considerable debate has been generated by the question of whether Britain faced a revolutionary crisis in 1831–2. The medium and longer-term effects of the Act upon the conduct and the nature of Victorian politics are also important.

Essay topics

How would you account for the passing of the Reform Act of 1832?
Did Britain face a revolutionary crisis in 1832?
What truth is there in the contemporary view that the Reform Act of 1832 gave power to the middle classes?

Sources and documents

H. J. Hanham, *The Nineteenth Century Constitution, 1815–1914: documents and commentary* (1969) has a selection of relevant documents, as has E. C. Black, *British Politics in the Nineteenth Century* (1970). G. D. H. Cole and A. W. Filson, *British Working Class Movements: select documents, 1789–1870* (1951) and D. J. Rowe (ed.), *London Radicalism, 1830–43: a selection from the papers of Francis Place* (1970) have documents on the radical side.

Secondary works

D. G. Wright, *Democracy and Reform, 1815–1885* (1970) is a brief outline. M. Brock, *The Great Reform Act* (1973) is the best modern study, but J. R. M. Butler, *The Passing of the Great Reform Bill* (1914) is an older narrative still of value. A broader survey can be found in J. Cannon, *Parliamentary Reform, 1640–1832* (1973). One of the issues which produced the break-up of the Tory dominance is discussed in G. I. T. Machin, *The Catholic Question in English Politics, 1820 to 1830* (1964) and K. Feiling, *The Second Tory Party, 1714–1832* (2nd end, 1951). The Whig Party is treated in A. Mitchell, *The Whigs in Opposition, 1815–1830* (1967) and the role of Grey in G. M. Trevelyan, *Lord Grey of the Reform Bill* (1920). The rise of 'public opinion' is discussed in D. Read, *Press and People, 1790–1850* (1960) and P. Hollis, *The Pauper Press: a study in working class radicalism in the 1830s* (1970). On the reform crisis J. Hamburger, *James Mill and the Art of Revolution* (1965) pursues the important argument that the radicals 'worked up' a crisis in order to force through the Bill. This argument is considered in J. Stevenson, *Popular Disturbances in England, 1700–1870* (1979) and M. Thomis and P. Holt, *Threats of Revolution in Britain, 1789–1848* (1977), ch. 4. See also D. Fraser 'The agitation for parliamentary reform' in J. T. Ward (ed.), *Popular Movements, c. 1830–1850* (1970). On the influence of continental events, see N. Gash, 'The French Revolution of 1830 and the reform crisis' in *Essays presented to Sir Lewis Namier* (eds. A. J. P. Taylor and R. Pares, 1956). The effects of the Reform Bill on the structure of politics are analysed in N. Gash, *Reaction and Reconstruction in English Politics, 1832–52* (1965) and his earlier *Politics in the Age of Peel* (1953). See also G. B. A. M. Finlayson, *England in the Eighteen Thirties. Decade of reform* (1969) and H. J. Hanham, *The Reformed Electoral System in Great Britain, 1832–1914* (Historical Association Pamphlet, 1968).

Articles

A. Briggs, 'Middle-class consciousness in English politics, 1780–1846', *P.P.* (1956); 'Thomas Attwood and the economic background of the Birmingham Political Union', *C.H.J.* (1947–9); 'The background of the parliamentary reform movement in three English cities, 1830–32', *C.H.J.* (1950–2) are important. See also H. Fergeson, 'The Birmingham Political Union and government', *V.S.* (1960). Also relevant are J. Milton-Smith, 'Earl Grey's cabinet and the objects of parliamentary reform', *H.J.* (1972); D. C. Moore, 'The other side of reform', *V.S.* (1961) and 'Concession or cure: the sociological premises of the first Reform Act', *H.J.* (1966); G.

Rudé, 'English rural and urban disturbances, 1830–31', *P.P.* (1967); D. J. Rowe, 'Class and political radicalism in London, 1831–2' *H.J.* (1970).

15. Peel, the Tory Party and the repeal of the Corn Laws

For some contemporaries the end of agricultural protection raised even greater passions than parliamentary reform, and the struggle over the Corn Laws has frequently been seen as marking a decisive shift in the balance of political power in nineteenth-century Britain. Strong support for 'repeal' from middle-class interests and opposition from sections of the landed interest produced a conflict with wide economic and political repercussions. It is important to see the Corn Law issue in the context of the 'Hungry Forties' and the debate about the 'Condition of England?'. In the passing of 'repeal' the role of the Anti-Corn Law League and the Manchester School has to be weighed against the personal influence of Peel over the timing of the measure. Peel's position in the Tory Party and the repercussions of the Corn Law issue for party alignments is an important aspect of the question.

Essay topics

Why did the struggle to repeal the Corn Laws arouse such passions in early Victorian Britain?
   Why did Peel repeal the Corn Laws?

Sources and documents

H. J. Hanham, *The Nineteenth Century Constitution, 1815–1914: documents and commentary* (1969) has some relevant documents, see also A. E. Bland, P. A. Brown and R. H. Tawney, *English Economic History: select documents* (1914), Pt III, section VI. Peel's memoirs *Memoirs by the Rt. Hon. Sir Robert Peel* (ed. Lord Mahon and E. Cardwell, 1856–7) reveal his own view of the situation. R. S. Surtees, *Hillingdon Hall* (1845) is a novel with some relevant social comment. See also A. Prentice, *History of the Anti-Corn Law League* (1853, reprinted 1968).

Secondary works

A. Briggs, *The Age of Improvement, 1783–1867* (1959), ch. 6, is a good brief introduction to the politics of the 1840s, see also the section in N. Gash, *Aristocracy and People: Britain 1815–1865* (1980). There is a useful discussion in W. H. Chaloner, 'The agitation against the Corn Laws' in J. T. Ward (ed.), *Popular Movements c. 1830–1850* (1970). More detailed studies include N. Gash, *Politics in the Age of Peel*, (1953) and *Reaction and Reconstruction in English Politics, 1832–52* (1965). R. Blake, *The Conservative Party from Peel to Churchill* (1970) has a brief outline, but see R. Stewart, *The Foundation of the Conservative Party 1830–1867* (1979) for a more detailed study. N. Gash's *Peel* (1976) or his *Sir Robert Peel* (1972) are the standard lives. See also A. Briggs, 'Sir Robert Peel' in H. van Thal (ed.), *The Prime Ministers*, vol. 1 (1974). N. McCord, *The Anti-Corn Law League* (1958) is essential on the famous pressure group, while W. D. Grampp, *The Manchester School of Economics* (1960) examines the economic issues. C. R. Fay, *The Corn Laws and Social England* (1932) and D. G. Barnes, *A History of the English Corn Laws* (2nd edn, 1961) analyse the long-term history of the Corn Laws. F. M. L. Thompson, *English Landed Society in the Nineteenth Century* (1963) is valuable on the position of the landed interest. G. Kitson Clark, *The Making of Victorian England* (1962), especially ch. 7, has a masterly analysis of the repercussions of the repeal of the Corn Laws. R. Stewart, *The Politics of Protection: Lord Derby and the Protectionist Party, 1841–1852* (1971) discusses one strand of Tory reaction to the Corn Law issue.

Articles

G. Kitson Clark, 'The repeal of the Corn Laws and the politics of the forties', *Econ. H.R.* (1951); B. Kemp, 'Reflections on repeal of the Corn Laws', *V.S.* (1961–2) and S. S. Fairlie, 'The nineteenth-century Corn Law reconsidered', *Econ. H.R.* (1965) are of general relevance. See also G. L. Mosse, 'The Anti-Corn Law League, 1844–46', *Econ. H. R.* (1947); J. A. Thomas, 'The repeal of the Corn Laws, 1846', *E.* (1929); M. Lawson-Tancred, 'The Anti-Corn Law League and the Corn Law crisis of 1846', *H. J.* (1960). G. Kitson Clark, 'The country gentlemen and the repeal of the Corn Laws', *E.H.R.* (1967) and 'The electorate and the repeal of the Corn Laws', *T.R.H.S.* (1951) are also relevant. The party political dimension is discussed in N. Gash, 'Peel and the party system', *T.R.H.S.* (1951) and A. Aydelotte, 'The House of Commons in the 1840s', *H.* (1954). The reactions of the landed interest are discussed in D. Spring, 'The English landed estate in the age of coal and iron', *J. Econ.H.* (1951); A. Aydelotte, 'The country gentry and the repeal of the Corn Laws', *E.H.R.* (1967); W. R. Ward, 'West Riding landowners and the Corn Laws', *E.H.R.* (1966); D. Spring, 'Earl Fitzwilliam and the repeal of the Corn Laws', *Ag.H.* (1954).

16. Chartism

The diversity of Chartism almost belies its status as a single movement or 'ism'. None the less, the agitations which focused around the People's Charter provide an important opportunity to examine the attitudes and motivations of the mass of unenfranchised workers in mid-nineteenth century Britain. Chartism drew both upon strong traditions of artisan radicalism and the immediate stimulus of distress in the 'Hungry Forties'. Historians are somewhat divided between those who argue that Chartism marked the end of a period of 'insurgent' working-class activity, replaced by the 'labourism' of the mid-Victorian period, and those who see greater continuity between the Chartist and post-Chartist periods, particularly when viewed from the local level. An acceptable approach is to study Chartism in the context of a particular region, which gives both some appreciation of the interplay of the Chartists with competing interests, such as trade unionism and the Anti-Corn Law League, and some awareness of the wide range of issues which flowed into Chartism. Some examination of what happened *after* 1848 is also useful.

Essay topics

Account for the rise and fall of Chartism.

How far does the local history of Chartism modify the view that it failed?

Sources and documents

Of the memoirs of Chartists, W. Lovett, *The Life and Struggles of William Lovett* (1876 and later editions) and R. G. Gammage, *History of the Chartist Movement* (1854 and later editions) are particularly valuable. See also B. Wilson, 'The struggles of an old chartist' in D. Vincent (ed.), *Testaments of Radicalism* (1977). G. D. H. Cole and A. W. Filson (eds.), *British Working Class Movements, 1789–1870* (1951); D. Thompson (ed.), *The Early Chartists* (1971); P. Hollis (ed.), *Class and Conflict in Nineteenth Century England, 1815–1850* (1973) also have relevant documents.

Secondary works

F. C. Mather, *Chartism* (Historical Association pamphlet, 1965) is a useful introduction. J. T. Ward, *Chartism* (1973) and D. Jones, *Chartism and the Chartists* (1975) are two fuller recent studies. The older studies by M. Howell, *The Chartist Movement* (1918) and J. West, *A History of the Chartist Movement* (1920) are also still of value. A. Briggs, *Chartist Studies* (1958) is essential on the regional background and G. D. H. Cole, *Chartist Portraits* (1940) on the leaders. The social background of the 1840s is discussed in J. L. and B. Hammond, *The Age of the Chartists* (1930) and G. D. H. Cole and R. Postgate, *The Common People, 1746–1946* (4th edn, 1949), section 5, but see the qualifications made by M. I. Thomis, *The Town Labour in the Industrial Revolution* (1974). D. Bythell, *The Handloom Weavers* (1969) deals with a group prominent in Chartist activity. F. C. Mather, *Public Order in the Age of the Chartists* (1959) and J. Stevenson, *Popular Disturbances in England, 1700–1870* (1979), ch. 12, discuss the public order side. The ideological background to Chartism is discussed in D. Thompson, *The Early Chartists* (1971); E. P. Thompson, *The Making of the English Working Class* (2nd edn, 1968), ch. 16; P. Hollis, *The Pauper Press: a study in working-class radicalism of the 1830s* (1970), chs 6 and 7. Individual biographies include D. Read and E. Glasgow, *Feargus O'Connor, Irishman and Chartist* (1961); A. Plummer, *Bronterre: a political biography of Bronterre O'Brien* (1971); D. Williams, *John Frost: A Study in Chartism* (1939); A. R. Schoyen, *The Chartist Challenge: a portrait of George Harney* (1958). Other aspects of Chartism are discussed in A. Hadfield, *The Chartist Land Company* (1970) and H. N. Faulkner, *Chartism and the Churches* (1916). The legacy of

Chartism is discussed in F. E. Gillespie, *Labour and Politics, 1851–1867* (1927) and J. Saville, *Ernest Jones: Chartist* (1952).

For the large and growing literature of regional studies of Chartism, see the bibliography in D. Jones, *Chartism and the Chartists* (1975).

Articles

Important articles include R. P. Higgins, 'The Irish influence on the Chartist movement', *P.P.* (1961); D. J. Rowe, 'The failure of London Chartism', *H.J.* (1968); I. Prothero, 'Chartism in London', *P.P.* (Aug. 1969) and 'London Chartism and the Trades', *Econ. H.R.* (May, 1971). H. Weisser, 'Chartist internationalism, 1845–8', *H.J.* (1971); D. J. Rowe, 'Some aspects of Chartism in the north-east', *I.R.S.H.* (1971); T.R. Tholfsen, 'The Chartist crisis in Birmingham', *I.R.S.H.* (1958); B. Harrison, and P. Hollis, 'Chartism, Liberalism and Robert Lowery', *E.H.R.* (1967).

17. Social reform in nineteenth-century Britain

The period from the end of the eighteenth century witnessed widespread adjustments of social policy to meet the needs of a rapidly expanding industrial society. Many aspects of government and society came under scrutiny and the result was a patchwork of measures and initiatives to deal with the consequences of population growth, industrialisation and urban development. The motives and tactics of reformers require analysis, as well as the adequacy of the solutions they provided. One theme of recent work has been to criticise such reforms as a mere means of 'social control', but this demands careful scrutiny. The repercussions of social reform for the conduct and nature of government have also stimulated discussion.

Essay topics

Did Victorian social reform amount to anything more than a 'sop to conscience'?

How would you characterise the nature of nineteenth-century social reform?

Sources and documents

Many of the classic texts and reports on social reform have been reprinted in modern editions. R. Owen, *A New View of Society* (1813–14) and *Report to the County of Lanark* (1821) contain the essentials of 'Owenism'. Of central importance is *The Report of the Royal Commission on the Poor Law* (1834, new edition with an introduction by S. G. and E. O. A. Checkland, 1974). On the public health question, see E. Chadwick, *Report on the Sanitary Condition of the Labouring Population of Great Britain* (1842; new edition with introduction by M. W. Flinn 1965). E. P.

Thompson and E. Yeo (eds), *The Unknown Mayhew* (1971) has selections
from Mayhew's investigations into London labouring life in the 1840s
and 1850s. There is an excellent selection from late Victorian social
enquiries in P. Keating (ed.), *Into Unknown England, 1866– 1913* (1976).
See also W. Booths' passionate *In Darkest England and the Way Out*
(1890, reprinted 1970). Documents on particular topics can be found in
M. E. Rose, *The English Poor Law, 1780– 1830* (1971); J. M. Goldstrom,
Education: elementary education, 1780– 1900 (1972); J. J. Tobias,
Nineteenth Century Crime: prevention and punishment (1972); E.
Midwinter, *Nineteenth Century Education* (1970). E. Midwinter, *Victorian
Social Reform* (1968) also has a selection of documents with
introduction.

Secondary works

Most of the general histories of nineteenth-century Britain include
sections on social reform. E. Halevy's *History of the English People in the
Nineteenth Century* (1924 and subsequent re-editions) is still an excellent
starting-point. J. P. Roach, *Social Reform in England, 1780– 1880* (1978)
and U. R. Q. Henriques, *Before the Welfare State: social administration in
early industrial Britain*, (1979) are two comprehensive modern studies of
the problem. H. Perkin, *The Origins of Modern English Society,
1780– 1880* (1969) is relevant, especially ch. 8, Specific reform
movements are discussed in J. T. Ward, *The Factory Movement,
1830– 1855* (1963); S. E. Finer, *The Life and Times of Sir Edwin Chadwick*
(1952); J. Burnett, *A Social History of Housing, 1815– 1970* (1979); M. E.
Rose, *The English Poor Law, 1870– 1930* (1971) and *The Relief of Poverty,
1834– 1914* (1972); G. W. Oxley, *Poor Relief in England and Wales,
1601– 1834* (1974); D. Fraser (ed.), *The New Poor Law in the Nineteenth
Century* (1976); J. J. Tobias, *Crime and Industrial Society in the
Nineteenth Century* (1967); T. A. Critchley, *A History of Police in England
and Wales, 1900– 1966* (1967); J. Hurt, *Education in Evolution* (1972);
P.H.J.H. Gosden, *The Development of Educational Administration in
England and Wales* (1966); A. T. Scull, *Museums of Madness: The Social
organisation of insanity in nineteenth century England* (1979); M.
Ignatieff, *A Just Measure of Pain: the penitentiary in the Industrial
Revolution* (1978).

There is an important local study in E. C. Midwinter, *Social
Administration in Lancashire, 1830– 1860* (1969) and of the problems
which remained to be solved in G. Stedman Jones, *Outcast London: A
study in the relationship between classes in Victorian society* (1971). The
role of state intervention in discussed in A. J. Taylor, *Laissez-faire and
State Intervention in Nineteenth Century Britain* (1972). For
administrative consequences see O. MacDonagh, *Early Victorian
Government* (1977) and D. Roberts, *Victorian Origins of the British
Welfare State* (1960). The 'social control' theme is discussed in A. P.
Donajgrodzki (ed.) *Social Control in Nineteenth Century Britain* (1977);
and P. McCanny (ed), *Popular Education and Socialisation in the
Nineteenth Century* (1977).

Articles

There is a large article literature which can be followed from the secondary works. See especially W. O. Aydelotte, 'The Conservative and Radical interpretations of early Victorian social legislation', *V.S.* (1967) on general issues. On poverty, see U. R. Q. Henriques, 'How cruel was the Victorian Poor Law?', *H.J.* (1968); D. Roberts, 'How cruel was the new Poor Law?', *H.J.* (1963); M. Blaug, 'The myth of the old Poor Law', *J. Econ. H.* (1963) and 'The Poor Law re-examined', *J. Econ. H.* (1963). More general issues are discussed in G. Kitson Clark, 'Statesmen in disguise', *H.J.* (1959); J. Hart, 'Nineteenth-century social reform: a Tory interpretation of history', *P.P.* (1965); B. Harrison, 'Philanthropy and the Victorians' *V.S.* (1966) and 'Religion and recreation in nineteenth century England', *P.P.* (1967); O. MacDonagh, 'The nineteenth-century revolution in government: reappraisal', *H.J.* (1958–9); V. Cromwell, 'Interpretations of nineteenth-century administrations: an analysis', *V.S.* (1966); H. Parris, 'The nineteenth century revolution in government: a reappraisal reappraised', *H.J.* (1960).

18. Trade unionism

There has been an enormous growth of interest in labour and trade union history in recent years. Discussions of nineteenth-century trade union history almost inevitably become bound up with wider interpretations of the development of British society in general. It is important to examine the relationship between trade unionism and the working population at large at a time when trade union members made up only a minority of the labour force and reflected primarily the interests of the more skilled and more favourably placed workers. The involvement of trade unionists with radical politics and the nature of 'respectability' are two of the themes which can be pursued.

Essay topics

Did the experience of nineteenth-century trade unionists suggest that 'respectability' paid better dividends than violence?

How effective were the early trade unions in protecting the interests of the working population at large?

Sources and documents

G. D. H. Cole and A. W. Filson (eds), *British Working Class Movements: select documents, 1789–1875* (1951) has a wide selection of documents; see also A. Aspinall, *The Early English Trade Unions* (1949). On the period up to 1850, P. Hollis (ed.), *Class and Conflict in Nineteenth Century England 1815–1850* (1973) has several documents on radicalism and trade unionism. On the 1860s, see E. Frow and M Katanka (ed.), *1868: year of the unions* (1968); S. Pollard, *The Sheffield Outrages* (1971); and on the later nineteenth century E. J. Hobsbawm (ed.), *Labour's Turning Point 1880–1900* (2nd edn, 1974).

Secondary works

A. E. Musson, *British Trade Unions, 1800– 1875* (1972) has a brief outline and helpful bibliography. H. Pelling, *A History of British Trade Unionism* (1963); G. D. H. Cole, *A Short History of the British Working Class Movement* (1948); S. and B. Webb, *The History of Trade Unionism* (rev. edn, 1920) are broader histories. On the early period, see the introduction in A. Aspinall, *The Early English Trade Unions* (1949); E. P. Thompson, *The Making of the English Working Class* (2nd edn, 1968); J. L. and B. Hammond, *The Skilled Labourer, 1760– 1832* (1919, new edn with introduction by J. Rule, 1980). G. D. H. Cole, *Attempts at General Union, 1818– 1834* (1953) and J. F. C. Harrison, *The Early Victorians, 1832– 51* (1971), especially chs 2 and 6, are important on the 1830s and 1840s. Biographies of early trade union leaders include G. Wallas, *The Life of Francis Place, 1771– 1854* (5th edn, 1951); R. G. Kirby and A. E. Musson, *The Voice of the People: John Doherty, 1798– 1854* (1975); I. Prothero, *Artisans and Politics in Early Nineteenth Century London: John Gast and his times* (1979). On the Victorian years, see F. E. Gillespie, *Labour and Politics in England, 1850– 1867* (1927); R. Harrison, *Before the Socialists: studies in labour and politics 1861– 1881* (1965); D. Kynaston, *King Labour* (1976); A. Briggs 'Robert Applegarth and the trade unions' in *Victorian People* (1954); K. Burgess, *The Origins of British Industrial Relations: the nineteenth century experience* (1975) and *The Challenge of Labour: shaping British society, 1850– 1930* (1980).

There are a number of important collections of essays, especially E. J. Hobsbawm (ed.), *Labouring Men* (1964); A Briggs and J. Saville (eds) *Essays in Labour History*, vol. 1 (2nd edn, 1967) and J. Saville (ed.), *Democracy and the Labour Movement* (1954). For the overlap between formal trade unionism and violence, see M. I. Thomis, *The Luddites* (1970); J. Stevenson, *Popular Disturbances in England, 1700– 1870* (1979), chs 11– 14; and for Wales, D. J. V. Jones, *Before Rebecca: popular protests in Wales, 1793– 1835* (1973), chs 3– 4. For particular trades and areas see the bibliography in A. E. Musson, *British Trade Unions, 1800– 1875* (1972), to which can be added H. Hikins, *Building the Union* (Merseyside) (1973); E. Ellen, N. McCord, J. F. Clarke and D. J. Rowe, *The North-East Engineers' Strikes of 1871* (1971); G. J. Barnsby, *The Working Class Movement in the Black Country, 1750– 1867* (1979); B. Trinder, *The Industrial Revolution in Shropshire* (1973); W. J. Rowe, *Cornwall in the Age of the Industrial Revolution* (1953); G. Stedman Jones, *Outcast London* (1971). For agriculture, see P. Horn, *Joseph Arch* (1971); and J. P. D. Dunbabin (ed.), *Rural Discontent in Nineteenth Century Britain* (1974).

For the ideology of trade unionism, see G. D. H. Cole, *Robert Owen* (1925); J. F. C. Harrison, *Robert Owen and the Owenites in Britain and America* (1969); J. Foster, *Class Struggle in the Industrial Revolution* (1974); H. J. Collins and C. Abramsky, *Karl Marx and the British Labour Movement: Years of the First International* (1965). There are also useful sections in H. Perkin, *The Origins of Modern English Society, 1780– 1880* (1969) and S. G. Checkland, *The Rise of Industrial Society in England* (1964).

Articles

M. D. George, 'The Combination Laws reconsidered', *E.H.* (1927) and
M. D. George, 'The Combination Laws', *Econ. H.R.* (1936) are important
revisions on the effects of the Combination Acts. Hobsbawm's four
articles, 'The labour aristocracy', 'The machine-breakers', 'Economic
fluctuations and some social movements' and 'Custom, wages and
work-load', reprinted in *Labouring Men* are all important. R. N. Price, 'The
other face of respectability: violence in the Manchester brickmaking
trade, 1859–1870', *P.P.* (1975) and S. Pollard, 'The ethics of the Sheffield
outrages', *T.H.A.S* (1953–4) bear upon the place of violence in trade
disputes. R. V. Clements, 'British trade unions and popular political
economy, 1850–1875', *Econ. H.R.* (1961); A. E. Musson, 'The Webbs and
their phasing of trade-union development between the 1830s and the
1860s', *L.H.S.B.* (1962); S. W. Coltham, 'George Potter, the Junta and the
Beehive', *I.R.S.H.* (1965) are also relevant.

19. Victorian religion

The popular image of Victorian Britain is of a religious society in which
Christian morality and principles played a greater part than in some other
periods. The accuracy of this picture requires some scrutiny, particularly
in regard to the working classes. The difficulties faced by churchmen in
keeping pace with rapid population growth, urbanisation and the threat
of secularism need examining, as do the nature and impact of revivalist
groups such as the Oxford Movement. The powerful influence of
nonconformity and the links with social and political issues are also
important.

Essay topics

How adequate was the response of organised religion to the needs of
industrial Britain between 1815 and 1900?
    Was Victorian Britain a Christian country?
    How relevant was the Oxford Movement to the problems of Victorian
Britain?

Sources and documents

The 1851 Religious Census occupies a central place in the textbooks; its
findings are reprinted in C. Cook and B. Keith, *British Historical Facts,
1830–1900* (1975) with some other relevant tables. John Wade, *The Black
Book: or corruption unmask'd* (1820) devoted its largest section to the
Church of England. General Booth, *In Darkest England and the Way Out*
(1890, reprinted 1970) is a remarkable comment on the social and spiritual
problems of late Victorian society. Charles Booth's famous survey, *Life
and Labour of the People in London* (1903) has an important section on
religion in the slums. By contrast, *Kilvert's Diary* (1938–40) is a beautiful
evocation of the life of a country cleric in the 1870s. Spiritual dilemmas

are well conveyed in E. W. Gosse, *Father and Son* (1907) (Darwinism) and
J. H. Newman, *Apologia pro vita sua* (1864) (Catholicism). E. Royle (ed.),
Radical Politics, 1790–1900: religion and unbelief (1971) has some
documents on secularist movements, and J. H. Y. Briggs and I. Sellars
(eds), *Victorian Nonconformity* (1977) on Nonconformity.

Secondary works

The relevant sections of A. Armstrong, *The Church of England, the
Methodists and Society, 1700–1850* (1973) are useful. K. S. Inglis,
Churches and the Working Classes in Victorian England (1963) poses the
major problems of urban growth. Much the most impressive analysis of
church-going and denominational affiliation is A. D. Gilbert, *Religion and
Society in Industrial England: church, chapel and social change,
1740–1914* (1976). There is also some useful material in W. G. Ward,
Religion and Society in England, 1790–1850 (1972). Two good surveys of
the state of religious development at the beginning and middle of the
period can be found in E. Halevy, *England in 1815* (1924), Pt III and G.
Best, *Mid Victorian Britain, 1851–75* (1971). The great study of the
Anglican Church is O. Chadwick, *The Victorian Church* (2 vols, 1966–70).
See also S. C. Carpenter, *Church and People, 1789–1899* (1959). Reform
movements are discussed in W. L. Mathieson, *English Church Reform
1815–1840* (1923); O. J. Brose, *Church and Parliament: the reshaping of
the Church of England, 1828–1860* (1959); D. Brown, *The Idea of the
Victorian Church: the role of the Church of England in state and society,
1833–1889* (1968); G. Best, *Temporal Pillars: Queen Anne's Bounty, the
Ecclesiastical Commissioners and the Church of England* (1964). For the
Oxford Movement see G. Faber, *Oxford Apostles* (1936); R. W. Church,
The Oxford Movement. Twelve years 1833–45 (2nd edn, 1932) and Y. T.
Brilioth, *The Anglican Revival, Studies in the Oxford Movement* (new
imp., 1934). See also D. Newsome, *The Parting of Friends* (1966). M. L.
Edwards, *After Wesley: a study in the social and political influence of
Methodism in the middle period, 1791–1849* (1935); R. F. Wearmouth,
Methodism and the Working-Class Movements of England, 1800–1850
(1937) and *Methodism and the Struggle of the Working Classes,
1850–1900* (1954); E. R. Taylor, *Methodism and Politics, 1791–1851*
(1935) are all relevant to the later history of Methodism, if somewhat
uncritical. R. Moore, *Pit-men, Preachers and Politics* (1974) is more
critical. On Nonconformity, see C. Binfield, *So Down to Prayers: studies
in English Nonconformity, 1780–1920* (1977).

The Roman Catholic community can be studied through J. Bossy, *The
English Catholic Community, 1570–1850* (1975) and G. A. Beck (ed.), *The
English Catholics, 1850–1950* (1950). The important theme of
anti-Catholicism is covered by G. Best, 'Popular protestantism in
Victorian Britain' in R. Robson (ed.), *Ideas and Institutions of Victorian
Britain* (1967) and E. R. Norman, *Anti-Catholicism in Victorian England*
(1968).

Articles

See K. S. Inglis, 'Patterns of worship in 1851', *J. Eccl. H.* (1960); D. M.
Thompson, 'The 1851 Religious Census', *V.S.* (1967); A. Smith, 'Popular

religion', *P.P.* (1968); W.L. Arnstein, 'The Murphey riots: a Victorian dilemma', *V.S.* (1975); K. T. Hoppen, 'The Oxford Movement', *H.T.* (1967).

20. British foreign policy in the nineteenth century

Britain's unique position of maritime supremacy after the Napoleonic Wars gave her a virtually free hand outside Europe, as well as a major voice in European diplomacy. The use which Britain made of this position and the role of her most famous foreign secretaries, Castlereagh, Canning and Palmerston, are traditional areas of concern. The considerations which affected the development of the Empire and colonial policy before the phase of the 'new imperialism' after 1870 have also attracted interest.

Essay topics

How did the foreign policies of Castlereagh and Canning differ?
   On what principles did Palmerston conduct British foreign policy?
   Did Britain have a coherent policy towards her colonies between 1815 and 1870?

Sources and documents

K. Bourne, *The Foreign Policy of Victorian England, 1830–1902* (1970) and J. B. Joll, *Britain and Europe: Pitt to Churchill, 1793–1940* (1950) are particularly helpful collections of documents. Also available are H. M. V. Temperley and L. M. Penson (eds), *Foundations of British Foreign Policy from Pitt to Salisbury* (1938) and K. N. Bell (ed.), *Select Documents on British Colonial Policy, 1830–1860* (1969).

Secondary works

P. M. Hayes, *The Nineteenth Century, 1814–80* (1975) has a general outline of foreign policy; see also the opening chapters of R. W. Seton-Watson, *Britain in Europe, 1789–1914* (2nd edn, 1955). The essential work on post-1848 diplomacy is A. J. P. Taylor, *The Struggle for Mastery in Europe, 1848–1918* (1954). The work of the two principal foreign secretaries of the early nineteenth century is considered in C. K. Webster, *The Foreign Policy of Castlereagh* (2 vols, 1931) and H. M. V. Temperley, *The Foreign Policy of Canning, 1822–27* (1925). See also H. A. Kissinger, *A World Restored: Metternich, Castlereagh and the problems of peace, 1812–1822* (1957). Biographical studies include C. J. Bartlett, *Castlereagh* (1966); J. W. Derry, *Castlereagh* (1976); P. J. V. Rolo, *George Canning: three biographical studies* (1965) and W. Hinde, *George Canning* (1973). On Palmerston, H. C. F. Bell, *Lord Palmerston* (2 vols, reprinted 1966) is the basic study, but see also D. Southgate, *'The Most English Minister . . .' The policies and politics of Palmerston* (1966). C. K.

Webster, *The Foreign Policy of Palmerston, 1830–41* (2 vols, 1951) deals
with the early period. J. Ridley, *Lord Palmerston* (1970) offers a general
biography. D. C. M. Platt, *Finance, Trade and Politics: British foreign
policy, 1815–1914* (1968) is an overall interpretative study. On particular
topics, see G. B. Henderson, *Crimean War Diplomacy and Other Essays*
(1947); H. M. V. Temperley, *England and the Near East. The Crimea*
(1936); V. Puryear, *England, Russia and the Straits Question, 1844–56*
(1931); C. Sproxton, *Palmerston and the Hungarian Revolution* (1919);
W. C. Costin, *Great Britain and China, 1833–60* (1937); D. Beales,
England and Italy, 1859–60 (1961).

For imperial and colonial issues, B. Porter, *The Lion's Share: a short
history of British imperialism, 1850–1970* (1975) and R. Hyam, *Britain's
Imperial Century, 1815–1914: a study of empire and expansion* (1976)
provide general outlines. B. Semmel, *The Rise of Free Trade Imperialism:
classical political economy, the empire of free trade and imperialism,
1750–1850* (1970) and D. K. Fieldhouse, *Economics of Empire,
1830–1914* (1976) discuss the economic dimension. See also A. H. Imlah,
Economic Elements in the Pax Britannica (1959) and L. H. Jenks, *The
Migration of British Capital to 1875* (1927). C. A. Bodelsen, *Studies in
Mid-Victorian Imperialism* (1924) is an important study, now amplified by
W. P. Morrell, *British Colonial Policy in the Age of Peel and Russell*
(1930, rev. edn, 1970). A. P. Thornton, *The Imperial Idea and its Enemies*
(1959) discusses policy, as does K. E. Knorr, *British Colonial Theories:
1570–1850* (1963). The later period is treated in J. Gallagher and R.
Robinson, *Africa and the Victorians: the official mind of imperialism*
(1961) and C. C. Eldridge, *Victorian Imperialism* (1978). J. M. Ward,
Colonial Self-Government: the British experience, 1759–1856 (1976)
offers a recent view of colonial government.

P. M. Kennedy, *The Rise and Fall of British Naval Mastery* (1976) is
particularly useful on the military aspects of the *Pax Britannica*.

Articles

J. Gallagher and R. Robinson, 'The imperialism of Free Trade', *E.H.R.*
(1953) raises important issues. G. B. Henderson, 'The foreign policy of
Lord Palmerston, *H.* (1938) and M. Beloff 'Great Britain and the American
Civil War', *H.* (1952) are both useful. See also as case studies, M. M.
Robson, 'Liberals and "vital interests": the debate on international
arbitration, 1815–72', *B.I.H.R.* (1959); R.R. Florescu, 'Stratford Canning,
Palmerston and the Wallachian Revolution of 1848', *J.M.H.* (1963); F. G.
Weber, 'Palmerston and Prussian Liberalism, 1848', *J.M.H.* (1963); K.A.P.
Sandiford, The British cabinet and the Schleswig-Holstein crisis, 1863–4',
H. (1973).

21. Gladstone and Liberalism

Victorian Liberalism is an elusive phenomenon which it is crucial to
understand for the tenor of politics in the latter half of the nineteenth
century, for the formation of the Liberal Party and for Gladstone's appeal
to a wide range of electors. Considerable research in recent years has

been devoted to the grassroots of Victorian politics, one of the most interesting aspects of the period. Gladstone himself is an enigmatic figure, at least as important for what he represented as for what he did. One line of interpretation has tended to undermine Gladstone's position as a 'heroic' crusader for good causes in favour of concentration upon the 'high politics' at the cabinet level, by which Gladstone sought to manage the coalition of interests which made up the Liberal Party.

Essay topics

What were the principal characteristics of mid-Victorian Liberalism and how were they represented in the formation of the Liberal Party?

Did Gladstone's performance in office justify his reputation as the 'poor man's friend'?

Sources and documents

Samuel Smiles, *Self-Help* (1859), represents the gospel of work and sturdy independence raised to an inspiration. J. S. Mill, *On Liberty* (1859) is the classic statement of Victorian Liberalism; see also his *Political Economy* (1848), Book VI, chs 10 and 11 on *laissez-faire*. W. Bagehot, *The English Constitution* (2nd edn, 1873) is a brilliant analysis of the mid-Victorian constitution.

Secondary works

G. Best, *Mid-Victorian Britain, 1851–75* (1971) has a wide-ranging survey of the mid-Victorian scene. Also valuable are G. Kitson Clark, *The Making of Victorian England* (1962); W. L. Burn, *The Age of Equipoise. A study of the mid-Victorian generation* (1964); G. M. Young, *Victorian England: portrait of an age* (2nd edn 1953); R. Robson (ed.), *Ideas and Institutions of Victorian Britain* (1967); W. E. Houghton, *The Victorian Frame of Mind* (1957). J. R. Vincent, *The Formation of the British Liberal Party, 1857–1868* (1966) is central; but see also D. G. Southgate, *The Passing of the Whigs, 1832–1886* (1962) and W. E. Williams, *The Rise of Gladstone to the Leadership of the Liberal Party, 1859 to 1868* (1934). J. R. Vincent, *Pollbooks: How Victorians voted* (1967) is an important illustration of how politics worked at the local level. H. J. Hanham, *Elections and Party Management: Politics in the time of Disraeli and Gladstone* (1959) is important for the development of parties; see also the early sections of R. T. McKenzie, *British Political Parties* (1955).

There are several biographies of Gladstone: J. Morley, *The Life of W. E. Gladstone* (2 vols, 1905–6), though old, presents a good picture of Gladstone the 'great man'. P. Magnus, *Gladstone. A Biography* (1954) is highly readable, while E. Feuchtwanger, *Gladstone* (1975) is a brief recent life. The introductions to M. R. D. Foot and H. C. G. Matthew (eds), *The Gladstone Diaries* (6 vols, 1968–78) are important recent reviews of Gladstone's career. The Second Reform Bill is discussed in F.B. Smith, *The Making of the Second Reform Bill* (1966) and M. Cowling, *1867: Disraeli, Gladstone and Revolution: The passing of the Second Reform Bill* (1967). R. T. Shannon, *Gladstone and the Bulgarian Agitation, 1876* (1963) examines the domestic repercussions of the Bulgarian crisis, and

T. O. Lloyd, *The General Election of 1880* (1968) studies an important
election. The later stages of Gladstone's career are discussed in D. A.
Hamer, *Liberal Politics in the Age of Gladstone and Rosebery* (1972); J. R.
Vincent and A. Cooke, *The Governing Passion: cabinet government and
party politics in Britain, 1885–86* (1974); and M. Barker, *Gladstone and
Radicalism: the reconstruction of Liberal policy in Britain, 1885–94*
(1975).

   On other Liberal figures, see D. Read, *Cobden and Bright* (1967); R.
Jay, *Joseph Chamberlain: a political study* (1981); D. Judd, *Radical Joe:
a life of Joseph Chamberlain* (1977); P. Fraser, *Joseph Chamberlain
Radicalism and Empire, 1868–1914* (1966); A Briggs, *Victorian People*
(1954).

   Local political allegiances are discussed in H. Pelling, *The Social
Geography of British Elections 1885–1910* (1967). On local politics see
also D. Fraser, *Urban Politics in Victorian England* (1976) and *Power and
Authority in the Victorian City* (1979); K. O. Morgan, *Wales in British
Politics, 1868–1922* (1963); A. Briggs, *Victorian Cities* (1963).

Articles

Of importance are J. A. Thomas, 'The system of registration and the
development of party organisation, 1832–70', *H.* (1950); J. F. C. Harrison,
'The Victorian gospel of success', *V.S.* (1957); T. R. Tholfsen, 'The
transition to democracy in Victorian England', *I.R.S.H.* (1961); F. H.
Herrick, 'The Second Reform movement in Britain, 1850–65', *J.H.I.* (1948);
R. Harrison, 'The British working class and the general election of 1868',
I.R.S.H. (1960); W. H. Mael, 'Gladstone, the Liberals and the election of
1874', *B.I.H.R.* (1963); C. H. D. Howard, 'Joseph Chamberlain and the
Unauthorised Programme', *E.H.R.* (1950); R. Kelly, 'Midlothian', *V.S.*
(1960); T. R. Tholfsen, 'The origins of the Birmingham caucus', *H.J.*
(1959); J. Dunbabin, 'Parliamentary elections in Great Britain
1868–1900: a psephological note', *E.H.R.* (1966).

22. Disraeli and the late nineteenth-century Conservative Party

Disraeli is often regarded as the founder of the modern Conservative
Party and the agent of its revival in the latter part of the nineteenth
century. It is important to discuss how essential and distinctive his
personal contribution was, particularly in the passing of the Second
Reform Bill, the fostering of imperialism and the promotion of 'Tory
democracy'. Some consideration must also be given to the effects of the
broader movements of electoral opinion, especially the growing
disillusionment of middle-class voters with liberalism and the rise of
working-class Toryism in places such as Lancashire. The character of
Conservatism under Salisbury should also be considered in any
discussion of late nineteenth-century conservatism.

Essay topics

What did Disraeli contribute to the Conservative Party?
  How would you account for the revival of the Conservative Party in the
latter half of the nineteenth century?

Sources and documents

Disraeli's novels provide some insight into his social views; see
especially *Sybil* (1845) or *Coningsby* (1844). T. E. Kebbel (ed.), *The
Selected Speeches of Lord Beaconsfield* (1882) is particularly useful for
the Crystal Palace speech of 1872. H. J. Hanham, *The Nineteenth
Century Constitution, 1815– 1914. Documents and commentary* (1969)
and P. Adelman, *Gladstone, Disraeli and Later Victorian Politics* (1970)
also have some relevant documents.

Secondary works

R. Blake, *The Conservative Party from Peel to Churchill* (1970) puts
Disraeli in context, but Disraeli's place in the earlier history of the party
can also be examined in R. Stewart, *The Foundation of the Conservative
Party, 1830– 1867* (1978). The standard life is R. Blake, *Disraeli* (1966), but
the older W. F. Monypenny and G. E. Buckle, *The Life of Benjamin
Disraeli, Earl of Beaconsfield* (2 vols 1929) is still useful. R. Blake 'The rise
of Disraeli in H. Trevor-Roper (ed.), *Essays in British History presented
to Sir Keith Feiling* (1965) is also relevant. H. J. Hanham, *Elections and
Party Management. Politics in the time of Disraeli and Gladstone* (1959)
and the early part of R. T. McKenzie, *British Political Parties* (1955)
discuss the political machinery of the period. The Second Reform Act is
treated in F. B. Smith, *The making of the Second Reform Bill* (1966) and
M. Cowling, *1867. Disraeli, Gladstone and Revolution. The Passing of the
Second Reform Bill* (1867). See also the chapter on 1867 in R. Harrison,
Before the Socialists: studies in labour and politics, 1861– 1881 (1965) for
a view which stresses the popular pressure for reform as opposed to the
'high politics'.

  P. Smith, *Disraelian Conservatism and Social Reform* (1967) and E. J.
Feuchtwanger, *Disraeli, Democracy and the Tory Party* (1968) examine
some of the wider aspects of Disraelian conservatism. R. McKenzie and J.
Silver, *Angels in Marble* (1968) has an appraisal of the appeal of
working-class Toryism. For the later period, see H. Pelling, *Popular
Politics and Society in Late Victorian Britain* (1968). H. Pelling, *The Social
Geography of British Elections, 1885– 1910* (1967) has a mass of
information on local politics. The major personalities of the late Victorian
Conservative party can be examined in R. Taylor, *Salisbury* (1975) and P.
Marsh, *The Discipline of Popular Government: Lord Salisbury's domestic
statecraft, 1881– 1902* (1978) and J. Cornford, 'The parliamentary
foundations of the Hotel Cecil' in R. Robson (ed.), *Ideas and Institutions
of Victorian Britain* (1967). Lord Randolph Churchill's influence on the
Tory Party is discussed in R. Rhodes James, *Lord Randolph Churchill*
(1959) and W. S. Churchill, *Lord Randolph Churchill* (new edn, 1952).
Joseph Chamberlain's gradual movement towards the Conservatives can
be followed in P. Fraser, *Joseph Chamberlain, Radicalism and Empire,*

1868–1914 (1966); H. Browne, *Joseph Chamberlain, Radical and Imperialist* (1974); D. Judd, *Radical Joe: a life of Joseph Chamberlain* (1977).

Articles

C. J. Lewis, 'Theory and expediency in the policy of Disraeli', *V.S.* (1960–1); E. J. Feuchtwanger, 'The Conservative Party under the impact of the Second Reform Act', *V.S.* (1959); J. Cornford, 'The transformation of conservatism in the late nineteenth century', *V.S.* (1963–4); J. P. Dunbabin, 'Parliamentary elections in Great Britain, 1868–1900: a psephological note', *E.H.R.* (1966). There is a review of the debate on the Second Reform Act in G. Himmelfarb, 'The politics of democracy: the English Reform Act of 1867', *J.B.S.* (1966). On party organisation see E. J. Feuchtwanger, 'J. E. Gorst and the central organisation of the Conservative Party, 1870–1882', *B.I.H.R.* (1959). R. Greenall, 'Salford working class conservatism, 1865–86', *N.H.* (1974) is an important case study of Lancashire politics. The role of the Liberal Unionists and Chamberlain is discussed in P. Fraser, 'The Liberal Unionist alliance: Chamberlain, Hartington, and the Conservatives, 1886–1904', *E.H.R.* (1962).

23. The Irish Question

Irish affairs exerted considerable influence upon British politics at various points in the nineteenth and early twentieth centuries. As well as general concern on the nature of the 'Irish Question', interest has tended to focus on particular phases of activity, notably the Home Rule period. In this area, studies have tended to move away from the view of Gladstone 'idealistically' struggling with the intractable problems of Ireland towards the role of the Irish Question in the conduct of late Victorian politics. This 'high politics' interpretation requires placing in the context of the broader studies of the rise of Irish nationalism. The period of agitation before, during and after the First World War is also beginning to attract fresh attention.

Essay topics

Why did Britain not grant self-government to Ireland during the nineteenth century?
    Why did Gladstone fail to solve the 'Irish Question'?
    How far were independence and partition for Ireland inevitable by 1914?

Sources and documents

T. C. and R. B. McDowell, *Irish Historical Documents, 1172–1922* (1977) has a comprehensive selection of documents. A. de Tocqueville,

Journeys to England and Ireland (ed. J. P. Mayer, 1958) has a perceptive account of conditions in pre-famine Ireland. Among later writers, see J. S. Mill, *England and Ireland* (1868) and G. B. Shaw, *The Matter with Ireland* (1962) and *John Bull's Other Island* (1907). A. V. Dicey, *England's Case Against Home Rule* (reprinted, 1973) is also relevant. See also the selection of documents in G. Morton, *Home Rule and the Irish Question* (1980).

Secondary works

J. C. Beckett, *The Making of Modern Ireland, 1603–1923* (1969) is an excellent outline of the complex history of Ireland; see also his *Short History of Ireland* (5th edn, 1976). F. S. L. Lyons, *Ireland Since the Famine* (2nd edn, 1973) devotes more space to economic and social conditions, while R. Dudley Edwards, *An Atlas of Irish History* (1973) has maps and tables on many aspects of Irish history. N. Mansergh, *The Irish Question, 1840–1921* (1965) is an important general interpretation; see also J. C. Beckett, *Confrontations: studies in Irish history* (1972); E. Strauss, *Irish Nationalism and British Democracy* (1951); J. E. Lee, *The Modernisation of Irish Society, 1848–1918* (1973).

The repeal period can be studied through A. D. MacIntyre, *The Liberator: Daniel O'Connell and the Irish Party, 1830–1847* (1965); R. B. McDowell, *The Irish Administration, 1801–1914* (1964); K. B. Nowlan, *The Politics of Repeal: a study in the relation between Great Britain and Ireland, 1841–50* (1965); G. O'Tuathaigh, *Ireland before the Famine, 1798–1848* (1972). On the land question, see R. D. Collison Black, *Economic Thought and the Irish Question, 1817–1870* (1960); J. E. Pomfret, *The Struggle for Land in Ireland, 1800–1923* (1930); B. Solow, *The Land Question and the Irish Economy, 1870–1903* (1971). R. Dudley Edwards and T. Desmond Williams (eds), *The Great Famine* (1956) is a more scholarly treatment than C. B. Woodham-Smith, *The Great Hunger* (1962).

For the Home Rule period J. L. Hammond, *Gladstone and the Irish Nation* (1938) represents the traditional view of Gladstone's involvement with Ireland. D. A. Hamer, *The Liberal Party in the Age of Gladstone and Rosebery* (1972) explains policy towards Ireland in terms of Liberal politics. J. R. Vincent and A. Cooke, *The Governing Passion: cabinet government and party politics in Britain, 1885–86* (1974) treat the Irish issue as an example of political manoeuvre among the top politicians. On the influence of Parnell, C. C. Cruise O'Brien, *Parnell and his party, 1880–90* (1957) is essential. F. S. Lyons, *Charles Stewart Parnell* (1978) is the standard biography; see also M. Hurt, *Parnell and Irish Nationalism* (1968) and A. O'Day, *The English Face of Irish Nationalism: Parnellite involvement in British politics, 1880–86* (1977). The relationship between the land question and the rise of the Home Rule issue is examined in P. Bew, *Land and the National Question in Ireland, 1858–1882* (1977). The attitude of the Conservatives is reviewed in L. P. Curtis, *Coercion and Conciliation in Ireland, 1880–1892: A study in Conservative Unionism* (1963). The rise of unionism is discussed in P. Buckland, *Irish Unionism 1885–1923: a documentary history* (1973); P. Gibbon, *The Origins of Ulster Unionism* (1975); A. T. Q. Stewart, *The Narrow Ground: aspects of Ulster, 1609–1969* (1977).

The later aspects of the Irish crisis are discussed in A. T. Q. Stewart, *The Ulster Crisis* (1967); R. D. Edwards and F. Pyle, *1916: The Easter Rising* (1968); F. S. L. Lyons, *The Irish Parliamentary Party, 1890–1910* (1951); K. B. Nowlan (ed.), *The Making of 1916: studies in the history of the Rising* (1969); R. D. Edwards, *Patrick Pearse: the triumph of failure* (1979); C. Townshend, *The British Campaign in Ireland, 1919–1921* (1979); D. Fitzpatrick, *Politics and Irish Life, 1913–21* (1977).

Articles

The most relevant include J. H. Whyte, 'Daniel O'Connell and the repeal party', *I.H.S.* (1958–9); M. D. Condon, 'The Irish Church and the reform ministries', *J.B.S.* (1963–4); C. H. D. Howard, 'Joseph Chamberlain, Parnell and the Irish "central board" scheme, 1884–85', *I.H.S.* (1952–3) R. R. James, 'C. S. Parnell', *H.T.* (1957); E. D. Steele, 'Gladstone and Ireland', *I.H.S.* (1970–1), 'John Stuart Mill and the Irish Question, 1865–1975', *H.J.* (1970), and his 'Ireland and the Empire in the 1860s: Imperial precedents for Gladstone's first Irish Land Act', *H.J.* (1968); D. A. Hamer, 'The Irish Question and Liberal politics, 1886–1894', *H.J.* (1969); M. Hurst, 'Ireland and the Ballot Act of 1872', *H.J.* (1965); L. J. McCaffrey, 'Home Rule and the general election of 1874', *I.H.S.* (1954–5); D. C. Savage, 'The origins of the Ulster Unionist Party, 1885–6', *I.H.S.* (1960–1); G. P. Taylor, 'Cecil Rhodes and the Second Home Rule Bill', *H.J.*, (1971); F. S. L. Lyons, 'John Dillon and the plan of campaign, 1886–90', *I.H.S.* (1964–5); L. P. Curtis, 'Government policy and the Irish Party crisis, 1890–92', *I.H.S.* (1962–3); J. Boyle, 'The Belfast Protestant Association and the Independent Orange Order 1901–10', *I.H.S.* (1962–3); H. W. McCready, 'Home Rule and the Liberal Party, 1899–1906', *I.H.S.* (1962–3); D. G. Boyce, 'British Conservative opinion, the Ulster Question and the partition of Ireland, 1912–21', *I.H.S.* (1970–1).

24. British imperialism

This is a very large topic, but one which in terms of British history is primarily concerned with the domestic causes and effects of overseas expansion. It is widely recognised that the latter part of the nineteenth century witnessed a rapid expansion of the British Empire in the phase of so-called 'new imperialism'. Differing explanations have been given for this process, the once fashionable economic interpretation being subjected to an increasing degree of qualification. The effects of imperialism on domestic politics can usefully be focused on the issues and conflicts raised by the Boer War.

Essay topics

What forces promoted the expansion of the British Empire in the latter part of the nineteenth century?

How far did the Boer War mark a turning-point in British attitudes towards the Empire?

Sources and documents

R. W. Winks (ed.), *British Imperialism: gold, god, glory* (1966) has a
useful selection of documents; see also H. M. Wright (ed.), *The New
Imperialism* (1961). G. Bennet (ed.), *The Concept of Empire: Burke to
Attlee, 1774–1947* (1953) also provides a range of documents. C. W.
Dilke, *Greater Britain* (1868) and *Problems of Greater Britain* (1890) and J.
R. Seeley, *The Expansion of England* (1883) are important contemporary
analyses. See also J. A. Hobson, *Imperialism: a study* (1902).

Secondary works

M. A. Chamberlain, *The New Imperialism* (Historical Association
Pamphlet, 1967) is a good survey of recent thinking on the question of
imperial expansion. Of the general histories, see especially B. Porter, *The
Lion's Share: a short history of British imperialism, 1850–1970* (1975); R.
Hyam, *Britain's Imperial Century, 1815–1914: a study of empire and
expansion* (1976); J. Bowle, *The Imperial Achievement: the rise and
transformation of the British Empire* (1977). C. A. Bodelsen, *Studies in
mid-Victorian Imperialism* (1924) covers the period c. 1837–87. J.
Gallagher and R. Robinson, *Africa and the Victorians: The official mind of
imperialism* (1961) is an important series of case studies of how
expansion occurred. On the 1860s and 1870s see also C. C. Eldridge,
Victorian Imperialism (1978). D. K. Fieldhouse, *The Colonial Empires*
(1966) and *Economics and Empire, 1830–1914* (1976) reconsiders the
economic arguments for imperialism. D. C. Platt, *Finance, Trade and
Politics in British Foreign Policy, 1815–1914* (1968) is an important study
which places imperialism in the context of British foreign policy. On
investment see A. K. Cairncross, *Home and Foreign Investment,
1870–1913* (1953); A. R. Hall (ed.), *The Export of Capital from Britain,
1870–1914* (1968); H. Feis, *Europe, the World's Banker, 1870–1914*
(1930); S. B. Saul, *Studies in British Overseas Trade 1870–1914* (1960).
On the diplomatic repercussions of imperialism see P. Kennedy, *The Rise
of Anglo-German Antagonism, 1860–1914* (1980) and W. Langer, *The
Diplomacy of Imperialism, 1890–1902* (1935), which also has an
interesting chapter on the public psychology of imperialism. This theme
is followed up in R. Price, *An Imperial War and the British Working Class:
working-class attitudes and reactions to the Boer War, 1899–1902*
(1972). Attitudes to empire are also the theme of R. Price, 'Society, status
and jingoism: the social roots of lower middle class patriotism,
1870–1900' in G. Crossick (ed.), *The Lower Middle Class in Britain* (1977)
and H. Pelling, 'British labour and British imperialism' in his *Popular Politics
and Society in Late Victorian Britain* (1968). A. P. Thornton, *The Imperial
Idea and its Enemies* (1959) and *Doctrines of Imperialism* (1965) discuss
ideologies of empire; see also J. Kemp, *Theories of Imperialism* (1967).

The collection of essays by C. J. Barlett (ed.), *Britain Pre-Eminent*
(1969) has several useful essays, see especially D. Southgate, 'Imperial
Britain'. Other collections of relevance are R. Hyam, *Reappraisals in
British Imperial History* (1975); D. A. Low, *Lion Rampant: essays in the
study of British imperialism* (1974); P. Kennedy, *The Realities Behind
Diplomacy: Background Influences on British External Policy, 1865–1980*
(1981).

On the political repercussions of empire, see D. Judd, *Balfour and the*

British Empire (1968); H. G. Matthew, *The Liberal Imperialists: the ideas and politics of a post-Gladstonian élite* (1973); B. H. Brown, *The Tariff Reform Movement in Great Britain, 1881–1895* (1943). Chamberlain's role is discussed in R. V. Kublicek, *The Administration of Imperialism: Joseph Chamberlain at the Colonial Office* (1969).

On the Boer War see T. Pakenham, *The Boer War* (1979); J. S. Marais, *The Fall of Kruger's Republic* (1961); E. Pakenham, *Jameson's Raid* (1960); S Koss (ed.), *The Pro-Boers* (1973).

Articles

See particularly H. Cunningham, 'Jingoism in 1877–78', *V.S.* (1971); J. Gallagher and R. Robinson, 'The imperialism of Free Trade', *Econ. H.R.* (1953); S. B. Saul, 'The economic significance of "constructive imperialism" ', *J. Econ. H.* (1957); D. C. Platt, 'Economic factors in British policy during the "New Imperialism"', *H.* (1968). Among a number of more detailed articles, see W. D. McIntyre, 'British policy in West Africa: the Ashanti Expedition of 1873–4', *H.J.* (1962); R. L. Tignor, 'Lord Cromer: practitioner and philosopher of imperialism', *J.B.S.* (1962–3); E. Stokes, 'Milnerism', *H.J.* (1962); W. Strauss, 'Joseph Chamberlain and the theory of imperialism', *P.A.* (1942). For South African affairs see E. Drus, 'The question of imperial complicity in the Jameson Raid', *E.H.R.* (1953); G. Blainey, 'Lost causes of the Jameson Raid', *Econ. H.R.* (1965).

25. The rise of the Labour Party

The formation and emergence of the Labour Party was one of the most important aspects of the period prior to 1914. Overhanging this topic and the next one is the question of why the Labour Party proved, eventually, to be able to rise at the expense of the Liberals. Although the development of mass trade unionism and the spread of socialist ideas provide the background, the question of why a separate, trade-union-backed political party emerged at all needs consideration, as it was not a pattern followed by all industrial countries. Proponents of a 'new Liberalism' have argued that Labour was in a relatively weak position prior to 1914 and not necessarily bound to succeed the Liberals; the evidence for the period 1906–14 needs particular attention.

Essay topics

Why did the Labour Party come into existence and what had it achieved by 1914?

Sources and documents

E. Hobsbawm (ed.), *Labour's Turning Point 1880–1900* (2nd edn, 1974) has a wide range of documents on trade union and radical politics at the end of the nineteenth century. See also H. Pelling (ed.), *The Challenge of Socialism* (1954). B. Webb, *My Apprenticeship* (1926) and *Our*

Partnership (1948) are eyewitness accounts by an early member of the
Fabians, of social movements before 1914. R. Tressell, *The Ragged
Trousered Philanthropists* (1955) is a remarkable novel of Edwardian
working-class life.

Secondary works

H. Pelling, *The Origins of the Labour Party, 1880–1900* (2nd edn, 1965) is
the standard account. See also his *Short History of the Labour Party*
(1961) and F. Bealey and H. Pelling, *Labour and Politics, 1900–1906: A
History of the Labour Representation Committee* (1958). Carl F. Brand,
The British Labour Party: a short history (1965) and J. H. Stewart Reid,
The Origins of the British Labour Party (1962) are alternative general
treatments. Trade union attitudes are discussed in H. Pelling, *A History of
British Trade Unionism* (3rd edn, 1976); J. Lovell and B. C. Roberts, *A
Short History of the T.U.C.* (1968); R. Gregory, *The Miners and British
Politics, 1906–1914* (1968). E. Hobsbawm, *Labouring Men* (1964) has a
number of important essays, see especially 'General labour unions in
Britain, 1889–1914' and 'Trends in the British Labour Movement since
1850'. The early political fortunes of Labour are discussed in P.
Thompson, *Socialists, Liberals and Labour: The struggle for London,
1885–1914* (1967) and H. Pelling, *The Social Geography of British
Elections, 1885–1910* (1967). The intellectual influences on the early
Labour and socialist movements are discussed in E. P. Thompson,
William Morris: romantic to revolutionary (1955); C. Tsuzuki, *H. M.
Hyndman and British Socialism* (1961); H. Pelling, *America and the
British Left* (1956); M. Cole, *The Story of Fabian Socialism* (1961); A. M.
McBriar, *Fabian Socialism and English Politics, 1884–1918* (1966); E. R.
Pease, *The History of the Fabian Society* (2nd edn, 1963); N. and J.
MacKenzie, *The First Fabians* (1977); S. Pierson, *Marxism and the Origins
of British Socialism* (1973); W. Wolfe, *From Radicalism to Socialism*
(1975).

R. McKibbin, *The Evolution of the Labour Party, 1910–1924* (1974)
discusses the growth of labour organisation, while the argument that
Labour's position was weakening prior to 1914 is made by R. Douglas,
'The strange death of Labour England, 1910–14' in K. Brown (ed.),
Essays in Anti-Labour History (1974). The rise of a more militant socialist
movement is discussed in W. Kendall, *The Revolutionary Movement in
Britain, 1900–21* (1969); R. Holton, *British Syndicalism, 1900–1914:
myths and realities* (1976); and B. Pribicevic, *The Shop Stewards
Movement and Workers Control, 1910–1922* (1959). For the industrial
disputes of the pre-1914 period, see E. Phelps Brown, *The Growth of
British Industrial Relations: a study from the standpoint of 1906–1914*
(1959).

The character of the Labour Party representatives in parliament is
discussed in D. E. Martin, '"The instruments of the people"?: The
Parliamentary Labour Party in 1906', in D. E. Martin and D. Rubinstein
(eds.), *Ideology and the Labour Movement: essays presented to John
Saville* (1979). On prominent labour personalities, see I. McLean, *Keir
Hardie* (1975), K. O. Morgan, *Keir Hardie: radical and socialist* (1975); F.
Reid, *Keir Hardie: the making of a socialist* (1978); A. Bullock, *The Life
and Times of Ernest Bevin*, vol. I (1960).

Articles

See P. Thompson, 'Liberals, Radicals and Labour in London, 1880–1900', *P.P.* (1964); R. I. McKibbin, 'James Ramsay MacDonald and the problem of the independence of the Labour Party, 1910–1914', *J.M.H.* (1970); K. O. Morgan, 'The New Liberalism and the challenge of Labour', *W.H.R.* (1973); G. A. Phillips, 'The Triple Industrial Alliance in 1914', *Econ. H.R.* (1971).

26. The Liberal Party in the age of Asquith and Lloyd George

The history of the Liberal Party in the early twentieth century is dominated by the question of its eventual decline and replacement by Labour as the other major party in British politics. Historians have debated whether the Liberals were already doomed by 1914 or whether a 'new Liberalism' had emerged sufficient to pre-empt Labour's appeal. For some, the decisive factor was the First World War and the splits produced in the party. Lloyd George is a fascinating figure whose career attracts considerable attention in the literature.

Essay topics

Was Liberalism a spent force by 1914?
  Was Lloyd George an asset or a liability to the Liberal Party?

Sources and documents

K. O. Morgan, *The Age of Lloyd George: the Liberal Party and British politics, 1890–1929* (1971) has an excellent selection of documents bearing directly on this topic. See also A. Bullock and M. Shock (eds), *The Liberal Tradition from Fox to Keynes* (1956) and T. Wilson (ed.), *The Political Diaries of C. P. Scott* (1970).

Secondary works

There is a good survey of the debate on the decline of Liberalism in K. O. Morgan, *The Age of Lloyd George*, chs 1–5; see also H. Pelling 'Labour and the downfall of Liberalism' in his volume of essays, *Popular Politics and Society in Late Victorian Britain* (1968). G. Dangerfield, *The Strange Death of Liberal England* (1936) argues the case for the decline of 'Liberalism' by 1914. P. F. Clarke, *Lancashire and the New Liberalism* (1971) argues in favour of a 'new Liberalism' by 1914; see the informative review by K. O. Morgan in *History* (1972). R. McKibbin, *The Evolution of the Labour Party, 1910–24* (1974) in essence contradicts this view; see also T. Wilson, *The Downfall of the Liberal Party, 1914–35* (1966) which locates the crucial period of decline after 1914. H. Pelling, *The Social*

Geography of British Elections, 1885– 1910 (1967) is a mine of
information on the complex electoral forces at work prior to 1914. See
also K. D. Brown (ed.), *Essays in Anti-Labour History* (1974) and C.
Cook, *A Short History of the Liberal Party, 1900– 1976* (1976). S.
Koss, *Nonconformity in modern British politics* (1975); H. W. Emy, *Liberals,
Radicals and Social Politics, 1892– 1914* (1973); H. G. Matthew, *The
Liberal Imperialists: the ideas and politics of a post-Gladstonian élite*
(1973); C. Wrigley, *David Lloyd George and the British Labour Movement*
(1976) deal with important themes. The ideology of Liberalism has
attracted increasing attention; see especially M. Freeden, *The New
Liberalism: an ideology of social reform* (1978); P. F. Clarke, *Liberals and
Social Democrats* (1978); M. Bentley, *The Liberal Mind, 1914– 1929* (1977).

There are several biographies of Lloyd George; see especially K. O.
Morgan, *Lloyd George* (1974); P. Rowland, *Lloyd George* (1975); J.
Grigg, *Lloyd George* (2 vols, 1973, 1978). Also available are M. Thomson,
Lloyd George (1951); F. Owen, *Tempestuous Journey* (1954); W. Watkin
Davies, *Lloyd George, 1863– 1914* (1939); A. J. P. Taylor, *Lloyd George:
rise and fall* (1961); C. L. Mowat, *Lloyd George* (1964). His later career is
ably discussed in J. Campbell, *Lloyd George: the goat in the wilderness,
1922– 1931* (1977). There are also a number of useful essays in A. J. P.
Taylor (ed.), *Lloyd George: twelve essays* (1971). For Asquith, see R.
Jenkins, *Asquith* (rev. edn, 1978) and S. Koss, *Asquith* (1976). Churchill's
early career is covered in R. S. Churchill, *Winston S. Churchill*, vols. I and
II (1966 and 1967). On other figures, see K. Robbins, *Sir Edward Grey*
(1971); D. A. Hamer, *John Morley* (1968); and A. Briggs, *Seebohm
Rowntree* (1961).

The effect of the First World War on the Liberals is discussed in C.
Hazlehurst, *Politicians at War, July 1914 to May 1915* (1971) and A. J. P.
Taylor, *Politics in Wartime* (1964).

Articles

Major topics are dealt with in J. F. Harris and C. Hazlehurst,
'Campbell-Bannerman as prime minister', *H.* (1970); F. Bealey,
'Negotiations between the Liberal Party and the L.R.C. before the
general election of 1906', *B.I.H.R.* (1956) and 'The electoral arrangement
between the L.R.C. and the Liberal Party', *J. M. H.* (1956); M. Peter, 'The
progressive alliance', *H.* (1973); P. F. Clarke, 'The progressive movement
in England', *T.R.H.S.* (1974); P. Thompson, 'Liberals, Radicals and Labour
in London, 1880– 1900', *P.P.* (1964); J. Howarth, 'The Liberal revival in
Northamptonshire, 1880– 95', *H.J.* (1969); J.G. Kellas, 'The Liberal Party
in Scotland, 1876– 1895', *S.H.R.* (1965); C. Hazlehurst, 'Asquith as prime
minister, 1908– 16', *E.H.R.* (1970); K. O. Morgan, 'Lloyd George's
premiership', *H. J.* (1970). For the influence of franchise arrangements on
party support, see H. C. G. Matthew, R. I. McKibbin and J. A. Kay, 'The
franchise factor in the rise of the Labour Party', *E.H.R.* (1976) and P. F.
Clarke, 'Liberals, Labour and the franchise', *E.H.R.* (1977).

27. The causes and consequences of the First World War

The origins of the First World War remain a major concern of historians. Although responsibility for the outbreak of the war has been variously allocated, the crucial question arises of how Britain became involved in a general European war in 1914. The rise of the alliance system and Britain's role within it is important, while the Anglo-German naval rivalry added a special dimension to Britain's relations with Germany. Particular attention needs to be given to the considerations affecting British policy in the summer of 1914. On the domestic front, historians have increasingly recognised the importance of war as a significant agent of social, economic and political change. The effects of the First World War on Britain can be studied either as a whole or through the examination of a major aspect, such as the impact of the war upon party politics, the labour movement, the role of women or social policy.

Essay topics

How much responsibility did Britain bear for the outbreak of war with Germany in 1914?

Were the social effects of the First World War of greater significance than the political ones?

Sources and documents

J. B. Joll (ed.), *Britain and Europe: Pitt to Churchill, 1793–1940* (1950); J. H. Wiener (ed.), *Great Britain: foreign policy and the span of empire* (4 vols, 1972); C. J. Lowe and M. L. Dockrill, *The Mirage of Power: British foreign policy, 1902–22* (3 vols, 1972) all have useful documents. Lord Grey, *Twenty-Five Years, 1892–1916* (2 vols, 1925) is a first-hand account by Britain's foreign secretary during the crucial period. See also W. S. Churchill, *The World Crisis, 1911–14* (1923). Both enjoyable and relevant is E. Childers *The Riddle of the Sands* (1903), a spy story about German invasion plans. K. O. Morgan (ed.), *The Age of Lloyd George: the Liberal Party and British politics, 1890–1929* (1971) has useful documents on political developments. Lord Beaverbrook's volumes, *Politicians and the War, 1914–16* (2nd edn, 1960) and *Men and Power, 1917–18* (1956) give a personal account of the political infighting. R. Roberts, *The Classic Slum: Salford life in the first quarter of the century* (1971) discusses the impact of the war on a working-class area. There is a wealth of war memoir material; see especially R. Graves, *Goodbye to All That* (1929) and Vera Brittain, *Testament of Youth* (1933, and later eds).

Secondary works

B. Schmitt, *The Outbreak of War in 1914* (Historical Association pamphlet, 1964) is a good overview of the traditional interpretation that the alliance system was to blame for the outbreak of war, a view increasingly under attack; see, for example, H. W. Koch (ed.), *The Origins of the First World War: great power rivalry and German war aims* (1972).

A. J. P. Taylor, The *Struggle for Mastery in Europe, 1848–1918* (1954) is a
major diplomatic study; see also R. W. Seton Watson, *Britain in Europe,
1789–1914, a survey of foreign policy* (1937). Z. S. Steiner, *Britain and
the Origins of the First World War* (1977) is the most detailed analysis of
British involvement. The classic study of Anglo-German naval rivalry is
E. L. Woodward, *Great Britain and the German Navy* (1935), now updated
on the naval side by A. J. Marder, *From the Dreadnought to Scapa Flow.
vol. i: The road to war, 1904–14* (1961) and on the political by P.
Kennedy, *The Rise of the Anglo-German Antagonism, 1860–1914* (1980).
Military preparations are discussed in M. Howard, *The Continental
Commitment: the dilemma of British defence policy in the era of two
world wars* (1972), ch. 2, and S. R. Williamson, *The Politics of Grand
Strategy: Britain and France prepare for war, 1904–1914* (1969). On the
Foreign Office, see Z. S. Steiner, *The Foreign Office and Foreign Policy,
1898–1914* (1969). A. Marwick, *The Deluge* (1965) surveys economic and
social life during the First World War; see also his *Britain in the Century
of Total War: war, peace and social change, 1900–1967* (1968). The
political repercussions of the war are discussed in T. Wilson, *The Downfall
of the Liberal Party, 1914–35* (1966); A. J. P. Taylor, *Politics in Wartime*
(1964); C. Hazlehurst, *Politicians at War, July 1914 to May 1915* (1971).
The early role of Lloyd George is considered in R. J. Q. Adams, *Arms and
the Wizard: Lloyd George and the Ministry of Munitions, 1915–1916*
(1978); but for the wartime developments, see also S. Koss, *Asquith*
(1976); R. Jenkins, *Asquith* (1978); P. Rowland *Lloyd George* (1975); M.
Gilbert, *Winston S. Churchill*, vols 2 and 3 (1971 and 1975). J. Ramsden,
The Age of Balfour and Baldwin, 1902–40 (1978) covers the Conservative
Party; see also the section in R. Blake, *The Conservative Party from Peel
to Churchill* (1970) and J. Stubbs, 'The impact of the Great War on the
Conservatives' in G. Peele and C. Cook (eds), *The Politics of Reappraisal,
1918–1939* (1975). For the Labour Party the crucial study is R. McKibbin,
The Evolution of the Labour Party, 1910–1924 (1974); see also H. Pelling,
A Short History of the Labour Party (1961). Trade union developments
can be followed in H. Pelling, *A History of British Trade Unionism* (3rd
edn, 1976) A. Bullock, *The Life and Times of Ernest Bevin*, vol I (1960),
and K. Burgess, *The Challenge of Labour* (1980). For the left-wing
movements, see W. Kendall, *The Revolutionary Movement in Britain,
1900–21* (1969); R. K. Middlemas, *The Clydesiders* (1965); J. Hinton, 'The
Clyde Workers' Committee and the dilution struggle' in A. Briggs and J.
Saville (eds), *Essays in Labour History, 1886–1923* (1971); I. McLean,
'Red Clydeside, 1915–1919' in R. Quinault and J. Stevenson (eds.),
*Popular Protest and Public Order: six studies in British history,
1790–1920* (1974); B. Pribicevic, *The Shop Stewards Movement and
Workers' Control, 1910–1922* (1959).

On the suffrage question, see M. D. Pugh, *Electoral Reform in War and
Peace, 1906–1918* (1978). There is a brief introduction to the women's
suffrage question in M. Pugh, *Women's Suffrage in Britain, 1867–1928*
(Historical Association pamphlet, 1980). C. Rover, *Women's Suffrage and
Party Politics in Britain, 1866–1914* (1967), D. Morgan, *Suffragists and
Liberals* (1975) and R. Fulford, *Votes for Women* (1957) provide detailed
accounts. See also J. Liddington and J. Norris, *One Hand Tied Behind
Us: the rise of the women's suffrage movement* (1978) and A. Rosen,
*Rise up Women! the militant campaign of the Women's Social and
Political Union, 1903–14* (1974). A. Marwick, *Women at War, 1914–1918*

(1977) has an excellent set of photographs with commentary. On other social issues, see B. B. Gilbert, *British Social Policy, 1914–1939* (1970), ch. 1; J. Harris, *William Beveridge: A Biography* (1977), chs 9 and 10; J. Burnett, *A Social History of Housing, 1815–1970* (1978), ch. 8; M. Swenarton, *Homes Fit for Heroes: the politics and architecture of early state housing in Britain* (1981).

Articles

The major themes are discussed in K. O. Morgan, 'Lloyd George's premiership', *H.J.* (1970); T. Wilson, 'The coupon and the British general election of 1918', *J.M.H.* (1964); P. Abrams, 'The failure of social reform: 1918–20', *P.P.* (1963); S. Koss, 'The destruction of Britain's last Liberal Government', *J.M.H.* (1968); J. M. Winter, 'Arthur Henderson, the Russian Revolution and the reconstruction of the Labour Party', *H.J.* (1972); N. Blewett, 'The franchise in the United Kingdom, 1885–1918', *P.P.* (1965); C. Hazlehurst, 'Asquith as prime minister, 1908–16', *E.H.R.* (1970). On the suffrage question, see M. D. Pugh, 'Politicians and the women's vote 1914–18', *H.* (1974); D. Close, 'The collapse of resistance to democracy: Conservatives, adult suffrage and second chamber reform 1911–28', *H.J.* (1977). On the social effects of the war, see J. M. Winter, 'Britain's "Lost Generation" of the First World War', *P.S.* (1977); 'The impact of the First World War on civilian health in Britain', *Econ. H.R.* (1977); and 'Some aspects of the demographic consequences of the First World War in Britain', *P.S.* (1976).

28. Britain in the 1920s

The fall of Lloyd George, the formation of the first Labour government, the emergence of Baldwin and the General Strike dominate the story of the 1920s. It was also a period when hopes of post-war reconstruction were quickly dashed by depression. It is worth asking how effective the political leaders of this period were and what, if anything, was achieved. The General Strike marked a major confrontation between organised labour and the Conservative government. Views differ as to whether it was the inevitable outcome of the growth of union power, a 'showdown' engineered by Baldwin, or an anachronistic conflict brought about by an unfortunate breakdown in negotiations. Above all, the General Strike needs placing in the context of Labour and trade union growth.

Essay topics

Was anything substantial achieved in British politics in the decade following the First World War?
    What was the significance of the General Strike?

Sources and documents

Lord Beaverbrook, *The Decline and Fall of Lloyd George* (1963) is informative, if biased. K. Middlemas (ed.), *Thomas Jones: Whitehall Diary, vol. I, 1916–25* and *vol. II, 1926–30* give an inside account of politics. On the 1920s see W. S. Churchill, *The World Crisis* (1923–31) and C. F. G. Masterman, *England after the War: a study* (1922). K. O. Morgan, *The Age of Lloyd George: the Liberal Party and British politics, 1890–1929* (1971) has documents on one strand of politics. R. Page Arnot, *The General Strike* (1926) has a comprehensive set of documents on the strike.

Secondary works

A. J. P. Taylor, *English History, 1914–45* (1965) and C. L. Mowat, *Britain between the wars, 1918–1940* (1955) are both important general studies; see also A. Marwick, *Britain in the Age of Total War: war, peace and social change, 1900–1967* (1968). K. O. Morgan, *Consensus and Disunity: the Lloyd George Coalition government, 1918–22* (1979) is the essential study of the Lloyd George Coalition. On his fall, see M. Kinnear, *The Fall of Lloyd George: the political crisis of 1922* (1973). R. McKibbin, *The Evolution of the Labour Party, 1910–24* (1974) and M. Cowling, *The Impact of Labour, 1920–24* (1971) take rather different approaches to the question of Labour's rise. R. W. Lyman, *The First Labour Government, 1924* (1957) and D. Marquand, *Ramsay MacDonald* (1977) consider Labour in office. The Liberals are discussed in T. Wilson, *The Downfall of the Liberal Party, 1914–35* (1966); C. Cook, *A Short History of the Liberal Party, 1900–1976* (1976), and in the essays by J. Campbell and C. Cook in G. Peele and C. Cook (eds), *The Politics of Reappraisal, 1918–39* (1975). S. Koss, *Asquith* (1976) and J. and K. O. Morgan, *Portrait of a Progressive: the political career of Christopher Addison* (1980) discuss personalities on the Liberal side. See also J. Campbell, *The Goat in the Wilderness: Lloyd George, 1922–1931* (1977) and S. Koss, 'Asquith versus Lloyd George: the last phase and beyond' in A. Sked and C. Cook (eds), *Crisis and Controversy: essays in honour of A. J. P. Taylor* (1976). For the Conservatives see J. Ramsden, *The Age of Balfour and Baldwin, 1902–40* (1978); J. Barnes and K. Middlemas, *Baldwin* (1969); H. Montgomery Hyde, *Baldwin* (1973); H. Pelling, *Winston Churchill* (1977). C. Cook, *The Age of Alignment: electoral politics in Britain 1922–1929* (1976) provides an analysis of the electoral shifts of the period.

The controversy about the conduct of economic policy and the return to the Gold Standard is covered in D. E. Moggeridge, *The Return to Gold, 1925: the formulation of economic policy and its critics* (1969) and R. S. Sayers, 'The return to gold, 1925' in L. S. Pressnell (ed.), *Studies in the Industrial Revolution* (1960); see also D. H. Aldcroft, *The Inter-War Economy: Britain, 1919–1939* (1970), ch. 9; S. Pollard, *The Development of the British Economy, 1914–1950* (1962), ch. 4; S. Glynn and J. Oxborrow, *Interwar Britain: a social and economic history* (1976), ch. 4.

On the General Strike see P. Renshaw, *The General Strike* (1975); G. A. Phillips, *The General Strike: the politics of industrial conflict* (1976); M. Morris, *The General Strike* (1976); W. H. Crook, *The General Strike* (1931). The strike from the trade union side is discussed in A. Bullock, *The Life and Times of Ernest Bevin*, vol. I (1960), see also H. Pelling, *A History of British Trade Unionism* (3rd edn, 1973). See also the essay by G. McDonald, 'The defeat of the General Strike' in G. Peele and C. Cook (eds), *The Politics of Reappraisal, 1918–1939* (1975).

Social policy is outlined in S. Glynn and J. Oxborrow, *Interwar Britain*, as well as the general works by Taylor, Mowat and Marwick. See also M. Bruce, *The Coming of the Welfare State* (1961) and D. Fraser, *The Evolution of the British Welfare State* (1973). See also the essays by Crowther, Ryan and Brown in P. Thane (ed.), *The Origins of British Social Policy* (1978).

Articles

See K. O. Morgan, 'Lloyd George's premiership', *H.J.* (1970); P. Abrams, 'The failure of social reform: 1918–20', *P.P.* (1963); S. Macintyre, 'British Labour, Marxism and working class apathy in the nineteen twenties', *H.J.* (1977); and H. C. G. Matthew, R. I. McKibbin and J. A. Kay, 'The franchise factor in the rise of the Labour Party', *E.H.R.* (1976).

29. Britain and the slump

The 1930s appear dominated by the theme of economic depression and mass unemployment. The years of the slump have been portrayed as a particularly turbulent period in which both fascism and communism seemed to challenge the established political parties. The reasons for the breakup of the Labour government in 1931 require close analysis, as does the reaction to the depression. Recent work has stressed the more prosperous side of the decade (at least for some) and the need to explain the relative weakness of radical discontent in the decade overall. Some consideration of the evolution of more interventionist strategies in the economy and social policy is useful, as well as the extent to which Labour was poised for electoral victory prior to the Second World War.

Essay topics

How would you account for the failure of political extremism in Britain after 1929?

What was the significance of the collapse of the Labour government of 1931?

Do the domestic policies of the National government deserve more credit than they have received?

Sources and documents

G. Orwell, *The Road to Wigan Pier* (1937) is a brilliant survey of social conditions and political attitudes. W. Hannington, *Unemployed Struggles, 1919–1936* (1936) is particularly useful on unemployed movements. J. Stevenson (ed.), *Social Conditions in Britain between the Wars* (1977) has documents on social conditions. H. Macmillan, *The Middle Way* (1938) represents an influential plea for a fresh approach to economic and social management. O. Mosley, *My Life* (1968) and *The Greater Britain* (1932) are important on British fascism. On the higher levels of politics see H. Macmillan, *Winds of Change, 1914–1939* (1966) and T. Jones, *A Diary with Letters, 1931–50* (1954).

Secondary works

C. L. Mowat, *Britain between the Wars, 1918– 1940* (1955); A. J. P. Taylor, *English History, 1914– 45* (1965); A. Marwick, *Britain in the Age of Total War: war, peace and social change, 1900– 1967* (1968) are all useful. There are a number of good surveys of economic affairs; see especially S. Pollard, *The Development of the British Economy, 1914– 1950* (1962); D. H. Aldcroft, *The Inter-War Economy: Britain 1919– 1939* (1970); S. Glynn and J. Oxborrow, *Interwar Britain: a social and economic history* (1976).

The essential study of the fall of the Labour government is R. Skidelsky, *Politicians and the Slump: the Labour government of 1929– 1931* (1967), but R. Bassett, *Nineteen Thirty-One: political crisis* (1958) is also useful. D. Marquand, *Ramsay MacDonald* (1977) provides a perceptive analysis of the role of the Labour leader. J. Stevenson and C. Cook, *The Slump: politics and society in the depression* (1977) focuses on the response to mass unemployment. On the communists see H. Pelling, *The British Communist Party* (1958) and R. Martin, *Communism and the British Trade Unions, 1924– 33* (1969). For the British Union of Fascists see C. Cross, *The Fascists in Britain* (1961) and R. Benewick, *The Fascist Movement in Britain* (1972). R. Skidelsky, *Oswald Mosley* (1975) examines the central figure in British fascism. See also K. Lunn and R. C. Thurlow (eds), *British Fascism: essays on the radical right in inter-war Britain* (1980). A useful guide to the Labour Party's subsequent history in the 1930s can be found in H. Pelling, *A Short History of the Labour Party* (1961); See also B. Pimlott, *Labour and the Left in the 1930s* (1977). For the Conservatives see R. Blake, *The Conservative Party from Peel to Churchill* (1970) and J. Ramsden, *The Age of Balfour and Baldwin, 1902– 1940* (1978). Trade union reactions can be followed in A. Bullock, *The Life and Times of Ernest Bevin*, vol. I (1960) and S. Pollard, 'Trade union reactions to the economic crisis' in his collection of essays *The Gold Standard and Employment Policies between the Wars* (1970). Social policies are discussed in D. Fraser, *The Evolution of the British Welfare State* (1973) and M. Bruce, *The Coming of the Welfare State* (1961).

Articles

R. McKibbin, 'The economics of the second labour government, 1929– 31', *P.P.* (1975); F. M. Miller, 'The unemployment policy of the National government, 1931– 1936', *H.J.* (1976); A. Marwick, 'Middle opinion in the thirties', *E.H.R.* (1964) are all useful. Two important articles on economic affairs are D. H. Aldcroft, 'Economic growth in Britain in the inter-war years: a re-assessment', *Econ. H.R.* (1967) and H. W. Richardson, 'The basis of recovery in the nineteen thirties: a review and a new interpretation', *Econ. H.R.* (1962).

30. Appeasement and British foreign policy in the 1930s

The conduct of British foreign policy in the 1930s has attracted controversy, primarily over the question of appeasement. Inevitably, judgements of appeasement as a policy demand some assessment of whether the dictators, especially Hitler, were appeasable. Even if appeasement might have worked, some appreciation is required of whether the policy was conducted effectively and what forces politicians were influenced by in adopting it. The Munich Crisis of 1938 occupies a central place in the literature, but some consideration of the evolution of foreign policy during the 1930s as a whole is necessary, as well as the role of Italy and Japan in shaping Britain's attitudes. Cowling's close study of the positions taken up in response to Hitler introduce a more complex dimension to the debate on foreign policy at the higher levels of politics.

Essay topics

What forces shaped British foreign policy in the 1930s?
   Had appeasement anything to be said for it as a policy?

Sources and documents

Lord Avon, *Facing the Dictators* (1962) and *The Reckoning* (1965) are important memoirs by a foreign secretary of the 1930s; see also W. S. Churchill, *The Second World War, vol. I, The Gathering Storm* (1949). G. Orwell, *Collected Essays, Journalism and Letters, vol. I, An Age Like This* (ed S. Orwell and I. Angus, 1970) expresses many of the political and intellectual conflicts of the decade.

Secondary works

There is a useful introduction to the topic in the historiographical essay by D. C. Watt in A. Sked and C. Cook (eds), *Crisis and Controversy: essays in honour of A. J. P. Taylor* (1976). For the general histories of foreign policy, see F. S. Northedge, *The Troubled Giant: Britain among the great powers, 1916–1939* (1966) and W. N. Medlicott, *British Foreign Policy since Versailles, 1919–1963* (rev. edn, 1968). See also W. N. Medlicott, *The Coming of War in 1939* (Historical Association pamphlet, 1963) and *Britain and Germany: the search for agreement, 1930–1937* (1969). A. J. P. Taylor, *The Origins of the Second World War* (1961) and M. Gilbert, *The Roots of Appeasement* (1966) are important and influential reappraisals of the period. See also J. L. Snell, *The Outbreak of the Second World War: design or blunder?* (1962); D. H. Lammers, *Explaining Munich: the search for a motive in British policy* (1966); F. L. Loewenheim, *Peace or Appeasement? Hitler, Chamberlain and the Munich Crisis* (1965). D. C. Watt, *Personalities and Policies: Studies in the formulation of British foreign policy in the twentieth century* (1965) has a number of important essays on the formulation of foreign policy. M. Cowling, *The Impact of Hitler: British politics and British policy, 1933–1940* (1975) re-evaluates the responses of politicians to foreign affairs. The role of public opinion is considered in M. Ceadel 'Fulham revisited' in C. Cook and J. Ramsden (eds), *By-Elections in British Politics* (1973); F. R. Gannon, *The British Press and Germany, 1936–1939* (1971);

R. B. McCallum, *Public Opinion and the Last Peace* (1944). Also valuable are K. Robbins, *Munich* (1968); K. Middlemas, *Diplomacy of Illusion: the British government and Germany, 1927–1939* (1972); S. Aster, *1939: The coming of the Second World War* (1974). See also M. Ceadel, *Pacifism in Britain, 1914–1945* (1980).

Particular episodes are discussed in K. G. Watkins, *Britain Divided: the effect of the Spanish Civil War on British political opinion* (1963); J. Edwards, *The British Government and the Spanish Civil War, 1936–39* (1979); D. Waley, *British Public Opinion and the Abyssinian War, 1935–6* (1975); T. R. Emmerson, *The Reoccupation of the Rhineland* (1976).

The attitude of Labour and the left towards appeasement is discussed in T. D. Burridge, *British Labour and Hitler's War* (1976); A. Bullock, *The Life and Times of Ernest Bevin*, vol. I (1960); H. Pelling, *A Short History of the Labour Party* (1961). See also S. Aster, 'Ivan Maisky and Parliamentary Anti-appeasement 1938–1939' in A. J. P. Taylor (ed.), *Lloyd George: twelve essays* (1971).

Military and economic considerations are the themes of M. Howard, *The Continental Commitment: the dilemma of British foreign policy in the era of two world wars* (1972) and G. C. Peden, *British Rearmament and the Treasury, 1932–1939* (1979).

Biographical studies of the major protagonists include M. Gilbert and R. Gott, *The Appeasers* (1963); J. Barnes and R. K. Middlemas, *Baldwin* (1969); K. Fielding, *The Life of Neville Chamberlain* (1946); M. Gilbert, *Winston S. Churchill, vol. 5, 1922–1939* (1976); H. Pelling, *Winston Churchill* (1977); D. Carlton, *Eden* (1981).

Articles

See D. C. Watt, 'Appeasement: the rise of a revisionist school?', *P.Q.* (1963); F. Coglan, 'Armaments, economic policy and appeasement', *H.* (1972); C. A. MacDonald, 'Economic appeasement and the German "Moderates" ', *P.P.* (1972); T. Mason, 'Some origins of the Second World War', *P.P.* (1964); D. H. Lammers, 'Fascism, Communism and the Foreign Office, 1937–1939', *J.C.H.* (1971); R. Helder, 'East Fulham revisited', *J.C.H.* (1971); R. Eatwell, 'Munich, public opinion and Popular Front', *J.C.H.* (1971); R. A. C. Parker, 'Great Britain, France and the Ethiopian Crisis, 1935–1936', *E.H.R.* (1974). Also relevant on British public opinion is A. Marwick, 'Middle opinion in the thirties', *E.H.R.* (1964).

31. Britain and the Second World War

The impact of 'total war' was perhaps even more significant in the case of the Second World War than the First. Domestic politics were dominated by the leadership given by Churchill to the coalition government and the remarkable mood of social optimism which gave rise to the Beveridge Report and the Butler Education Act. The reasons for Labour's victory in the 1945 general election require explanation, as well as some assessment of what it accomplished.

Essay topics

Why did the Labour Party win the general election of 1945?
Assess the impact of the Second World War on British politics and
society.

Sources and documents

G. Orwell, *Collected Essays, Journalism and Letters, vol 2. My Country
Right or Left* (ed. S. Orwell and I. Angus, 1970) provide an interesting
commentary on contemporary attitudes. T. Harrisson, *Living Through the
Blitz* (1976) contains the Mass Observation reports on the impact of
bombing on civilian morale and attitudes. See also H. Macmillan, *The
Blast of War, 1939–1945* (1967) and W. S. Churchill, *The Second World
War* (6 vols., 1949–54). See also the collection of photographs with
commentary in A. Marwick, *The Home Front: the British and the Second
World War* (1976).

Secondary works

Of the general studies, A. Marwick, *Britain in the Century of Total War:
war, peace and social change, 1900–1967* (1968) and A. J. P. Taylor,
English History, 1914–45 (1965) have relevant sections. P. Addison, *The
Road to 1945: British politics and the Second World War* (1975) has a
brilliant analysis of wartime politics. See also H. Pelling, *Britain and the
Second World War* (1970) and the essays by P. Addison and A. Marwick
in A. Sked and C. Cook, *Crisis and Controversy: essays in honour of
A. J. P. Taylor* (1976). For Churchill see R. Rhodes James, *Churchill: a
study in failure* (1973); H. Pelling, *Winston Churchill* (1977); R. Blake, *The
Conservative Party from Peel to Churchill* (1970). For the Labour Party see
H. Pelling, *A Short History of the Labour Party* (1961) and C. F. Brand, *The
British Labour Party: a short history* (1965). Major personalities of the
period are covered in J. Harris, *William Beveridge: a biography* (1977); A.
Bullock, *The Life and Times of Ernest Bevin*, vol. II (1967); B. Donoughue
and G. W. Jones, *Herbert Morrison* (1973). A. Calder, *The People's War*
(1969) discusses the war from the point of view of the civilian population.
The effects of the war on social policy are surveyed in M. Bruce, *The
Coming of the Welfare State* (1961) and D. Fraser, *The Evolution of the
British Welfare State* (1973); see also the essay by J. MacNicol, 'Family
allowances and less eligibility' in P. Thane (ed.), *Origins of British Social
Policy* (1978) and J. Harris, 'Social planning in war-time: some aspects of
the Beveridge Report' in J. M. Winter (ed.), *War and Economic
Development* (1975).

The general election of 1945 is analysed in R. B. McCallum and A.
Readman, *The British General Election of 1945* (1947). Post-war politics
are discussed in E. Watkins, *The Cautious Revolution* (1950) and R.
Brady, *Crisis in Britain* (1952). See also M. Sissons and P. French (eds),
The Age of Austerity (1963); J. D. Hoffman, *The Conservative Party in
Opposition, 1945–1951* (1964); F. Boyd, *British Politics in Transition,
1945–63* (1964). M. Foot, *Aneurin Bevan 1945–60* (1975) is valuable on
the Labour leader. For economic affairs see S. Pollard, *The Development
of the British Economy, 1914–67* (2nd edn, 1969) and A. Milward, *War,
Economy and Society 1939–45* (1977).

Articles

See A. Marwick, 'Middle opinion in the thirties', *E.H.R.* (1964) and 'The
Labour Party and the Welfare State in Britain, 1900–1948', *Am. H.R.*
(1967).

32. Decolonisation and foreign policy since 1945

While the theme of imperial expansion has attracted considerable
attention, no less important was the dismantling of Britain's overseas
Empire and the decline of influence in many different parts of the world.
The Suez crisis provides one focal point for the discussion of Britain's
changing role in the world. Britain's withdrawal from her remaining
colonies and the entry into the European Common Market bring the topic
up to the 1970s.

Essay topics

Why did Britain grant independence to so many of her colonies after
1945?
    What was the significance of the Suez crisis for the conduct of British
foreign policy in the post-war period?

Sources and documents

The later sections of G. Bennet (ed.), *The Concept of Empire: Burke to
Attlee, 1774–1947* (1953) are relevant. See also N. Mansergh (ed.),
Documents and Speeches on Commonwealth Affairs, 1952–1962 (1963);
Lord Avon, *Full Circle* (1960) and *The Reckoning* (1965), and W. Strang,
Britain in World Affairs (1961).

Secondary works

General studies of foreign affairs include C. M. Woodhouse, *British
Foreign Policy since the Second World War* (1961); F. S. Northedge,
British Foreign Policy, The Process of Readjustment, 1945–1961 (1962)
and *Descent from Power: British foreign policy, 1945–73* (1974); W. N.
Medlicott, *British Foreign Policy since Versailles, 1919–63* (1968).
    For the Empire, see the survey by B. Porter, *The Lion's Share: a short
history of British imperialism, 1850–1970* (1975). C. Cross, *The Fall of the
British Empire 1918–1968* (1968) is an outline of decolonisation; see also
N. Mansergh, *The Commonwealth Experience* (1969); D. Goldsworthy,
Colonial Issues in British Politics, 1945–61 (1971); D. C. Watt,
Personalities and Policies (1965). Other features of British policy are
considered in P. S. Gupta, *Imperialism and the British Labour Movement,
1914–64* (1975); P. Darby, *British Defence Policy East of Suez 1947–1968*
(1973); P. M. Kennedy, *The Rise and Fall of British Naval Mastery* (1976);
C. J. Bartlett, *The Long Retreat: a short history of British defence policy,*

1945–70 (1972); M. Gowing and L. Arnold, *Independence and Deterrence: Britain and atomic energy, 1945–1951* (1974).

The immediate post-war period is discussed in M. A. Fitzsimmons, *The Foreign Policy of the British Labour Government, 1945–51* (1953); A. Bullock, *The Life and Times of Ernest Bevin*, vol. II (1967); M. Edwards, *The Last Years of British India* (1963); M. and T. Zinkin, *Britain and India: requiem for empire* (1964).

The background to the Suez affair can be found in E. Monroe, *Britain's Moment in the Middle East, 1914–56* (1963). On the crisis itself, see H. Thomas, *The Suez Affair* (1966); S. Lloyd, *Suez 1956: A Personal Account* (1978); A. Nutting, *No End of a Lesson* (1967).

On attitudes to Europe, see E. Barker, *Britain and a Divided Europe, 1945–70* (1971); R. B. Manderson-Jones, *The Special Relationship: Anglo-American relations and Western European unity, 1947–56* (1972); M. Camps, *European Unification in the Sixties* (1967); U. Kitzinger, *The Second Try: Labour and the EEC* and *Diplomacy and Persuasion: How Britain joined the Common Market* (1973).

33. Britain since 1951

Although many of the official documents and papers relating to Britain's recent history are still not available, the main features of these years are beginning to receive serious historical analysis. Economic difficulties are one dominant theme of the period, which in recent years has begun to be debated in terms of the 'decline' of Britain. The nature of post-war politics and the adequacy of existing institutions to meet the demands of a more sophisticated electorate provides another approach to the period. Some analysis of the most significant social changes of the period is beginning to be possible.

Essay topics

How appropriate is it to speak of the 'decline' of Britain in the period since 1951?

Was Britain well governed in the years after 1951?

Sources and documents

Of the political memoirs of the period, see Lord Avon, *Full Circle* (1960); R. A. Butler, *The Art of the Possible* (1971); the later volumes of Harold Macmillan's *Memoirs* (6 vols, 1966–73); H. Wilson, *The Labour Government, 1964–1970: a personal record* (1971). R. H. S. Crossman, *The Diaries of a Cabinet Minister* (1975–7, abridged edn, ed. A. Howard, 1979) are the outstanding set of memoirs with provocative insights into the workings of modern British politics. A. H. Halsey (ed.), *Trends in British Society since 1900* (1972) has a wealth of statistics on social developments, while A. Sampson, *Anatomy of Britain Today* (1965) is an interesting survey of Britain in the 1960s.

Secondary works

A. Sked and C. Cook, *Post-War Britain: a political history* (1979) provides a survey of the major political events. See also D. Childs, *Britain since 1945: a political history* (1979); C. J. Bartlett, *A History of Post-war Britain, 1945* (1977); M. Proudfoot, *British Politics and Government, 1951–1970* (1974).

V. Bogdanor and R. Skidelsky, *The Age of Affluence, 1951–64* (1970) and D. McKie and C. Cook, *The Decade of Disillusion: British politics in the 1960s* (1972) are two books of essays bearing on several aspects of the period. Economic developments are discussed in S. Pollard, *The Development of the British Economy, 1914–67* (2nd edn, 1969) and J. C. R. Dow, *The Management of the British Economy 1945–1960* (1968). Major political figures of the period are discussed in P. Williams, *Hugh Gaitskell* (1979); M. Foot, *Aneurin Bevan, 1945–60* (1973); N. Fisher, *Iain Macleod* (1973). Particular topics are discussed in S. Haseler, *The Gaitskellites* (1969); C. Cook, *A Short History of the Liberal Party, 1900–1976* (1976); S. Brittan, *The Treasury under the Tories* (1964); F. Parkin, *Middle Class Radicalism: the social bases of the British Campaign for Nuclear Disarmament* (1968); F. Stacey, *British Government 1966–75: years of reform* (1975); J. Morgan, *The House of Lords and the Labour Government* (1975); P. Foot, *Immigration and Race in British Politics* (1965); R. Taylor, *The Fifth Estate: Britain's unions in the modern world* (1978). Other issues are considered in C. Harvie, *Scotland and Nationalism: Scottish society and politics, 1707–1977* (1977); A. Butt Phillips, *The Welsh Question: nationalism in Welsh politics 1945–70* (1975); M. Walker, *The National Front* (1977).

Social developments are considered in P. Calvocoressi, *The British Experience, 1945–1975* (1979); P. Gregg, *The Welfare State from 1945 to the Present Day* (1967); A. H. Halsey, *Change in British Society* (1978). See also the longer-term appraisal in F. Bedarida, *A Social History of England, 1851–1975* (1979). Recently published is A. Marwick, *British Society Since 1945* (1982).

Index